D0906690

The Nazi Concentration Camps, 1933–1939

The Nazi Concentration Camps, 1933–1939

———— A DOCUMENTARY HISTORY————

EDITED AND WITH AN INTRODUCTION BY

CHRISTIAN GOESCHEL AND NIKOLAUS WACHSMANN

ORIGINAL GERMAN DOCUMENTS TRANSLATED BY EWALD OSERS

UNIVERSITY OF NEBRASKA PRESS   LINCOLN & LONDON

This publication is supported by the
Arts and Humanities Research Council.

  Arts & Humanities
Research Council

Library of Congress Cataloging-in-Publication Data
The Nazi concentration camps, 1933–1939: a documentary history /
edited and with an introduction by Christian Goeschel and
Nikolaus Wachsmann; original German documents translated
by Ewald Osers.
p.   cm.
Includes bibliographical references and index.
ISBN 978-0-8032-2782-8 (cloth: alk. paper)
1. Concentration camps—Germany—History—Sources. 2. World
War, 1939–1945—Concentration camps—Germany—Sources.
3. World War, 1939–1945—Prisoners and prisons, German—
Sources. 4. World War, 1939–1945—Atrocities—Germany—
Sources. 5. Nationalsozialistische Deutsche Arbeiter-Partei—History
—Sources. I. Goeschel, Christian. II. Wachsmann, Nikolaus.
III. Osers, Ewald, 1917–2011.
DD256.5.N3553 2012
940.53′185309043—dc23   2012000594

Set in Sabon by Bob Reitz.

CONTENTS

MAP

ACKNOWLEDGMENTS

This book is the result of a major research project at Birkbeck College, University of London, generously funded by the British Arts and Humanities Research Council. Additional funding for the translation was provided by the Fritz Thyssen Stiftung and Birkbeck College's Faculty of Arts. We are grateful for this additional support, which enabled us to complete this volume.

We are also greatly indebted to the four doctoral students connected to this research project, namely, Christopher Dillon, Julia Hörath, Paul Moore, and Kim Wünschmann. While working on their dissertations on aspects of the prewar Nazi concentration camps, they made many significant contributions to our work and also supplied us with a number of documents. Thanks are also due to Paul Moore, who provided help with the final editing of the manuscript. We also want to thank Ina Sondermann and Kyle Simonsen for their editorial work.

At the University of Nebraska Press, Heather Lundine and Bridget Barry have been a source of support and encouragement throughout. We are also very grateful to Jonathan Lawrence and Sabrina Stellrecht for their excellent editorial work.

During our work on this book we have benefited greatly from the help and advice of many friends and colleagues. At Birkbeck we would especially like to thank Sean Brady, Catharine Edwards, David Feldman, Daniel Pick, Jessica Reinisch, Lucy Riall, Jan Rüger, Julian Swann, and Frank Trentmann. We would also like to thank the many librarians and archivists in Austria, Britain, Germany, Switzerland, and the United States who helped us with material for this book. Many colleagues, too, including Carina Baganz, Wolf Gruner, Susanne Heim, Stefan Hördler, Angelika Königseder, Daniel Palmieri, and Dirk Riedel, sent us copies of documents, often at short notice. Jürgen Matthäus and Joseph Robert White gave us some important advice on sources.

We would also like to thank Richard Bessel, Donald Bloxham, Jane Caplan, Richard J. Evans, Mary Fulbrook, Neil Gregor, Jeremy Noakes, and Richard Overy for their support of this project on numerous occasions. Geoffrey Giles and Alan Steinweis deserve our special thanks for their most useful comments on an earlier draft of the manuscript.

We have been fortunate to present some elements of this book at several workshops and conferences, including the Cambridge Modern European History Seminar and Alan Kramer's conference on the international history of concentration camps, held at Trinity College, Dublin. We also gained important insights at an informal workshop in London in July 2007, and would like to thank the participants for their helpful feedback. Above all, we would like to thank all the speakers at our international conference at Birkbeck College in July 2008, the first such conference on the history of the prewar Nazi camps. In the United States we gained from the presentation of our project at the Lessons and Lessons Conference at Northwestern University in fall 2008; our thanks to Alan Steinweis, Doris Bergen, Suzanne Brown-Fleming, Donald Schilling, and Theodore Z. Weiss for inviting us.

Finally, we would like to pay tribute to Ewald Osers, who undertook the challenging task of translating the documents assembled in this book, but passed away before its completion.

Extracts from Paul Martin Neurath's *Die Gesellschaft des Terrors* and Ruth Andreas-Friedrich's *Der Schattenmann* are reproduced with kind permission of Suhrkamp Verlag. Extracts from *The Times* are reproduced with permission of News International. Finally, the extract from Ludwig Bendix's memoirs is reprinted with permission of the Leo Baeck Institute, New York. Every effort has been made to trace the copyright holders of the extracts selected for the present volume. We apologize for any inadvertent omission, which will be rectified in a subsequent reprint.

The Prewar Nazi Concentration Camps

Few regimes have burned as many powerful images into historical memory as the Third Reich. Although its reign of terror lasted for just twelve years, the Nazi dictatorship wreaked unprecedented destruction and left tens of millions dead, many more scarred and displaced, and entire countries in ruins. Left behind were many pictures impossible to forget. Among the most searing images are those from the concentration camps. Indeed, popular memory of the Nazi camps has been shaped by photos and newsreel shot immediately after liberation in 1945. These pictures of piles of corpses, mass graves with hundreds of dead people, their emaciated arms and legs entangled, half-dead survivors, barely able to stand, staring into the camera, bewildered, sick, and starved, went around the world, augmented with reports by Allied soldiers, politicians, and journalists, as well as survivors themselves. All these images and testimonies, which still haunt us today, had a profound and long-lasting impact on the concentration camps' public perception.[1]

Since 1945, the concentration camps have come to symbolize the Third Reich's horrors. References to camps like Auschwitz—the largest and most deadly of them all—have become shorthand for Nazi inhumanity. The camps are the subject of films, plays, novels, and countless books and articles. Historians, philosophers, psychologists, sociologists, and many others have continued to grapple with the camps, which Hannah Arendt identified as "the true central institution of totalitarian organizational power."[2] Literature on the camps, which has continued to grow with immense speed in recent years, is now so vast that no historian can hope fully to master it.[3]

Most historians of the concentration camps have focused on the last, cataclysmic years of World War II. This was the time when the camp system of the Schutzstaffel (Protection Squad, or SS) grew beyond bounds. Inmate numbers shot up from 110,000 in September 1942 to a staggering 715,000 in mid-January 1945. The number of camps rose dramatically, too, as the regime set up hundreds of new satellite camps, often near factories, with the regime using all remaining resources for the war effort. Death dominated the concentration camp system during its final years. Initially, this was true above all for Auschwitz and Majdanek, which operated as both concentration and extermination camps during the Holocaust. In Auschwitz alone, the Nazis murdered around one million Jews. But extermination, exploitation, violence, neglect, and disease also gripped many other concentration camps, where death rates rose dramatically as the war came to an end: up to half of all the prisoners in the camps in early 1945 died before the end of the war, either during death marches from abandoned camps or inside the last remaining ones. By the time the Allies arrived, the camps had become vast zones of the dead and dying.[4]

This, then, is the most familiar image of the Nazi concentration camps: huge numbers of abused, sick, starved, and dying prisoners crammed into camps whose macabre features included gruesome medical experiments, lethal forced labor, and gas chambers, with the camps as central sites of the Nazi extermination of European Jewry. But this picture only captures the latter stages in the concentration camps' history. In fact, the camps were a product of neither World War II nor the Holocaust: by the time Auschwitz was set up in 1940, the Dachau camp, the first one to be established by the ss, had operated for more than seven years. Overall, and quite understandably, given the devastation of the war and the Holocaust, the history of the camps is dominated by their end. But what about their beginnings?

The Nazi camps were as old as the regime itself, with the first camps set up weeks after Adolf Hitler's appointment as Reich Chancellor on 30 January 1933. Initially established in an improvised manner, as places of repression for real and suspected political enemies, the camps were soon coordinated by the ss. They became permanent fixtures of the Nazi racial state, and their function also gradually changed: by the late 1930s, camps grew in size and filled up with social outsiders and German Jews. Prisoners faced constant brutality from the Camp ss, a tightly knit group of committed activists who became experts in abuse long before the outbreak of World War II.

However, the history of the prewar Nazi concentration camps remains widely unknown, especially outside Germany, and comparatively little has been written on the camps' emergence. As a result, misconceptions abound. After the war, several writers passed over the distinctiveness of the prewar period, suggesting that few prisoners had survived and that, by 1939, there were more than one hundred camps holding a million prisoners.[5] But this was simply reading history backwards; in reality, almost all prisoners survived the prewar camps, and mass murder and mass detention did not generally hit until the war. By 1939 there were no more than six main camps, with little more than twenty thousand prisoners. These were not the only obvious differences from the wartime years. Before the war the vast majority of prisoners were German, with only a few foreigners; economic motives played no more than a peripheral role; and Jewish prisoners were almost always in a small minority.

In recent years a more nuanced picture of the concentration camps before the Holocaust has begun to emerge. Since the 1990s, in particular, many local studies of individual camps have appeared, in addition to important monographs on the wider camp system.[6] However, this new research has, on the whole, been more encyclopedic than systematic or analytical, and many questions remain.[7] One major reason for the pervasive ignorance of the prewar Nazi camps is the lack of accessible documentary material. Key documents are scattered across archives throughout the world, while most published survivors' memoirs have long been forgotten or gone out of print. Until now, no effort has been made to pull this material together into a single volume. The present book is the first such attempt in either English or German.

As the camps were instruments of the political elite of the Third Reich, an examination of the camps promises to reveal much about the thinking of the Nazi leadership. Moreover, given the unprecedented terror in the concentration camps during the war, it is imperative to understand what "preceded the unprecedented."[8] To grasp more fully how the camps could turn into mass graves we need to examine their entire history, from the beginning. For there were obvious continuities: some of the roots of wartime terror — ss control over the camps, for example — reach back to the period well before 1939.

At the same time, we have to remain alert to breaks. Just as the road from prewar anti-Semitism to the Holocaust was a twisted one, there was no straight line from early terror in Dachau to Auschwitz. The prewar camps did not inevitably lead to mass extermination.

Before turning to the primary documents from the camps, it is necessary to briefly delineate the prewar history of the concentration camps. The camps developed in three distinct phases, with their function, living conditions, and appearance undergoing dramatic changes along the way.

The Early Camps, 1933–1934

In 1933 the Third Reich supplanted the Weimar Republic, Germany's first democracy established after the defeat in World War I. Political violence was an integral part of Weimar politics from the beginning, but it reached new heights in the early 1930s when the Weimar state was in terminal decline, paralyzed by economic depression, political deadlock, and social unrest. Bloody riots and clashes took place all over Germany, above all between the uniformed wings of the Social Democrats and the Communists, and the rising Nazi movement, in particular their paramilitary units, the Sturmabteilung (Stormtroopers, SA) and the SS (initially, the SS was a small unit within the SA that was used to protect Nazi meetings). Their ferocious fights were the most extreme manifestations of the deep divisions — political, regional, cultural, and social — that tore Germany apart. By then the Weimar Republic was effectively dead, but it was not clear what would take its place. Most Germans did not support Nazi rule: the parties of the left, though deeply hostile to one another, still outnumbered the Nazi Party in the last free elections held in November 1932. It took the machinations of a few national-conservative power brokers to install Adolf Hitler as German chancellor on 30 January 1933. Hitler headed a coalition government with the Deutschnationale Volkspartei (German National People's Party, DNVP), with only three Nazi ministers in his cabinet.[9] Hitler's appointment as chancellor was not the end of the Nazi seizure of power, but rather its beginning.[10]

A warning sign of the new regime's radical nature came after the Reichstag Fire of 27 February 1933. After years of political warfare against the left, the Nazis immediately blamed the Communists for the fire. Blinded by their paranoia about an imminent left-wing uprising, the Nazis ignored the evidence that the fire had been the work of a lone protester. During the night, the police and Nazi activists rounded up Communist functionaries and other opponents. The next day, the cabinet agreed on the fateful Decree for the Protection of People and State, which suspended basic civil rights, including the right to personal freedom. This was the flimsy basis for the practice of so-called protective custody (*Schutzhaft*), which legitimized the indefinite detention of individuals, bypassing due legal process.[11] By the time of the national elections of 5 March 1933, the first and last multi-party vote in the Third Reich, as many as five thousand individuals had already been arrested.[12] But these arrests were just a prelude to the Nazi war on political opponents.

Over the following months, Germany rapidly turned into a one-party dictatorship as the Nazis made a total claim over almost all aspects of life. Many Germans enthusiastically backed the new regime and gladly fell into line. Many others, however, were pressured or beaten into submission. Some historians have downplayed the significance of political violence in 1933 and argue that the Nazi revolution "did not begin with a sweeping onslaught on German society" as it could build on the support of the great majority from the start.[13] But consent only went so far, and violence—from the threat of force to open terror—proved indispensable in intimidating millions of Germans who had proved resistant to the lure of Nazism. The Nazis used violence to secure their precarious hold on power, both nationally and in the regions. Meanwhile, local activists celebrated their new powers by settling scores with political rivals. The Nazis were anything but magnanimous in victory, determined to extract brutal revenge against all those who had stood in the way of their movement.[14]

Mass detention of alleged opponents was at the center of Nazi terror in 1933. The great majority of them were male left-wing activists, above all Communists. Some were arrested by the police and turned over to the regular justice system for trial and sentencing; like other civil servants, German judges and prosecutors largely supported the Nazi regime and became experts in using and abusing existing and new legislation to fight the left. But most prisoners never came before a judge: tens of thousands were kidnapped by SA or SS men, and many more—one hundred thousand or more—were placed in protective custody.

The practice of extralegal political detention quickly led to a scramble for places of confinement. The new rulers grabbed whichever spaces they could and used existing places, such as prisons and workhouses. Yet, there were far more prisoners than could be accommodated in older structures; also, Nazi activists themselves were often keen to lock up prisoners elsewhere. It was in this context that the camps emerged. In the spring and summer of 1933, hundreds of early camps were set up across Germany. The focal points were major cities and industrial areas, due to the large size of the local working-class opposition. In Berlin alone, SA and SS troops established more than 170 torture cellars to detain and abuse alleged opponents. But early camps were also set up in the countryside.[15]

When they came to power, Nazi leaders had no clear master plan for the camps. Indeed, there was no central coordination as local and regional authorities created a bewildering landscape of camps in all shapes and sizes. Some held just a handful of prisoners, others several hundred or more. The treatment of prisoners varied greatly, too, from comparatively lenient conditions to outright sadism, though murders were still rare because the early camps' primary purpose was to break the opposition, not physical extermination. Still, the early camps could hardly have been more diverse. Terminology, too, was still unsettled. The Nazi authorities and the press described some early camps as "concentration camps"; other terms used at the time included "collection camp," "work camp," "protective custody camp," "prison camp," and "transit camp."[16]

Historians of the Third Reich have tried to differentiate the various types of Nazi camps that emerged in 1933. In the 1960s, Martin Broszat distinguished between the later state concentration camps and earlier "wild" camps run by Nazi Party formations, especially the SA.[17] But such references to "wild" camps are somewhat misleading, as many of these camps had close links to regional state authorities or soon developed them. This collaboration was a result, not least, of the early blurring between party and state in the Nazi dictatorship. As early as the spring of 1933, SA and SS men occupied posts in German police forces, from senior positions right down to rank-and-file auxiliary offices. This was one reason why the federated German state authorities were so heavily involved in extralegal detention from the start. Indeed, many German states already established their own large camps in the spring of 1933.[18]

Reflecting the camps' diversity, some historians have preferred to speak of "early concentration camps." This term was coined by the political scientist Johannes Tuchel in his elaborate typology of prewar Nazi camps. However, Tuchel's approach has its limitations. The rigid definition of different types of "early concentration camp" imposes too much order on the dynamic early period of Nazi rule. Also, the camps subsumed by Tuchel under this term often had little in common with each other or, even more importantly, with the later SS concentration camps.[19]

In the final analysis, then, an inclusive, all-embracing definition is most helpful: all sites of extralegal detention in 1933 — ranging from small SA torture cellars to protective custody wings in regular prisons — can be described as early camps.[20] Of course, we need to acknowledge the differences between these early camps, as diversity and dissimilitude were their very hallmarks. Some of these camps were, to an extent, prototypes of the later system of SS concentration camps, but most early camps left no such obvious legacy.

During 1933 the early camps were in constant flux, as was Germany as a whole. There was no clearly defined type of Nazi concentration camp. But the regime was edging closer. Certainly, the landscape had changed considerably by the end of the year. For the great majority of sites of terror only operated for a few weeks or months — they were never supposed to be permanent.[21] Similarly, most SA torture chambers had closed down by the summer of 1933, though a few lasted considerably longer. Still, by the end of 1933 the overall number of early camps had fallen sharply. Central state authorities emerged as the dominant forces that coordinated and rationalized the camps. This process was reflected in the sharp fall in prisoner numbers: there were now substantially fewer inmates than only a few months earlier, as the Nazi regime, becoming more entrenched, now scaled back its assault on the opposition. The regime publicly celebrated this new approach in the run-up to Christmas 1933, with much-publicized releases of thousands of prisoners from the early camps. At the end of the year, only Bavaria and Prussia still ran large camps with more than a thousand prisoners, and both states had developed rival visions for a future camp system.

In Prussia, as in several other German states, the ministerial authorities pursued the setting up of state camps from the spring of 1933. Having left much of the initiative to regional authorities in March 1933, the Prussian Ministry of Interior, headed by Hermann Göring, decided in April to establish several large camps for thousands of prisoners in the Emsland region near the Dutch border (the largest of these camps was Esterwegen). The first inmates arrived in the Emsland in June, and by September there were some three thousand prisoners. Under the Prussian model, which was also applied to several other state camps (such as Lichtenburg), the Ministry of Interior remained in ultimate control, at least on paper, appointing civilian officials as camp directors who in turn supervised the commanders of the guard details. In practice, however, this model never really worked, as ss and sa guards refused to submit to the control of civil servants. Moreover, Prussian planning for the camps was never fully streamlined, with different agencies pulling in different directions. In late November 1933 the Ministry of Interior eventually lost control over the camps; they passed instead to the newly independent Prussian political police office, the Gestapa, also controlled by Göring. Over the coming months, Prussian policy was characterized by drift and chaos.[22]

While Prussian policy remained contradictory and confusing, extralegal detention in Bavaria was coordinated much more effectively under ss leader Heinrich Himmler. With single-minded determination—confronting senior government officials in Bavaria and the Reich—Himmler established Dachau as the central Bavarian camp, run by the ss and holding well over half of all registered protective custody prisoners in the state.[23] Dachau was also a new kind of institution, a product of both party and state. The political police largely controlled arrests and releases, and the ss ran the camp. Crucially, both ss and political police were in Himmler's hands. Here was the template for the ss concentration camp system that emerged between 1934 and 1937.

The Formation of the ss Camp System, 1934–1937

In early 1934 the future of the camps was still uncertain: there were various types of early camps, run by different authorities under different sets of rules, with substantial discrepancies between individual German states. And yet, by the end of the year the contours of an ss system of camps had become visible. It was shaped, above all, by ss leader Heinrich Himmler, whose relentless rise to the top of the German police determined the fate of the camps. By April 1933 he had already accumulated major powers as commander of the increasingly independent Bavarian political police. But it quickly became clear that Himmler's ambition would not be confined to his regional base in Bavaria. With forceful persuasion, he gradually gained control of the political police forces in all other German states too, culminating in his appointment on 20 April 1934 as Inspector of the Prussian Secret State Police (though Hermann Göring was still nominally in charge). With the political police playing a decisive role in extralegal detention—cemented in the first nationwide rules for protective custody, also passed in April 1934—Himmler was now in pole position to gain control over the early camps. He lost no time to act.[24]

Since late 1933, Himmler had been confident that control over the German political police would enable him to coordinate the early camps and create a system of concentration camps.[25] His vision was simple: the remaining early camps would either be taken over by the ss and reorganized along the lines of Dachau, or they would be closed down. In the spring of 1934, just a few weeks after he had taken charge of the Prussian political police, Himmler took the first step and ordered the ss to restructure the Lichtenburg camp, overseen by his loyal enforcer, Dachau commandant Theodor Eicke.[26] Meanwhile, Himmler was already planning to bring further camps in Prussia, as well as Sachsenburg in Saxony, under his control.[27] The speed of the ss takeover of the camps accelerated after the so-called Night of the Long Knives, which eliminated the sA as a major political force and further boosted the standing of the ss. More generally, it marked the consolidation of the Nazi regime's power. By the summer of 1934, any serious internal opposition to Nazi rule had been crushed. In the wake of President Hindenburg's death in early August 1934, the army, the final obstacle to total Nazi domination of the state, swore an oath of allegiance to Hitler, who took the title Führer and Reich Chancellor.

Now the regime had to decide the future shape of its terror apparatus. After it had turned into an established dictatorship, would the camps still be necessary? In the mid-1930s their future was far from certain. To be sure, by late 1934 the foundations for a nationwide ss concentration camp system were in place, headed by the newly promoted Theodor Eicke as Inspector of the Concentration Camps, a title he had been using since late May 1934 (officially from July 1934). In December 1934 an office was added to Eicke's title—the Inspectorate of the Concentration Camps, in Berlin—which now directed the fledgling ss camp system.[28] But the camps' future was still uncertain. The number of prisoners in protective custody continued to fall in 1934, with leading Nazi figures like Göring and Reich Interior Minister Wilhelm Frick calling for even further cuts. In just one year, the official number of Prussian protective custody prisoners declined from nearly 15,000 (31 July 1933) to just 1,243 (8 August 1934).[29] As a result, prisoner figures inside the newly minted ss concentration camps remained small: by the summer of 1935, the Camp Inspectorate under Eicke controlled just five camps (the Columbia-Haus in Berlin, Dachau, Esterwegen, Lichtenburg, and Sachsenburg), with a total of no more than 4,000 prisoners. Even in Himmler's flagship camp at Dachau, prisoner numbers first declined and then stagnated: the record figures of late 1933 were not reached again until 1938.[30]

Meanwhile, the regular legal apparatus had turned itself into an effective instrument of terror against political and social outsiders. Indeed, in the prewar period the regular prison system dwarfed the ss camps, at least in terms of numbers. By late June 1935 there were more than 107,000 state prisoners (twice as many as in 1931), including almost 23,000 inmates classified as political prisoners. These inmates were held in hundreds of prisons across Germany, including some former early camps that had been turned into state prisons. For many legal officials, the camps now seemed superfluous because the judiciary was perfectly capable of detaining any political opponents and social outsiders.[31]

Of course, judges and prosecutors often cooperated closely with the Gestapo and the ss. These officials were all too ready to sacrifice legal principles on the altar of Nazi ideology, bending over backwards to excuse brutal excesses. Yet, they still wanted to maintain some measure of law and order to prevent Germany from sliding into complete anarchy. For Himmler, by contrast, disdain for the law was a matter of principle and pride, deeply entrenched after years of fighting against the Weimar state. For him, the ultimate arbiter was not the written law or constitution, but Hitler's will. This ss ethos was reflected in the first Dachau regulations, dating from May 1933, which threatened prisoners with the death penalty, blatantly contravening the criminal code. The resulting conflict between the legal authorities and the ss was inevitable. Already in 1933, some ss murders in Dachau were pursued by state prosecutors. Several more investigations of abuses in other camps followed in 1934 and 1935. In all, more than thirty camp officials were eventually convicted (though only a few of them actually served their sentences). These verdicts did little to enhance the reputation of the camps among conservative government officials, and Himmler's newly created camp system came under some pressure to justify itself.[32]

It took several crucial interventions by Hitler in 1935 to secure the camps' future.[33] The camps turned from temporary, improvised sites of terror into a permanent feature of the Nazi state. Why did Hitler save the camps? His distrust of the traditional legal system was even greater than Himmler's, and he was determined to maintain the camps as places of punishment under the Nazi leadership's direct control. But beyond Hitler's direct involvement, structural factors also aided the survival and later blossoming of the camps. For the camps, as they emerged under Himmler, were perfectly suited for the type of rule that emerged in Nazi Germany. The Third Reich never settled down, as it was no traditional dictatorship. Rather, its "cumulative radicalization" (Hans Mommsen) pushed the regime toward ever more extreme policies, and there was no more extreme space for discipline and punishment than the concentration camp.[34]

By 1935 the ss camp system was firmly established. But it was not yet fully formed. The system of ss camps was still emerging, during a lengthy, complex process of coordination that lasted until 1937. Early on, for example, a significant proportion of prisoners in protective custody still remained outside the grasp of the ss Inspectorate.

In Prussia, police figures for June 1935 reveal that almost 40 percent of protective custody prisoners (693 of 1,770) were detained in regular state prisons, not in ss camps.[35] There were also still some early camps outside the control of the ss Inspectorate, and these were only gradually closed down or redesignated. Bad Sulza, for example, which had been staffed by sa troops since its foundation in October 1933 by the Thuringian Ministry of Interior, was not turned into an ss concentration camp until 1 April 1936.[36] Throughout this formative phase, the ss Inspectorate was engaged in hectic activity, taking over camps, closing down camps, and building new ones.

The dust finally settled toward the end of 1937. By then, the landscape of the camps had been transformed. There were four central ss concentration camps; of these, only two, Dachau and Lichtenburg, had been established in 1933. In addition, the Camp Inspectorate had established two new camps, built from scratch: Sachsenhausen near Berlin began operation in July 1936, and Buchenwald in Thuringia followed in July 1937. Conditions inside the camps also changed. Discipline and terror became more standardized, with similar rules and regulations across almost all the remaining concentration camps, applied by a professional corps of guards and officers, the so-called Death's Head ss.[37]

The Expansion of the ss Camp System, 1937–1939

The concentration camps proved to be highly dynamic weapons of Nazi repression and control, and in the late 1930s their function changed yet again. The camps' changing focus reflected the increasing radicalization of the Nazi regime, which would not tolerate deviance or dissent. Prisoner numbers rapidly shot up as a result. Numbers had already started to creep up after the camps' future was secured, rising from 4,761 on 1 November 1936 to around 7,750 by the end of 1937. Yet these numbers were still considerably lower than those for the early camps of 1933. Only after the ss camp system had been firmly established did prisoner numbers expand rapidly, especially in 1938. By the end of June 1938 the camps were already packed with some 24,000 prisoners. Existing camps, growing at breakneck speed, were transformed into large, overcrowded compounds. In Buchenwald, for example, the prisoner population tripled in less than five months, rising from 3,000 at the end of April 1938 to 7,723 at the end of June, before reaching 10,471 by the end of September 1938.[38]

In the late 1930s the ss expanded the entire camp system. In just one year it opened three new concentration camps in quick succession. Flossenbürg in Bavaria, close to the Czechoslovakian border, opened in May 1938. Mauthausen in Upper Austria followed in August 1938, just months after the German annexation of Austria. Finally, Ravensbrück was opened in May 1939; north of Berlin, it replaced Lichtenburg as the central concentration camp for women. Initially, these new camps remained in the second tier behind the older ones, as almost all their prisoners arrived from existing camps, not directly from the police. Also, these new camps were considerably smaller than the big three at Buchenwald, Dachau, and Sachsenhausen.[39]

From 1937 the Third Reich entered a new, more aggressive phase. By this time the regime was firmly established, with Hitler riding a wave of popularity. Nazi radicals became more powerful than ever and helped to push forward more extreme policies, both at home and abroad. In foreign policy, Hitler was pondering conquests, mapping out a risky military move against Austria and Czechoslovakia, the first stepping stone to his dream of German "living space." He succeeded faster than even he could have expected. By the spring of 1939, Germany had annexed not only Austria but also controlled large parts of Czechoslovakia. Rapid success made the regime even more radical and reckless, and Hitler moved next against Germany's neighbor to the east. It was the invasion of Poland on 1 September 1939 that triggered World War II, culminating nearly six years later in the collapse of Hitler's "Thousand Year" Reich. Inside Germany the period from late 1937 was also marked by renewed radicalism, fueled by heightened ideological zeal. The regime stepped up attacks on community aliens, that is, those regarded as alien to the so-called national community. In particular, the Nazis subjected Jews to an unprecedented wave of discrimination and terror to drive them completely out of German social and economic life.[40]

Inevitably, Himmler's police and ss—as the weapons of choice of the political leadership—would play a major part in the escalation of the Nazi policy of exclusion. The German police, united since 1936 under Himmler's command, became more aggressive and widened its persecution of community aliens, dragging ever more victims straight to the ss concentration camps. It continued to keep a close watch on left-wing political prisoners, as it had done since 1933. Himmler's hatred for Communists, in particular, did not diminish, even though the back of their resistance had already been broken. Still, the Gestapo started to move beyond the usual political suspects. In the early years the great majority of political prisoners in the camps had come from the organized working class, but from the mid-1930s onward they were joined by an ever more heterogeneous mix of other political detainees. Among them were German émigrés who had returned to the Third Reich, individuals who had criticized the regime, and a number of Jehovah's Witnesses, who defied the total claims of the Nazi state on religious grounds. The prisoner population also became more international in 1938–39 with the arrival of several thousand political prisoners from Austria and Czechoslovakia, foreshadowing the vast numbers of foreign prisoners during the war.[41]

Needless to say, concentration camps were more than instruments of political repression. In the final years before the war they also played a short but crucial part in Nazi racial policy. In 1938 the camps briefly turned into sites for the mass detention of Jews. In the spring and summer of 1938 the Nazis detained thousands of Jews in the camps after various police raids inside the Reich, targeting in particular Jewish men who were accused of being criminal or work-shy.[42] This was a significant development. The Nazi racial war against Jews changed the camps; and it escalated dramatically just a few months later, when anti-Semitic terror reached new heights during and after the November 1938 pogrom.[43] Up to twenty-six thousand male German Jews were taken to the camps on Hitler's orders: within a few days the prisoner population in the concentration camps had almost doubled. Conditions inside the camps were dreadful. Of course, anti-Semitic excesses were nothing new; such outrages had occurred since 1933. But in the late fall of 1938 the ss opened a new page in its assault on Jews. In the wake of the nationwide pogrom, camp guards felt emboldened to unleash their own orgy of violence, which lasted for several weeks.[44]

Yet, Nazi racial policy was not yet geared toward mass murder. Rather, the main aim was to terrorize Jews into leaving Germany. This was why most Jewish men arrested in November 1938 survived the camps and were released after some weeks or months inside the camps. From mid-November 1938 the Gestapo ordered the successive release of sick, disabled, and elderly Jews, including war veterans, as well as the release of those who "sold" (at knockdown prices) their businesses to non-Jews. Others were released if they promised to emigrate. They joined the exodus of German Jews after the pogrom (an estimated 115,000 Jews in the ten months preceding the outbreak of war in September 1939).[45] The pogrom and the subsequent violence in the camps had the effect desired by the Nazi leadership. It made clear, once and for all, that Jews had no place, no hope, and no future in Nazi Germany. The mass detention of Jews was a brief, though significant, chapter in the history of the prewar camps. Afterward, the number of Jewish prisoners quickly fell again. By the spring of 1939 they were once more a rather small prisoner group in the camps.

In general, prisoners were by this time detained much longer than they had been in the early camps. Even though releases still occurred, they were becoming less frequent.[46] This was one reason for the general rise in the prisoner population in the camps. The main reason, however, was a different one. In the late 1930s the concentration camps filled up with social outsiders. It was the regime's large-scale attack on the homeless, beggars, and petty criminals, not its persecution of political opponents or Jews, that was behind the rapid expansion of the ss camp system in this period.

As soon as the Nazis had captured power, they pushed ahead with a wide range of disciplinary measures against criminals, the mentally ill, and others on the margins of society. In September 1933, for example, well over ten thousand alleged work-shy people and beggars were temporarily taken into police custody.[47] Inevitably, the Nazi desire to remodel German society also had an impact on the concentration camps. Already in 1933, the police took hundreds of prostitutes, beggars, and homeless to the camps. And in November 1933, the Prussian Ministry of the Interior introduced indefinite preventive police custody (*polizeiliche Vorbeugungshaft*) for so-called professional criminals, a measure later extended to the whole Reich.[48] Only a few months later, in the spring of 1934, the Bavarian Ministry of the Interior defended the practice of locking up social outsiders—including those accused of "alcoholism," "immoral lifestyle," and "work shirking"—in Dachau. This practice, it noted, was very much in line with the spirit of National Socialism.[49] Over the coming years even more social outsiders were targeted, including homosexual men, who were pursued by the police with unprecedented force. In 1935, for example, some 325 of 711 prisoners in the Lichtenburg camp were classified as homosexuals.[50] But the decisive assault against social outsiders was still to come.

In 1937 and 1938 the police conducted several high-profile, large-scale raids. Police orders included detailed arrest quotas, often exceeded by zealous local officials. So-called professional criminals and asocials were the chief targets of these raids. Both terms were more than misleading: the former was regularly applied to harmless petty offenders or to those merely suspected of criminal intentions, while the latter was a vague, catch-all term that could be applied to all kinds of deviant behavior, including begging and prostitution.[51] Inside the camps, the prisoner population underwent a decisive shift. In the past, political prisoners had dominated the camps. This now changed. In Sachsenhausen, for example, the SS counted some 1,668 protective custody prisoners at the end of 1938, compared to 441 criminals and 4,753 asocials.[52] This transformation had a profound impact on prisoner relations. Inmates had never formed a unified group, but the prisoner population now became more fractured than ever.

When the Nazis launched World War II on 1 September 1939, 21,400 men, including a small number of women, were held in the six SS concentration camps. This figure was around seven times higher than when Himmler had seized the camps in 1934–35.[53] Soon, prisoner numbers shot up even higher, from thousands to tens of thousands and then hundreds of thousands, while murder became the norm. The SS transformed the camps from places of brutal abuse and torture into sites of mass murder. But despite the profound changes to the SS camp system during the war, there was no complete rupture. On the contrary, there were obvious continuities, including the camps' administrative structure and the use of prisoner functionaries in supervisory positions. In other words, when setting up new camps such as Auschwitz, the SS could build on their years of abuse and domination.[54] The transformation of the camps into sites of unprecedented terror was possible not least because the SS had conceived the camps as flexible and expandable spaces. Here was a system of mass detention that prepared the ground for virtually unlimited Nazi wartime terror against political, racial, and social outsiders.[55] The documents in this book will shed light on its emergence and development between 1933 and 1939.

Some Comments on This Volume

This volume brings together documents on the prewar concentration camps, drawn from a large number of archives and libraries in Austria, Germany, Britain, Switzerland, and the United States. Most have never been published before, and some have only recently been discovered. For example, we have drawn on documents from the recently opened archives of the Red Cross's International Tracing Service, which allow new insights into the persecution and background of social outsiders, long marginalized in the historiography.

As far as possible, we have selected documents that date to the period before World War II. Such sources illustrate the twists and turns, the contradictions and complexities in the evolution of the ss camp system, without presenting it as inevitable. They also offer the advantage of immediacy: contemporary prisoner testimonies, for example, were not yet colored by knowledge of the camps' later descent into mass extermination and the Holocaust. However, we have occasionally gone beyond contemporaneous sources. Some key aspects of the camps were only fully described during and after the war; in such cases we felt it appropriate to offer readers a more expansive insight into the camps rather than stick too rigidly to self-imposed selection criteria.

The selected documents explore the camps from many different perspectives and shed light on the intricate relationships between terror, state, and society in the Third Reich. The vast majority of the texts selected for this volume were originally written in German, though there are also some reports by foreign observers. Before World War II and the extension of the camp system across Europe, the Nazi concentration camp was an almost exclusively German space. In that period, camps were located inside Germany, their leaders and guards were German, and so were almost all prisoners.

The documents originate from a great variety of sources and include official ss documents, Nazi legal files and trial records of former camp officials, articles in Nazi and foreign newspapers, secret police reports, published and unpublished accounts by former prisoners, reports from Social Democratic agents, and many more. Rather than reproduce these documents in their entirety—which would provide more texture—we have decided to present selected extracts, allowing us to include a much larger and more diverse body of sources.[56] The omission of text is always indicated by ellipses.[57] Still, no source collection—however comprehensive—can ever be complete; the Nazi bureaucracy alone left behind tens of thousands of documents. We have included documents that, in our view, offer the most telling insights in the camp system before the war. With few exceptions, the focus is on written sources. There are, of course, many other sources from the camps—including photographs, mostly taken by the ss for documentary or propaganda purposes, as well as prisoner drawings and architectural plans—but it was not possible to include them in this edition.[58]

The present volume is divided into six chapters, each of which has further thematic subdivisions. Each chapter contains primary sources, presented in broadly chronological order. All chapters open with a short general introduction, and each subdivision starts with a brief survey which places the sources that follow in their historical context. There are brief descriptive headings for each document, including date and author. In addition, notes provide further material on the individual sources.

Overall, this book's structure is thematic. It would have been possible to group the documents more chronologically along the lines of the three phases of the prewar camps outlined above. However, this would have resulted in too much overlap between individual sections and made for repetitive reading. Instead, the selected documents center on key themes from the prewar camps. The only exception is chapter 1, in which we felt that the differences between the early camps and the later ss camp system were so significant that the two could not be subsumed under the same thematic headings. Instead, chapter 1 explores the early camps only (1933–34), from a wide range of perspectives. The themes first introduced here all resurface in the following chapters on the ss concentration camps between 1934 and 1939. Chapter 2 explores the consolidation and growth of the ss camp system and examines the pervasive influence of ss leader Heinrich Himmler as well as the place of the camps within the network of Nazi repression and control. Chapter 3 turns to the Concentration Camp ss, the professional corps of perpetrators running the camps. Theodor Eicke was the most dominant figure here, but there were also powerful commandants, such as Karl-Otto Koch. Sources in this chapter also explore rank-and-file ss guards, who have long been neglected by historians of the camps. Chapter 4 is the first of two chapters on camp inmates; it analyzes life and death in the camps, while chapter 5 looks more closely at different inmate groups and their relations to one another. Finally, chapter 6 discusses the public face of the concentration camps, showing that the camps were never entirely hidden from the public, neither in Germany nor abroad.

TRANSLATOR'S NOTE

The style and tone of the documents in this volume vary a great deal—from the professional journalistic style of the newspaper articles to the "command style" of orders and instructions, to the informal narrative style of ex-prisoners recalling their experiences. An attempt has been made to convey these styles in the English translation. No attempt, however, has been made to reproduce the frequent grammatical mistakes.

ss ranks have been left untranslated and are italicized—with the exception of Himmler's title of Reichsführer, which has been rendered as "Reich Leader" in line with practice in British and U.S. publications. Instead, a table showing ss ranks with corresponding ranks in the German and U.S. Armies has been appended as guidance for the reader.

DNVP Deutschnationale Volkspartei (German National People's Party)

KPD Kommunistische Partei Deutschlands (German Communist Party)

NCO noncommissioned officer

NSDAP Nationalsozialistische Deutsche Arbeiterpartei (National Socialist German Workers' Party)

SA Sturmabteilung (Stormtroopers)

SD Sicherheitsdienst (Security Service)

SS Schutzstaffel (Protection Squad)

SPD Sozialdemokratische Partei Deutschlands (German Social Democratic Party)

ss Concentration Camps, 1934–1939. This map—using the German borders
of summer 1939—shows all camps under the ss Camp Inspection as well as
Moringen, the first central camp for women.

The Nazi Concentration Camps, 1933–1939

ONE

The Early Camps, 1933–1934

In early March 1933, just before the Reichstag elections, a Weimar newspaper published a short article on the opening of a "collection camp" for Communists. What was at the time worth nothing more than a few newspaper inches opened, in retrospect, a new chapter in the history of the nascent Third Reich. For the Nohra camp, established by the Thuringian Interior Ministry on the site of a former airport, was one of the first early camps. It was not a coincidence that this camp was located in Thuringia, a central German state already led by the Nazis since August 1932, months before Hitler became German chancellor (**document 4**).[1] How and why did camps like Nohra, places where large numbers of people were detained without trial, emerge so swiftly during the Nazi seizure of power in the spring of 1933?[2]

A week before the March elections, on the night of 27 February, the Reichstag building had been set on fire. The Nazis, with their longstanding hatred of the Communists and the Social Democrats, used the fire to fulfill their promise to destroy the left and the civil liberties guaranteed by the democratic Weimar Constitution. Arrests of left-wing activists began already on the night of the Reichstag fire. Meanwhile, Ludwig Grauert, a national-conservative senior official in the Prussian Ministry of the Interior, drafted a decree to legalize the arrests. The following day, the Reich cabinet, led by Hitler, extended this decree to cover the arrests throughout Germany, going far beyond a mere legalization of the mass arrests. Reich President Paul von Hindenburg signed what became known as the Reichstag fire decree (3).[3] The police, assisted by the SA and the SS, appointed in February 1933 as auxiliary police in Prussia, Germany's largest state, were now entitled to tap telephones, intercept mail, and, most significantly, arrest anyone suspected of undermining the new government.

Over the following weeks and months, the new rulers of Germany unleashed a wave of terror against Communists, Social Democrats, and other political opponents, taking them into so-called protective custody.[4] This ambiguous term left it vague as to who was to be protected: the detainee or the state. On paper, "protective custody" was a practice that built on the mid-nineteenth-century precedent of "police detention," also used to detain hundreds of Socialist activists and strikers in World War I. Yet in 1933 the Nazis applied protective custody on an unprecedented level and to different ends: to destroy the German left.[5]

Despite an atmosphere of massive Nazi violence against the left, the national elections on 5 March 1933 did not result in a Nazi triumph. The Nazi Party and its junior partner, the DNVP, gained no more than 52 percent of the vote. Germany was still deeply polarized, undermined by the Great Depression, mass unemployment, and years of political unrest. For Hitler and the Nazis, therefore, 1933 was all about securing power. After the elections, Nazi persecution of the left greatly intensified, encouraged by Hitler and sanctioned by the regime. Meanwhile, the Enabling Act, passed on 23 March 1933 by all remaining parties represented in the Reichstag except for the Social Democrats, gave a further boost to Nazi terror. This act, initially valid for four years but renewed in 1937, enabled the Hitler cabinet to pass legislation without any parliamentary interference. Effectively, the Reichstag had dismissed itself.[6]

In 1933 perhaps as many as two hundred thousand people, mostly men, were detained on political grounds throughout Germany.[7] Many of the prisoners ended up in early camps. Precise numbers are impossible to obtain because there were continual arrests, with the detainees often released again after a few weeks. Furthermore, many prisoners were simply kidnapped on the street by storm troopers, and these arrests did not find their way into official statistics.[8] Official figures for protective custody, such as those from the Reich Chancellery files from July 1933, are therefore probably underestimates (12).

Improvisation and arbitrariness dominated the early camps, just as it characterized Nazi terror as a whole, prompting one senior SA officer to complain about the chaotic nature of arrests (11). Hitler, concerned that Nazi Party interference could endanger his regime's stability and

The Early Camps, 1933–1934

popular support, announced on 6 July 1933 that the Nazi revolution was complete.[9] The growing consolidation of the new regime was reflected in the prisoner numbers of the early camps, which fell from the autumn of 1933. By then, most early camps had already closed down again, with more closures following in late 1933 and early 1934.[10]

1.1. The Nazi Regime and the Camps

There was no blueprint for the Nazi concentration camps. True, Hitler and the Nazis had announced several times during the Weimar Republic that enemies of the state would be locked up in concentration camps (1 and 2), but such statements were little more than political rhetoric. When the Nazis came to power in 1933 there was no detailed strategy for setting up camps, just as there were no precise plans on how to implement their ideology. As a result, the early camps' establishment and operation was accompanied by improvisation and administrative chaos.[11]

In particular, the authorities faced a logistical challenge amid the mass arrests. Dozens of early camps were set up hastily in derelict buildings, former pubs, sports grounds, hotels, and even on ships. Among the most notorious of these new camps was a former brewery in Oranienburg near Berlin, established in March 1933 by the local SA.[12] Many protective custody prisoners, by contrast, were held not on new sites but in special wings, tracts, or cells of existing places of confinement, illustrating the collaboration between Nazi Party and state authorities. Workhouse officials were happy to see their institutions, which had often been half-empty in the Weimar period, fill up with newly arrested political prisoners. And legal officials also allowed extralegal detention in prisons as a temporary measure, even though protective custody was a potential rival to the established system of judicial imprisonment. Regular prisons soon became overcrowded: on 3 April 1933, for example, the Bavarian penal institutions alone held some 4,533 protective custody prisoners, among them a number of women sent to the prison and penitentiary in Aichach (20).[13] In Hamburg, Germany's second-largest city, the judicial authorities also detained political opponents on the site of a penitentiary, in Fuhlsbüttel (since March 1933). Here, detainees were guarded by prison warders, as well as SA and SS men who, at least initially, could not easily abuse prisoners because they were still supervised by the prison governor. This situation changed in September 1933 with the official opening of the Fuhlsbüttel concentration camp. Then a different spirit entered the camp (13).[14]

Extralegal detention in existing places of confinement left its mark on the early camps. Prisons and penitentiaries had long been run along notions of strict discipline and forced labor, and some of these penal practices now found their way into the early camps (13).[15] The same was true for early camps set up on the sites of Voluntary Labor Service premises, initially established by the Weimar Republic's Brüning government in 1931 for unemployed people; authorities in charge of these camps claimed that volunteers would be reformed through physical labor for the community.[16] Another important influence on the early camps was the military. Many camp officials were obsessed with military discipline, drill, and blind obedience, often drawn from their own experiences in the German army during World War I, and applied the mores of the German army to the early camps, albeit in a perverted form. Yet, in spite of all these institutional precedents and existing ideas for the large-scale detention of the regime's enemies, the early camps soon developed their own distinct practices and traditions of terror and domination.

What is particularly striking about the setting up of the early camps is the interplay between Nazi Party and state authorities. This was especially clear in Bavaria. On 20 March 1933, Reich Leader SS Heinrich Himmler, in his new role as Munich Police President, announced the opening of a concentration camp in Dachau near Munich. Some five thousand prisoners would be detained in it, Himmler declared (5). Set in an abandoned ammunitions factory, owned by the Bavarian state, Dachau would soon become emblematic of the close nexus between the SS, the police, and the concentration camps. The Bavarian political police, soon also controlled by Himmler, ordered arrests and releases, and before long the SS ran the camp.[17]

In Dachau, the first SS commandant, Hilmar Wäckerle, oversaw arbitrary violence and brutal rules that openly threatened prisoners with the death penalty for acts of resistance (8).[18] Because of this SS regime of terror and torture, Dachau was the early camp with the highest death rate. Here at least twenty-five prisoners were murdered in 1933. To deny responsibility, camp guards claimed that they had shot these inmates while they were trying to escape or that these prisoners had committed suicide. Despite these blatant murders in Dachau, however, the power of Himmler and the SS was far from absolute.

The legal authorities investigated several cases of inmate deaths in 1933, and the autopsies revealed that the ss had killed these detainees (9 and 10). Eventually Himmler was forced to remove Commandant Wäckerle, whose regulations for the camp were completely illegal under German law.[19]

Himmler replaced Wäckerle with Theodor Eicke, under whose command Dachau turned into the model camp of the ss. Once appointed commandant in the summer of 1933, Eicke was not slow to implement a more formalized set of punishments, at least on paper. At Dachau, Eicke pioneered features of the later concentration camps, establishing a strict military organizational structure. He enacted new draconian camp regulations and official punishments and also set up a distinctive professional corps of ss men, composed of self-proclaimed "political soldiers."[20] Still, Eicke's new regime did not put an immediate stop to the run-ins with legal officials who continued to investigate suspicious deaths in Dachau (17). Elsewhere, too, murders and other cases of torture and maltreatment in the early camps led to initial investigations by the legal authorities (24).

Meanwhile, a different model for the early camps began to emerge in Prussia, Germany's largest state, under Minister President Hermann Göring, who as interior minister was also in charge of the Prussian political police. After the initial chaos of March 1933 when various authorities had opened camps, state authorities such as the Prussian Ministry of the Interior, concerned with maintaining their own power and the bureaucratic regulation of protective custody, soon began to try to coordinate the camps. Göring's Prussian administration established large state-run concentration camps, for instance in the Emsland, a desolate region near the Dutch border where prisoners were put to work in the moors (6).[21] Other German states established camps too, such as the Hessian authorities (7).

Unlike Dachau, the Prussian state camps were run by a civilian director appointed by the Prussian Ministry of the Interior and initially guarded by ss units. This constellation soon led to conflicts of power between the ss and the civilian administration, as leading ss officers refused to take orders from civilian directors, their nominal superiors. In the autumn of 1933 the Ministry of the Interior tried to assert its authority after reports about abuses and murders in the

Emsland camps. The ministry relieved ss guards of their duties in November 1933 and replaced them initially with police units. Ultimately, however, this incident revealed the Prussian model's illusory premise. Radical sa or ss activists would never take orders from civil servants. Also, the Prussian administration never had a monopoly of political detentions, as party formations still ran and set up their own camps, for instance the notorious ss-run Bredow camp near Stettin on the Baltic coast.[22] By October 1933, Göring's administration declared that all such camps were to be closed and that the remaining prisoners must be transferred to state-run camps (**14**), an order that had to be repeated several months later (**21**); also, special forms for the arrest of prisoners were drawn up (**15**).[23]

In the end, though, it was Himmler's concept of the camp, not the Prussian state administration's, that prevailed. By April 1934 Himmler was in charge of all political forces across Germany (including Prussia), which came to be known as the Gestapo. The Prussian model of state-run camps failed because Himmler's vision of the concentration camps proved more radical and dynamic than that of his rivals. For Göring and Reich Interior Minister Wilhelm Frick, and for others like the Bavarian Reich governor Franz von Epp (a former army officer and a grandee of the Nazi movement), the camps were temporary sites for the extralegal detention of political enemies. It was for this reason that Frick and Epp complained about the very high numbers of arrests by Himmler's Bavarian police (**22**). But Frick's attempt to place limits on the use of protective custody fell on deaf ears. Reinhard Heydrich, under Himmler the Bavarian political police chief, laconically commented on Frick's demand of 9 January 1934 to limit the use of protective custody that "quick and harsh" arrests were still necessary if the police thought so (**19**).[24] Plans to limit Nazi terror were doomed to failure because leading Nazis, above all Hitler, saw the state bureaucracy as ineffective, bound by outdated laws and due legal process, and therefore inadequate for the implementation of the Third Reich's racial and social agenda. Himmler's dual function as de facto head of the political police and Reich Leader of the increasingly powerful ss allowed him to pursue his radical vision of the concentration camp.

As we have seen, the early camps' primary purpose in 1933 was to repress the political opposition. And the Nazis succeeded with this strategy as the camps played an important part in securing the new regime. But the early camps also had other functions. Almost from the start, the authorities detained social outsiders in the camps. In November 1933, for example, Göring enacted the Prussian decree for preventive custody of "professional criminals," allegedly dangerous repeat offenders who had to be locked away for the protection of the people's community (16).[25]

Yet, once more it was the Bavarian authorities who pursued the most radical policy. Himmler's vision of the camps went beyond the assault of real or suspected opponents of the new regime. Rather, Himmler envisioned the camps as permanent institutions for the exclusion of a wide range of so-called community aliens.[26] His Bavarian political police used its powers of protective custody to place anyone who fell short of Nazi expectations of proper members of the German national community in the Dachau camp, highlighting the arbitrary nature of protective custody. An official statistic of protective custody prisoners in Bavaria of 10 April 1934, compiled at Himmler's orders, shows that of the 2,450 prisoners in protective custody, 2,009 were political prisoners while 441 had been detained for other reasons. Among these 441 prisoners were 96 alleged racial pests, 82 so-called asocials, and 23 purported alcoholics. Two people had been arrested for offenses against forest laws (*Holzfrevel*).[27] To be sure, the use of the camps as sites of social discipline was not without critics among the new ruling elite. Some high-ranking Nazis, such as Epp, complained to Himmler about the apparent misuse of protective custody (22). But again, Himmler's policy prevailed, as is already prefigured in a sharp riposte to Epp (23), and the camps continued to play their part in the Nazi war on social outsiders, which soon escalated further.

DOCUMENTS

1. *Völkischer Beobachter*: Article by Adolf Hitler on the treatment of supposed traitors to the nation, dated 13 March 1921[28]

Traitors to the national cause of the people should be strung up once and for all. In future let us regard as a traitor not only a person who denounces a cannon or a rifle, but also one who, in the nation's most desperate need, still sees nothing in his fellow Germans other than an object of exploitation. Let our fine luxury establishments be swept out and let this whole pack of bone-idle drones be the first to be locked into the national labor service. [. . .] Let us stop the Jews from undermining our nation, if necessary by keeping their germs safely in concentration camps. In short, clean our nation of all poison above and below. Only with a cleansed people will it be possible to face the difficult times to come, not with a riffraff. Now, at long last, the slogan of this pack of international stock exchange and financial bandits must no longer be: Negotiate at any price, but resistance to the end!

2. *Völkischer Beobachter*: Article on the National Socialists' plans for seizing power, dated 11 August 1932[29]

A National Socialist emergency decree would have swept through quite differently here:[30] on the negative side by the immediate arrest and sentencing of all Communist and Social Democrat Party functionaries, the concentric smoking-out of the deadliest districts and the accommodation of suspects and intellectual instigators in concentration camps. On the positive side, however, through the reconstruction of the national education system which the November Revolt[31] of the present usurpers of government power in 1918 has broken up.

3. Order of the Reich President for the protection of people and state, dated 28 February 1933[32]

On the basis of Article 48, Section 2 of the Reich Constitution it is hereby ordered as follows for the prevention of Communist acts of violence endangering the state:

§ 1. Articles 114, 115, 117, 118, 123, 124 and 153 of the Constitution of the German Reich are suspended until further notice. In consequence restrictions of personal liberty, of the right to free expression of opinion, including the freedom of the press, the right of association and assembly, interventions in the secrecy of correspondence, postal, telegraphic and telephonic secrecy, instruction of domestic searches and of confiscation and restriction of property are permissible beyond the legal limitations otherwise set hereto [. . .]

§ 6. This Order comes into effect on the day of its proclamation.

The Reich President von Hindenburg
The Reich Chancellor Adolf Hitler
The Reich Minister of the Interior Frick
The Reich Minister of Justice Dr Gürtner

4. *Weimarische Zeitung*: Report on the opening of the Collection Camp Nohra in Thuringia, dated 4/5 March 1933[33]

Mass transportation. It is reported that, in the course of the police action against the Communists some 400 functionaries have been taken into protective custody in Thuringia. Where the prison space was insufficient to take in the arrested, the Communists are accommodated in two large collection camps. Already on Friday a large number of KPD functionaries from a number of localities were transported by trucks into these camps under heavy police guard. It is expected that some 300 Communists will be held in these two collection camps.

5. *Münchner Neueste Nachrichten*: Report on the opening of the Dachau Concentration Camp, dated 21 March 1933[34]

At a press conference the Acting Police President of Munich Himmler announced:

On Wednesday the first concentration camp will be opened near Dachau. It has a capacity of 5,000 persons. Here all the Communist and — as far as necessary — Reichsbanner[35] and Marxist[36] functionaries who threaten the security of the state will be concentrated as it is not possible in the long run, if the state apparatus is not be greatly overstressed, to leave the individual Communist functionaries in local court prisons. On the other hand, it is not acceptable to set these functionaries free again. Individual experiments made by us have shown that they continue to agitate and attempt to organize. We have taken this measure without regard to petty misgivings, in the conviction that we are thereby calming the national population and acting in its spirit.

6. Circular of the Prussian Minister of the Interior on political detainees in protective custody, dated 24 April 1933[37]

For the maintenance of state security in the face of state-threatening subversion originating chiefly from the Communist side the need arose, especially in the first few weeks of the past month, to make use, on a major scale, of the possibility of imposing police detention in line with § 1 of the Emergency Order of 28 February 1933. The large number of persons detained includes also some whose arrest under the conditions then prevailing seemed advisable, but whose further detention no longer appears absolutely necessary given the consolidation of the national government that has taken place since, as well as the general calming of the political situation. It should also be remembered that the further imposition of police detention upon such persons, most of whom are unable to meet the resulting costs from their own means, gives rise to considerable costs to the state. I therefore request that a reexamination be embarked upon as soon as possible of the extent to which the restrictions on personal freedom then imposed should be further maintained.

In such an examination one will have to proceed from the view that all such detainees should continue to be kept under detention who, in view of their past political activity, may safely be assumed that, after possible release, they will again engage in activities of a seditious character. This includes primarily persons who have drawn attention to themselves in the Communist Party, its auxiliary and affiliated organizations, or pacifist groups, as leading functionaries, deputies, speakers at meetings or otherwise as agitators, especially also in literary form. It goes without saying that in all cases any possible consideration for a detainee's personal circumstances must take second place to the requirements of the maintenance of state security. In cases of doubt my decision is to be requested.

After the conclusion of this speedy reexamination I am to be informed on its outcome with an accurate number of the persons retained in detention. I would add in this connection that I have set in motion the establishment of three large concentration camps with a capacity of 2 to 3,000 persons for those to be kept in protective custody also in future, where these persons are to be moved after [the camps'] completion.

I request that release from police detention be made dependent in all cases on the signature of an obligation note the wording of which obliges those released to refrain in future from any seditious political activity, especially any participation in high-treason or state-treason subversion. They are also to supply a written undertaking that they cannot make any claims on the grounds of the police measures taken against them.

7. Instruction by the State Commissioner for Police in Hesse, Werner Best,[38] concerning the opening of the Osthofen concentration camp,[39] dated 1 May 1933[40]

For the implementation of police detention to be imposed for political reasons in accordance with § 1 of the Order of the Reich President for the protection of people and state of 28 February 1933 it is hereby ordered:

1. For the state [*Land*] of Hesse a concentration camp is being established, in which all persons taken *into police detention for political reasons* are to be accommodated, provided that their detention has already run for more than a week or is to be extended by more than a week [. . .].

2. The Hessian concentration camp is being established on the grounds of the paper factory in Osthofen, District Worms [. . .].

4. ss *Sturmbannführer Karl d'Angelo* is appointed honorary *head of the Hessian concentration camp*. He is subject to supervision by the Police Office Worms. The camp service is done by auxiliary police officers called up by the Police Office Worms; their names are to be reported to me.

5. The Police Office Worms has to work out a *camp order* and submit it for my approval.

8. Special regulations for the Dachau camp decreed by Commandant Hilmar Wäckerle, May 1933[41]

For the persons accommodated in the Dachau camp the following special regulations are hereby decreed:

A. General

§ 1. Martial law is imposed on the Dachau camp and the following regulations are in force with immediate effect:

§ 2. In the event of attempted escape by prisoners the guard and escort unit may make use of its firearms without a warning call.

B. Penal regulations

§ 3. The following punishments may be imposed on the prisoners:

1. Confinement.
2. Punitive transfer within the existing prisoner categories.
3. Death.

Confinement can be light, medium or severe. The maximum duration of the two former categories is 8 weeks, that of stricter confinement is 3 months. As a rule implementation of the punishment of confinement is in solitary confinement. In medium confinement the punished person receives hard bedding and is fed with bread and water. Severe confinement is practiced in the same way as medium, but in a totally dark cell.

§ 4. The prisoners must show respect and obedience to every member of the camp commandant's office, as well as to those of the guard units, and must obey their orders punctiliously. Equally they must obey the instructions of the persons assigned to the security and escort service.

§ 5. Punishment of confinement or punitive transfer is imposed on [an individual]:

1. who offends in any way against § 4,
2. who knowingly speaks an untruth to a member of the camp commandant's office or the guard personnel,
3. who does not comply, or comply correctly, with an order given to him,
4. who offends against the house or camp rules,
5. who insults or defames a member of the camp commandant's office or the guard personnel,
6. who bases a complaint on untrue allegations or submits it, or attempts to submit it, other than by the prescribed official channels,
7. who criticizes the institutions of the camp, the instructions and orders of the camp commandant's office or the authorities

subordinated to it, or takes part in consultations pursuing that aim,

8. who collects signatures for a joint complaint,
9. who refuses labor service,
10. who without permission is in any kind of contact with persons outside the camp or seeks such contact,
11. who performs sabotage of any kind [. . .]

§ 8. The death penalty is imposed on [any individual]:

1. who physically resists, or attempts to assault, a member of the camp commandant's office or the guard personnel,
2. who encourages, or attempts to encourage, another prisoner to deny obedience to members of the camp commandant's office or the guard personnel [. . .].

C. Classification of prisoners:

§ 10. The prisoners are divided into three categories.

§ 11. The prisoners in all 3 categories have to do labor service; its duration and scope is determined by the camp commandant.

§ 12. All prisoners are initially placed in Category II unless otherwise decreed in the following.

§ 13. In Category II the prisoners receive ordinary bedding and appropriate food.

§ 14. Category II prisoners who behave well and are willing to work can be transferred to Category I. In this category the prisoners receive good bedding and sufficient food [. . .]

§ 15. Prisoners who behave badly are transferred to Category III. In this category the prisoner receives hard bedding and as food hot meals reduced in size by one-quarter of the ration.

§ 16. Category III can also have prisoners transferred to it who have behaved well during their stay in the camp, but whose previous life justifies a particularly severe supervision in the interest of calm and order in the camp [. . .].

D. Jurisdiction

§ 18. Jurisdiction within the camp regarding the prisoners is exercised exclusively by the camp commandant, unless the case is an offense under § 8. All cases coming under § 8 are judged by a camp court composed of the camp commandant, one or two officers to be appointed by the camp commandant and an ss man belonging to the guard personnel.

9. Report from the investigation records of the Munich State Prosecutor's office on prisoner deaths in the Dachau camp, dated 30 May 1933[42]

Schloss Louis, 55, widower, merchant from Nuremberg.

In the afternoon of 16.5.1933 the Public Prosecutor's Office was informed by the gendarmerie station Dachau that Schloss had hanged himself in his solitary confinement cell in the camp. A judicial postmortem examination was performed the very same day in the presence of the Provincial Court physician Dr. Flamm [. . .]. Because, in the course of it, it was found that the corpse exhibited numerous weals on the body and because the cause of death seemed doubtful, an autopsy was performed on 17.5.33. According to the preliminary expert opinion death by hanging could not be proved. The extensive destruction of fatty tissue found was considered adequate for explaining the death by autointoxication and fat embolism.

10. Report of the Munich Senior State Prosecutor Wintersberger to the Bavarian Minister of Justice Hans Frank on a conversation with Heinrich Himmler about deaths in the Dachau camp, dated 2 June 1933[43]

In accordance with instructions I had a lengthy conversation at noon on 1 June 1933 with Herr Police Commander Himmler at his office at Munich police headquarters about the incidents at the Dachau concentration camp [. . .] and reported to him in particular on the cases Schloss, Hausmann, Strauss and Nefzger, on which he seemed to be already informed, and showed him the photographs kept with the investigation records. I pointed out that the four cases named, in particular, even on the results of the findings so far, justify the urgent suspicion of grave punishable actions on the part of individual members of the camp guards and camp officials and that both the Public Prosecutor's Office and the police authorities that have become aware of these incidents should, without regard for any persons whatever, conduct a criminal prosecution of the above incidents. I requested Herr Police

Commander Himmler to support me most vigorously in this task. I declared that I have ordered and am conducting a judicial preliminary investigation of the four cases named and that I shall request a judicial detention order because of fear of collusion against the persons who are gravely suspected of criminal involvement in these cases [. . .]

On my request, Herr Police Commander Himmler agreed to issue an order that during the inquiry into the Dachau camp, conducted by myself and the investigating judge, no difficulties whatsoever would be put in our path and all our questions would be answered [. . .]

11. Letter from SA-*Gruppenführer* Schmid to the Bavarian Minister-President Siebert with a complaint about arbitrary arrests, dated 1 July 1933[44]

Everybody is arresting everybody, bypassing the prescribed official procedure, everybody threatens everybody with protective custody, everybody threatens everybody with Dachau. Businesses are forced to dismiss any number of employees, businesses are forced to engage employees without checking their knowledge of the job [. . .]. Down to the smallest gendarmerie station a veritable uncertainty about who is responsible for what has gripped the best and most reliable officials; this, quite simply, is bound to have devastating and state-eroding effects.

Surely I cannot be counted among the pussy-footers, which is precisely why I have to point out that, if the revolution is to be transformed into an orderly relationship of state and people, the state apparatus must be kept entirely safe from all revolutionary interference by the street. Both in the practical and the personal regard it must absolutely be left to the responsibility of the state ministries alone on how the revolutionary ideas are transformed into action for the national community [. . .]. Every last street sweeper nowadays feels responsible for things whose connections he has never understood at all.

12. Survey, from Reich Chancellery records, of the number of persons in protective custody on 31 July 1933[45]

Prussia	14,906
Bavaria	4,152
Saxony	4,500

Württemberg	971
Baden	539
Thuringia	16
Hesse	145
Hamburg	682
Meckl[enburg]-Schwerin	35
Braunschweig	248
Oldenburg	170
Anhalt	112
Bremen	229
Lippe-Detmold	17
Lübeck	27
Meckl[enburg]-Strelitz	16
Schaumburg-Lippe	24
Total	26,789

13. Address by Max Lahts, Acting President of the Hamburg prison administration, to the detainees of the Fuhlsbüttel camp, dated 4 September 1933[46]

I have had you fall in today to inform you that the Herr Reich governor[47] has, effective today, subordinated the protective detainees to the prison administration. The motivation and reason for this is the realization that a major number of you are not willing to abandon your hostile attitude to the new state, as has time and again been made obvious by your general behavior. In particular it transpires that you have made fun of protective custody as practiced hitherto, compared it to a small children's crèche and made the wildest inflammatory speeches in the community halls. These are intolerable conditions and, as President of the Prison Administration, I will utterly eliminate them. The prison administration will inflexibly, implacably and ruthlessly, with the use of all means, prove to you, as avowed enemies of the National Socialist state, that no one may with impunity disrupt Adolf Hitler's state in its reconstruction effort. [. . .]

The new protective custody order will give you an opportunity to prove whether you are willing to abandon your subversive attitude of the past, so that I can then with a good conscience return you to freedom as full members of the German nation [. . .]. Otherwise you will only have yourselves to blame if I keep you here until I am convinced of your complete about-face.

Under the new protective custody order you will be placed under stricter supervision, especially in the community halls. In place of the hitherto voluntary labor you are all now subject to compulsory labor.

The new protective custody order that I am here bringing to your notice in rough outline envisions 3 categories:

The first category

will include those of you who have behaved impeccably. Your food remains as before. You may receive mail from your relatives once a month and write to them once a month. You are permitted to smoke only during your free time. You may receive visitors only with the special approval of the camp commandant.

The second category

embraces all those who have refused to submit to the institutional regulations and who have not behaved impeccably, as well as those who, because of the gravity of their past actions for which they were taken into protective custody, do not deserve the privileges of the first category. They are therefore not granted any kind of privileges. So they are not permitted to write. They are subject to a smoking ban and they may not receive any visitors.

The third category

embraces those of you who have behaved with especial recalcitrance and impropriety and on whom, because of their especially hostile attitude to the nation and the state, protective custody was imposed. Members of the third category are kept in solitary confinement. Naturally they are not permitted to write, they are under a smoking ban and may not receive any visitors. In addition they receive a hot meal and soft bedding only every 3rd day. Those particularly recalcitrant among them will have detention in a darkened cell imposed on them.

Release of protective detainees is only with my approval through the camp commandant.

You will be notified of your assignment according to your behavior to date. Your treatment will depend on your behavior in the past and in the future. It will be hard but just. It will be done for the protection of the German people and will be appropriate to yourselves so long as you are enemies of the German nation and state.

14. Circular from the Prussian Minister of the Interior to the Provincial Administrations and the Secret Police Office in Berlin, regarding the detention of protective custody prisoners in state concentration camps, dated 14 October 1933[48]

1. Persons who, in accordance with § 1 of the Reich President's Order for the protection of nation and state of 28 February 1933, have for political reasons been placed [. . .] under *police detention* are in *principle* to be accommodated in *state concentration camps*, provided that, because of the reason for their arrest, they need not be available at any time to the police authority for investigation purposes and provided that the restriction of their freedom is not envisioned for a relatively short time. If transportation to a state concentration camp is not, or not yet, immediately required, then the protective detainees are to be held in state or local police prisons. *Any other detention is inadmissible in future.*

2. Only those camps that have been *expressly confirmed* by me as such are *state concentration* camps. At present the following are to be regarded as concentration camps:

   a) Camp Papenburg Distr. Osnabrück
   b) Camp Sonnenburg Distr. Frankfurt-Oder
   c) Camp Lichtenburg Distr. Merseburg
   d) Camp Brandenburg Distr. Potsdam

   Until further notice the sections of the Provincial Institution Brauweiler nr. Cologne and of the Provincial Workhouse Moringen nr. Hanover, which have been adapted for the accommodation of political detainees, are put on an equal footing with the state concentration camps listed.

   Other facilities for the accommodation of political detainees are not recognized by me as state concentration camps; insofar as they still exist they will shortly, in any case by the end of this year, be dissolved. *Any new admission of protective detainees to such institutions is therefore forbidden.*

3. Regardless of the regulations issued for the imposition and cancellation of political protective custody, in the interests of orderly

accountancy any *assignment* of detainees to *state concentration camps* and any *release* from them will in future be effected *only through the mediation* of the office established for that purpose in *my ministry* [. . .].

4. The *costs* of detainees accommodated in the state concentration camps Papenburg, Sonnenburg, Lichtenburg and Brandenburg are borne by the state and made available directly by myself, so that the police authorities responsible for the imposition of protective custody are no longer concerned with the costs once the detainee has been transferred to a State concentration camp.

15. Blank form for an application for transfer to a Prussian state concentration camp, presumably from fall 1933[49]

Secr[et] State Police Office
The Police President / Director
The District Prefect
The Chief Burgomaster (as District Police authority)

By enactment of _____/_____ 1933 _____ Reference
_____ (first and last name)
resident at _____ district _____ Admin. province _____
occupation _____ religion _____
born on _____ in _____ district _____
nationality _____
personal status: single, married, widowed, divorced
recipient of old-age pension _____
[. . .] has been taken into political custody. The detainee is at present in police custody / judicial prison in _____
The detainee is capable of work and is in good health.
The detainee suffers from _____
The detainee is permanently unfit for agricultural work
I request the detainee's transfer to a state concentration camp.

16. Decree of the Prussian Minister of the Interior on the application of preventive police detention of professional criminals, dated 13 November 1933[50]

Preventive police custody (meaning detention designed to prevent a crime) is to be imposed primarily on persons who are known to the criminal police as professional criminals, who live wholly or partially on the proceeds of criminal actions. The formal condition for the application of preventive custody is that the person concerned has been sentenced three times to penitentiary or prison at home or abroad for a period of at least 6 months for a deliberate crime or offense committed through greed and that a period of less than 5 years has elapsed between the separate criminal deeds. [. . .]

Beyond the range of persons described it is also possible exceptionally to take into protective police custody persons who, without being professional criminals with a record, by their actions display a criminal intent aimed at murder, robbery, theft or arson and who, though not yet breaking a particular legal provision, reveal an intent that is a danger to public safety. Cases like those of the Saß brothers in Berlin,[51] who repeatedly proved their intent to commit burglaries by their actions, but had to be let off each time because [their cases were] not actionable under criminal law — making a mockery of the authorities — should be impossible in a National Socialist Germany.

The imposition of preventive police custody is the exclusive personal right of the heads of the state [*Land*] criminal police authorities and must be thoroughly and reliably justified, so that no doubt should arise as to the legality of the detention [. . .]. Preventive police custody is executed in special state concentration camps. In the selection of professional criminals with a record the first choice, given equal danger, should be single persons, followed by childless married persons. Preventive police custody may, moreover, be for as long as its purpose requires.

17. Letter from the Bavarian State Minister of the Interior Adolf Wagner to the Bavarian State Minister of Justice Hans Frank on deaths in the Dachau camp, dated 29 November 1933[52]

Dear Herr Party Comrade, State Minister Dr. Frank,

The Political Police Commander in the State Ministry of the Interior [Himmler] submitted to you an application on 18.11.1933 to the effect that the investigation proceedings in the cases of [the deceased] protective custody prisoners Hugo Handschuh, Wilhelm Franz and Delwin Katz be quashed on grounds of state policy [. . .].

Meanwhile it was once more pointed out to me in a conference with the Political Police Commander Reichsführer-ss Himmler that carrying out the investigation procedures would cause great damage to the standing of the National Socialist state because these proceedings are directed against members of the SA and SS and that the SA and the SS, the main exponents of the National Socialist state, would therefore be directly affected. For this reason I am supporting the application of the Political Police Commander in the State Ministry of the Interior, submitted to you on 18.11.1933, for the quashing of the investigation proceedings.

The Political Police Commander Reichsführer-ss Himmler informs me that he had a lengthy conversation with you in this matter. It has also been discussed in the Council of Ministers. The result was that the Ministry of Justice has detailed a delegate to the Political Police. I firmly hope that these are the last cases to compel the Herr Reich governor and the Council of Ministers to intervene in the interest of the state. I have made it very clear to the agencies of the Political Police that in similar cases in the future I will not find myself ready to apply for investigation proceedings to be dismissed. On the other hand, I do not deny the absolute necessity of providing a means, especially to the guards in concentration camps, enabling them, in the event of physical attack, of disobedience or even of serious infringements of concentration camp discipline, to intervene by immediate use of their firearms or execution under martial law. Only thus will it be possible to maintain order in every respect in the concentration camp that, as is well known, holds chiefly criminal individuals. I should be very grateful, Herr Minister of Justice, to learn your opinion.

Heil Hitler!

18. Announcement of the Prussian Minister President Hermann Göring on releases from concentration camps, dated 9 December 1933[53]

In view of the favorable result of the Reichstag elections[54] especially in the concentration camps [. . .] it is my intention to effect releases from the concentration camps. I have decided on this measure all the more readily as, through my assumption of the leadership of the political police in connection with the proposed reorganization,[55] I believe that a guarantee for the maintenance of order in the state and the suppression of the Marxist-Communist movement now exists even with a mitigation of the protective custody measures.

Given the calming of the domestic political situation and in view of the completed stabilization of the National Socialist regime I consider it acceptable for some 5,000 prisoners to be released in this manner by Christmas [. . .]. The prisoners to be released are to be made to understand in particular my intention to reintegrate them, in line with the Führer's wishes, into the National Socialist people's community. However, they are not to be left in any doubt that those who repay the National Socialist state's generosity with renewed seditious activities will be strictly, mercilessly, and forever rendered harmless by me.

19. Circular from Reich Minister of the Interior Wilhelm Frick to the State [*Land*] governments on the abuse of protective custody, dated 9 January 1934[56]

In view of the complaints received by me I cannot avoid the impression that protective custody is in some cases used in a manner not compatible with its purpose. Even though the Reich President's Order for the protection of nation and state of 28 February 1933 does not contain any formal conditions for the imposition of protective custody, this does not relieve the responsible authorities of their duty of closely examining in each case whether a justified reason for the imposition of protective custody exists [. . .]. Protective custody must not therefore be imposed as a "punishment," i.e. as a substitute for judicial or police punishment, moreover with a duration limited in advance. It is therefore not admissible in principle for protective custody to be imposed instead of the opening of criminal proceedings.

20. Letter of the Governor's Office of the Penitentiary and Prison Institution Aichach (Upper Bavaria) to the Munich General State Prosecutor, dated 15 February 1934[57]

The protective custody detainee Hedwig L. is accommodated here on the instruction of the Police Directorate Nuremberg-Fürth. As criminal proceedings are pending against her she has to be kept in solitary confinement, as are three other protective custody detainees. As penal detainees are not to be accommodated next to protective custody detainees and as protective custody detainees are not suitable cell neighbors, two cells have to be kept unoccupied next to the detention cell in order to make isolation complete. This, however, is no longer possible in future as the occupation of the institution is increasing all the time. Added to this is the fact that they must also, in the exercise yard, walk separately from the rest of the protective custody detainees.

21. Letter from the Prussian Minister President Hermann Göring to the Inspector of the Prussian Secret State Police, Rudolf Diels, regarding unauthorized concentration camps, dated 11 March 1934[58]

It has repeatedly come to my notice that Police Presidents have, alongside the police prisons, opened other prisons that bear the character of concentration camps, especially as guard duties are performed by SA or SS personnel.

I forbid in principle the opening of such secondary prisons or camps. Insofar as prisons or camps of the kind described exist, they are to be dissolved at once [. . .]. Furthermore I forbid SS or SA personnel to serve any longer in prisons or concentration camps. The tasks of education and exercise, which are the duty of these units, are not compatible with such use. Existing SA or SS guard personnel are to be relieved instantly and replaced by police staff. Such police staff naturally also include SS or SA men serving not in this capacity but as members of a state guard unit and are accordingly uniformed or made identifiable by special badges.

Implementation of the present instruction is to be reported to me by 17 March.

22. Letter from the Reich governor in Bavaria, Franz von Epp, to the Bavarian Minister-President Siebert, on the excessive number of protective custody detainees in Bavaria, dated 20 March 1934[59]

The number of persons still in protective custody in Prussia, as announced in the press during the past few days — 2,800 — is considerably below the number that was recently reported to me by competent quarters in Berlin. This, as well as the closure of the Oranienburg concentration camp that has taken place in the meantime, leads one to the conclusion that the number of releases in Prussia has recently been continued on a considerable scale.

The Early Camps, 1933–1934

The latest monthly report of the Political Police Commander Bavaria [Himmler] gives the number of protective custody prisoners in Bavaria as 3,500, of whom 2,200 are in Dachau. This disproportion does not make sense given the size of the states [*Länder*] Prussia and Bavaria, as well as the fact that the organizations hostile to the National Socialist state, especially the Marxist ones, cannot be compared with their corresponding organizations in Bavaria in terms of numbers, extent, or radicalism of views and actions. The disproportion only begins to make sense when one examines the protective custody justifications given by the Bavarian authorities. Alcoholism, ill-treatment of wife, trapping of songbirds, firewood theft, embezzlement of moneys belonging to an organization, immoral lifestyle, public disturbance, work shirking, etc. There is a major volume of protective custody cases for insults of communal councilors, mayors, local and district party leaders, *Gauleiters* [Nazi Party regional leaders], SA men and leaders, special commissioners, senior dignitaries of the Reich and the states [*Länder*]. There has also been an increase recently of cases when protective custody was imposed because of "anti-social behavior" (payment of wages below tariff, poor housing conditions of employees, violence against workers or employees, etc.) or because of derogatory criticism of some laws or directives. Finally, protective custody is still being imposed for "threat to personal safety."

This list shows that the authorities entrusted with the imposition of protective custody have lost the understanding of the meaning and purpose of protective custody and a sense of the responsibility associated with the imposition of this measure. Above all else, such a practice shakes the confidence in the law, which is the foundation of every state, and stands in opposition to the state of law and order demanded and proclaimed by the Führer. The Reich President's Order of 28.2.33, which is the basis of protective custody and which is unambiguous in its formulation and aims, was issued at a time of greatest political turmoil and fiercest political struggle. It provided the instruments for rapidly and thoroughly rendering strong and well-organized enemies of the state innocuous. The total National Socialist state, as it exists today, will and can apply a different yardstick to the use of those instruments, all the more so as subsequent laws and orders have created a series of legal provisions that make protective custody dispensable. I merely mention the Reich President's Order for the Repulsion of Malicious Attacks against the Government of National Resurgence and the Law against the Formation of New Parties.

From the above it follows:

It is not for the authorities to decide at will whether punishable actions are criminally prosecuted or whether protective custody is imposed for them. In all cases involving criminal facts the case must go before a judge; if detention seems necessary, by handing over the accused. The establishment of special courts[60] and the regulations on fast-track procedure guarantee a rapid judgment [. . .].

I moreover request that—beyond the "protective custody amnesty" decreed on the occasion of the anniversary of the assumption of responsibility by the National Socialist government—an immediate examination be conducted in this spirit of all pending protective custody cases and the gradual release of all protective custody detainees concerned be ordered by 15 April 1934 at the latest. In this connection the two months' suspension of release ordered by the Bavarian Political Police with effect from 22 February 1934 regarding the protective custody detainees in the Dachau concentration camp will have to be regarded as nonexistent.

23. Reply by the Bavarian Minister of the Interior Wagner to the Bavarian Minister-President Siebert, dated 14 April 1934[61]

It is presumed that the number of protective custody prisoners in Prussia, as published in the press (viz. 2,800) is correct. It should, however, be emphasized that, as far as is known here, only those protective custody prisoners are statistically recorded in Prussia who are in concentration camps for a lengthy period. Not recorded undoubtedly are the protective custody prisoners accommodated in Prussian prisons [. . .]. Beyond dispute is the fact that especially the Marxist organizations have always been far stronger and larger, in numbers and extent, in Prussia than in Bavaria. But there is no reason whatsoever for seeing in this a disproportion in the numbers of protective custody prisoners in the two states [Länder] [. . .]. It can already be guaranteed that in the event of the release of a mere 1,000 medium-ranking KPD functionaries from the Dachau camp the Bavarian KPD districts will soon equal the Prussian districts in extent and strength [. . .].

The observation that imposition of protective custody for alcoholism, firewood theft, embezzlement of moneys belonging to organizations, immoral lifestyle, work shirking, etc., do not correspond to the letter of the valid regulations, is entirely accurate. They do, however, correspond to National Socialist sentiment. Struggle against a lifeless bureaucratism, struggle against an incompetent legislation—these were among the main arguments of the National Socialist struggle against the former state. If the same tendencies were to reappear today, those that we fought against in the old state, then this would not be understood by the fighters for the National Socialist idea. It is certainly a fact that the protective custody detention of persons for the criminal offenses listed above has undoubtedly played the most essential part in the decline of criminality in Bavaria. Fear of protective custody detention dissuades many habitual criminals, who base their activity on the loopholes in the law, from continuing their former lifestyle [. . .]. The continuous criticism by the Reich governor's office of protective custody matters that come under the authority of my own ministry[62] is solid proof to me that the Reich governor's office fails to bring the necessary confidence to the handling of protective custody cases by my ministry. I suggest that the protective custody issue be, for a change, approached from a different point of view and that the necessary confidence be shown in my ministry that deals most painstakingly with all protective custody matters. I ask therefore that the fact that protective custody has frequently to be imposed also in criminal matters be seen not, as has been the rule until now, as a failure of the authorities subordinated to me, but as proof that the legal instruments for a quick judicial sentencing of those cases just do not exist.

24. Report of the Wuppertal-Elberfeld Senior State Prosecutor to the Central State Prosecutor's Office of the Prussian Ministry of Justice about ill-treatment at the Kemna camp, dated 9 July 1934[63]

The protective custody prisoners are said to have been grossly ill-treated during their interrogation in order to force them to make statements.

One prisoner is said to have been laid across a table, to have had his mouth tied up by a towel to prevent him from screaming, several guards are said to have held the prisoner down while other guards were hitting the prisoner with so-called bullwhips until he lost consciousness [. . .]. It is further asserted that the protective custody detainees had been forced to eat unwashed salted herrings soaked in axle-grease, human excrement and urine. If the prisoners vomited as a result, they are said to have also been forced to lick up their vomit [. . .].

Postscript. Some prisoners are said to have died of their injuries.

1.2. Life and Death Inside

As there was little central coordination of the first arrests and the early camps' establishment, conditions for prisoners varied very widely. Nazi treatment of prisoners was completely arbitrary and often included abuse and torture. In Berlin and elsewhere, storm troopers arrested suspects on the streets, detaining them in camps, cellars, and SA barracks (25).[64] Most inmates of the early camps later remembered their arrival as a particularly humiliating ritual, accompanied by constant beatings and degrading ceremonies, such as being forced to run the gauntlet. In some camps, prisoners were stripped of their clothes on arrival and given some worn uniforms or rags, while in other makeshift camps, prisoners kept their own clothes and shoes.[65] Likewise, in some camps prisoners received sufficient food, while in others they were left to starve. At Dachau, prisoners often received very poor food, yet rations were initially sufficient. Prisoners with access to money were able to buy extra rations and tobacco at the camp canteen, and most prisoners were allowed to receive one parcel per month with fresh underwear and food. In Dachau, at least, prisoners also had some access to lavatories and showers.[66]

Prisoners in many of the early camps were forced to live according to strict rules. They had to wake early and follow a military-style schedule, including roll calls and meticulous cleaning of their living quarters and clothes. Work, often dirty and strenuous with no real economic use, was compulsory in most early camps. For the Nazis, forcing the prisoners to work was a means of control and supposedly also of education. Military exercise, often nothing but abuse, was also the rule in most camps, and Nazi officials were keen to degrade elderly and unfit prisoners by forcing them to march and run.[67] For all prisoners and their relatives, the complete uncertainty as to when they would be released was one of the most unsettling aspects of detention. Yet at the same time it is important to stress again that the vast majority of the early camps' prisoners *were* released within weeks or months of their arrest.

Terror and violence were particularly rife in SS- and SA-run detention centers. Conditions in early camps officially controlled by judicial authorities were generally better than in Nazi-run camps. When the Hamburg-Fuhlsbüttel camp was officially transformed into a concentration camp in early September 1933 and effectively put under control of the Hamburg *Gauleiter*, conditions immediately deteriorated. Backed by the increasingly Nazified Hamburg judiciary, who remained nominally in charge, ss guards were let loose on the prisoners. Among them was the German Jewish journalist Fritz Solmitz held in Fuhlsbüttel since May 1933, who managed to make secret notes about the ss torture. He wrote his final message just hours before his death in Fuhlsbüttel (29).[68] On top of the abuse, some prisoners in makeshift detention facilities were left without food and medical help for days. Here, at local level, ss and sa men took revenge on their left-wing enemies whom they had long fought in street battles in the final crisis-ridden years of the Weimar Republic. Nazi guards unleashed their violence most forcefully against individual Communists and against Jews (28 and 30). This was not at all surprising given that anti-Bolshevism and anti-Semitism were the Nazi Party's core ideologies.[69]

Yet even in the most notorious camps like Kemna and Dachau, prisoners tried to adapt to camp life.[70] Many prisoners engaged in cultural activities to escape the harsh reality of the concentration camp. In many camps detainees made music together, and some even gave theater performances (32). This soon aroused the suspicion of the camp authorities, as they feared that such performances alluded too directly to life in the camps.[71]

DOCUMENTS

25. Report of Hans Dammert, suspected of Communist agitation, on his detention in Berlin, apparently written in 1933[72]

On 7 March at 5 in the afternoon I was arrested straight from the office where I worked. Under escort I was taken to the Nazi barracks Hedemannstr. 6.[73] In the doorway of the building I was immediately received with blows to my head. Then I was taken upstairs into a corridor that was lined with Nazis in civvies. Anyone who passed had to call out "Heil Hitler" and received a smacking box on the ears. Then one came to the common room where one's personal data were recorded. After a while several SA men appeared who were talking provocatively of the horrors of the Russian Revolution and the murders committed by the Communists, and were also speaking about the abuses that they had just been performing in other rooms of the same barracks. Evidently they were trying to get themselves into the mood and instill fear into us. After about half an hour a big SA man swung the door open with the words: "Ah, here we have the murderers of XX" (I have unfortunately forgotten the name of the SA man whom we had allegedly killed). Our protests against this outrageous accusation were answered with blows. Two SA men were working on me and the colleague arrested along with me with a revolver butt and a whip handle. We were being constantly hit on the head until we were both lying on the floor. Then one of the SA men tried to trample on me, but he was too drunk to stand on his own feet. When they noticed that I was still not unconscious, they made me get up and repeat sentences like: "My love for Adolf Hitler is great, but it is hard to stand up straight." Even if I had wanted to, I couldn't speak anymore because my jaw was broken twice on one side and once on the other. I was thereupon taken to a very dirty washroom where there were traces of the drunkenness of the SA. Equipped with a rag and a bucket I had to mop up the floor of that washroom, next to me stood an SA man with a whip. When they had enough of this I was put, with all my clothes on, under a cold shower and time and again dipped into the water. When I was eventually half-unconscious as a result, I was taken, wet as I was, back to the common room, where I was left lying without medical help the whole night and the following day until late in the evening. There I was repeatedly threatened with execution by shooting. Also, in spite of my seriously wounded condition, whenever a new SA man entered the room, I had to stand up and call out "Heil Hitler." When my condition had so deteriorated the following evening that they evidently feared trouble, I was dismissed under the most serious threats and, at the orders of the barracks commandant Bruckmann (or Bruggmann) taken to a hospital by two SA men. There they diagnosed the following injuries: triple fracture of the jaw, injury to the temporal bone, light concussion, several wounds to the face, contusions on the thorax and on the right hand, a wound on the left thigh caused by kicks. Before leaving the barracks I had to write a letter to my parents that I had been well treated, that I was all right and that I would see them tomorrow. My colleague had suffered such a severe injury to one of his eyes that a few days after our joint release one of his eyes had to be removed. In spite of being seriously ill he was rearrested about 3 weeks later and had to spend many weeks in the state hospital.

26. Report by Gerhart Seger on SA leaders of the Oranienburg camp, published in 1933[74]

Since the establishment of the camp the commandant was *Sturmbannführer* Schäfer[75] from Oranienburg. He had been a police officer cadet but had not been accepted as a police officer under Severing.[76] He then worked as a minor bank official and, on the side, was active as organizer and leader of an SA *Sturmbann*. In this capacity he became commandant of the concentration camp set up in the area of SA *Standarte* 208.

Schäfer is a veritable underling of a person. His hatred of Social Democrats is boundless. He enjoys practicing it by insulting helpless prisoners, who, following the camp rules, have to stand to attention in front of him, in an obscene manner. Schäfer did not often let himself go to indulge in physical maltreatment by beatings, but he was all the more generous with the imposition of disciplinary punishment: confinement in a dark cell, postal and visitors' bans and detailing to penal squads [. . .].

Sturmbannführer Krüger from Trebbin was, until October, the chief sadist of the Oranienburg camp. Employed by the Secret State Police, he held interrogations in Room 16; he has the two dead from Anhalt on his conscience, probably even more. One is reluctant to put on paper the full scale of this not-yet-30-year-old SA leader's crimes of unbridled raving sadism, of physical ill-treatment and moral torture of the prisoners [. . .]. Krüger felt especially strong when there were National Socialist visitors to whom he could present us. Like a self-important tamer in a small touring circus he would then stride around the camp, summoning the "VIPs" of the camp and introducing them to the visitors with vile remarks. "Just look at these shepherds! This here is another overfed mayor of the SPD! This Jewish swine here opened his filthy trap against our Führer!" and other insults of this

The Early Camps, 1933–1934

kind—and the prisoner always had to silently stand at attention and let himself be abused! In October, for reasons not accurately known to us prisoners, Krüger was removed; first he was transferred to the Blumberg branch camp as a kind of "prisoner-of-honor" and then he was completely dismissed and sent home, as was reported by visitors from Trebbin. But the "tradition" of Room 16, which he created, continues to exist.

The person continuing it is *Sturmführer* Stahlkopf,[77] who already was a keen participant in all crimes in Krüger's day. While Krüger had a certain daredevil brutality, Stahlkopf is the type of the creepy, particularly infamous sadist, whose character has a downright unimaginable vileness. The abysmal meanness of this man is perhaps best revealed in an episode that took place on the day before my escape.

A married prisoner is called to Room 16 for interrogation. Stahlkopf asks him, "How long have you been in custody?" "Six months," the prisoner answers. "So who is f——ing your wife back home?"

A special peculiarity of *Sturmführer* Stahlkopf was that at night, when he was slightly drunk, he would collect prisoners from the dormitories in order to beat them or to put them through some drill in the courtyard. This he did above all with the unfortunate members of the so-called Jewish company, which existed for a while and to which the former leader of the Social Democrat Party in the Prussian Diet Ernst Heilmann[78] had been detailed during his stay in the Oranienburg camp.

27. Description of the Dachau camp in summer 1933 by the former detainee Wenzel Rubner,[79] published in 1934[80]

I am describing the Dachau camp as it looked at my release in September 1933. After the escape of the Communist Deputy Beimler [see 33] in April 1933 the fortifications were greatly strengthened. The Dachau camp is very large, some 235 hectares. To circle it would take two hours. The entire ground is surrounded by a high wall. In addition to the buildings, inside the wall, are a gravel pit, a sizable pond and some woodland. It is said that the complex of buildings used to belong to a brewery. During the war it was developed and enlarged as a gunpowder factory and ammunition store [. . .]. The more sizable and spacious buildings of the camp are reserved for the administration and ss staff. The prisoners are accommodated at night in ground-level huts. On the cold walls of the dining hall a Communist from Kempten, on orders from the ss but obviously not without enjoying this bad deed himself, had painted caricatures of Social Democrat leaders. The Prussian Minister President Otto Braun,[81] the Berlin Police President Albert Grzesinski,[82] Philipp Scheidemann[83] (with a needle through his forehead), the Center Party leader Marx,[84] the "Ullstein Jew" Georg Bernhard[85] (with temple ringlets and a Jewish skullcap) were represented in that gallery. There were also disgustingly distorted pictures of the murdered Rathenau and Erzberger and of the dead Gustav Stresemann.[86] One wall near the dining hall bears the portrait of an sa man with a swastika flag. Next to it is a motto that has become symbolic of Herr Hitler's movement not only in Dachau: "Forward over graves!" The narrow concrete cells behind the huts, dark confinement cells, built by the prisoners themselves in compulsory labor, differ but little from medieval dungeons [. . .].

The camp is protected as follows: facing the wall inside is barbed wire. The space between barbed wire and the wall is continually patrolled by ss details, on top of the three-meter-high wall there is more barbed wire. The wall is intersected by four towers with loaded machine guns manned day and night. A fifth mg tower stands in the camp opposite the main guardhouse. The towers are equipped with powerful searchlights that light up the camp at night. The prisoners' huts form a barbed-wire enclosed camp within the camp wall. At night this wire is charged with high-voltage electric current. When the inmates line up to receive their food, ss sentries with rifles with mounted bayonets stand next to them; a loaded mg is aimed at all times on the prisoners by the kitchen entrance.

28. Report by the Communist Alfred Benjamin, a German Jew, on his detention at the Esterwegen concentration camp in August 1933, written in 1933[87]

I was assigned to the Papenburg camp no. 3 near Esterwegen. This camp is situated far from any human habitation amid heath, moor and sand. Immediately upon arrival we Jews were isolated. On the way to the camp we were beaten with iron sticks and rifle butts, jabbed with bayonets, had a revolver with its safety catch off held to our heads.

With vile insults which, for reasons of decency, one cannot even approximately reproduce, they tried to humiliate and insult us—in short, we were tormented by all imaginable means and methods. It should be said—because this will make various things more credible—that only ss men served as staff, moreover without exception people of no more than thirty, including some absolute sadists whose pleasure at ill-treating us can only be explained as sexual deviation. General living conditions in the camp were disastrous—added to this there was a special position for "Jews, criminals and functionaries" in the form of concentration in a "Special squad." The camp administration tried to turn the other comrades against us, they said it was our fault that they were here, they promised everything possible to get them to kill us in our hut at night, but—the workers displayed icy faces and declared their solidarity with us. It is perhaps not inopportune to give a brief outline of the living conditions. Food was not only insufficient but also often inedible. For instance, for weeks there was only rice with noodles without any meat, extremely seldom there was thick bean soup that was filling. And that with heaviest ten-hour daytime labor. The work consisted of moor drainage, a daily stint of 15 cubic meters had to be accomplished. Anyone unable to keep up because of weakness or illness has to expect most severe punishment as a "work refuser." I myself am sick with my lungs—yet once, when I collapsed during work, I did not succeed in getting to the doctor. With a heavy hippopotamus whip I was whipped out of the sick bay before I could speak a word [. . .]. The camp lacks the most primitive hygienic conditions. For 1,000 people there was only one water pump, which was often out of order. Drinking of unboiled water resulted in many cases of dysentery. Many developed rheumatism from standing for hours up to their knees in the ice-cold moorland water. The huts were without stoves right into October. We could not sleep restfully because even at night we were fetched out of the huts to be tormented. Over two months I witnessed five executions "while trying to escape."

29. Excerpts from secret notes of the German Jewish journalist Fritz Solmitz from the Fuhlsbüttel concentration camp to his wife, Karoline, 13 to 18 September 1933[88]

On 13.9. at 2 in the afternoon Senator Schröder, accompanied by President Lahts, appeared on the threshold of my hall. After the latest news from Karoline I had to assume that the visit meant my release [. . .]. Minutes later my section guard Robert Etzert [. . .], *Scharführer* in the *Marinesturm*,[89] pub-keeper by occupation, formerly a sailor, returned to the hall. He shouted: "Solmitz, pack your things!" Long pause, all my blood flowed to my heart, this is the moment I've been waiting for for more than six months. "Category 3, solitary confinement."[90] Category 3 is the terrible treatment that alleged recalcitrants, in fact all Communist leaders, have to suffer, but also Meitmann [a Hamburg Social Democrat]. Strictest solitary confinement, [. . .] no light in the evening. While daylight lasts, tow picking. It is 1,000 times worse than penitentiary. You don't get fresh air at all. E., who had been persecuting me with anti-Semitic insults from the first day on, drove me, wildly cursing, into the solitary cell. I had no time to pack my things even in a makeshift way. I am skipping the next half-hour, which was full of insults. I was then taken to the corridor, where the *Sturmführer* of the ss *Sturm* was waiting for me with his dog-whip in his hand. I was driven into the cellar, then into a bay that had probably served as a potato store in the past. In addition to E. and a roughly 25-year-old *Sturmführer* there were another 7 men present. Command: "Bend over." I remained standing upright, immediately received terrible blows to my face with the dog-whip and the bullwhip. I reeled and fell. Short pause. "The swine's pretending." Up. Stand up. "Bend over." I was beaten down three times. After the third time I still had strength enough to shout: "I'm not bending over." But I believe that in the end, in a half-conscious state, I nevertheless did so. I don't know how long this torture lasted. I was still being beaten as I was lying on the floor, until the skin on my head split and blood squirted out. The longed-for loss of consciousness still had not come. With curses and blows I was driven upright and bleeding heavily had to run to my cell at a trot. There I was allowed to wash. A medical orderly came to bandage me. He was told by my tormentors that the window flap had fallen on my head. "The Jew has such a soft noddle." (When the doctor came the following day, I was forced to tell him the same lie by my chief torturers.) Then I had to clean my totally blood-soaked things and my blood-spattered cell. An hour later E. brought me dark bread and tea. As I greedily reached for the tea, he called out: "Stop. Everything back immediately, you won't get anything to eat, Jew, for 3 days. Commandant's orders." Since then I've now and again received one piece of dark bread or a can of coffee. But I hardly eat that. Hunger no longer hurts me. In the evening I take a Veramon tablet, the last but one. ("Why don't you swallow the whole lot, so you croak," E. had said while searching me. Unfortunately there were only 2 tablets left.) I didn't want to have my fate decided by those idiots [. . .]. On 15th I eventually dared ask for what reason I was punished with Category 3 and starvation, whether on the grounds of my political past or my behavior here. E. replied that there was nothing to find fault with in my behavior here, but they knew now what a swine I had been before [. . .]. 16.9. [. . .] Repeatedly asked to be examined by the doctor. No answer. To every word from me their reply "Trap." I am quite still. The tow picking also does me a lot of good [. . .].

Monday, 18 Sept. evening.

Today there was tea. Just as I was sipping it, E. entered with 5 men from the *Marinesturm* to inform me after some sneeringly friendly questions that I would be whipped again the next day. After all, the noddle has healed up. A very long ss man steps on my toes and yells: For me you'll bend over. "Oi, say yes, you pig." Another: "Why don't you hang yourself? Then you won't get whipped!" The seriousness of the threat is not to be doubted. God, what shall I do? Karoline, my love, this was your birthday. Everything I've written down is God's truth. May it serve to save others. Fly away, far away, K. with the children and everything that bears my name. Get away soon. Make good use of these lines if they reach you. But be careful doing it. Help those who can still be helped. Let Heiner be a fatherly friend to my children. His road is the right one.

Farewell for ever!

for Frau Karoline Solmitz from Lübeck.

30. Report of Rubin Weinmann, a German Jew, on his arrest in Berlin, written on 13 November 1933[91]

On 23 August 1933 at 1 o'clock at night sa men of the Secret Police, identified as such by their cap ribbons and badges, occupied the building

Berlin, Weinbergsweg 4, where I was living, in order to prevent a possible escape [. . .]. We were taken to the SA *Sturm* Lokal 35/6 on Alte Jakobstrasse, where a crowd of cheerful looking SA men received us with howls of delight. We were immediately taken to the cellar of the place. They sat my mother on a chair and tipped a water bucket over her head so she should not hear me scream from the ill-treatment. I was taken to a small side room, where several SA men tore down my trousers, unbuttoned their shoulder straps and forced me to count every blow. When I had got to roughly 40 they asked me where the copying device was [the SA men accused him of printing illegal leaflets]. I had until then pretended not to know what they were talking about [. . .]. [With two other prisoners, I] had to scrub the floor and tolerate several buckets of water being poured over our heads. Suddenly the SA people discovered that our hair was too long and my friend, named Horst Rosenzweig, first had to cut my hair with scissors and then I, his. We had to collect the hair that had dropped on the floor and put it into our pockets. The two of us were assigned the dirtier jobs, whereas the other boy, who was a Christian, was assigned better work. From the conversation of the SA people I learned that in a further room of the cellar there was a girl, named Edith Baumann, who allegedly had an affair with Horst Rosenzweig, and that girl, who was a Christian, was told that nothing would be done to her if she made detailed statements about the Communist activity of Horst Rosenzweig, which apparently she didn't do [. . .]. During my detention in the kitchen of the SA premises we were most vilely insulted with such expressions as "Jewish whoremongers," "Galician onion Jews" and "We'll castrate you so you can't molest Aryan girls anymore" [. . .]. A senior SA functionary named Witzar and called "Fritz Meyer," who had also played a leading part in the interrogation, came in, said "Jeeew" and spat into my face. Then he came and led me into a remote room where an SA man was sleeping. "Fritz Meyer" closed the windows to prevent any screams being heard outside as mechanics were working on the opposite side of the building. I had to take my trousers down, hold up my shirt and, in ducked position, allow myself to be struck on my naked buttocks. For any shout he threatened me with five further blows of the cane. The SA man who had until then been asleep in the little room had woken up with the flogging; angrily he asked "Fritz Meyer" to leave the flogging to him. I had to kneel down, support myself with my hands on the floor while he beat me. "Fritz Meyer" then hung up a picture of the former Reich President Ebert on the wall and I had to say a few Hebrew words in front of that picture. Then I had to dress again, but before I did so he said to me: "Let's see if you've been circumcised."

31. Report by the Social Democrat prisoner Fritz Ecker on Dachau ss guards, published in 1934[92]

On Sunday, 22 October 1933, the commandant of the Dachau concentration camp, ss *Oberführer* Eicke, ordered the nearly 2,500 prisoners of the camp to fall in. In front of these prisoners, who had to suffer or watch horrible atrocities every day, he raved against the "villains" who were spreading abroad horror stories about the Dachau camp. In his address Eicke then announced that the protective custody detainees Altmann, Dr. Katz, Dr. Rosenfelder and Willy Franz had tried to smuggle out notes sewn into a cap about incidents in the camp. "Two of the arrested traitors," Eicke said literally, "have already been transferred to the Beyond: the Jew Dr. Katz and his helper Willy Franz.[93] We still have enough German oaks to hang anybody on them who opposes us. There are no atrocities and there is no Cheka cellar in Dachau. Anybody whipped, deserves to be whipped!" [. . .]

The most feared flogging hero and murderer was Hans Steinbrenner,[94] who maltreated prisoners day after day and soon acquired various nicknames: "Murdering fire-raiser," "The long terror" and "Ivan the Terrible" he was called in turn [. . .]. If a prisoner was to be specially tormented he was handed over to this "Ivan" for treatment. His first order as a rule was for them to clean the lavatory [. . .].

In July and August 1933 the ss men had yet another way of cheating the prisoners out of their money. Hans Steinbrenner checked the purses and made "house searches" on his own initiative. Wherever he found, or suspected, any money he suggested, by striking the person's face, a "donation" for a purpose named by him. Where these donations went was clear from the constant drunkenness of Steinbrenner and his friends.

32. Report of the Communist Wolfgang Langhoff on the "Zirkus Konzentrazani" in the Börgermoor camp, published in 1935[95]

"I tell you, you're crazy!" remarked an old worker from Düsseldorf. "The ss are our mortal enemies and now you actually want to play to them! When they see this they'll say, these people are still much too well off. We haven't beaten them up enough!" "You've got to understand, Willi! We're prisoners here. All right, but they've also managed to intimidate us! To break us morally! We hang our heads in shame and run about the camp like whipped dogs. But if we now show them that we are real chaps and that with their ill-treatment they can get stuffed, you just wait for the impression this'll make on them! Get it? Surely they regard us as subhumans. But if they now see how we stick together then some ss man or other, who is just as much of a proletarian as we are, may ask himself if the way they're treating us now is the right one. Already we'll have gained something. And then our own boys themselves! If the performance is good they will all be proud of it and will wonder if we might not do something else, something more important, together in the camp!"

"Quite right," our room eldest interjected [. . .]. I had inquiries made in every hut about what artistic, humorous or other talents existed and was amazed at the quantity of offers made to me. Everything was represented: acrobats, gymnasts, singers, animal imitators, jugglers and so on. We rehearsed behind our hut in the evening and nobody was allowed to watch. Only the ss men patrolling the barbed-wire corridor stopped and watched our rehearsals with curiosity. I could feel how they welcomed such a diversion, because from within themselves they were in no position to develop any form of entertainment [. . .]. Sunday came. In the morning we were still rehearsing the new song that our miner colleague had written and to which a commercial employee had made the tune. Meanwhile "Kerl," a permanent joker, who his comrades say is a little "daft," ran with a large poster that Hans K. had painted for us all around the camp and even in front of the commandant's office. "*Zirkus Konzentrazani*! Today great gala performance! Gigantic animal show! The greatest oxen in the world. Never seen before. August—the greatest comic! Opening at 2.30" [. . .]. Except for the seats that we had kept for the ss and the Commandant the place was sold out. We had deliberately placed the ss so they had to look into the sun, just in case any of them had thought of bringing a camera along and snapping. In addition we had also decided to break off the performance if a camera was spotted [. . .]. We, who are no longer leading the lives of humans, had dared to decide about ourselves for a few hours, without orders, without instructions, just as if we were our own masters and as if such an institution as a concentration camp did not exist!

1.3. The Prisoners

In the overwhelming majority, the early camps' prisoners were Communists, followed by Social Democrats.[96] Prominent left-wing politicians such the former leader of the SPD group in the Prussian assembly Ernst Heilmann were treated especially badly by the Nazis (26). Men were in the vast majority, though the early camps also held some women, sometimes the wives of left-wing activists.[97] Women taken into protective custody were mostly held in small special wings in state prisons (such as Gotteszell in Swabia and Aichach in Bavaria) or workhouses (such as Brauweiler in the Rhineland).[98]

Yet, despite all the Nazi terror, prisoners were not passive victims and formed groups of solidarity with inmates from backgrounds similar to their own. Political prisoners, in particular, often developed close ties with fellow inmates. Communists, for example, often shared the food they had received in parcels from relatives and gave food rations to those in the arrest cells where they were left to starve for a few days. Some political prisoners also took over the role of prisoner representatives who negotiated with the camp authorities on behalf of other inmates. Meanwhile, the camp authorities delegated the responsibility for certain aspects of day-to-day life, such as cleaning the barracks, to prisoner supervisors (sometimes known as Kapos). These supervisors (or prisoner functionaries), soon a fixed feature of the camps, were in a difficult position as they had to deal directly with the guards. Prisoners thought to be collaborating were ostracized and often punished by fellow inmates.

Political prisoners in the early camps shared the expectation that the Nazi regime would not last long, providing them with a sense of hope. Yet conflict, not solidarity, often characterized relations between Social Democrats and Communist prisoners, reflecting the long antagonism between the two parties in the Weimar Republic. In the early camps, Social Democrats, such as the former Reichstag deputy Gerhart Seger, accused Communists of collaborating with Nazi guards, while Communist prisoners accused the Social Democrats of doing just the same (34).[99]

The Early Camps, 1933–1934

Apart from Social Democrats and Communists, there were also Jews and prisoners from other backgrounds in the early camps. Most Jews were detained in the camps as left-wing activists. However, some, including the preacher Max Abraham, were arrested by the Nazis simply because they were Jewish. From the beginning, Jewish prisoners were on the lowest rung of the hierarchy of prisoners that gradually began to emerge. Nazi camp guards, often extremely anti-Semitic, abused Jews particularly badly, torturing them and forcing them to carry out the dirtiest jobs (30 and 37).

Purported criminals and beggars also began to arrive in the camps in the autumn of 1933, amid the escalating Nazi terror against social outsiders. In Bavaria, for instance, officials in charge of the increasingly overcrowded Rebdorf workhouse began to transfer to Dachau inmates who soon came to be known as asocials, a catch-all term for beggars, tramps, alcoholics and other people not conforming to the behavior expected. And in Prussia, hundreds of purported habitual criminals, often people with a string of convictions for petty offenses, were detained in concentration camps such as Esterwegen and Lichtenburg (38) in the wake of the November 1933 Prussian decree on preventive custody (see section 1.1).[100] It is unclear how these prisoners from social minorities, marginalized already before 1933, fit into the prisoner population. Clearly, they were treated with suspicion by political prisoners who shared common prejudices against them and accused them of stealing from their fellow prisoners (39).[101]

DOCUMENTS

33. Report of the former Communist Reichstag Deputy Hans Beimler on his detention in the arrest cell of the Dachau camp, published in 1933[102]

Fourteen days of strict arrest, I thought to myself, that'll be "great." As I was sitting on the edge of the primitively knocked-together wooden bunk, the only item of furniture, reflecting upon my further fate, the door of my cell was kicked open and three ss men, their hands behind their back, led by Steinbrenner, entered with the words:

"Now we got you, you agitator, you traitor to your country, you traitor to the workers, you Bolshevik swine, you bigwig." Saying this,

Steinbrenner strikes me several times on my head and my shoulders [. . .]. Half an hour may have passed and again the door opens. Vogel, the Administrator, the man "responsible" for what happens in the hut that contains the cells, stands before me.

"Have you got any request—a wish or a complaint?" was his question to me. My hatred and disgust for this gang of murderers was too great for me to lower myself by voicing a request or a wish. A complaint? I didn't want to be a figure of ridicule. "None of the three," was my answer. Now he handed me a two-meters-long rope the thickness of a finger and invited me to hang it from the water tap. After a brief reflection I took the rope in my hand—and again reflected. "Yes, yes," he said, "just climb on the bed and hang the rope from the tap."

34. Report of the Social Democrat politician Gerhart Seger about disputes between Communist and Social Democrat inmates in the Oranienburg camp, published in 1934[103]

Probably by far the most painful experience for anyone who has dedicated himself body and soul to the German workers' movement will be that not even in a concentration camp, in the face of jointly suffered torments, inflicted on everybody by the common political opponent, was it possible to create a minimum of comradeship [. . .]. One evening *Sturmbannführer* Krüger stepped before the line of prisoners and announced that the following day the "fully-gorged Social Democrat bigwig Fritz Ebert"[104] would be delivered to the camp, that Marxist pig who was one of the November criminals who had hurled Germany into misfortune, well, the SA would know how to deal with that swine.

So what happened after this speech with its disastrous announcement at the end? From the ranks of the Communist prisoners came loud calls of Bravo! The Communists concerned, themselves victims of the chief SA sadist standing before them, were not ashamed to applaud the murderer of their own party friends when this National Socialist promised to have a go at a Social Democrat!

35. *Der Gegen-Angriff*: Article dated 24 February 1934. The Dutch Communist Nico Rost criticizes Gerhart Seger's account of the Oranienburg camp[105]

If, albeit Dutch, one had, because of one's views, to spend some time (fortunately only briefly) in "protective custody" in the Oranienburg concentration camp, one is probably duty bound to comment on Gerhart Seger's book "Oranienburg" [. . .].

We will disregard the fact that it is wrong to announce Seger's book as "the first authentic account of one who escaped from the concentration camp" because—quite apart from numerous reports of escapees in the anti-fascist press—we have had for six months the shocking report of Hans Beimler (actually a colleague of Seger from the Reichstag) [. . .]. However, Seger's book contains, whenever it deals with Communists, only distortions and deliberate falsehoods. In his entire mentality Seger has remained the old SPD leader who, even in the concentration camp and in spite of all his assertions to the contrary, sees an enemy in a Communist worker [. . .].

During the time of my stay in the Oranienburg camp, in April 1933, there was complete solidarity between KPD and SPD workers [. . .].

36. Report by Kreszentia Mühsam on the solidarity of the inmates in Oranienburg in the years 1933 and 1934, published in exile in 1935[106]

The greatest joy that I could give Erich [her husband] was with food parcels. As the nutrition in Oranienburg was very deficient in fat and I had no money at home to buy delicacies, I brought along a roast pork belly every visiting day, so he could eat his fill in the evening with his comrades. When he saw the parcel he asked me: "How many comrades do you think I can invite this evening?" and when I said: "Ten to twelve," his eyes shone with pleasure as though nothing bad had ever happened to him.

37. Report of the Jewish preacher Max Abraham about his detention in the Börgermoor (Emsland) camp in 1933, first published in 1934[107]

The Jews mainly on the Sabbath were assigned to work in the latrines [. . .]. "Today you have Shabbes again, you bastards. We'll see where your God of vengeance is when we teach you a thing or two in the pigsty." The Jewish high holidays were approaching. We asked ourselves nervously whether the dates were known to the SS men, because we were fearing even worse torments. We agreed therefore to avoid any hint of the approaching holidays. I had originally had the firm intention of requesting the camp commandant to release the Jewish company from work, but had to let myself be convinced by my comrades that such a request would not only be in vain, but might have regrettable consequences.

We had not made allowance for our relatives who, ignorant of what was happening in the camp, sent us good wishes for the New Year. As the letters went through the censorship the dates became known to the ss and there was now nothing to keep secret. So I went to the camp commandant after all and asked for exemption from work and for permission to hold divine service. Answer: "There's no such thing here!" On the first holiday, at six in the morning, we Jewish inmates were called up into a special squad. At quick-march speed we were chased across the courtyard. In front of a dung pit the command "Halt" was given. We had to step down into the pit and form up in it. I was snatched from the ranks of my comrades and put in the middle of the pit. ss *Scharführer* Everling yelled at me: "Well, Rabbi, you can hold your divine service here!" Everything in me rebelled against having our faith—quite literally—dragged into the mud. I remained silent.

Everling: "You refuse to obey the order?"

"I don't hold divine service in a dung pit!"

Everling got me out of the pit—rubber truncheons and rifle butts crashed down on me. Unconscious I was taken to my bunk. For two hours I lay there unconscious. In the afternoon we were taken to the same dung pit where the others had had to work in the morning. Now Everling invited me to give a lecture on Judaism and other religions. I began: "The Jewish religion, like other religions, has as its basis the Ten Commandments and the beautiful biblical sentence: 'Love thy neighbor as thyself!'" Everling interrupted: "Stop, you swine, we'll teach you what's meant by neighborly love!" Now I was ill-treated so terribly that I developed high fever and went into spasms. My body was beaten bloody. I could neither sit nor lie. Thus I spent a frightful night full of confused and cruel hallucinations. Next morning I was taken to the sick bay in an alarming condition.

38. Report of Wolfgang Langhoff on the arrival of so-called professional criminals at the Lichtenburg camp in the autumn of 1933, published in 1935[108]

One should not think that one can tell "professional criminals" by their appearance. They are not crooks with a kerchief and cap. On the contrary, they are very well dressed, in elegant overcoats, shiny polished shoes, with decent bourgeois hats on their heads. They look like "gentlemen." A few ss men wander curiously around them. We are standing by the window with throbbing hearts and clenched teeth. After all, we know what is in store for them. They do not know it themselves. They are unsuspecting . . .

Now the "Black Man"[109] comes across the courtyard. We hear a command "Attention!" He looks the people over. Thoroughly and slowly. "How many years did you get?" "My last sentence was two years and three months." "How long altogether?" "Seven years in all." "What for?" "Burglary and insurance fraud." He questions each one of them. Very calmly, in a soft voice. His eyes under the peak of his cap are wandering ceaselessly over the group. Suddenly he shouts: "Will you kindly look straight ahead! What's there to whisper about? Gone mad, what? Scum! Pack of criminals! Lousy thieves! There's no room for you any longer in the new Germany! Did you think Adolf Hitler would idly stand by while you contaminate the national body and cheat our people? We'll open your eyes for you! You are the last shit, not worth the grub you'll get here! Under the black-red-gold government[110] you were making hay! End of your story! I don't care if you rot here or if you croak—but none of you will ever get out of here! Don't you believe that we are humane! We don't give a monkey's for humanity! Humanity is the mark of the weak!" [. . .] Along the yard wall, past the latrine, the prisoners are galloping in a circle. At a crazy speed. They race along like lunatics, across the softened ground, through mud, snow and puddles. Their suitcases and parcels fly into the mud. They stumble, they fall. Flogging raises them to their feet again. They extend their arms, imploringly. They howl.

39. Report by Fritz Ecker on the "self-justice of the prisoners" in the Dachau camp, published in 1934[111]

It is to the credit of the political prisoners that, during the many months of my stay in the camp, not one of them committed an offense. It was always the criminals, people from the workhouse.

The sinners who were caught were always handed over to the 5th Corporal's Unit of the 1st Company.[112] There were several "tall-as-trees" Communists, roofers by trade, who undertook the office of judges. The thief was bound hand and foot, a board was hung round his neck and he was carried around the camp.

Later a far worse method of punishment was invented. Before the company was lined up for the evening meal, the thief was taken into the kitchen—and handed over to the ss people. Brummer, the "kitchen bull," as I witnessed myself, struck such a prisoner in the face with his fist, about twenty times, till the blood spurted from his nose and mouth. The man was then put on a crate and a board was hung round his neck: "I am the thief of First Company. I am a criminal." ss man Brummer then poured [. . .] four buckets of cold water over the head of the bleeding victim, took a scrubbing brush and scrubbed his face.

1.4. The Camps and the Public

From the outset, the concentration camps had a public remit. For the Nazis, the camps' public purpose was primarily about the deterrence of any potential left-wing opposition and resistance. It was for this reason, above all, that the regime was keen to publicize the early camps' establishment. Local newspapers in particular, both Nazi and those that had not been associated with the party before 1933, ran reports on the opening of the early camps, written in the context of widespread terror and the increasing Nazi control of the press. Communists and Social Democrats had to be locked up, according to these reports, because they endangered the new order (48): in the camps, left-wing rabble-rousers would be turned into full members of the German national community under a regimen of tough military discipline and work. At the same time, the regime was keen to portray the camps as highly regulated places where torture was impossible — not least to counter widespread rumors and reports about abuses in the camps, which soon spread across Germany and beyond.

News of the early camps had quickly spread abroad. Some foreign observers bought into Nazi propaganda: German officials set the camps up for foreign delegations' official visits and threatened prisoners with severe punishment if they told the truth about the brutal life in the camps. Yet most foreign observers and journalists realized that terror and torture were integral aspects of the early camps and of the Third Reich more generally. Many ex-prisoners who escaped abroad publicized their shocking experiences of the camps too.[113]

The German authorities, including the foreign office, were deeply concerned about the impact of such exile and foreign reports on public opinion in both Germany and abroad, roundly dismissing them as "atrocity propaganda" (*Greuelpropaganda*), a term with which Germans had been familiar since 1914 when Allied newspapers had reported German war atrocities in Belgium.[114] German propaganda articles explicitly refuted alleged "atrocity propaganda." There was even a live radio broadcast from the Oranienburg camp on Germany's international radio station in which an inmate was forced to say that he was being treated extremely well (56). Moreover, Werner Schäfer, Oranienburg's commandant, published a book in response to exile publications. He claimed that while he and his guards had indeed cracked down on the Communists, he was looking after his prisoners so well that he even received letters from former inmates thanking him for their good treatment (61). Schäfer, keen to ingratiate himself with Hitler, sent his Führer a copy of the book. While there is no evidence that Hitler actually read it, one of his aides wrote to Schäfer that Hitler gladly accepted this present. This was not surprising, because the book reaffirmed Nazi propaganda about the camps as places of discipline and reeducation.[115]

The Nazis even forced ex-prisoners to write letters to the editors of foreign newspapers to refute alleged "atrocity stories." Such was the case of Dr. Ludwig Levy, a state prosecutor, from Potsdam, who was imprisoned at Oranienburg in 1933. A former prisoner mentioned Levy's name in a long report about atrocities in Oranienburg which he published in *The Times* on 19 September 1933 after his release from the camp and his subsequent escape from Germany. This report evidently infuriated the Nazi authorities, which put Levy, recently released from Oranienburg, under heavy pressure, probably including the threat of immediate rearrest in the camp or worse. Levy thus had little choice but to refute *The Times*'s article in a letter to its editor (54).[116]

The Nazi regime also worked hard to manage public knowledge of the camps inside the Reich to preserve the official Nazi picture of the camps. To this end, camp officials forced inmates to write postcards to their relatives that they were being treated well. And upon their release, prisoners had to sign a declaration promising that they would not talk about their experiences inside the camps lest they be rearrested and never set free again (60). The authorities were so concerned about their public image that telling negative stories about the regime became a criminal offense under the Reich President's Decree against Malicious Attacks of 21 March 1933. Special courts sentenced numerous people to prison terms for talking about abuses in the camps.[117]

Still, unauthorized reports about the camps spread quickly through Germany. Despite the threats, many prisoners talked about their experiences upon their release. These reports soon spread further, together with other rumors about the camps (53). Moreover, Socialist and Communist pamphlets and leaflets published abroad soon found their way back to Germany. Furthermore, in some early camps, such as Börgermoor, wives were allowed to visit their imprisoned husbands and also transmitted news from the camps to their friends and families (51). Many relatives of prisoners also wrote to the authorities, pressing for their relatives' release. Sometimes even senior civil servants tried to intervene on behalf of prisoners—very much to the annoyance of some Nazi leaders (50). The regime almost always rejected such applications, even when Louise Ebert, widow of the Weimar Republic's first Reich President, wrote to Hindenburg, asking for her son's release in July 1933 (47).

Further details emerged from the local population living near camps. Most of the early camps were located in or near cities, towns, and villages, in earshot or eyesight of residents and passersby. For readers of local newspapers, the camps were not abstract prison camps but places in the immediate vicinity where the regime's potential and real enemies were detained. The contacts between the camps and the surrounding population were manifold and complex. Initially, local businesses and local councils hoped to profit from having a camp in town (43), welcoming the establishment of camps in their localities as an opportunity for tradesmen and businesses at a time of mass unemployment.[118] One Oranienburg citizen even proposed to the mayor that camp inmates should be used for public building projects (46). And indeed, some camp authorities did "lend" prisoners for a fee to local councils, and prisoners also carried out construction works.[119] Yet not all local people were "proud of having a camp in town," as one historian has claimed.[120] Local left-wing sympathizers were, of course, dismayed and deterred by the camps. A local paper from Dachau, a Communist stronghold in the Weimar Republic, even warned people of approaching the camp's perimeter fence, suggesting that the camp authorities were afraid of a Communist attack at a time when the Nazi regime had not yet fully established its power (42).[121] Moreover, in Dachau the local community did not benefit immediately from the setting up of a camp, which soon led to some disillusionment.[122]

All in all, it is clear that most Germans knew of the early camps from both official and unofficial sources. What they made of the camps is a more complex question. Clearly, reactions varied. Rumors of arbitrary terror probably offended some law-abiding citizens, concerned about revolutionary chaos. At the same time, many middle-class Germans no doubt welcomed the crackdown against the left. Nazi propaganda could build here upon anti-Bolshevik fears prevalent since the Russian revolution of 1917 and the German revolution of 1918. In Nazi propaganda the early camps were depicted as civilized and harmless compared to what the Communists would have done to the Nazis and the German middle classes if they had come to power.[123] Still, by no means did all Germans accept or tolerate the early camps.[124] Most obviously, the organized working class did not approve of camps where tens of thousands of their representatives were locked up and abused. Many workers saw the camps as instruments of outright terror against them by an alliance of Nazis and capitalist exploiters. Such must have been the workers' impression when in 1934 a Leipzig firm threatened workers with confinement in a camp if they talked about company secrets.[125] Still, German workers' attitudes were ambiguous, too. Opposition to Nazi terror could often go hand-in-hand with support for the regime's crackdown on social outsiders. In short, Germans' attitudes toward the early camps were as varied as their attitudes toward the early Nazi regime as a whole.

DOCUMENTS

40. *Kasseler Post*: Article about the protective custody authority in the Kassel *Karlshospital*, dated 5 April 1933[126]

Thus arose the "Protection Wing of the Karlshospital," which is nothing more and wishes nothing more than, upon official instruction, providing the protection that is granted to every German and to every person living in Germany. A reliable squad of efficient and well-tried SA men has assumed the guarding of this location and provides the guarantee that all those who have either been brought into custody or have submitted to it voluntarily are securely looked after. Who would have thought that the large hut at the *Karlshospital* has now assumed the task of a protective custody wing? In the great, spacious "theater hall" straw mattresses have been set up for fifty persons; the adjoining room, formerly the school room, serves as a day room [. . .]. Here they are all together, persons from the most varied political camps, with the most varied views. They all feel how the seriousness of the age and the hardships of the people demand a personal stance from them. For many of them it is no doubt difficult, perhaps everything will be buried that had been seen by one or the other as a great aim in life, ever since their childhood. The SA comrades are trying, by standing together with those entrusted to their custody, to show them the direction and the road [. . .].

41. *Berliner Illustrirte Zeitung*: Article about the Oranienburg concentration camp, dated 30 April 1933[127]

A large number of persons taken into protective custody in the past few weeks have now been concentrated in camps. Such camps were first established in southern Germany and then also in Prussia and Saxony. The Württemberg camp on the Heuberg hill is, according to police information, equipped for 1,500 protective custody detainees, the Bavarian camp near Dachau is said to have a capacity of 5,000 inmates. The Oranienburg camp near Berlin and the Saxon camp on the Hohnstein hill are designed for lesser numbers.

42. *Amper-Bote*: Article warning the Dachau citizens regarding the Dachau concentration camp, dated 2 June 1933[128]

Warning!

On 30 May two persons were observed at the peripheral wall of the Dachau concentration camp as they were trying to look over the wall. Of course they were immediately arrested. They claimed to have looked over the wall out of curiosity about what the camp was looking like from inside. To enable them to satisfy their thirst for knowledge and to provide them with an opportunity to do so, they were kept in the concentration camp for one night. Hopefully their curiosity is now satisfied, even though this has happened in an unforeseen manner. In case any other curious individuals do not refrain from acting against the ban and look over the wall, they should, for the satisfaction of their curiosity, take note that in future they will be given not just one night but a more prolonged opportunity to study the camp. The curious are hereby warned again.

The Delegate of the Supreme SA Command
Special Commissioner Friedrichs

43. Copy from the minutes of the board meeting of the Oranienburg savings bank (*Sparkasse*) on 26 June 1933[129]

In view of the expected economic advantages for the town, the board is prepared to promote the financing of the development of the concentration camp and to make up to 7,000 RM available at 70% for lending on creditors' claims, subject to the following conditions:

[. . .](b) All moneys of the concentration camp administration shall pass through the Oranienburg savings bank.

(c) Payment of the 7,000 RM shall be made direct to the business people entitled.

(d) Any supplies and orders shall, providing competitive prices and equal-value materials, only go to local business people and craftsmen.

44. Letter from the SA *Standarte* 208 of the Oranienburg concentration camp to the Oranienburg mayor with a request for the assignment of weapons to the guard units, dated 29 June 1933[130]

As a result of the sudden increase in the number of detainees the guard units find themselves in the awkward position of not having sufficient weapons. However, as a large number of confiscated weapons are lying at the local police administration, I humbly request that these may be ceded on loan to the camp. I humbly request that this application be treated as *especially urgent* since transports are still arriving.

45. From the diary of Walter Tausk, a German Jew from Breslau, entry of 30 June 1933[131]

As more and more persons who formerly held high positions [. . .] arrive in the concentration camps, posterity should know how the former *Oberpräsident* [a senior civil servant supervising administrative matters in a Prussian province] of Lower Silesia, the Social Democrat Lüdemann,[132] was—after his arrest in Berlin—brought to the Dürrgoy camp last week:

1st Act: Lüdemann is led by Heines,[133] who, in a deliberately very spiteful manner tears a strip off him and concludes: "Dismissed, protective custody inmate Lüdemann!"

2nd Act: He is taken in a triumphal procession from police

headquarters across Schweidnitzer Stadtgraben, Graupenstraße, Roß-markt, Blücherplatz, Ring, Ohlauer Straße to the *Oberpräsidium* (his former office) and led through the building. During the entire procession SA men walk in front of him, alongside him and behind him. Those in front bawl: "Down with Marxism!" Those in the middle roar curses against Lüdemann—in which the hired shouters on the pavements join in "creating an atmosphere that is hostile and that would have led to violence had the SA men not been present." The SA men at the back bawl: "Long live Hitler!" The tail of the procession is made up by the sadist Edmund Heines, the Police President, in his princely motorcar!

3rd Act: Now the procession, in the same form, moves from the *Oberpräsidium* via Albrechtstraße, Schweidnitzer Straße to the Kaiser Wilhelm Monument, where an SA band is "making music." Here Heines orders a halt and publicly addresses the people, again tearing a strip off Lüdemann. Lüdemann is wise enough to keep silent to all that and to swallow his anger!

4th Act: The procession moves on, as before, to the Dürrgoy camp.[134]

5th Act: In the camp all the inmates are on parade—Lüdemann is introduced to them, with Heines again tearing strips off him, and is then finally left in peace by that sadist. At the end Heines generously announces that, in exchange for this super-bigwig, he'll set ten lesser Social Democrats free. The whole business was, in bold type and with a picture, in *Schlesische Tagespost*, Breslau's leading Nazi paper, the following day.

46. Letter from Martin Aust, an Oranienburg citizen, to the Oranienburg major with suggestions for the employment of camp inmates, dated 14 July 1933[135]

Dear Herr Doktor,

Following my discussions with the gentlemen from the Oranienburg industry, the gentlemen named by you would like to put the following suggestions to you on how the inmates of the concentration camp might be employed. To begin with I would like to point out that industry is, naturally enough, reluctant to see concentration camp inmates do any work that might disadvantage the trade [. . .]. The principal occupation of the concentration camp inmates will, as I see it, be in the area of working the earth productively. Many a factory will not have such work or clearing work done because the costs do not justify it. If therefore labor could be provided in this field by having such work done for lower wages, work that would otherwise not be done at all, then free trade will not be disadvantaged and the concentration camp administration would have its expenses reduced. [. . .]. The town itself could have earthwork carried out, making it more attractive to visitors—thus this work would be productive in the long term. This is what I have in mind:

1. Beautification of the Schlosspark: with its wonderful trees it could be transformed into a tourist attraction. Landscape architects would no doubt be ready, in the interest of the town, to make beautification proposals free of charge. [. . .]

Whether or not it will be possible to have concentration camp inmates cultivate vegetables and potatoes on town land I am unable to judge. At any rate this would also provide an opportunity to overcome unemployment [. . .].

Heil Hitler!

47. Letter from Louise Ebert to Reich President Paul von Hindenburg concerning her son, dated 14 July 1933[136]

Dear Herr Reich President,

You have repeatedly, dear Herr Reich President, said very kind words to me in recognition of the work done for Germany by my husband. This gives me the courage to turn to you, Reich President, in a private matter.

Without being given any reason whatever, my son, a Member of the Reichstag, was arrested on 1 July and taken to the Berlin Police Headquarters.[137] National Socialist newspapers have already reported on the plan to deliver my son to a concentration camp. In order to avoid this I am turning to you, Herr Reich President, with my request. The terrible fate of so many of my son's friends gives me no rest. Having sacrificed two sons to the Fatherland[138] and having had my husband die also in service to nation and Fatherland, I would wish, also on behalf of his young wife and his children, to spare my son, who himself fought at the front throughout the war, from being exposed to the arbitrariness of young people as a humiliated laboring prisoner. I am not asking for preferential treatment for my son, who would emphatically reject that himself; I beg most humbly that with your help, your kind help, he might be spared the degrading compulsory labor. When a mother, worried about her son, turns to you, Herr Reich President, she can surely expect to be forgiven by you.[139]

48. German Foreign Ministry note to all representative offices, translated into English as "The Facts Concerning the German Concentration Camps," dated July 1933[140]

In view of the false statements made concerning the concentration camps in which elements inimical to the new order are being detained, it must be emphasized that the heads of such establishments have been given the strictest orders that inmates must not be touched by hand. This precludes the maltreating and torturing of such prisoners of which there has been talk.

These concentration camps are intended to be at once penal and educational institutions for those who have committed high treason, are guilty of sedition[141] [. . .].

The concentration camps were established for two reasons: In the first place it was the duty of the new state in Germany to protect itself against hostile propaganda and overt acts, and, again, it is deemed desirable to educate the former antagonists in the new state idea, and thus make them worthy fellow citizens in the new Germany. Internees who for a considerable period conduct themselves properly are released and are then at liberty to live where they want.

49. NS-*Nachrichten für den Kreis Niederbarnim*: Article on the Oranienburg concentration camp, dated 19 August 1933[142]

Hence the new government ordered the establishment of concentration camps, such as Oranienburg, which was one of the first and very much at the center of public interest. The large buildings of the former Munich Brewery were rented and on the "opening day" 39 erring counter-revolutionary fellow Germans were in custody in the place where formerly the stuff in Gambrinus's honor was brewed and where subsequently biscuits and other delicacies (*Buma-Werke*) and later still radio sets (Schauer & Co) were made. As one would expect, the inmates changed frequently right from the start. Departures and arrivals—the latter on a rising graph—took place almost every day. In consequence the security and administration apparatus, consisting of SA men from our *Sturmbann* and well-tried party members, developed into an organism such as the proper battalions of the old army as well as of our Reichswehr would be proud of. A visit to the camp under the friendly guidance of the camp adjutant Daniels (the camp commandant is *Sturmbannführer* Schäfer) is instructive in several respects. Amazing what has been created in three months out of the long neglected complex of buildings! Here walls had to be erected anew, elsewhere existing ones had to be torn down. Here huge spaces were subdivided by new walls, elsewhere walls had to come down in order to create more space. Earth moving, cleaning and clearing work, new building and reconstruction, creation of barracks-type furnishings, beds and tables—everything *through the work of the political prisoners*, who had to work as bricklayers, joiners, carpenters, plumbers, etc. They created their "home" themselves. Yes, a home! I call on all *Landsturm* troopers called up and drilled to bear witness for me. Who, I ask, would have, in the emergency barracks or the "quarters" of abandoned fortresses, experienced such practical and healthy sleeping conditions, such utterly simple but healthy canteens, such light and pleasant shower equipment, such hygienically faultless provisions for human needs, such care in the sick bay as that enjoyed by our fellow Germans in the concentration camp on Berliner Straße? And they are still extending and improving it [. . .].

Not all, by far not all, faces are attractive. There are some one would not like to meet in a dark alley. On some one can see how years of incitement can transform a person's features into something brutal, mean, or also sly, false and insidious. In other types you can see, even if you are not an expert on skull dimensions or physiognomy, how the owner of this or that semi-animal face cannot be anything other than an incorrigible Bolshevist. No instruction can help in these cases; even the most draconian education would be fruitless. Such atavisms have always existed. There, curious fellow Germans, you see the three-tier bunks, a straw mattress of coarse gray cotton, ditto pillow, neatly folded blanket. Of course the quarters have to be properly built. The high, dry and well-ventilated rooms, where once the national beverage of the Germans ripened until it was ready, are certainly not a bad place to sleep.

50. Prussian Chief of the Secret State Police to all Reich and Prussian Ministries, regarding the interventions by civil servants in protective custody matters, published 26 August 1933[143]

There has recently been a striking increase of occasions when senior civil servants, without official instruction, have demanded information on the location and the reasons for the detention of political protective detainees. In this context I have had to discover that these inquiries almost exclusively concern detainees who are not from the working class. [. . .] I should point out that the Herr Reich Chancellor Adolf Hitler has repeatedly condemned this malpractice. The fact that senior civil servants have been ready, at the request of relatives of the protective detainees, to intercede for them has not remained unknown. Its consequence is that more recently persons asking for information frequently proceed to threaten interventions by ministers, state secretaries and senior National Socialist leaders, because they evidently believe that such declarations are capable of influencing the decisions of my officials. Care should be taken that all cases to be examined by the Secret Police Office [. . .] are examined as speedily as possible without regard to the person concerned.

51. Report by the Communist Hanne Höttges on her visit in the summer of 1933 to her husband in the Börgermoor camp, published in 1975[144]

The sentries allowed us through over the bridge of the Ems Canal as far as a toolshed. We got out, put down the parcels and now began the most difficult part — obtaining permission to visit. We chose a deputation of six women, who submitted our wish to the sentry; we were refused on the grounds that the commandant was not present. The women should simply leave their parcels, the recipients would get them all right, but they should drive back home as fast as possible. But we didn't want to do that. We had agreed that, if necessary, we would wait until morning, because then the men would be marched out to work in the moor and we would see them then. We negotiated some more and after many efforts we succeeded in obtaining visitors' permits, but the women were supposed to go in one at a time. Further negotiations, until it was agreed that all the men would come together. One and a half hours was the time for conversation, after that it was parting again. How long for, was the anxious question.

52. Report of a prisoner who escaped from the Sonnenburg concentration camp, published in the *Braunbuch* in 1933[145]

In the Sonnenburg penitentiary 414 political prisoners are accommodated, among them Carl von Ossietzky,[146] who had been arrested on 28 February. A fellow prisoner, who had spent thirteen days in the Sonnenburg penitentiary and has since succeeded in reaching the frontier, saw Ossietzky in the sick bay. Stooping attitude, emaciated features, his face sickly yellow, nervous gesticulations with his hands, unsteady gait—this is how he described Ossietzky. The other Sonnenburg prisoners: Dr. Wiener, his entire body beaten green and blue; the Communist Bernstein, whose kidneys had been smashed and who can only walk with a stick now, [. . .] Erich Mühsam, who, along with [the Communist prisoner] Kasper, had to dig a grave for himself on the grounds that they would both be shot the next morning. Erich Mühsam, too, looks disfigured because his beard had been cut off. During the night the window of Kasper's cell had been smashed, a pistol had been pushed through and he was threatened with execution. Then they burst into the cell and worked on Kasper with a rubber truncheon.

53. From the verdict of the Berlin Special Court on the joiner Willi P. for offenses against the Decree against Malicious Attacks of 21 March 1933[147]

On 27 September 1933 toward 12:30 at night the former SA man, now Reichswehr soldier, Roloff and the SA man Gerstenberger were approached by a prostitute at the corner of Kraut and Frankfurter Street in Berlin. The accused joined them and for his part began a conversation. He declared that he knew a good deal of the place, he was frequently in that neighborhood. When the two SA man took their leave they used the Hitler salute. The accused [Willi P.] beckoned them to come back again, which they did. Now the accused, assuming the two to be persons who shared his views, stated: "The government will surely be overthrown within six months. The business with van der Lubbe[148] will have a postscript," and in the further course of the conversation "that he had been in the Oranienburg concentration camp, where he had not been given anything to eat for 14 days. Had been made to work a lot and had been beaten a lot."

54. *The Times*: Reader's letter from Dr. Ludwig Levy, dated 29 September 1933[149]

Sir,

Having seen that an article about the concentration camp at Oranienburg near Berlin was published in *The Times* of September 19, and that my name is mentioned, I declare as follows: During the whole time of my detention in the concentration camp at Oranienburg near Berlin (not from March 1933, but from June 28 to July 25, 1933), I did not see any political prisoners maltreated; I myself was never maltreated in the least; I was never deprived of breakfast or of receiving a visit. On the contrary, my treatment there by everyone concerned was always thoroughly good and even respectful.

55. *The Times*: Reader's letter from a former fellow inmate of Levy, dated 4 October 1933[150]

Sir,—I have read with interest the letter from Dr. Ludwig Levy in *The Times* of September 29 referring to the article on the Oranienburg concentration camp which you published on September 19. May I, in my turn, make a few comments on this letter?

If it is to be taken as a true and spontaneous statement of fact, I can only congratulate Dr. Levy on having survived a month in a Nazi concentration camp with a whole skin, and the Nazi propaganda department on having found a Jewish ex-prisoner who could give a certificate to that effect. I presume that the article in *The Times* was brought to Dr. Levy's notice by the Nazis, as he knows no English and is unlikely to be a regular reader of your paper.

Dr. Levy lived in the same room as myself at Oranienburg. I saw him constantly, and often talked with him. A few days after his arrival at the camp in June—his inclusion in the list of those who had been there since March was due to a slip in the translation of my statement[151]—I saw Dr. Levy with his left eye black and swollen and blood running from it. About a fortnight later his right eye was in the same condition. On both occasions he was fresh from an interview with the camp "leaders." I also saw him kicked and knocked about by the guards, like the rest of us, many times.

I do not blame Dr. Levy for making the statement which you have published, as I am well aware of the kind of pressure to which he, still living in Potsdam, must be exposed. I must, however, assure you that the statements contained in the article on Oranienburg are not only true but carefully restrained. The facts can be confirmed at any time by witnesses who shared my experience.

I am, Sir, your obedient servant
The Author of the article.

56. Radio report from the Oranienburg concentration camp for the foreign program of *Deutschlandsender* and *Deutscher Kurzwellensender,* recorded on 30 September 1933[152]

[Announcer]: The young National Socialist Germany defends itself against lies and atrocity stories spread by part of the foreign press. Truthfulness is the path of honest working people. Lies and deception destroy a person and destroy the destiny of a nation if it lives a sham existence in lies and falsehood [. . .]. One lie chases another. We therefore bring you today a factual item from Greater Berlin's concentration camp. We have wandered out with our microphone to Oranienburg and will now try to bring the truth to you and to the world, a mirror of the life and the doings of the misguided, incited and culpable fellow Germans taken into protective custody in the concentration camp there. This concentration camp in Oranienburg holds prominent leaders of the SPD [Social Democrat Party] and functionaries of the KPD [Communist Party], persons who have become guilty of robbing the German people's assets, who have offended against custom and morality, against state and nation, against the philosophy of the German man. [. . .]

[Reporter, addressing a prisoner]: Now what do you think we National Socialists would have been given to eat if you Communists had been at the helm? I think you would not have treated us as decently as you are being treated here [. . .].

The Early Camps, 1933–1934

[Commandant Schäfer]: We didn't even have two ha'pennies to rub together then to establish this camp, but we got down to the job with the necessary National Socialist drive and what you are seeing today was built up not with any government help but with our own energy in absolute thrift [. . .].

[Schäfer]: The discipline among this compacted mass, compacted from all parts of Germany [. . .] and when we asked: Who's that saluting over there? The answer was: an *Amtsgerichtsrat* [local judge] of the SPD who committed offenses against the nation and state. The worker, the little man, the big man are dressed alike here in the community of protective custody [. . .]. May I take this opportunity to point out again that at least 52 percent of the inmates here have a criminal record, that is, burglars, thieves, people who somehow got into conflict with the criminal law — what's more not once, but some people here have had seventeen previous convictions, some even 20 [. . .].

[Reporter]: The fellow German standing before me, this incited Communist, doesn't know me and I don't know him, he has not been coached for this but has just been called over to us. We will ask him now how he feels here, whether he is satisfied with the food. I want to make one thing clear to him straightaway. You don't have to worry, you will not be punished even if you tell me that you are dissatisfied. You need say nothing more than the truth.

[Inmate]: Yessir.

[Reporter]: Tell us how you feel about the food.

[Inmate]: The food here is good and plentiful.

[Reporter]: Have you been ill-treated in any way? [. . .] Has anything at all happened to you here?

[Inmate]: Nothing has happened to me. [. . .]

[Reporter]: Now tell your comrades in Moscow and in Holland and all Jewish agitators, what you ultimately, what you still think of the KPD, in other words if you still have that conviction today to distribute illegal leaflets once you've been released?

[Inmate]: I honestly have the impression that, when I'm released again, I will no longer [. . .] distribute any material against the [. . .] existing government and I would recommended to all fellow Germans that they should no longer regard the propaganda that's been made until now, as the truth. Because I have the impression that the people here are treated as human beings.

57. *Völkischer Beobachter*, article about the opening of a concentration camp for beggars, dated 4 October 1933[153]

On the initiative of the *Landrat* Merker-Meseritz a concentration camp for beggars and vagabonds has been set up at Gumpersdorf near Meseritz in order to counteract the mischief of beggars and vagabonds; at present it holds 50 inmates. The beggars are employed there on agricultural work, so that, after a probation period, they can be employed as agricultural laborers.

58. Report by F. C. Robinson, British Vice-Consul in Dresden, on his visit to the Hohnstein camp, dated 10 October 1933[154]

The Camp itself is a model from all points of view — the kitchens (in a quarter formerly used as a hostelry for young girls run however under communistic influence) would not disgrace a good hotel. We inspected the food which was good, and I was informed that the "garrison" eats precisely the same food as the prisoners. A warm midday meal is conveyed in field kitchens to those working outside the Camp. Sleeping quarters were airy and adequate, a plentiful water supply for all purposes including baths and douches being available. [. . .]

The object of these Camps, I am informed, goes beyond the immediate scope of merely segregating elements poisonous to the community. It aims at moral and social reformation, and that in turn decides more or less the length of time the internment shall last in each case. The methods of inculcating and subsequently testing this regeneration are interesting — and I should imagine effective.

59. Postcard from the Communist Karl Ibach to his parents from the Kemna concentration camp, dated 13 October 1933[155]

My dear parents,

This is the first sign of life that I can give you in a long time. I can report of myself that I am still feeling physically well. A much more serious question for me is how you are. I hope you are not worrying too much unnecessarily, everything will be all right. There are a few things that I still need, i.e. my old blue jacket, a pair of long socks,

2 handkerchiefs, the blue shirt, brown shoe polish. Please send me also a little bread spread (margarine, jam). Perhaps also some potato pancake, plum pancake or potato salad. Please pack the things in a strong carton that I could also use as a clothes carton. Parcels can now only be handed in on Tuesday or Friday until 6 p.m. Every sign of life from you is a great joy to me, showing me that I have not been forgotten. I warmly embrace you and wish that we will all see each other again soon. Loyally your Karl. At last I can catch up with something and congratulate my dear father on his birthday.

60. Declaration signed by a prisoner on his release from the Kemna concentration camp, dated 16 October 1933[156]

I hereby undertake to refrain in future from any political activity hostile to the state, in particular from any participation in high- or state-treasonable machinations. It was explained to me that protective custody will again be imposed on me, moreover for an unspecified period, if I again engage in seditious activity. I further declare that no claims will be made by me on the grounds of the political measures taken against me. It was also explained to me that, if necessary, I may again choose protective custody voluntarily.

61. From the *Anti-Braunbuch* by SA-*Sturmbannführer* Werner Schäfer, commandant of the Oranienburg camp, published in 1934[157]

It would be foolish and also quite incomprehensible to conceal that some of the arrested have meanwhile received a none too gentle treatment. Incomprehensible because such treatment met an urgent necessity. For many years persecuted, for many years chased, beaten bloody, outlawed, expelled from their jobs and their homeland—the moment had at last come when our old SA men were able to refresh the memory of some of these, in the past, politically especially exposed agitators [. . .]. Meanwhile—I had intervened to bring some order into the chaos of the first delivery [of prisoners]—the badly lit room was filling. Familiar faces of Oranienburg Marxists emerged from the semi-darkness. Accustomed to showing their contempt for us with truly loutish bearing and street gestures, they arrived—hands up to the elbow in their trouser pockets, caps pulled to the back of the neck or low into the face—and—within an instant they relearned. Rarely have I seen such wonderful educators as my old SA men, most of whom come from a proletarian background themselves, who were now accepting these especially loutish Communist bigmouths with exceptional dedication. I am often reminded of the story of the man who vigorously boxed a boy's ears when he caught him stealing apples in the market. What splendid significance there is in this slight, but to us maturing humans instructive, story! Years later a respected man thanked his "educator," who had shown him the right way with his healthy box on the ears [. . .].

A released inmate wrote on 2 November 1933:

Dear Herr Kommandant,

I take the liberty of writing a few lines to you. Am happily back with my family. I sincerely thank you for my good treatment and everything else. People tried to make my life difficult for me again. But I'm holding out.—I also wish the Herr Adjutant much joy with his room. I hope I'll find some work soon.

My son-in-law is also an SA man.

Most respectfully,
G. H. Fräser, formerly 1097

62. Postcard from the Political Department of the Dachau camp to the Kaindl family, dated 18 November 1933[158]

In reply to your card we inform you that the protective custody detainee Otto Kaindl is in good health. The reason why he cannot send you any news is that the subversive activities of a few Communist rascals have made a postal shutdown necessary. We do not know here when he will be released. This is decided in each individual case by the Bavarian Political Police in Munich.

63. *Berliner Lokal-Anzeiger*: Article on professional criminals in the concentration camps, dated 25 November 1933[159]

Concentration camps for criminals: Statements by Police General Daluege:[160] Every German shall be able, also in the evening, to walk confidently even through lonely streets.

[. . .] The Prussian criminal police is said [. . .] to have already accommodated a considerable number of criminals in police prisons. A special concentration camp, where they should, under close guard and strict discipline, learn to work again is already being established. Anyone who has a record of repeated punishment for criminal actions committed from common greed and who, with a probability bordering on certainty, would work as a professional criminal also in today's state, will now in future in Prussia, even without evidence of a new criminal action, be placed in a concentration camp [. . .]. It is the firm will of the Minister President [Göring] and of all judicial and police officials subordinated to him [. . .] that every German should be able to walk in the evenings in complete safety even along deserted streets. He should be able to keep his windows open without being afraid of cat burglars. Above all, he should be able to sleep tranquilly again in the knowledge that we are guarding him.

64. Report in a Wuppertal Protestant-Lutheran community paper of 17 December 1933 on Christmas in the Kemna camp[161]

The management of the Kemna concentration camp has given permission for a Christmas celebration to be held for the prisoners, when they may also receive presents. The camp commandant has lifted the existing smoking ban for the feast days until 1 January. Who is willing to help by giving the prisoners a gift of a few cigarettes or tobacco? Also greatly in demand by the prisoners are butter or margarine or lard to spread on their bread. [. . .] Gifts for this Christmas celebration are requested either via the district pastor or to the post office check account *Evangelische Kirchengemeinde* Langerfeld: Cologne 84915.

Pastor Altenpohl
Pastor to the concentration camp

65. Recollections of the British citizen Madeleine Kent of her visit with others to Hohnstein in June 1934, published in 1938[162]

It was painful to me to sit consuming coffee and whipped cream in a café garden directly opposite the grim castle gate, but as they had not known Hohnstein in the old days, I could not expect them to share the thrill of horror it gave me to see the barbed wire and the armed sentries at the entrance to what had once been a kind of Abbey of

Theleme. [D]riving slowly away, we passed a gang of prisoners toiling under armed guard at the making of a new road [. . .]. The men were so obviously not navvies by trade, any more than they were criminals. I knew most of them to be professors, doctors, lawyers, schoolmasters, and former deputies of the Saxon diet. And now, painfully thin, barefoot and in rags, they were carrying hods of sand uphill under the broiling sun or wielding picks with arms that visibly trembled.

66. Public appeal of the Prussian Minister President Hermann Göring regarding the Christmas amnesty 1933[163]

The Prussian Minister President does not wish such fellow Germans to be disadvantaged only because they have been in a concentration camp, so that e.g. acceptance of an employment is made impossible to them only because they are former protective custody detainees.

67. Report of the Württemberg Ministry of the Interior to the Reich governor in Württemberg, forwarded to the German Foreign Ministry, on the visit of an American Consul to the Oberer Kuhberg camp near Ulm, dated 14 April 1934[164]

On 5 April 1934 the American Consul approached me with a request for permission to visit the Kuhberg protective custody camp. As this was an opportunity to counteract the foreign atrocity propaganda, I gave permission for the visit and personally accompanied the American Consul and his Vice-Consul to the protective custody camp. There we inspected the accommodation quarters of categories 1–3, as well as protective custody detainees who happened to be working. The administrative quarters, the workshops and the kitchen were likewise inspected. In the inmates' kitchen we sampled the evening meal. It was pea soup with garnish. The food was very good, as the American Consul noted appreciatively. He also, unprompted, noted the good appearance of the protective custody detainees. On this occasion both gentlemen suddenly remarked to me that all the protective custody detainees they had seen "did not have good heads." In the course of the conversation between the two gentlemen and myself, partly in English, the gentlemen added that it struck them that all the protective custody detainees held here had definite criminals' heads. The visitors asked to have the entire organization of protective custody and of the protective custody camp explained to them, which I did in great detail. In this connection it emerged that the Consul had believed that we also kept criminal prisoners in the protective custody camp and that he also believed that detention of a protective custody prisoner was done on the basis of a judicial order of arrest. He noted with satisfaction that under our regulations a person can only be arrested on the basis of a written warrant of arrest issued by the Ministry of the Interior and after interrogation of the accused. He greatly commended the organization as explained to him. He then inquired whether the prisoners had any reading matter at their disposal, which I confirmed and of which the Consul personally convinced himself. He particularly liked the fact that we have a loudspeaker system for the prisoners in the camp, which he was able to witness in operation.

Summing up, I gained the definite impression that the tribute by the American Consul, who was only transferred here from Marseille two months ago, came from a full heart and was sincerely meant, rather than being just the performance of an international courtesy.

TWO

The ss Concentration Camp System

By April 1934, as we have seen, Reich Leader ss Heinrich Himmler had secured de facto control of all political police forces across Germany, including Prussia. As these police forces were largely in charge of the detention and release of protective custody prisoners, Himmler was now in a strong position to bring the early camps under ss control.[1] The ss soon reorganized some remaining early camps along the lines of the Dachau ss camp and closed down other camps. The first camp to fall into the hands of the ss was Lichtenburg, one of the largest Prussian camps: Dachau Commandant Theodor Eicke took it over in late May 1934 on Himmler's orders. Eicke immediately sacked the civilian camp director and even arrested him temporarily. He also fired other guards and replaced them with ss men. The Prussian bureaucracy's model for state-run concentration camps was officially abandoned as control through civil servants was replaced by ss rule.[2]

The "Night of Long Knives" of 30 June 1934 offered a welcome opportunity for Himmler and the ss to boost their standing within the Nazi dictatorship. Prompted by fabricated rumors about an imminent sa uprising, Hitler decided to liquidate senior sa leaders. Eicke himself shot sa chief Ernst Röhm at the Munich-Stadelheim prison. His actions proved both his ruthlessness and his blind loyalty to his superiors.[3] The so-called Röhm putsch led to the decline of the sa and simultaneously increased the ss's reputation as the regime's ideological and radical vanguard. Furthermore, the ss became an independent organization that reported directly to Hitler. Also, Himmler felt confident enough to take over several more early camps in Prussia and Saxony that had previously been staffed by sa units: Hohenstein, Esterwegen, Oranienburg, and Sachsenburg.[4] Himmler chose his paladin Theodor Eicke to realize his ideal of a system of permanent ss concentration camps. Dachau, which Eicke had shaped, soon became the model for the ss camps' organizational structure as well as training site for many of the camp ss officers.[5]

But the future of the camp system had not been settled yet. The vast majority of political prisoners had already been freed, following regular releases and amnesties. In April 1934, Hermann Göring claimed in an interview that there were between 4,000 and 5,000 prisoners in the Prussian camps and 6,000 to 7,000 in all of Germany. Real numbers in the non-Prussian camps were probably higher, as there were more than 2,000 prisoners left in Dachau alone.[6] Still, prisoner numbers were much lower than in 1933 and they continued to fall: by late 1934 an estimated 3,000 prisoners were left in protective custody.[7] Apart from the releases, another major reason for the significant drop in prisoner numbers was the fact that political repression in this period was increasingly transferred to the regular legal system. Courts tried and sentenced political suspects, often using new repressive laws introduced since the spring of 1933.[8]

Most importantly, perhaps, not all Nazi leaders shared the ss plans for the camps. In fact, the camps' expansion was accompanied by conflicts among various state and party institutions.[9] Reich Interior Minister Wilhelm Frick was concerned about the increasing influence of Himmler and his political police, which curtailed the state bureaucracy's power.[10] Similarly, the judiciary, led by the national-conservative Reich Minister of Justice Franz Gürtner, worried that the camps were turning into permanent places of detention beyond its control.[11]

Himmler could not care less about these bureaucratic interventions, because his model of the camps rested on Hitler's unconditional support. Hitler backed Himmler's rise to the top of the German police, and he also underwrote Himmler's vision that the camps must become permanent extralegal instruments of terror for safeguarding the national community. Himmler did not see any reason to get rid of the concentration camps, not least because they were a source of his own increasing power within the Nazi regime.[12] And as the contours of the ss camp system emerged, Himmler's radical vision of the camps began to take effect.

The ss Concentration Camp System

2.1. Heinrich Himmler and the Creation of the ss Camp System

The so-called Röhm putsch on 30 June 1934 marked a watershed in the development of the ss camp system. ss and police units arrested leading SA men. Some of the prisoners ended up in ss camps, prompting protests by SA officials about torture and abuses. Nothing could have demonstrated more powerfully the growing ss domination of the camps (70). The ss also executed a number of SA men, as well as representatives of the conservative elites, in the Dachau camp (69). Meanwhile, Eicke—since July 1934 the official Inspector of the Concentration Camps—brought further camps under ss control. On 4 July 1934, for example, ss units under his command entered Oranienburg. Prussian police units had disarmed the Oranienburg SA guards a few days before, and Eicke quickly closed down the entire camp (68).[13] He also closed down Hohnstein and several other early camps.

Himmler lost little time in seizing the momentum of the Röhm purge and quickly created a bureaucratic structure for the camps' administration, culminating in the establishment of the Inspectorate of the Concentration Camps, led by Eicke (72). Housed in the notorious Gestapo headquarters at 8 Prinz-Albrecht-Strasse in Berlin, this office was nominally part of the Gestapo, a state institution under Himmler's control (as head of the ss guard troops, Eicke remained subordinated to Himmler as ss leader) (80).[14] Only Eicke's office, Himmler declared, was in charge of the concentration camps. Himmler made it clear that he would not tolerate any interference from the state bureaucracy or the judiciary in matters concerning the concentration camps (73). In December 1934 he insisted in a letter to Göring that the concentration camps were an absolutely necessary instrument for the total suppression of political dissent and deviant behavior (71).

The year 1935 was decisive for the concentration camps. In the summer of that year, Hitler made several vital interventions. He opposed additional releases of prisoners and secured the camps' financial future. He agreed that the funding for the camps would come from the Reich budget (75). In addition, Hitler backed the brutal regimen inside the camps and did not order Himmler to cut down on the number of deaths. Finally, Hitler intervened in court cases against camp guards suspected of abuses.[15] As a result, judicial investigations, always rare, petered out. In effect, the concentration camps became extralegal sites of incarceration, even though some of the underlying conflicts between the ss and the judiciary over the formal jurisdiction of the camps continued until 1939.[16]

At the same time, the coordinated persecution of the regime's political adversaries was stepped up amid the more general escalation of the Nazi regime's domestic and foreign policies on the road to war. This resulted in several orders and decrees in 1935 and 1936. For example, in July 1935 Himmler ordered that one thousand former Communist functionaries be detained in the camps (74), an order extended by Himmler's lieutenant Reinhard Heydrich to also include those whom the authorities merely suspected of being Communist activists. The following raids, which led to more than two thousand arrests throughout Germany, reflected Himmler's general demand for radical action against the left, expressed in an internal speech in March 1936 (78).[17] In the draft of this speech, Himmler insisted that the mass releases of Communist prisoners in 1933 and 1934 had been one of the Nazi regime's most serious mistakes. He deleted these remarks from his manuscript, probably because he did not want to openly criticize other Nazi leaders.[18] But this was not all. In 1936, Reinhard Heydrich ordered Gestapo offices across Germany to register all potential enemies of the state in a vast database to facilitate their arrest in the event of war (77). Meanwhile, prisoners detained in the camps for a second time were to be treated especially harshly, Himmler ordered in 1936. These decrees particularly targeted Communists (79 and 83).

A significant development was Himmler's appointment as Chief of the German Police on 17 June 1936, which strengthened his powers further as all police forces throughout Germany came under his ultimate control; Himmler and the ss were now well placed to implement the radical social-hygienic vision of German society in the concentration camps and elsewhere (83). The following day, Eicke began to secure the grounds for the construction of a major concentration camp on the outskirts of Berlin (81). This new camp, Sachsenhausen, opened that summer. Another new camp followed in July 1937 when

The ss Concentration Camp System

the ss established Buchenwald in Thuringia, set in a picturesque forest near Weimar, one of Germany's cultural centers during the late eighteenth and early nineteenth centuries.[19] This was part of a wider process in the second half of the 1930s. In the mid-1930s the ss closed down several camps, including Esterwegen, the Columbia-Haus, and Sachsenburg (85 and 87), so a December 1936 list of camps compiled by the German Foreign Office was soon outdated (82).

Sachsenhausen and Buchenwald, the major new ss camps, consisted of rows of prefabricated huts, pointing to the ss camps' future architecture. Yet the ss was still experimenting with the camps' design, and the ambitious model used in Sachsenhausen for a new type of camp proved unworkable in practice and soon had to be altered.[20] Nevertheless, the ss's intention was clear. The new camps would be very different from almost all early camps, as they would be large, permanent compounds, flexible and easily expandable, cut off from outside view and interference. Dachau was rebuilt along these lines in 1937 and 1938 (86).[21] Prisoners had to build the new compounds from scratch, often in extremely harsh conditions (88).

By late 1937 the camps had been streamlined under ss control (arrests and releases of camp prisoners, meanwhile, were in police hands [84]). With the exception of the central women's camp at Lichtenburg (operational from December 1937), each of the ss camps had a specific geographical remit: Dachau was the camp for prisoners from southern Germany, Buchenwald for those from western Germany, and Sachsenhausen for those from eastern, central, and northern Germany (90). Two more camps for men were added in 1938. Flossenbürg, located near quarries close to the Czechoslovakian border, was opened in the spring (93).[22] And in the summer the ss opened the Mauthausen camp near Linz in Austria, set next to two quarries, which would soon become a notorious place of murderous slave labor (92).[23] Finally, in May 1939, the ss established the Ravensbrück camp, the first purpose-built women's camp, to replace Lichtenburg as the central concentration camp for women (258). Himmler's vision of the camps as sites for the extralegal detention of social, political, and racial outsiders, articulated in speeches in 1937 (83) and 1938 (94), had materialized.

68. Felix von Papen's recollections of 30 June 1934 as a prisoner in the Oranienburg camp, published around 1939[24]

To begin with, it was on 30 June at 9 o'clock in the evening that fifty men of the Hermann Göring *Stabswache*, a military formation,[25] appeared. They demanded that the SA hand over all weapons, the captain in command explaining with a friendly smile: "We just shot an SA man dead, the fellow refused to hand over his rifle." It would have been easy enough, with the well-placed machine guns, to deal very quickly with the captain and his entourage. But who was to give the order? In Germany an order is indispensable. Our almighty Herr Stahlkopf [a senior SA guard] suddenly became afraid. He showed them the arms depots since none of his men intended to die, especially when they didn't quite know what for. Three days later the SS turned up. They were more cautious than the purely military *Stabswache* because, in the SS too, they would rather live than die. They first surrounded the depot that was now bare of all weapons and had actually brought two tanks along with them. It looked alarming. After these precautionary measures of Party comrades against Party comrades the Herr SS *Brigadeführer* Eicke, Chief of all concentration camps in Germany, made his entrance. The SA showed no composure. The sentry on duty at the gate dropped his rifle in alarm. [. . .] In a rasping voice Herr Eicke informed his SA comrades that he was now taking over the running of the camp, that the SA were now only guests in the camp. Every SA man had a duty to find a civilian occupation as quickly as possible. [. . .] Suddenly the SA men were our chums. They were looking to us for help. "Friends," they insistently urged us—no longer shouting but quite softly— "surely we must now stick together against these black devils." However, the black devils lost no time explaining to us: "It's our turn now. We come straight from murdering in Munich."

69. Report of the prisoner Hans Deller on the murder of SA men in the Dachau camp on 1 July 1934, published in 1967[26]

In the evening of Sunday, 1 July 1934, we saw, at a distance of roughly 200 meters, a gallows on which a body with black trousers and a brown shirt was hanging and, according to the direction of the wind, was swaying first one way and then the other. At sunset we then had to form a circle in the camp; the place of execution was in the background. One side along the bank of the Würm (name of the river flowing through the camp) was formed by the lined-up ss; the delinquents were then led one by one over the little wooden bridge to the place of execution. Naked to the waist, they had to face the execution squad. After the execution of the first victim of the Röhm coup in Dachau the ss men present gave a round of applause.

70. Secret letter from *Oberregierungsrat* (a senior civil servant) and SA-*Obersturmbannführer* Lothar Schiedlausky to the General of the Prussian State Police Kurt Daluege about incidents in the Columbia-Haus camp during the Röhm purge, dated 9 August 1934[27]

I attach two reports by members of SA departments with the dissolution of which I have been entrusted—men who have been in protective custody. As I feel responsible for the fate of persons entrusted to me, I request that everything be done at your end to call the culprits to account. I leave it to you to decide whether to pass on this material to the Reichsführer-ss for the purpose of expelling the guilty persons from the NSDAP [the Nazi Party] and the ss.

Moreover I request an examination in principle whether other than police bodies can ever be drawn upon for guard duty. After what I found in the Papenburg and Sonnenburg concentration camps, and more recently in Lichtenburg, the need for an immediate replacement of all non–civil service guard personnel would seem to be a necessity.

Heil Hitler!

[. . .] *Copy*

Berlin, 9 August 1934

Guard duty at the *Police prison Kolumbiastrasse* from 30.6. to 2.7.34 was in the hands of ss *Standarte* 42.

One of the [SA men in] protective custody taken there during those days reports ill-treatment committed by the guard personnel not only against him but also against other inmates.

The protective custody inmate was obscenely insulted, spat at and struck in his face by the guard personnel. The protective custody detainee was made to stand nearly an hour outside the guardhouse and made the butt of hatred and the vilest loutish behavior [. . .]. The protective custody detainee experienced considerable pain in the kidney area as a result of his ill-treatment in the courtyard of the police prison and observed traces of blood in the form of red threads while urinating.

71. Letter from the Inspector of the Secret State Police Heinrich Himmler to Hermann Göring, rejecting the application made by the Society of Friends for the concentration camps to be abolished, dated 6 December 1934[28]

Although time and again we have pointed out that the concentration camps were established because of an absolute necessity to protect not only the German people but ultimately human society against seditious and asocial elements, the Society of Friends, evidently in ignorance of German conditions prior to 30 January 1933, has now requested the abolition of the concentration camps.

The concentration camps in their present form represent institutions in which political enemies of the state and saboteurs have to be accommodated in the interest of the national community. [. . .] With all the recognition that one may have for the good intentions of the Quakers, the welfare of the entire people must not be put in jeopardy by abolishing an institution that at present is the most effective means against all enemies of the state, or by rendering it ineffective through some relaxation.

72. Directive by Heinrich Himmler on the establishment of the Inspectorate of Concentration Camps, dated 10 December 1934[29]

With effect from 10.12.1934 the office of "Inspector of Concentration Camps" is established with residence in the office building of the Secret State Police in Berlin, Prinz-Albrechtstr. 8 (Ground floor, Rooms 30–34) and directly subordinated to me. Matters of organization, administration and economic management of the concentration camps hitherto dealt with by Office II 1 D of the Secret State Police are removed from it as from the date mentioned and transferred to the new office, whereas processing of material (political) matters of protective custody continue to come under Office II 1 D.

—In matters concerning the ss guard personnel employed on guard duties in the concentration camps the Inspector of Concentration Camps answers to the Chief of the ss Office in the Reich Leadership of the ss.

—The Inspectorate of the Concentration Camps is headed by ss *Gruppenführer* Eicke.

73. Memorandum by Heinrich Himmler to officials of the Secret State Police concerning the exclusive competence of the Inspectorate of Concentration Camps for matters concerning concentration camps, dated 8 July 1935[30]

I have repeatedly noticed that both written and oral, and especially telephonic, queries on concentration camp matters, in particular of a budgetary or organizational character, are not processed or answered by the "Inspectorate of Concentration Camps" set up specially in accordance with my directive of 10 December 1934, but by other departments in the house. I point out again that *all* matters regarding concentration camps—with the exception of the conduct of budgetary negotiations (establishment of the budget and cash estimates)—are processed by the independent I.K.L. [Inspectorate of Concentration Camps]; in future therefore all relevant inquiries, both oral and written, are to be passed on to the Inspectorate of Concentration Camps or inquirers to be referred to that office.

74. Himmler order to Reinhard Heydrich concerning a detention campaign against Communists, dated 12 July 1935[31]

Reichsführer-ss has ordered that the number of protective custody inmates from the ranks of former KPD functionaries be increased next month by one thousand.

75. Letter from Oswald Pohl,[32] Chief of Administration of the ss, to Ludwig Grauert, State Secretary in the Prussian Ministry of the Interior, regarding the financing of concentration camps, dated 4 December 1935[33]

On 27 August 1935 a conference was held at the Reich Ministry of the Interior between representatives of the Reich Ministry of Interior, the Bavarian Ministry of Finance and the Reich Leadership of the ss.

On the agenda was the financing of the Dachau concentration

camp until 31.3.1936. The conference resulted in fundamental agreement to the effect that financing should be regulated between the Reich and the *Land* Bavaria, seeing that the NSDAP (Reich Leadership of the SS) had borne 80 percent of these expenses in the years 1933/34.

Meanwhile a quarter of a year has passed without any sign of the outcome of that conference. The Reich Leader SS has therefore instructed me to ask you to put your foot down now to ensure that this precarious affair is finally sorted out. The situation in Dachau, where the spotlight is primarily on state matters, is worse than disastrous. The Reich Leadership of the SS, which, in expectation of an early settlement has time and again advanced amounts, has got itself close to bankruptcy in this matter. It is, in consequence, totally unable to contribute even one more Pfennig. Considering the state function of the camp, the Reich Treasurer of the NSDAP—in my opinion rightly so—likewise refuses to make any contribution.

76. Secret decree by Reinhard Heydrich as Head of the Gestapa to the Prussian state police authorities concerning the recording of Social Democrats and Communists in a card index, dated 12 December 1935[34]

In order to be able at any time to deal a painful blow against left-wing radical anti-state elements, I hereby order that separate lists of Communists and Marxists be *immediately* prepared, who, if necessary, could instantly be taken into protective custody upon instruction from *here*. In particular this concerns persons who, because of their political attitude, represent a threat to the existence of the state. The lists, to be most suitably prepared in the form of card indexes, are constantly to be kept up to date.

77. Secret letter from Reinhard Heydrich as Head of the Gestapa to the Prussian State Police authority of the district Aachen, concerning the registration of all enemies of the state in a card index, dated 5 February 1936[35]

The task of the Political Police is the protection of the state. This task makes it necessary for the Political Police to be most accurately informed not only about the activities of the enemies of the state but also about their whereabouts, to ensure that there is the possibility, in the case of extraordinary events (war), for all enemies of the state, or the enemies of the state of a certain political color, to be taken into protective custody at one blow throughout the Reich territory.

I therefore order:

(1) The State Police authorities and the Political Police of the *Länder* are immediately to prepare a card index (the A-card index) of all enemies of the state who—to give an example—absolutely have to be taken into protective custody in the event of war.

(2) Enemies of the state within the meaning of this instruction are all such persons who may be expected to become active on the lines of their former attitude and activity, or on the basis of their present attitude, as inciters or rabble-rousers, as saboteurs or intelligence agents or in a similar manner endangering the public safety and order.

(3) In particular this concerns

    (a) all radical left-wing elements (KPD, SPD, SAP[36]), including their associated organizations,

    (b) all leaders of oppositional or reactionary movements,

    (c) all influential members of Bible researcher associations,[37]

    (d) all economic saboteurs,

    (e) all political confidence tricksters,

    (f) all other persons who are viewed as hostile to the state within the meaning of Subsection 2.

78. Address by Heinrich Himmler to the *Staatsräte* on 5 March 1936[38]

The method of the first weeks and months, of the first year [of Nazi rule], was improvised since what mattered first of all was to settle the hash of an opponent who was active in the street. The brutal violence of the red partisans had to be opposed by an equally brutal violence of the state and the Movement.[39] [. . .] In the course of 1934 came the time when we, in German decency—if I may say so—~~completely~~ misjudging the adversary cleared the concentration camps except for a negligible number. ~~This was one of the worst political mistakes the National Socialist state could have made.~~[40] [. . .] The belief that the political struggle against the adversaries—Jewry, Bolshevism, worldwide Freemasonry and all the forces that do not want a newly risen Germany—is over is, in my opinion, a grave error, for Germany stands only at the beginning of what may well be a conflict lasting centuries, perhaps the decisive worldwide conflict with those forces of organized subhumanity. I would even say that we, our generation, also in this respect, can only give the Political Police and the state's fighters against the worldwide political adversary the beginning, the foundation, the tradition which then, over the centuries, as an enduring institution, will enable Germany to be victorious in its struggle. [. . .]

The adversary:

May I now explain to you in rough outline how we view the *adversary* for the struggle against whom we believe that we need the apparatus and institution of the Secret State Police. I would like to go back to what I said at the beginning of my address about the struggle against Communism and against the enemies of the state in the year 1933/34. I said at the end of my characterization that his methods have changed and I also emphasized that I regarded the release of the Communist prisoners as a wrong political move. I believe we Germans make a *serious mistake* inasmuch as we are measuring the *political adversary* by our *own decent yardsticks*. Thus we believe, for instance, that a political adversary whom we have released would regard this as a sign of decency and would therefore no longer undertake anything because he would somehow feel obliged to us, because he felt he had to be grateful to us that, as a leading Communist, he was not executed by firing squad while, as he himself knows, if things had gone the other way, every leading National Socialist would have had to face death. [. . .]

This chivalrous attitude, however, must be seen as madness if applied to Jewry or to Bolshevism, which has immorality, fraud and lies as a prerequisite of its political struggle and which, according to a typically Jewish principle, regards any non-annihilation of the opponent as weakness. [. . .] All in all it should be stated here that we Germans *must at long last learn* that the Jew and any organization trained by Jews should not be viewed as humans of our species or exponents of our way of thinking.

We had our *practical experience* on a major scale with the *above mentioned release* of the Communist protective custody detainees from the concentration camps. The past roughly two years have shown us that these minor, medium and sometimes overlooked major functionaries, who were then released, have not by any means given up their activities but have, most of them, gone to *Moscow for courses* and in these courses were retrained in a *new kind of illegal activity*. Newly schooled, with *new passports* and a *changed appearance*, they returned to Germany, but are now working in regions where they had not yet been previously. [. . .] The frequently heard phrase: "Why don't you release the man from the prisoner camp and put him under *surveillance*," sometimes, more emphatically, by saying: "We shall put the man under *intensified surveillance*," is a real *impossibility* to every expert. If I really want to place somebody under surveillance, so that I can guarantee that he does no harm, I need for every one of those louts and villains at least three officials per day, for whom this would be the hardest service that an official of the criminal police can be assigned to.

79. Instruction by Himmler to the Inspector of Concentration Camps, Theodor Eicke, regarding the treatment of inmates brought into a concentration camp for the second time, dated 23 March 1936[41]

Secret!

Special sections are to be set up in all concentration camps of inmates detained in a concentration camp for the second time. As a matter of principle the protective custody records of all persons brought into a concentration camp for the second time are to be resubmitted only after three years.[42] The customary quarterly detention reexaminations are abolished for these inmates. For such inmates I authorize correspondence permits four times in a year — for writing and for receiving a letter. Working time 10 hours a day. Smoking is not permitted. Receipt of money from their home no more than 10.00 RM per quarter. No parcels to be received at all.

80. Decree on the appointment of a Chief of German Police in the Reich Ministry of the Interior, dated 17 June 1936[43]

I. To ensure a uniform concentration of police tasks in the Reich a Chief of German Police is appointed in the Reich Ministry of the Interior; at the same time the management and processing of all police matters within the scope of the Reich and Prussian Ministries of the Interior are transferred to him.

II. (1) The Deputy Chief of the Secret State Police in Prussia, Reich

Leader ss Heinrich Himmler is appointed Chief of German Police in the Reich Ministry of the Interior.

(2) He is subordinated, personally and directly, to the Reich and Prussian Minister of the Interior.

(3) Within his jurisdiction he deputizes for the Reich and Prussian Minister of the Interior in the latter's absence.

(4) His official title is: Reich Leader ss and Chief of German Police in the Reich Ministry of the Interior. [. . .]

The Führer and Reich Chancellor
Adolf Hitler
The Reich Minister of the Interior
Frick

81. Secret letter from Theodor Eicke to the Prussian Forestry Office Sachsenhausen with the demand for the release of land for the construction of the Sachsenhausen concentration camp, dated 18 June 1936[44]

On this land a state concentration camp is to be established immediately with completion by 1 October 1936. I attach a building plan for safekeeping. As a building site an equilateral triangle of 1 km per side is considered sufficient. The apex of the triangle points toward Sachsenhausen railway station. On the road side and on the east side toward Sandhausen a security strip of c. 80–100 m will continue to exist.

I request that this application is dealt with speedily as I have only three months at my disposal for the overall construction of the camp. [. . .]

Justification:

(a) The state concentration camp Esterwegen nr. Papenburg has to be dissolved on 1 October 1936 and handed over to Reich Labor Leader State Secretary Hierl against payment of expenses incurred for the new construction of the Sachsenhausen concentration camp.

(b) The inmates of the Esterwegen concentration camp and 1 ss Death's Head *Sturm* as guard personnel will be transferred to the new Sachsenhausen concentration camp by 1 October 1936.

(c) The "Columbia" concentration camp, Berlin, will similarly be dissolved by 1 October 1936; the buildings are being handed over to the Reich Aviation Ministry on the same date. The inmates of the Columbia concentration camp will likewise be transferred on that date to the new Sachsenhausen concentration camp. [. . .]

Establishment and maintenance of concentration camps is a police matter and, as such, continues to be the responsibility of the *Länder*, in the present case of the *Land* Prussia. In these circumstances I request that you waive any payment for the value of the land ceded [. . .] and let me have it, for the purpose indicated, free of charge.

82. Circular of the Political Department of the German Foreign Ministry to diplomatic missions and consulates, regarding concentration camps, dated 8 December 1936[45]

The following camps are concentrated under uniform direction as concentration camps: Dachau, Lichtenburg, Sachsenburg, Sachsenhausen and Sulza. For female protective custody inmates a women's protective custody camp has been attached to the *Land* Workhouse in Moringen. There are no longer any other concentration camps. According to the latest compilation in the Reich, as of 1 Nov. of this year 4,761 persons were accommodated in concentration camps. Of these, 3,694 persons were held in detention as political protective custody detainees and 1,067 persons as professional criminals and other asocial elements.

83. Speech by Heinrich Himmler on "Character and Task of the ss and the Police" at the National-Political Course of the Wehrmacht from 15 to 23 January 1937[46]

We still have the following concentration camps in Germany to-day—and let me say straightaway that I do not believe that they will become fewer; in my opinion there will have to be more in certain circumstances—1. Dachau near Munich, 2. Sachsenhausen near Berlin, this is the former Esterwegen camp in the Ems country. I dissolved this camp in the Ems country in response to the arguments of Reich Labor Leader Hierl, who pointed out to me, just as he did to the judiciary, that it was wrong to tell one person that service in the moor, the service of reclaiming the land, was a privilege, while we send some-body else there, as a detainee, telling him: You wait, I'll teach you *mores*, I'm sending you into the moor. This is indeed illogical and after six or nine months I dissolved the camp at Esterwegen and moved it to Sachsenhausen near Oranienburg. Next, there is a camp at Lichtenburg near Torgau, a camp at Sachsenburg near Chemnitz and, in addition, a few smaller camps. The number of protective custody inmates is 8,000. Let me explain to you why we have to have so many, why we have to have even more. We used to have a superbly organized KPD [Communist Party]. This KPD was smashed in 1933. Some of its functionaries went abroad. Another lot of them was then held by us as part of the very high number of protective custody inmates of 1933. Because of my very accurate knowledge of Bolshevism I have always opposed the release of these people from the camps. Surely we must clearly realize that the broad masses of the workers are entirely accessible to National Socialism and the present state, so long as they are not turned again to other ideas by these well-instructed, well-prepared and financially richly supported functionaries. It's obvious: anyone who was a Communist for years is prone to Communism, even if he was one of them from the best of motives. [. . .] In response to the urgings of the ministries we released a large number of protective custody detainees in 1933, in Prussia and in other German *Länder*. Only I in Bavaria didn't give in then and didn't release my protective custody detainees. [. . .]

I have now gradually begun, with the Führer's approval, to rearrest a major part of these functionaries, as far as we can get hold of them, and thus ensure tranquillity. Especially in view of any foreign-policy danger we shall increase the number to such an extent that we can genuinely guarantee that the establishment of any new illegal organization becomes impossible if only for a lack of functionaries and leaders.

Beyond this it would be [. . .] enormously instructive for anyone to take a look at such a concentration camp. When you have seen this, you'll be convinced: none of them is there unjustly; they are the scum of criminality, of failures. There is no better demonstration of the heredity and racial laws, that is, for the things that Dr. Gütt[47] spoke to you about, than such a concentration camp. There are people with hydrocephalus, squinting eyes, malformed individuals, half-Jews, a vast

The ss Concentration Camp System

amount of racially inferior rubbish. All that is there together. Of course we differentiate among the inmates between those whom we put in for a few months, actually for education, and those whom we have to keep there for a long time. Education, on the whole, is only through order, never by any ideological instruction, because in most cases the inmates are slavish souls; there are only few with real character. These slavish souls would pretend anything one demands of them, they would repeat parrot-fashion what the *Völkischer Beobachter*[48] says, but in reality they remain the same. Education is therefore by orderliness. This orderliness begins with having the people live in clean huts. This is something only we Germans accomplish, few other nations would be so humane. Their linen is frequently changed. The people are getting accustomed to having to wash twice a day and they are made familiar with the use of a toothbrush, which most of them have not seen before.

I repeat: you wouldn't believe such types were possible. There's an infinite number of people with previous convictions, especially among the political criminals. In one camp we have the so-called professional criminals, 500 of them from Prussia and the other *Länder* with the most serious previous convictions. There isn't a single man among them who has not at least 8 to 10 years of penitentiary. There are people among them who have 31 previous convictions. I always visit the camps myself once a year, and I arrive suddenly without previous notice in order to see how they are run. Quite recently, last year, I saw a man of 72, who had just committed his 63rd indecent assault. It would be an insult to animals to call such a person an animal, because animals don't behave that way. Because criminality in Germany is still too high for me, I am beginning to lock up professional criminals on a much greater scale than hitherto after just a few convictions, after three or four times, and not let them walk free again. One can't assume the responsibility for this sort of thing any longer, especially we with our wallowing in humanity and our inadequate laws, letting those people loose on mankind again, especially the killers, people who commit robbery with violence, car theft, etc., whose prosecution then costs us a pile of money. What do you suppose the prosecution of a car thief costs us? I was once told, in a lecture in the Prussian State Council:[49] This, you know, is how the matter stands in this case, why don't you release the man, he's been inside for a year. You only need to put him under careful surveillance. I have to say to this: Only a layman can talk like that. What does it mean, putting a man under surveillance? For that I need at least three officials per day—there are 24 hours in a day—these three officials need two cars, because if the fellow is at all clever, he'll leap from one streetcar onto another, from one cab to another. So it can't be done without five officials. It so happens that during our struggle we were also illegal once and therefore—this is bad luck for the Communists—we're familiar with this sort of thing. [. . .]

These people therefore are now in a concentration camp. The main education is through orderliness, painstaking order and cleanliness, painstaking discipline. It's obvious that, when a superior appears, the man takes off his cap and stands to attention. Of course he is forbidden to salute with "Heil Hitler!" When the people are marching, it is obvious that at the first step they have to start singing. And it is obvious that no national songs are sung, but only popular or wanderers' songs. All these things have to proceed with absolutely rigid, soldierly discipline and order. The concentration camps are guarded by these Death's Head Units. It is impossible [. . .] to take married people for this guard service, because no state could pay for that. It is also necessary to have a relatively high number of these guard troops for the concentration camps—they number 3,500 men in Germany—because no other service is more devastating and strenuous for the troops than just that of guarding villains and criminals.

The better class of inmates works in workshops. If somebody is due for release, then we only release him when we have also found a job for him. [. . .] It makes no sense to release a person, thrusting him into hardship and hunger. The families of the inmates are cared for by the NS-*Volkswohlfahrt*[50] and other welfare bodies, so the dependents don't have to suffer hunger. Again something that's possible only in Germany, no other nation would do anything like it.

The camps are surrounded by barbed wire with an electric wire. Obviously, if anyone enters a forbidden zone or a forbidden path, shots will be fired. If anyone even tries to escape, let's say in the moor or on road works, or anywhere else, shots will be fired. If someone is cheeky or recalcitrant, and that happens now and again, or even if he just tries to be, he is taken into solitary confinement, into dark confinement with

The ss Concentration Camp System

bread and water, or—and I ask you not to be alarmed: I have taken the old penitentiary regulation of Prussia, dating from 1914–1918—he may, in bad cases, receive twenty-five lashes.[51] Atrocities, sadism, as frequently asserted by the foreign press, are quite impossible. For one thing, the punishment can only be imposed by the Inspector of all camps, not even by the camp commandant, and for another the punishment is executed by a guard company, so that there is always one platoon, 20 to 24 men, present; and finally there is a doctor present at the punishment and a minute-taker. One can't do more by way of meticulousness. Here, too I would like to say: These things are necessary; otherwise we would never have any control over those criminals.

84. Decree by Reinhard Heydrich as Head of the Gestapa regarding releases from concentration camps, dated 16 January 1937[52]

With effect from 25.1.1937 I hereby order that releases of protective custody inmates or schooling inmates[53] from concentration camps are only to be effected with my approval. All proposals for release are to be submitted through the section leader on a special proposal list as per specimen below, with detailed personal data and an attached photograph.

85. Letter from Reich Leader ss and Chief of German Police Heinrich Himmler to the Reich Ministry of Justice, regarding the sale of the Esterwegen concentration camp, dated 8 February 1937[54]

I request that you use your influence to ensure that *this sale sum* [1,050,000 RM for the sale of Esterwegen to the Reich Ministry of Justice] *is adhered to* [. . .], as even this amount is not fully adequate to meet *all* the construction costs of the replacement camp in Sachsenhausen, set up initially for 3,000 persons. Otherwise any excess costs for the Sachsenhausen camp, over and above the sales sum, will have to be taken over by the Reich. [. . .] I request that, when you examine my above request, you also acknowledge the achievement of all those involved in strenuous, laborious and dedicated day and night work under especially difficult and dangerous conditions in such an astonishingly short time. In the place of the simple Esterwegen camp, built at the time, in the first days of the Revolution in the moorland on the northwestern border of the Reich, a completely new, modern and up-to-date concentration camp, capable of expansion at any time, has now been created with comparatively small means in close proximity to the Reich capital—a camp equal to any kind of demands and requirements, one that guarantees the security of the Reich from enemies of the state and persons damaging the state in peacetime as well as in the event of mob[ilization].

86. From the notes of the Dachau camp gatekeeper Alfred Hübsch, a political detainee, on the reconstruction of Dachau by inmates during 1937 and 1938, written ca. 1960[55]

The new camp was constructed in 1937. 4 o'clock reveille, 5:30 fall-in, 6 o'clock start of work. Until May 1938 not one day off except for Christmas Day. Parade ground torn up, the whole camp made lower, the woodland cleared, gravel and soil removed.

87. Minute of the State Police Office Dresden regarding the dissolution of the Sachsenburg concentration camp, dated 13 July 1937[56]

The Sachsenburg concentration camp was dissolved on 12.7.37. The protective custody detainees were transferred to the Sachsenhausen concentration camp near Oranienburg. In future, male protective custody detainees will be taken to the Lichtenburg concentration camp (District Torgau). For reasons of economy of costs individual transports are no longer admissible in future. [. . .] The State Police offices will receive further instructions regarding the staging of collective transports.

88. Report of the former detainee Herbert Thiele about the construction of Buchenwald, written in 1979[57]

The first 149 detainees, coming from Sachsenhausen, arrived on the Ettersberg, which originally gave its name to the concentration camp to be built, toward the afternoon of 16 July 1937. They were received by the camp leader, ss *Hauptsturmführer* Weiseborn,[58] who with the vilest insults threatened that anyone who might even think of escape would be shot. Initially there was only one incomplete hut that these detainees had to complete by nightfall, while they were being driven on with blows from the ss. Some of these comrades were detailed to tree felling since the whole future camp consisted at first only of woodland. During the first few nights this hut was occupied half by the detainees and half by the ss. The detainees initially slept on the floor on straw spread there and could only inadequately cover themselves with old army coats. It was forbidden to leave the hut, in which there was neither water nor a toilet; anybody nevertheless risking it was instantly shot by the sentry. In 12 to 14 hours of the heaviest daily physical labor one hut was completed nearly every day during the time that followed. The first inmates' hut proper was Hut No. 7, completed on 28 July 1937. Meanwhile a second transport had come in from Sachsenburg with 70 criminal detainees. This was immediately followed by the first major transport from Lichtenburg with the entire illegal leadership of the KPD organization there.

89. Letter from Theodor Eicke to Heinrich Himmler, regarding the naming of the Buchenwald concentration camp, dated 24 July 1937[59]

The name "C. C. Ettersberg," as instructed, cannot be used because the NS Cultural Community in Weimar is objecting to it, as Ettersberg has connections with the life of the poet Goethe. *Gauleiter* Sauckel has also requested me to give the camp another name. [. . .] I suggest to the Reichsführer to name the camp "C. C. Hochwald, post Weimar."

90. Letter from Heinrich Himmler to the Reich governor in Thuringia, Fritz Sauckel,[60] with the instruction for protective custody detainees to be placed in the nearest concentration camp, dated 20 September 1937[61]

Following the reduction of the number of concentration camps to the three camps in Sachsenhausen, Buchenwald and Dachau for male detainees, assignment to the individual camps will almost inevitably be from the geographically neighboring territories, viz. assignment

(a) *to Sachsenhausen*: protective custody detainees from the eastern, northern and central regions,
(b) *to Buchenwald*: protective custody prisoners from the western and northwestern regions of the Reich, as well as from Saxony, Thuringia, Hesse and the northern parts of Bavaria, roughly north of the line Würzburg-Bamberg-Bayreuth,

(c) *to Dachau*: protective custody prisoners of the southern German State Police authorities.

However, given the over-occupation of one camp or another, e.g. in connection with initiatives in certain parts of the country, changes in the assignment to camps will occasionally be unavoidable. In such cases — provided assignments were ordered by the Secret State Police Office — general instructions will be issued on assignment on a case-by-case basis.

91. Letter from *Magistratsdirektor* (a senior municipal public servant) Hornek to the mayor of the City of Vienna regarding the establishment of the Mauthausen concentration camp, dated 7 April 1938[62]

Sturmbannführer Ahrens from the ss *Reichsführung* in Munich, Karlstraße 10, and Professor Dr. Schadler, the geologist of the *Land* Museum in Linz, called on me today to inform me that a state concentration camp for 3,000 to 5,000 persons is to be established in Mauthausen. Under consideration are two quarries belonging to the City of Vienna: the "Wiener Graben" quarry, which is not in operation, and the "Bettelberg" quarry, which is in operation. [. . .] The two gentlemen have asked for a basic agreement by 1600 today that the two quarries will be put at the disposal of the ss *Reichsführung*. [. . .] I therefore request approval of the following settlement:

[. . .] To the ss *Reichsführung*, Munich, Karlstraße 10

Further to the oral request made today, you are informed that the City of Vienna is, in principle, willing to make the quarries "Wiener Graben" and "Bettelberg" in Mauthausen, which are under its ownership, available to the ss *Reichsführung* for the establishment of a concentration camp.

92. Report of the political detainee Erwin Gostner on the Mauthausen concentration camp in 1938, published in 1945[63]

After a one and a half hour's march we approach the camp. It is situated in a hilly landscape. [. . .] We turn into a quarry and learn from the escorting ss men that this is our future place of work. Past a few building huts and huge granite blocks the path leads to a stairway[64] rising upward in a steep arch. We climb numerous steps, on our right the forrest drops almost vertically, below on our left glistens a lake. [. . .] With suspense we await the camp huts. For another ten minutes our way is slightly uphill, then we reach the camp situated on a large hill. We pass several ss huts and stand before a guard tower of massive stone blocks with a wooden superstructure. On the tower is a machine-gun post. Threateningly the machine-gun barrels reach out over our heads.

93. Minutes of a meeting of the Flossenbürg Parish Council on 20 July 1938 regarding the development of the local concentration camp[65]

At today's parish council meeting, in the presence of Herr *Gruppenführer* Eicke and Herr *Sturmbannführer* Weiseborn, building on the Plattenberg was on the agenda. A parish plot on the Plattenberg is being leased to the ss *Reichsführung*. On it the ss *Reichsführung* will put up blockhouses for the camp's married ss staff. The lease contract runs for an indefinite period. If ever the parish wishes to open a quarry on the leased land, the blockhouses, where necessary, will again be removed. In that event the lease expires.

94. Speech by Heinrich Himmler at the ss *Gruppenführer* Conference in Munich on 8 November 1937[66]

I now come to the concentration camps. In the past we had the Dachau camp and the Sachsenhausen camp near Berlin and two smaller camps, Lichtenburg and Sachsenburg, and finally another small one in Thuringia. The small camps Lichtenburg and Sachsenburg have been dissolved in favor of a big camp near Weimar, the Buchenwald concentration camp. The other two camps, Dachau and Sachsenhausen, have been enlarged to 6,000 inmates each; Buchenwald is envisioned for 8,000 inmates. I am convinced — and it is good to say so openly — that in the event of war they will still not be sufficient. I believe instead that a large number of criminal and political criminals — this year we actually locked up 2,000 criminal felons with at least 6 previous convictions and 6–7 years' penitentiary, after which the crime figures dropped quite significantly — have to be kept in the camps for many years of their lives, at least until they have got used to order, not that we believe that they have become orderly persons but because their will has been broken. There will be a great many whom we must never release. Let's be clear about this: broad sections of our people will, over the next few years or decades, again sometime become vulnerable to the poison of Bolshevism that is being handed out to them in ever-new forms and in homeopathic doses by the most sophisticated propaganda. If we release the functionaries then the people become addicts to the poison; if, however, we deprive them of the heads and the corps of leaders, if we keep them locked up, then the good spirit in each German will prevail in serious times, even in one who was a serious Communist in the past, and he will follow the good spirit. If we did not do this, I have to say that I would be very pessimistic already and even more so if things were to take a serious turn.

The ss Concentration Camp System

2.2. Ways into the Concentration Camps

From the mid-1930s the ss and the police began to extend their scope of persecution, reflecting the Nazis' increasingly wide-ranging definition of the "enemy" that had to be destroyed for Germany's survival. Of course, political opponents were still central to Nazi persecution in the camps, as we have seen, and the definition of who was a political enemy stretched further and further. For example, the Jehovah's Witnesses—a small religious group whose members refused to perform military service, reintroduced in Germany in 1935—increasingly found themselves persecuted by the regime, accused of being a Communist front. Many Jehovah's Witnesses were dealt with by courts. At the same time, the police began to detain Jehovah's Witnesses in concentration camps, often after they had been acquitted by ordinary courts or after their release from prison (96). In the summer of 1935 about 400 prisoners of the Sachsenburg camp were Jehovah's Witnesses. Such high numbers were not unusual. In the Lichtenburg women's camp at least 470 Jehovah's Witnesses arrived between late 1937 and 1939, making them the camp's largest prisoner group.[67]

Meanwhile, the Nazis' virulent racial anti-Semitism began to have an ever greater effect on German Jews. Nazi anti-Semitism manifested itself in social marginalization, economic expropriation, and legal discrimination. In the spring and summer of 1935 local Nazi activists targeted Jewish shops and attacked Jews who were in relationships with non-Jews. These waves of local anti-Semitism provided a crucial impetus for further national discriminatory legislation, as the regime was keen to affirm its control and leadership in racial policy. Therefore the regime passed the Nuremberg Laws in September 1935, which effectively reduced Jews to second-class citizens and racial outcasts.[68]

Many German Jews, some sixty thousand in 1933 and 1934 alone, emigrated because of the radicalization of Nazi policy, as the ss, in particular, was keen to force as many Jews out of Germany as possible.[69] Yet many German Jews found it very hard to make a living abroad. Entry permits soon elapsed for those who did not find permanent employment abroad, and many countries denied entry to families during the worldwide economic depression. Those Jews who returned to Germany were soon caught up in the web of Nazi terror. In Prussia the Gestapo had started to arrest returning Jews in January 1934. In the following year, the German authorities intensified the persecution. Many returning Jews were now taken into protective custody, with men sent to the Dachau concentration camp and women to Moringen. These Jewish returning émigrés would only be released if they offered a guarantee that they would get out of the country within two weeks (95).[70]

Nazi discrimination of Jews was stepped up further during the second half of the 1930s. The regime, concerned with public opinion abroad, only ordered a temporary letup of state-sponsored anti-Semitism before and during the summer Olympics of 1936. Nazi terror from below and above continued. Waves of racial terror increasingly destroyed the hope that Jews could still live in Germany. The annexation of Austria in March 1938, accompanied by anti-Semitic excesses, led to a further escalation of anti-Semitism across Germany.[71]

More Jews were arrested and taken to the camps, which became a testing ground for more radical forms of Nazi anti-Semitic terror.[72] Around mid-1938 more than two thousand Jews with previous convictions, often for petty offenses or transgression of the regime's harsh anti-Semitic legislation, such as the Nuremberg Laws, were detained in the concentration camps amid police raids throughout Germany and Austria against so-called asocials (103). Over the previous weeks the Viennese Gestapo had already taken many hundreds of Jews with previous convictions, often trivial ones, to Dachau, where the ss separated them from the other prisoners and brutally abused them. In charge of these mass arrests was Adolf Eichmann, an ss officer who would later play a key role in the extermination of European Jewry during World War II (102). Yet in 1938 the aim of Eichmann and the ss was forced emigration, not genocide, although the ss was always prepared to use extreme physical violence.

Nazi anti-Jewish policy reached its bloody prewar climax in the late autumn of 1938. On 7 November, Herschel Grynszpan, a young Polish Jew raised in Germany, entered the German Embassy in Paris, drew a gun, and shot Ernst vom Rath, a junior diplomat. Grynszpan's

The ss Concentration Camp System

act—a protest against the deportation of his family, together with thousands of other Polish residents, from Nazi Germany—prompted hitherto unseen violence on a massive level against Jews all over Germany. In the evening of 9 November, Nazi leaders unleashed a pogrom. Hitler himself gave the green light, and soon senior party officials were mobilizing their troops in the regions. Throughout the night and into the following day, Nazi activists went on the rampage, killing well over a hundred Jews.[73]

Already in the late evening of 9 November, Hitler ordered that twenty-five to thirty thousand Jews be arrested immediately (107). At five minutes to midnight, Heinrich Müller, one of the Gestapo's leaders, then telexed initial orders to regional police commanders throughout Germany (108). Police officials did not have to wait long for more specific orders, sent by Reinhard Heydrich, the Chief of the Security Police (a national police agency formed in 1936, after Himmler's appointment as Chief of German Police, which included both political and criminal police) (109).

For several days the Gestapo (assisted by regular police and storm troopers) carried out mass arrests all over Germany.[74] In all, about twenty-six thousand Jewish men were taken to the three main camps in Dachau, Buchenwald, and Sachsenhausen—far more than in any previous mass arrests.[75] For the first time, Jews made up the largest group of prisoners, though not for long, as most Jewish prisoners were released after some weeks, normally only if they promised to leave Germany. From mid-November 1938, Heydrich ordered the successive release of many arrested Jews, including war veterans and those who transferred their businesses to Germans (110).[76]

Despite the anti-Semitic excesses in the late 1930s, concentration camps were not primarily an instrument of anti-Jewish terror but rather of the repression of social outsiders. As we have seen, the practice of detaining so-called asocial elements and criminals in camps had begun as early as 1933, and it continued over the following years (99) before escalating dramatically in the last years before the war. In May 1938, Himmler requested that all male workhouse inmates able to work should be handed over to the concentration camps (101). More importantly, in 1937 and 1938 the police carried out several large-scale raids across Germany. In March 1937 the police arrested about 2,000 former convicts and suspected offenders in the camps, followed by 1,500 to 2,000 supposedly work-shy people in April 1938. More arrests soon followed. In June 1938 at least 9,000 men, most of them homeless or beggars, were sent to the camps in what was officially known as the Reich Action against the Work-Shy (Aktion Arbeitsscheu Reich).

The basis for these arrests were several decrees and directives issued by Himmler and Heydrich (100 and 103). Formulated deliberately widely, these decrees effectively allowed for the arrest of anyone labeled as asocial (104). Local police or welfare authorities made keen use of their powers and often targeted individuals who had been on their books for years, as in the case of Rudolf S. from Essen (105). Officials overwhelmingly shared the Nazi belief that deviant behavior was rooted in biological defects and that many social outsiders had to be removed from the national community. Initiative from below was important as local welfare and police authorities detained more people than was ordered by the police leadership. Furthermore, local police authorities often used the new decrees to arrest Jews and other so-called undesirables. Apart from their socio-biological component, such raids sent a clear message to all Germans: under no circumstances would the regime, preparing for war, tolerate any deviant behavior. As a result of all these initiatives, social outsiders outnumbered political prisoners in the camps after June 1938.[77]

Among those arrested were also other outsiders, in addition to alleged criminals, beggars, and homeless. The police persecution of homosexual men had increased soon after the Nazi seizure of power, leading to large-scale arrests of men who had long been discriminated against in Germany and elsewhere in Europe. Nazi persecution increased markedly after the Röhm putsch, when Himmler claimed that SA leader Ernst Röhm, more or less openly gay, had tried to establish a homosexual dictatorship that would have ruined Germany. In late 1934 police forces across Germany carried out raids against men accused of having sex with other men. Most of these men were dealt with by the judiciary, but some were sent to the concentration camps as a deterrent to others. In Bavaria some fifty-four men were taken into protective custody to Dachau, where they were housed in a separate hut. Inside, the lights were kept on at night. During the day, the prisoners had to carry out hard labor. They received smaller food rations than the other prisoners. The police suggested that the men should be kept at Dachau for at least three months, or for at least six months in particularly severe cases.[78] This order reflected the pervasive paranoia about the "threat" posed by homosexual behavior to other prisoners as well as the belief that homosexuality could be cured with hard work and tough discipline.[79]

In 1935, paragraph 175 of the German criminal code, which banned homosexual relationships among men, was made more severe. But this was not enough for Himmler. Soon, he ordered the compilation of a Gestapo card index of all known homosexuals which formed the basis of the Reich Central Office for the Combating of Homosexuality, created in October 1936. In the wake of the December 1937 decree against dangerous habitual criminals, the persecution of homosexuals continued. Himmler even announced that homosexual ss men would be taken to the camps, where they should be shot "while trying to escape" (98). Furthermore, many homosexuals who had earlier been convicted by the courts were now transferred to the concentration camps upon the completion of their judicial sentence. Estimates suggest that in all between five thousand and ten thousand homosexuals were taken to the concentration camps between 1933 and 1945, where they were subjected to especially brutal treatment by both the guards and fellow inmates.[80]

DOCUMENTS

95. Decree of the Bavarian Political Police regarding measures against returning émigrés, dated 7 March 1935[81]

Most recently there has been a steady increase in the number of returning émigrés, with Jewish repatriates accounting for by far the highest percentage. The repatriation of these fundamentally unwelcome elements has already in several instances given rise to anti-Jewish excesses, invariably caused by the arrogant demeanor of the repatriates. There can be no doubt that the German émigrés have contributed nothing at all to the raising of the reputation of the German Reich abroad. Indeed it is just they, in view of the boycott and atrocity propaganda supported by them, to whom the discrediting of Germany in the world is largely due. With their paeans of hatred in the émigré press they have appreciably damaged not only the German national honor but also the German national economy.

A repatriation on a major scale, such as observed at present, opens up, as instances have already shown, sources of danger to internal peace and to the security of the Reich. The cause of this is to be found in the mentality of the repatriates, who are not familiar with the principles of the National Socialist Germany. [. . .] On the other hand, one cannot deny that among the repatriates there is sometimes human material that, with appropriate guidance and schooling, can be reintegrated into the German national body. It seems therefore appropriate to provide the repatriates with ideological schooling to help them understand the new conditions in Germany. For reasons of effectiveness such schooling is to be performed in community camps.[82]

For this schooling process to be effected, every returning émigré, regardless of person, is to be instantly arrested without special instruction when passing through the frontier control or after arriving at his inland residence.

96. Decree of the Bavarian Political Police regarding the protective custody of Jehovah's Witnesses, dated 23 September 1935[83]

There are good grounds for issuing new directives regarding the detention and duration of protective custody imposed on followers of the International Bible Researchers' Association. It is therefore decreed with immediate effect as follows:

1. Persons caught out for the first time of being active for the "International Bible Researchers' Association" are to be taken into protective custody for up to seven days, unless a judicial warrant of arrest has been issued, and then, after a severe warning and a possible imposition of reporting duty, to be released. In the event of *leaders* of the I.B.R.A., protective custody may be extended up to two months.

2. If, after being released, a person is again active on behalf of the International Bible Researchers' Association, he is to be taken into protective custody and application is to be made, as hitherto, for transfer to a concentration camp. [. . .]

3. Extension of protective custody beyond the duration ordered can

only be considered if the protective custody detainee has attempted, during his stay in the concentration camp, to canvass among the other inmates for the ideas of the International Bible Researchers' Association or if he has seriously offended against the camp regulations and discipline. In such cases a thorough application is to be made, to which a report from the concentration camp commandant is to be attached about the person's behavior.

97. Letter from the Bavarian Political Police to the commandant of the Dachau concentration camp, regarding the detention of beggars in Dachau, dated 10 July 1936[84]

The head of the Transportation Department of the Police Directorate Munich [. . .] today informed me by telephone that in connection with the action ordered by the State Ministry of Interior by Decree No. 2074 a 4 of 22.6.36 against beggars and vagabonds the following transports will, for the time being, arrive at the Dachau concentration camp:

1st Transport:

120 persons on Wednesday, 15 *July* 1936 *at* 1630 at Dachau railway station. These 120 persons will, on three railway wagons, be directly transported from Dachau railway station into the Dachau concentration camp via the freight track.

2nd Transport:

120 persons on Friday, 17 *July* 1936 *at* 1400 at the main railway station Munich-transportation track. These 120 persons in two large prisoner transportation wagons of the Police Directorate Munich and the Bavarian Political Police will be handed over directly to the Dachau concentration camp from the Munich main railway station.

3rd Transport:

Eighty persons on Saturday, 18 *July* 1936 *at* 1645 at the main railway station Munich-transportation track. These 80 persons will likewise be directly handed over to the camp in large prisoner transport wagons.

98. Speech by Heinrich Himmler at the ss *Gruppenführer* Conference in Bad Tölz on 18 February 1937, mentioning homosexual ss men[85]

These people [homosexual ss men] are of course publicly degraded in every case and expelled and handed over to the court. After serving the punishment imposed by the court they are, upon my instruction, taken to a concentration camp and in the concentration camp shot while trying to escape.

99. Decree of the Reich and Prussian Minister of the Interior, Wilhelm Frick, regarding preventive police custody, dated 14 December 1937[86]

The reorganization of the criminal police throughout the Reich calls for a uniform regulation also of preventive police measures. Systematic surveillance, as hitherto practiced successfully in Prussia and other *Länder* [states], is to be retained; preventive police custody is to be extended in light of past experience and the insights gained from criminal-biological research. The obligation to fulfill the general duties of the police (and hence also of the criminal police) as defined by National Socialism, to protect the community by whatever measures are required against anyone intending to damage it, is not abolished by the special provision below. [. . .]

The following can be taken into preventive police custody:

(a) a professional or habitual criminal [. . .]

(b) a professional criminal if he was at least three times lawfully sentenced either to penitentiary or to imprisonment for at least 6 months for criminal offenses committed from greed.

(c) a habitual criminal if he was at least three times lawfully sentenced either to penitentiary or to imprisonment for at least 6 months for criminal offenses committed from a criminal impulse or from criminal inclination.

(d) anyone who, because of a serious criminal offense committed by him and because of the possibility of a repetition, represents such a major danger to the general public that it would be irresponsible to leave him at liberty, or anyone displaying by his actions an intention which aims at a serious criminal offense, actions that currently fall short of meeting the provisions of an existing criminal offense.

(e) anyone who, without being a professional or habitual criminal, endangers the general public by his asocial behavior. [. . .]

The ss Concentration Camp System

Preventive police custody is effected in closed reform or labor camps or in any other way ordered by the Reich Criminal Police Authority. It runs for as long as its purpose demands.

100. Decree of Heinrich Himmler regarding protective custody for work-shy persons, dated 26 January 1938[87]

In connection with the reorganization of the criminal police throughout the Reich, the Reich and Prussian Minister of the Interior, by Circular Decree dated 14.12.1937 [. . .] has effected a comprehensive and uniform system of the regulations regarding the preventive fighting of crime by the police. In this Decree, which has meanwhile been sent to the authorities concerned — including the State Police headquarters and the State Police stations — the criminal police is authorized, under certain conditions, to take professional and habitual criminals, as well as asocial elements, into preventive custody.

Because of the scope and the diverse composition of the circles in question, the smooth and complete implementation of the measures planned will take some time. This gradual implementation does not impede the rounding-up of the major part of the elements concerned, such as professional or habitual criminals [. . .] as these represent a well-defined and readily identifiable circle of persons.

Matters are different regarding those persons who, merely because of their proven reluctance to work, must be ranked with the asocial elements within the meaning of the above-mentioned Decree. These may be expected, after the promulgation of the measures envisioned, to feign instant willingness to work without, however, doing any fruitful work any more than before. In order to achieve a genuine cleaning-up by the effective round-up also of these asocial elements, a once-only, comprehensive and surprise strike is necessary.

For the execution of this action I order:

1. Work-shy within the meaning of this Decree are men of working age whose suitability for work has recently been confirmed, or is still to be confirmed, by a duty doctor's certificate and who in two proven cases have, without justifiable reason, declined the work offered to them or else have accepted the work but after a short time, without valid reason, given it up again.

2. The local labor offices have already been instructed to identify the work-shy persons known to them during the period from 18.2. to 4.3.1938 and report them to the State Police directorates and stations. [. . .] The total of work-shy persons identified up to 3.3.1938 is to be reported by telex by 3.3.1938.

3. After completing the identification, the State Police directorates and stations are to arrest the persons identified in the period from 4.3. to 9.3.1938. [. . .]

For protective custody a minimum duration of three months is initially laid down as a matter of principle. The review of custody (*Haftprüfung*) by the Secret State Police is to take place every three months. [. . .] The protective custody detainees are to be exclusively assigned to the Buchenwald concentration camp near Weimar.

101. Telex from Himmler to ss *Oberführer* Werner Best, dated May 1938[88]

May I remind you of the visit to State Secretary Pfundtner.[89] I request that you discuss with him what he is in principle already willing to do: that all male inmates of the Workhouses under autonomous provincial administration, who are capable of work, are handed over to the concentration camps.

I request an immediate issue of a relevant Order by the Reich Ministry of the Interior and an immediate examination by the Gestapo of all Workhouses and the transfer of men capable of work to the concentration camps.

102. Minutes of ss *Untersturmführer* Adolf Eichmann[90] (of the sd *Oberabschnitt* Austria) regarding the deportation of Austrian Jews to the Dachau concentration camp, dated 30 May 1938[91]

Over the next few weeks 5,000 Jews from Austria are to be taken to the Dachau concentration camp. To date about 650 have been rounded up to leave for Dachau by special train at 17.35 on 30 May. The next special transport is expected to leave on 1 June 1938; the rest will be deported after Whitsun. The Jews are predominantly elements with previous convictions or asocial elements. Of the above-mentioned 5,000 Jews, 4,000 have been rounded up in Vienna, the rest in the provinces.

The ss Concentration Camp System

103. Decree by Reinhard Heydrich to Criminal Police directorates regarding preventive crime fighting by the police, dated 1 June 1938[92]

As criminality is rooted in asocial behavior and constantly replenishes itself from it, the Decree of the Reich and Prussian Ministry of the Interior of 14 December 1937 [. . .] provided the Criminal Police with far-reaching opportunities to round up not only professional criminals but also those asocial elements whose behavior is a burden on the community and therefore damages it. However, I have had to observe that the Decree has not so far been applied with the necessary incisiveness. The strict execution of the Four-Year Plan requires the employment of all forces capable of work and does not tolerate asocial persons avoiding work and thereby sabotaging the Four-Year Plan.

I therefore order:

1. Regardless of the special action carried out by the Secret State Police against asocial elements in March of this year, the Decree of 14 December 1937 is to be most rigorously applied and, during the week from 13 to 18 June 1938, *at least* 200 male work-capable (asocial) persons are to be taken into preventive police custody by Criminal Police directorates at your end.

The following are to be particularly borne in mind:

(a) vagabonds, who are at present drifting from one place to another without work,

(b) beggars, even if they have a permanent place of residence,

(c) gypsies and persons wandering about in gypsy fashion, if they have shown no liking for regular work or have committed criminal offenses,

(d) pimps, who were involved in serious criminal proceedings—even if not enough evidence could not be found—and who still move in circles of pimps and prostitutes, or persons under strong suspicion of acting as pimps,

(e) persons with numerous previous convictions for affray, bodily harm [. . .] and suchlike, who have thereby demonstrated that they do not wish to integrate into the order of the people's community. [. . .]

2. Likewise in the week from 13 to 18 June all male Jews of the Criminal Police Directorate's district, who have served a prison sentence of no less than one month are to be taken into preventive police custody. [. . .]

Those arrested are to be deported immediately to the Buchenwald concentration camp near Weimar without confirmation or instruction by me.

104. Letter from the head of the Criminal Police office Gleiwitz to the Senior State Prosecutor in Neisse, dated 15 June 1938[93]

In a major special action against asocial elements (the work-shy, vagabonds, beggars, gypsies, pimps, resisters, persons causing bodily harm, brawlers, trespassers, etc.) who, along with professional criminals, are seen as the main cause of existing criminality, the Chief of the Security Police of the German Reich [Reinhard Heydrich] has ordered the nationwide arrest of such persons and their deportation to a labor camp, in order that, by performing work of use to the public within the framework of the Four-Year Plan, they are once more educated into becoming useful members of the people's community. Over the past few days a substantial number of asocial elements at present at liberty have been arrested and deported. Experience shows, however, that a large number of such persons are still in local court prisons serving longer or shorter detention and prison sentences. In order to make the improvement and educational opportunities available to them also, it is requested that persons with relevant previous convictions, who are still in those prisons but serving only brief residual prison sentences and who would anyway be released during the next 3 months, be, by way of suspension of sentence with the longest possible probation or of stayed execution of sentence, identified and simultaneously handed over to the Criminal Police station in Gleiwitz or to police units instructed by the above. We ourselves will ensure their immediate deportation to labor camps. As I have to pass on the number of those to be arrested no later than 20.6.38 I would be grateful if you could transmit to me the names of those concerned in writing or by telephone (Gleiwitz 3331, extension 361 or 367). At the same time I request information on the date of the detainee's release as well as his place of detention.

105. Instruction of the Head of the Criminal Police station Essen, regarding preventive police custody against Rudolf S., dated 18 June 1938[94]

S. is known here as a work-shy person who only does occasional work when compelled to do so in order to ensure his livelihood. Most of the time he receives welfare support and is therefore a burden to public care. He is divorced from his wife and lives in a barn in which he has put up an old bed. He converts the most part of his welfare support as well as of his wages into alcohol, so that he is always drunk. He is generally known as a drunkard.

106. Report by the SD *Oberabschnitt* Elbe, in a minute of the SD Staff Chancellery, dated 22 June 1938[95]

In the course of the action for the deportation of Jews who had been in prison for more than one month at the time of the Seizure of Power,[96] as well as of work-shy and asocial elements, altogether 162 persons, instead of 80 as envisioned, among them c. 30 Jews, have been deported to the Buchenwald concentration camp by the Criminal Police station Weimar in cooperation with the *Unterabschnitt* [a smaller SD administrative district].

107. From the diaries of Joseph Goebbels, dated 10 November 1938[97]

The Führer has ordered that 2[5]–30,000 Jews are to be arrested immediately. That will be a hit. They should see that the measure of our patience is exhausted.

108. Secret telex from Heinrich Müller of Gestapo headquarters to all State Police directorates and State Police stations, dated 9 November 1938 at 23.55[98]

Actions against Jews, particularly against their synagogues, will take place throughout Germany very shortly. These actions are not to be interfered with. [. . .] Preparations are to be made for the arrest of about 20–30,000 Jews in the Reich. Above all, wealthy Jews are to be chosen. Detailed instructions will follow in the course of this night.

109. Secret telex from Reinhard Heydrich to all State Police directorates and State Police stations, dated 10 November 1938 at 1.20[99]

As soon as the course of events of this night permits the employment of officers for this purpose, as many Jews—especially wealthy ones—are to be arrested in all districts as can be accommodated in the available detention quarters. To begin with, only healthy male Jews, not too elderly, are to be arrested. When the arrests have been effected contact is to be made without delay with the appropriate concentration camps regarding the fastest possible accommodation of the Jews.

110. **Circular from Reinhard Heydrich to all State Police directorates and State Police stations on the release of Jewish protective custody prisoners, dated 31 January 1939**[100]

The Reichsführer-ss and Chief of German Police has decided:

(1) that Jewish race defilers can also be released from protective custody provided they have not otherwise exposed themselves in a political or criminal respect *and* wish to emigrate. [. . .]

(3) In principle, Jewish protective custody prisoners may be released if they are in possession of emigration papers to other European states—i.e. not only overseas.

(4) The verbal threat of lifelong deportation to a concentration camp should continue to be made in every case, in the event that the person concerned, having been released from protective custody for the purpose of emigration, later returns without permission.

2.3. The Camps in the Nazi Web of Terror

According to some historians, the sharp fall in prisoner numbers in the concentration camps in the mid-1930s shows that Nazi terror against the German population had become negligible.[101] Yet, Nazi terror was never restricted to the camps. It manifested itself in many different ways. And while it did not hit all Germans, or even most of them, it was certainly visible to all. In addition to the everyday terror on the streets by gangs of Nazi thugs, who targeted German Jews, political suspects, and others branded as outsiders, a far-reaching and institutionalized policy of exclusion developed that involved several different state and party offices across Germany. Many hundreds of discriminatory laws and decrees were passed at local, regional, and state levels, some aimed at individual suspects, others at wider sections of the population. By 1939, for example, at least 300,000 men and women had been forcibly sterilized in Nazi Germany for alleged hereditary defects (in reality, the authorities' social and moral prejudices were often decisive). At the center of the policy of exclusion stood detention, with more Germans locked away than ever before. Apart from the new camps, there were reformatories, asylums, workhouses—institutions that all developed some links to the concentration camp system (232).[102] Above all, there were the state prisons, run by the legal authorities, not the ss. Since 1933 the German judiciary had gained formidable new weapons against political and social outsiders, and the hundreds of state prisons across Germany held some 116,000 inmates by late June 1937.[103]

Legal officials, led by Reich Minister of Justice Franz Gürtner, were determined to maintain their control over the punishment of lawbreakers against the encroaching ss and police apparatus. They were concerned, for example, about the growing cases in which police officers arrested defendants—who had just been acquitted by the courts—and took them straight to the camps.[104] As far as senior legal officials were concerned, the early camps may have been necessary during the Nazi capture of power, but courts and prisons were well placed by the mid-1930s to punish single-handedly any threats to the Nazi regime. Unsurprisingly, therefore, conflicts between the legal authorities and the ss continued. Hitler and Himmler regarded the judiciary useless at the implementation of the Nazi racial and social agenda because it was based on laws and ideas of legal process. The camps, on the other hand, were designed as places beyond the reach of the law, a notion that Hitler supported in 1935 (121).[105]

Apart from the legal authorities, others in the Nazi state were also keen to limit the ss's power of holding prisoners indefinitely without trial. As we have seen, Reich Minister of the Interior Wilhelm Frick was particularly concerned about the increasing power of Himmler's ss and police empire. On several occasions, therefore, Frick, a committed Nazi himself, challenged the ss's control of the camps. In January 1935, for example, he demanded an explanation why the authorities in Himmler's stronghold of Bavaria held more than half of all the around three thousand protective custody detainees in Germany (114). Yet Frick's intervention was ignored, as Himmler and Hitler rejected further legal or bureaucratic limits on Nazi terror.[106]

Some judges and state prosecutors were still determined to challenge the most outrageous ss crimes inside the camps; for them, camp commandants and guards were not above the law. Already in 1933, as we have seen, state prosecutors had investigated ss murderers in Dachau, and several more investigations of abuses in other camps followed in 1934 and 1935. In May 1935 a Dresden court sentenced the commandant and twenty-two guards of the Saxon Hohnstein camp to prison terms for torturing inmates. Nazi officials, including the Saxon *Gauleiter* Martin Mutschmann, demanded their immediate release and acquittal. The case eventually reached Hitler, who decided in late 1935 that the guards must be freed and amnestied, demonstrating his open disregard for the judiciary and his fundamental belief that he and the regime stood outside legal norms.[107]

Another prominent case was the legal investigation against officials of the Stettin-Bredow camp, a notorious camp where corrupt camp leaders and guards had systematically tortured and robbed prisoners, with the Stettin police's backing (112). The Prussian Central State Prosecutor's Office, set up in July 1933 to investigate criminal actions by sa and ss members, soon became involved, concerned with the impact of the atrocities on public opinion in Germany and abroad.

Eventually, a Stettin court sentenced camp officials to penitentiary or prison terms, yet once again most defendants did not serve their full sentences. Moreover, Fritz-Karl Engel, a high-ranking ss officer and Stettin's police president, who had ultimately been in charge of the Bredow camp, was actually acquitted, following Himmler's direct intervention (111, 112, and 113).[108] In the end, then, the ss largely prevailed over the judiciary.

Nonetheless, the legal apparatus, led by Franz Gürtner, was not prepared to accept that the ss camps were places entirely beyond the law, and Himmler's newly created camp system was still under some pressure to justify itself.[109] Gürtner repeatedly complained to Himmler about abuses and killings by the Camp ss (130), particularly about the cases in which murders were apparently covered up to prevent legal investigations.[110] The Reich Ministry of Justice, increasingly a spectator outside the camp perimeter, continued to keep an eye on such cases, even after the dissolution of the Central State Prosecutor's Office in 1937, replaced in 1938 by a commission for the investigation of cases in which prisoners had been "shot while trying to escape" (132). As he insisted that the camps were extra-territorial, Himmler was vehemently opposed to the legal representation of camp prisoners by attorneys. After a high-profile case where several pastors had been held in the Sachsenburg camp in 1935, Himmler, backed by Hitler, rejected any legal representation of camp prisoners (116 and 121).[111]

Yet it would be a mistake to view the relationship between the ss and the judiciary only in terms of conflict.[112] After all, the overwhelming majority of judicial officials, in office since the Weimar Republic, had long been sympathetic to the aims of the nationalist right, and once the Nazis were in power they believed that the regime would back efforts to push through tough laws and restore the state's authority, which had allegedly been undermined by the various Weimar governments.[113] All in all, the judiciary largely cooperated with the regime in the process of undermining the rule of law, for example, in the amnesties of March 1933 and August 1934 that protected hundreds of Nazi killers from prosecution.[114] Gürtner himself insisted at a 1939 conference with leading judges that the "cross-link with the State Police be maintained" (134). Both agencies agreed on the Third Reich's core policy of excluding social and racial outsiders as well as political opponents.

Before long, the legal authorities reconciled themselves to extra-legal detention in the concentration camps becoming a permanent feature of the Nazi state (123). Indeed, legal officials directly supported it. While they successfully blocked ss and police demands to hand over some regular state prisoners before the end of their sentences (127)—initiatives that owed less to the economic reasons cited by Himmler and Heydrich than to their desire to extend their influence—there was close collaboration between the judiciary, the ss, and police when it came to handing over prisoners who had completed their sentences in regular jails. Many thousand state prisoners were indeed transferred to concentration camps. On 18 December 1934 the Reich Ministry of Justice decreed that all political prisoners sentenced for treason must be reported to the Gestapo one month before their release from judicial detention, an order later extended to prisoners convicted of high treason. Often prison authorities wrote dismissive reports about these prisoners to the Gestapo, reflecting their hatred toward Communists and Socialists. After the end of their sentence, such inmates were often not released but detained by the police and then transferred to a concentration camp. Such was the case of Karl Elgas, a former KPD deputy in the Reichstag imprisoned in the Luckau penitentiary. Shortly before his sentence for attempted high treason came to an end, the prison governor reported him to the Gestapo, which then transferred him to Sachsenhausen, from where he was not released until April 1939 (124). There was also regular traffic of concentration camp inmates to state prisons, following prison sentences by courts. Such inmates were held in prisons for the duration of their formal judicial sentences before the authorities transferred them back to the camps (126).[115]

This collaboration between the judiciary and the ss went far beyond the suppression of political prisoners. More and more regular state prisoners were denounced to the police just before their impending release, to facilitate their detention in a concentration camp. From the mid-1930s, as the police increasingly targeted social outsiders, the judiciary began to give advance warnings about the releases of other inmates regarded as dangerous outsiders, including Gypsies,

Jehovah's Witnesses, and men sentenced for so-called race defilement under the 1935 Nuremberg Laws.[116]

To some legal officials, the increasingly powerful ss and police apparatus probably appeared like a monolithic bloc vis-à-vis the judiciary. But did the entire ss and police leadership work together unanimously on the camp system? Some historians argue that there was considerable tension, for example, between Eicke and the Gestapo leadership, represented by Heydrich and Dr. Werner Best. In several postwar trials, Best later tried to downplay his responsibility for the camps, despite the fact that it was the Gestapo, not the ss, that presided over arrests and releases from protective custody.[117] Still, Best and Eicke often worked together. For example, when Bernhard Lichtenberg, a Berlin priest, complained about atrocities in the Esterwegen camp, Best wrote a sharp riposte and appended Eicke's aggressive and threatening comments (120).[118] Eicke's authority over the camps was clearly not absolute, not least because Oswald Pohl, a former naval officer, was increasingly in charge of economic matters concerning the ss camps.[119] In short, there were various conflicts within the ss apparatus itself. But rather typical of the Third Reich, these were struggles of power, not of principle.

DOCUMENTS

111. Letter from State Prosecutor von Haacke to the Prussian Minister President Hermann Göring, regarding legal proceedings against the guards of the Bredow camp, dated 7 April 1934[120]

In Stettin there has been, over the past few months, a rule of absolute arbitrariness, rightly compared by the presiding judge with Communist Cheka[121] methods.

112. Interrogation of ss officer Heinz Flume, on 15 May 1934, by the Central Public Prosecutor's Office of the Prussian Ministry of Justice, regarding events at the Bredow camp[122]

In my capacity as crime officer of the Stapo station Stettin I deal with events regarding the Bredow concentration camp. One of my principal official duties was the provision of financial means for the camp. I had to approach associations, businessmen, etc., to persuade them to make donations to the camp. [. . .] I understood fines to be amounts that were imposed on the persons concerned as punishment. Whether this was done in a legal manner I am unable to say.

113. Report of the Central State Prosecutor's Office of the Prussian Ministry of Justice regarding the criminal case against ss *Oberführer* Engel and companions, dated 21 June 1934[123]

When ss *Oberführer* Engel[124] was appointed to Stettin as Police President in the autumn of 1933 he set up a small concentration camp in an administrative building of the Vulkan shipbuilding yard in Bredow near Stettin. This camp, in which Engel always showed great interest, was under the immediate direction of ss *Sturmführer* Dr. Hoffmann. [. . .] In this camp, which held about 25–40 inmates, serious ill-treatment of prisoners occurred from the start. This ill-treatment took place through the application of so-called wind speeds, with "Wind Speed 1" meaning 50 and "Wind Speed 2" 100 lashes with coachman's whips on the naked buttocks. Instructions on the application of the wind speeds were given to the camp in writing or by telephone from the Police President's office, as a rule by Dr. Hoffmann, and subsequently executed in the camp in a bunker in the basement, with the camp leader supervising and counting the lashes. In addition, especially during the past few months, there were numerous instances of ill-treatment performed, beyond the orders received, by the increasingly brutal guard personnel, especially Fink. Whereas initially the wind speeds were ordered essentially against enemies of the state and criminals dangerous to the public, [. . .] other inmates, including [Nazi] Party comrades and sa men were later ill-treated for some kind of accusations that subsequently often proved unsubstantiated or had been unfounded from the start. Along with the frequency of ill-treatment its severity also gradually increased, so that, when the camp was dissolved, altogether four persons, including a woman, were in hospital, some with life-threatening injuries. [. . .] When an investigation of the events was initiated by the Public Prosecutor's Office at the beginning of March 1934, the numerous cases of ill-treatment resulting in charges included those of Dünkmann (Party member since March 1931), Bieck (sa man as early as 1930), Fornell, Anna Rademacher, Schramm (since 1925 in the nationalist movement, since 1931 in the SA), Weiss (since 1918 close to the nationalist movement) and Barwa. The Great Criminal Court of the *Land* Court Stettin passed the following sentences [against SS men from the camp] for joint grievous bodily harm, in some cases accompanying crimes and offenses against official position:

Dr. Hoffmann to 13 years penitentiary, 5 years loss of civic rights; Salis to 5 years prison; Pleines to 5 years penitentiary, 3 years loss of civic rights; Fink to 10 years prison; Hermann to 6 years prison; Richter to 2 years prison and Treptow to 9 months prison. [. . .]

The former Police President Engel, who has been in remand custody in this matter since 3 June 1934, denies—as initially also the accused Dr. Hoffmann—to have known about these instances of ill-treatment or having given instructions for them. [. . .] For his exculpation Engel states the following: He had been sent to Pomerania in order to take up there the struggle against enemies of the state, especially the notorious Pomeranian Reaction. From everything that had been said to him in Berlin he had gained the firm conviction that he was being sent to Pomerania as the strongman who would not flinch from merciless sweeping measures. At Gestapo HQ he had been told by its head, *Ministerialrat* [a very senior civil servant] Dr. Diels, or by other officials in the presence of *Ministerialrat* Diels: "You're receiving a difficult inheritance, but you'll cope! You don't flinch from touching people belonging to the Reaction. You'll have to set up a bunker, the *Columbiadiele* should really be brought to Pomerania!"[125] In Stettin he had found very unfavorable conditions, and important local National Socialists had confirmed him in the view, instilled in him in Berlin, that merciless and brutal measures were needed. He had held three offices—that of an SS *Abschnittsführer*, of a Police President and of head of the difficult State Police station Stettin—and the work had grown above his head. He had always acted in the honest conviction of serving the state and the Movement. Engel also states that, after the announcement of the sentence against Dr. Hoffmann and companions, he had, through the mediation of a friend, been summoned to the Führer and that, when Engel had reported the entire case to him, the Führer had told him he need not worry and had then, by way of *Gruppenführer* Brückner,[126] sent him to Reich Minister Hess.[127] When Engel had reported everything to him, Reich Minister

Hess had explained that in the interest of our reputation abroad the execution and publication of the proceedings against Dr. Hoffmann and companions was most welcome, but that he would have a word with Minister President Göring to make sure the matter was now definitely closed for Engel. [. . .]

Although the above-mentioned circumstances make the offenses of the accused Engel appear in a much milder light, the Head of the Penal Department of the Ministry of Justice and the official signed below do not believe they could support a quashing of the proceedings, unless the statement of the accused Engel that the Führer had granted him immunity proved correct. [. . .] As the incidents at Bredow have become widely known among the general public of Stettin and Pomerania, the public—including the National Socialist public—expects that not only the subordinate culprits but also the culpable Police President Engel is called to account for these deeds.

114. Secret letter from the Reich Minister of the Interior, Wilhelm Frick, to the State Chancellery of Bavaria, with a complaint about excessive protective custody figures, dated 30 January 1935[128]

I have repeatedly pointed to the disproportionately high figures of protective custody inmates in Bavaria without any adequate explanations being supplied by the Bavarian Political Police or without a serious attempt being made to reduce the number of inmates. Although I fully believe that the intensifying Communist activity lately observed demands a harsher approach and that, especially with recidivist protective custody inmates a substantial duration of protective custody is appropriate, I cannot leave the disproportion uncriticized any longer, seeing that even according to the latest tables the number of Bavarian protective custody inmates is greater by several hundreds than the total of protective custody inmates in all other states, including Prussia.

115. Letter of the Reich Minister of Justice, Franz Gürtner, to the Reich Minister of the Interior, Wilhelm Frick, regarding the ill-treatment of Communist inmates, dated 14 May 1935[129]

If, however [. . .], one is to assume that a need exists in the concentration camps for the introduction of punishment by

The ss Concentration Camp System

whipping, then it seems indispensable for this disciplinary punishment and the manner of its execution to be uniformly and unambiguously regulated for the entire Reich territory.

It has happened that the camp regulations of certain concentration camps have issued unusually harsh rules [. . .], which are communicated to the inmates for deterrence, while the guard units are officially told that these rules, most of them dating back to 1933, are no longer applicable. Such a state of affairs is equally dangerous to the guard units and to the inmates. [. . .]

The criminal law valid at present, whose application is part of my duties, threatens officials who commit ill-treatment in office—especially if such ill-treatment is committed in order to obtain confessions or statements—with especially heavy punishment. That this legal regulation is also in line with the will of the Führer and Reich Chancellor emerges from the fact that the Führer, on the occasion of crushing the Röhm Revolt, ordered the execution by firing squad of three ss members who had ordered the ill-treatment of prisoners in Stettin.[130] [. . .] Experience of the first few years of the Revolution has shown that those persons who are instructed to execute whipping, after a short period lose the sense of the purpose and meaning of their actions and let themselves be guided by personal feelings of revenge or by sadistic inclinations. Thus members of the guard personnel in the former Bredow concentration camp near Stettin totally undressed a prostitute who had some differences with one of the guards and struck her with whips to such an extent that two months later the woman still had two open festering wounds on her right buttock, measuring 17.7 by 21.5 cm and 12.5 by 16.5 cm, as well as such a wound of 7.5 by 17 cm on her left buttock. In the Kemna concentration camp near Wuppertal inmates were locked in a staff locker and tortured by cigarette smoke being blown in, by the locker being knocked over, etc. Sometimes the inmates were first given salted herrings to eat in order to create in them a strong and tormenting thirst. In the Hohenstein concentration camp in Saxony inmates had to stand below a specially constructed dripping device until the skin on their heads showed suppurating injuries from the water dripping on them at regular intervals. In one concentration camp in Hamburg four inmates were—continually—once for three days and nights and once for five days and nights, tied to a railing in crucified position and so sparingly fed dry bread that they nearly starved to death.

These few examples reveal such a degree of cruelty, mocking any German feeling, that it is impossible to consider any mitigating circumstances. [. . .]

It therefore seems urgently necessary for the competent portfolio Minister to issue for all protective custody inmates a uniformly valid camp order that would quite clearly and unambiguously regulate the question of whipping as a disciplinary punishment and the question of the use of firearms by the guard personnel. [. . .]

It seems necessary for the competent portfolio Minister to issue to all police authorities of every kind an unreserved prohibition of ill-treatment of inmates to obtain statements under duress. [. . .] All instances of ill-treatment wholly or partially due to personal motivations must be prosecuted and punished as harshly as possible in close collaboration by all state authorities concerned.

Heil Hitler!

116. Letter from the Leipzig attorney Dr. Johannes Weygand to the Reich Minister of Justice, Franz Gürtner, regarding the detention of Protestant pastors at the Sachsenburg concentration camp, dated 17 May 1935[131]

Dear Herr Reich Minister,

The 18 *Saxon Protestant pastors*, who had been arrested during the period from the end of March until mid-April and some even later, as well as the Head of the Chemnitz Confessional Community, *Studienrat Küntzelmann* (known throughout Saxony ever since 1919 as an especially courageous, indefatigable and selfless fighter against the proletarian Freethinkers and Communist godless), are still prisoners in the Sachsenburg concentration camp [. . .]. According to reliable information, further arrests are to be expected. Since 6 May there has been an intensification of the measures against the imprisoned pastors. On that day Reich Governor Mutschmann personally attempted in Sachsenburg to offer the pastors summoned for this purpose their release in exchange for written declarations that they repented having committed offenses against the state and that they promised

The ss Concentration Camp System

never to do so again. None of the pastors had been ready to do this, and Reich Governor Mutschmann thereupon immediately imposed an absolute prohibition of visitors. As a result, the wives are no longer permitted to see their husbands [. . .]. This treatment and everything else that has been done to the pastors, their families and their congregations over these weeks is—as cannot be doubted—due exclusively to Reich Governor Mutschmann. The Saxon Ministry of the Interior and the Secret State Police have not initiated anything of this, any more than the local police authorities [. . .]. *Regulation of attorney representation* is therefore more urgent than ever. After all, there are no fewer than 18 protective custody proceedings pending in Saxony alone over the past few weeks, with detention in the intensified form of the concentration camp practiced against Protestant pastors who are not charged with anything other than resistance to attacks against Christianity demanded by the conscience of every Christian pastor. [. . .] To this day neither the Public Prosecutor's Office nor the ecclesiastical authority has initiated an investigation against any of the imprisoned pastors, let alone charged them with anything. To this day they are robbed of their freedom solely by the Reich Governor's intervention, without any kind of interrogation or regular proceedings; they are cut off from contact with the world outside and are not even able to communicate with their defending attorneys. I urgently appeal to you, Herr Reich Minister of Justice, to put an end to this state of affairs, which is incompatible with the avowal of a state based on law and order, as repeatedly pronounced by authoritative quarters.

117. Circular of the Reich Minister of Justice, Franz Gürtner, to the General State Prosecutors, regarding deduction of time spent in protective custody from the duration of judicial imprisonment, dated 17 June 1935[132]

By Decree of 7 June 1935 the Führer and Reich Chancellor has let me know his basic attitude to the question of allowing for the time spent in protective custody in calculating the duration of punishment: as a rule the period in protective custody is to be counted as part of the duration of punishment, unless it is a case of Communist functionaries on whom protective custody has been imposed as a general defense measure independently of and without connection to a specific offense.

118. Submission from the Berlin Cathedral Chaplain Bernhard Lichtenberg to the Prussian Minister President Hermann Göring, regarding conditions in the Esterwegen concentration camp, dated 18 July 1935[133]

While the application of the punishment of whipping in the concentration camps was substantially restricted in 1934, a systematic application of that punishment can now again be observed. Execution of the punishment of whipping, for instance, in the Esterwegen camp near Papenburg, is as follows. The inmates have to form a square. The fourth side of the square is taken up by the guard personnel. One of the leaders of the guard personnel reads out the punishment order, which says that inmate so-and-so has been sentenced to punishment by whipping and is to receive 25 strokes with the stick. The punishment orders are invariably signed by ss *Gruppenführer* Eicke, Gestapo Berlin, whose name is always read out as well. The inmate to be punished is tied with leather straps to a buck placed in the square. Execution is by a bullwhip, the delinquent himself having to count the strokes. [. . .]

Intake of new protective custody inmates has recently very often been as follows. The inmates have to form a square. The buck for the execution of the punishment is placed in the middle. The new arrivals have to stand next to the buck. One of the leaders reads out a whipping order against one of the inmates. The delinquent is strapped to the buck and execution of punishment follows as described above, with the new arrivals having to stand directly next to it.

On 13 April the Leader of the German Miners' Union, the former Social Democrat Reichstag Deputy Fritz Husemann,[134] was shot dead in the Esterwegen concentration camp. Fourteen days later the Communist Röver (or Römer) from Bremen was shot dead while working outside the camp (2 shots in his neck). The following day his corpse was laid out in a crate on the camp street, in dirty, unwashed, bloodstained condition, in his old working uniform. The prisoners had to fall in single file and march in line past the dead body. The first few in the line paid homage by removing their caps. This was stopped: honoring that swine would be the last thing! These incidents made the Jewish artist Loewy lose his head. The following morning he simply walked away during work outside the camp. He was fired upon. L. was taken to the sick bay with a bullet in his thigh and in his left hand. Some time later the Communist Ohl from Frankfurt/Main tried to hang himself. He was caught and cut down in time. As punishment for the attempt he had 25 strokes added; these were applied to him in the square with the bullwhip in the manner described. On the following day Ohl walked away from work outside the camp and was shot dead. [. . .]

So-called dragging along the camp street is performed as follows: To start with, the prisoner is made to run the 200-meter stretch there and back. Then comes the command: Attention. In this position he has to fling himself down and, with his arms tightly against his body, roll the stretch there and back. When he gets back it is: On your feet, march, march! The prisoner, trying to stand up and get into running stride, collapses because his physical strength is no longer sufficient. [. . .]

The Jews in particular have to suffer. Mostly they have to transport manure, clean out the latrine pits, sometimes with their hands. If commanded to roll, they must roll in the manure.

In the course of a search, allegedly for firearms, devotional books, Bibles and prayer books, hymn books, etc., were taken from the inmates and then torn to shreds by the guard personnel. Catholics had their rosaries taken from them and crushed by boots on the ground.

119. Circular letter from the Bavarian Political Police to all Bavarian police directorates and state police stations, regarding the transfer of criminal detainees to a concentration camp after serving their sentence, dated 5 September 1935[135]

On several occasions lately persons hostile to the state, who were imprisoned for high treason, were released from the institution after they had served their sentence, with no further surveillance or protective custody for deportation to a concentration camp taking place.

In order to avoid this abuse in the future it is ordered that for *all* persons sentenced by the *People's Court*[136] the question be raised with the Public Prosecutor's Offices of the Superior *Land* Courts concerning their envisioned date of release and the camp of their release in order that the re-transfer of these enemies of the state may be applied for in good time. This request could be made either simultaneously with the dispatch of the investigations initiated there or else after the sentence. In the case of persons sentenced by the *criminal benches* of the Superior *Land* Courts an examination is necessary, on a case by case basis, whether in view of their former activity re-transfer should be initiated when they have served their term.

120. Letter by Dr. Werner Best to the Prussian Minister President Hermann Göring, regarding the complaint of the Berlin Cathedral Chaplain Bernhard Lichtenberg, dated 27 September 1935[137]

On the individual points of the complaint the following is stated:

Execution of the punishment of whipping in the Esterwegen concentration camp is always done according to the regulations. Never has punishment by whipping been ordered or executed without the appropriate prescribed regulation on punishments. There is no obligation for the inmates to count the blows. If he does so nevertheless, he is doing so voluntarily and in his own interest. The punishment is executed in the presence of the other inmates only if it is for a particularly vile deed, or in the case of mutiny or refusal to obey orders. In other cases it is performed in the presence of the entire guard force and the responsible leader, but never without supervision. [. . .] All the shootings of inmates occurred during work outside the camp, in the moor or in the forest. The sentries are obliged to make immediate use of their firearms without warning in the event of an inmate's escape or an attack. All cases have been examined on the spot by the judge and found in order. [. . .]

That the Jews have to clean out latrine pits with their hands and have to roll in manure are atrocity stories just as the report that hymnbooks and Bibles were torn to shreds or that rosaries were taken from the Catholics and crushed underfoot on the ground. If there was a confiscation of Bibles at all, then only of members of the "Serious Bible Researchers' Association," so that these writings cannot be used in the camp for continuing their state-eroding activity.

Regarding the submission of Chaplain Lichtenberg, the Inspector of Concentration Camps, ss *Gruppenführer* Eicke has commented as follows:

The constant attacks on state concentration camps with atrocity lies serve the sole purpose of systematically undermining and shaking the state leadership's confidence in its institutions and bodies. [. . .] The agitation apostle Lichtenberg probably does not know that the undersigned is constantly on the highway week after week in order to exercise control over the state concentration camps. Doing my duty is my prime object; as a result my own family has to be neglected. It is regrettable that, in spite of my other burden of work, time has to be found to wipe off the poisonous state-eroding saliva of agitating chaplains.

I declare upon my official oath and my honor as an ss leader that in the official area entrusted to me, the concentration camps, proceedings are orderly and clean. It must therefore be demanded that more weight is attached to such a declaration on my honor than to the atrocity lies spread by Lichtenberg against his better knowledge. If the agitation apostle Lichtenberg keeps his official area, his altar, as clean as the responsible ss leaders are keeping their official area, then all would be well in the Third Reich. But so long as these undermining moles are eating up our foreign currency and leave their excrement on the altars, so long as the state-eroding political breath of hatred makes the altar candles flicker, so long those ultramontane state-destroying forces have no right to interfere in affairs of the state. It is the fury of Rome's black agents that is expressed here because the whole ss camp personnel of Esterwegen has voluntarily severed itself from the servants and institutions of an international anti-state Church that preaches hatred and subversion. [. . .] I request that the atrocity liar Lichtenberg be taken into protective custody for malicious attacks on the state, so that, in the Esterwegen camp he can convince himself of the order and cleanliness and is encouraged to introduce such order also in his ecclesiastical shop.

121. Letter from Heinrich Himmler to the Reich Minister of Justice, Franz Gürtner, dated 6 November 1935[138]

On 1.11.1935 I reported to the Führer and Reich Chancellor about the request submitted to us regarding permission for attorneys to be included in protective custody cases.

The Führer has forbidden the inclusion of attorneys and has instructed me to inform you of his decision.

122. Internal briefing for the Reich Minister of Justice, dated 29 November 1935[139]

Herr State Secretary Dr. Meißner[140] has just telephoned me, at 10.30, asking me to pass on the following to the Herr Minister, whom he has been unable to contact:

In the matter of the pardon for the persons sentenced for ill-treatment in the Hohnstein concentration camp, Herr Bouhler[141] had—he said—informed him yesterday that he had reported to the Führer the result of the latest investigations performed by himself and Reich Governor Mutschmann.[142] The Führer, he said, had decided to remit the remainder of all punishments. Would Herr State Secretary Meißner please report this to the Ministry of Justice for the issue of an appropriate decree. He, State Secretary Meißner, had pointed out that the Minister of Justice had, at the time, also been instructed by the Führer to undertake special investigations to establish in what cases the ill-treatment had been committed from sadistic motives and a pardon was therefore not appropriate. The Minister of Justice should therefore be given the possibility to submit to the Führer his view based on the still ongoing investigations. Herr Bouhler had thereupon said that the Minister of Justice would not be deprived of this. The Führer would only request him to speed up his investigations as much as possible so that his opinion might be received before the end of the following week, and in any case to submit a decree with full pardon.

123. Article in the legal journal *Deutsches Recht* on the legal basis of protective custody, dated 15 April 1936[143]

The authorities of the Secret State Police are, in an exemplary fashion, working hand in hand with the regular courts in order not to give dangerous enemies of the state a chance to continue their subversive machinations to the detriment of the community as a result of being released, however temporarily. [. . .] Only those who still mourn a past liberalistic era will regard the application of protective custody measures as too harsh or even illegal. [. . .] In the case of former Communist functionaries the deduction of protective custody from their punishment must be considered out of the question. Although protective custody as such is nothing to do with punishment, the Secret State Police has in practice repeatedly found that illegal Communist or other subversive efforts cannot be fought with the criminal law alone. It is the task of the Secret State Police to use the harshest means at its disposal against the real enemies of the state. It will therefore never content itself with letting, for instance, active Communist functionaries be sentenced only to criminal-law conviction by the legal authorities. It is part of its duties to keep such elements under strictest surveillance even after their release from penal detention and, if necessary, to take protective custody measures against them. [. . .]

There is probably no need to point out that recidivist protective custody detainees, i.e. persons who after release from protective custody resume their former subversive and disruptive activity, cannot expect particular leniency from the state. Instead the well-being and protection of the general public demands that such elements are kept in protective custody for as long as possible.

124. Report by the governor of the Luckau penitentiary for the Secret State Police, regarding the prisoner and former Communist Reichstag Deputy Karl Elgas, dated 9 July 1936[144]

The punishment does not appear to have impressed him in any significant way. Judging by the general impression of his personality, Elgas cannot give security that he will leave his seditious activities behind him in future. I therefore suggest that, following his penitentiary sentence, protective custody be imposed on Elgas.

125. Letter from ss *Obergruppenführer* Eicke to Heinrich Himmler, dated 10 August 1936[145]

Rumors are circulating in the Secret State Police office that the ss Death's Head units are to be withdrawn from my command in the autumn of 1936 and subordinated to the ss *Oberabschnitte* [a larger ss administrative unit]. These rumors issue from the office of Dr. Best. ss *Standartenführer* Dr. Best from the Gestapo office declared at a certain place that there was a disgusting mess in the concentration camps; the time had come to subordinate the camps again to the Gestapo.

126. Letter from the State Police post for the District Berlin to the Sachsenhausen concentration camp, dated 30 October 1936[146]

Upon demand of the General State Prosecutor's office in Berlin the protective custody detainee Fritz S., born at Fürstenwalde on 12.1.81, was transferred on 23.7.36 from the Esterwegen concentration camp to the Moabit remand prison. Tried on 15.9.36 by the Berlin Special Court, S. was sentenced to one year's imprisonment and to payment of the trial costs for the incident[147] which had been dealt with here by protective custody. This earlier protective custody was fully deducted from his punishment.

127. Reich Ministry of Justice minutes regarding Himmler's suggestion to transfer selected state prisoners to the camps, dated 15 February 1937[148]

The undersigned [officials from the Reich Ministry of Justice] were received by the Reichsführer [Himmler] on 13.2. The Reichsführer first of all announced that he had received from Minister President Göring the special task of ensuring that all persons capable of work but not yet working are employed on the targets of the Four-Year Plan, especially to remedy the existing shortage of agricultural workers (there is a shortfall of about 200,000 agricultural workers). For that purpose, he said, he was having a few work-shy elements taken to the camps from places where there are still some unemployed. These work-shy elements had to work there up to 14 hours a day; this was intended to show them, and others, that it is better to seek work in freedom than running the risk of being taken to such a camp. Within the framework of the instruction given to him he also intended to employ any judicial prisoners as yet not employed. [. . .]

In this connection the Reichsführer touched on the question of whether it might not be possible to bring state prisoners in security confinement[149] into his camps.

In reply to a question the Reichsführer stated that the existing work and enterprises of the state prisons should not be disturbed by the measures suggested by him. Finally, he asked that the Herr Reich Minister of Justice be accordingly informed and that he should let him, the Reichsführer, have the name of the official competent for dealing with these questions.

128. Report of the commandant of the Sachsenhausen concentration camp to the State Police Berlin, regarding the protective custody detainee Fritz S. (imprisoned since December 1935 for "seditious remarks"), dated 4 May 1937[150]

Behavior and work performance of S. are negligent and lazy. S. is a bad character and his detention so far has had no improving or instructive effect. The political attitude of S. today is still entirely Communist. In view of the seditious attitude of S. and his quite considerable previous convictions, he represents, in the event of release, a permanent danger to the people's community.

In any case I reject a release.

129. Report of the Jena General State Prosecutor to the Reich Minister of Justice, Franz Gürtner, regarding the construction of Buchenwald, dated 30 September 1937[151]

The Thuringian concentration camp in Bad Sulza has been closed down. Since the beginning of August the "Buchenwald" concentration camp is being constructed on the Ettersberg near Weimar — presumably for the whole of central Germany. In mid-September it accommodated about 2,200 inmates and will, it is believed, be equipped for 8,000 persons. An ss regiment is envisioned for guard duties. One will have to wait and see what effect the camp will have on the activity of the State Prosecutor's Office and on the nearest penal institutions. During the first few weeks seven inmates have been shot dead by the guard posts while trying to escape. The judicial proceedings have been stayed. Cooperation between the camp management and the State Prosecutor's Office has so far been good.

130. Letter from Heinrich Himmler to the Reich Minister of Justice, Franz Gürtner, regarding the shooting of concentration camp inmates while trying to escape, dated 16 May 1938[152]

Dear Herr Minister,

About two months ago you put to me your view that in the concentration camps too many people were being shot while trying to escape. Although personally I did not share your view, as in the instances that have occurred so far firing was always done from a distance of 30, 40, 50, 60 or 80 m, I ordered ss *Gruppenführer* Eicke to impress again on the Death's Head units who are doing guard duty in the concentration camps that fire is to be opened only in extreme necessity.

The result is shocking to me! The day before yesterday I was in the Buchenwald camp and was shown the corpse of a decent 24-year-old ss man, who had his skull shattered with a shovel by two criminals. The two criminals escaped [see section 4.2].

I looked again at the inmates of the camp and am profoundly saddened by the thought that owing to excessive leniency, which always acts as a brake on the official regulations regarding shooting in the event of an attempted escape, one of my decent men had to lose his life.

Permit me to inform you that I have revoked my order to shoot only in cases of extreme necessity and have put into force again the old regulation that, strictly in accordance with service regulations, fire is opened after three warnings or in the event of a physical attack without warning.

Two further criminals, who evidently knew about the attempted escape, were, after the ss man had been killed, shot dead from a distance of 50 or 60 m while trying to escape on the way back into the camp. As for the two actual murderers I have mobilized all means of a search in order to get hold of them.

Permit me to inform you already that I will request the Führer, whenever the regular court has handed down a death sentence against both of them, to let it be executed not in the courtyard of a state prison but in the camp in front of the fallen-in 3,000 inmates — and if possible by the rope on the gallows.

131. Letter from Himmler's office [signed by Heydrich] to the Reich Minister of Justice, Franz Gürtner, requesting the transfer of selected state prisoners to concentration camps, dated 28 June 1938[153]

Within the framework of the Four-Year Plan and for the provision of building materials for the construction projects ordered by the Führer in Berlin and elsewhere, I have been assigned special tasks. One of these tasks is the exploitation of large granite quarries near Flossenbürg (Bavarian Forest) and Mauthausen (Donau) by the inmates of concentration camps. The inmates held, however, are far from being sufficient for these extensive tasks. As, on the other hand, the prisons subject to your administration contain a large number of persons sentenced to security confinement, I request that these, insofar as they are male persons and capable of work, be transferred to the concentration camps for employment.

132. Letter from the Inspectorate of Concentration Camps to the commandants of Dachau, Buchenwald, Flossenbürg, Sachsenhausen, and Mauthausen regarding the shooting of inmates while trying to escape, dated 27 July 1938[154]

A department for processing instances of "*Shot while trying to escape*" has been set up at the Reich Ministry of Justice. The department is headed by Senior State Prosecutor von Haacke. His deputy is State Prosecutor Jaeckel. This is being brought to the notice of camp commandants along with the request for a continued most careful supervision of the processing of such incidents.

133. Letter from Oswald Pohl, ss administration leader, to Theodor Eicke, regarding the development of the Flossenbürg concentration camp, dated 31 August 1938[155]

The general building plan [for the Flossenbürg camp] was received by me yesterday, 30.8.1938. I now have it before me. I gather from it that 15 residential houses ordered without my participation are situated on land that does not actually belong to us (the Reich) yet. An agreement was allegedly reached with the Flossenbürg parish, whereby the latter will lease the land to the concentration camp for 25 years. This, of course, is quite preposterous. I would like to know who actually launched this nonsense. I am really sorry to have to ask that I am at least involved in these questions which cannot be solved without me anyway.

134. Minutes of a conference, on 24 January 1939, of Reich Minister of Justice Gürtner with leading regional legal officials, regarding protective police custody[156]

[The Chief President of the County Court] Hamm (Schneider): Protective custody detention is practiced today with more consideration for the reputation of justice. [. . .] There are judges who in cases of doubt issue detention orders so as to avoid protective custody. [. . .]

[The Chief President of the County Court] Düsseldorf (Schwister): Frequent requests for re-transfer [into the concentration camp] in cases where judicial warrants for arrest are rejected. It has even been found that appropriate arrangements had been made between examining and investigative judges and the State Police. [. . .]

The Herr Minister closes the discussion with the remark that it is the task of Chief Presidents to ensure that arrests by the State Police in the courtroom are avoided; otherwise he recommends that the cross-link with the State Police be maintained.

2.4. The ss Economy and the Camps

Forced labor was an integral aspect of the camps. The camps could draw on well-established disciplinary traditions here. In workhouses and prisons, exhausting forced labor had long been seen as an instrument of retribution and rehabilitation. It was supposed to punish past misdeeds and, for the future, instill discipline in "work-shy" prisoners. In the camps, of course, there was always a large gap between any lofty educative pretensions—such as the Prussian Interior Minister's plans for prisoners cultivating the moors of the Emsland camps in 1933 (**135**)—and the reality of institutionalized labor. If economic considerations came into play at all in the early years of the camps, they remained secondary. Indeed, prisoner labor was at times completely pointless, at least from an economic point of view—nothing more than abuse and torture, as in cases when prisoners had to cart sand or stones from one end of the camp to the other, and back again.[157]

Economic factors became more significant in the camps from the late 1930s onward as the Nazi regime began to prepare for war, articulated most clearly in the Four-Year Plan of 1936. At the time, Himmler's police and ss apparatus was expanding on all fronts, including the economy, and haphazard early ventures such as the Dachau camp's workshops (**138** and **139**) were now coordinated, and ss managers pushed ahead with more ambitious new projects. Before long, the concentration camps, where plenty of cheap labor was available, began to play a key role in the ss's economic plans. In April 1938 the ss established a new company (Deutsche Erd- und Steinwerke) to supply bricks and stones for Hitler's gigantic project of rebuilding Berlin and other German cities.[158] Much of the required labor force was supposed to come from the camp system.

This was a major reason why the new concentration camps for men (Flossenbürg and Mauthausen) were set up near quarries. The ss also established brickworks near Buchenwald (**140**) and Sachsenhausen. The Sachsenhausen brickworks, designed with great hubris, soon turned into an economic disaster. The ss's ambitions far outstripped its technical and managerial abilities. In fact, the new factory failed to produce any high-quality bricks for Hitler's program of rebuilding German cities (**144**).[159] Yet, the ss was still pressing ahead with these plans. In the autumn of 1938 it acquired grounds in Neuengamme outside Hamburg and soon opened a Sachsenhausen subcamp (*Aussenlager*) there, where inmates would build yet another brick factory (**141**).[160]

Clearly, the growing ss economic ambitions contributed to the mass arrests of social outsiders in the late 1930s, as the camps needed more and more forced workers. At the same time, wider economic considerations were at play. Above all, the regime had an eye on the camps' deterrent effect: the arrests sent out a warning to workers at large that supposedly work-shy elements would be punished at a time of rearmament and labor shortages (**127**).[161]

In all, the new economic policy of the ss marked a decisive shift in the history of the camps, paving the way for the later mass exploitation of prisoners for the German war machine.[162] This new approach also foreshadowed another wartime development: mass death of prisoners through forced labor. For work in the quarries was particularly exhausting—one reason it had long been championed by some leading Nazi figures (**136**). It also offered the ss new possibilities for prisoner abuse. Soon, the quarries were among the most lethal labor commandos in the camp system, contributing to the growing fear, misery, and death in the months before World War II. ss officials were well aware of the prisoners' suffering, of course, but they still moved ahead with their plans for the exploitation of prisoner labor. Indeed, some officials openly advocated the use of prisoners in lethal jobs. For example, one high-ranking ss official proposed that camp prisoners should be sent into the notorious radium mines in the annexed Sudeten region of Czechoslovakia (**142**). The proposal came to nothing, but Himmler's enthusiastic response (**143**) clearly demonstrates the murderous mind-set of ss leaders, which would reveal itself fully during the war.

The ss Concentration Camp System

135. Letter from Ludwig Grauert from the Prussian Ministry of the Interior to the district administrator (*Regierungspräsident*) in Osnabrück, dated 22 June 1933[163]

More than anything else it seems necessary to employ those detainees, of whose release there is no question during the next few years, in a way that creates value for the general public and simultaneously reduces the state's costs of support and eventually frees it from them altogether.

Such value-creating employment of the protective custody detainees, whose number is about 10,000 at present and will continue to be at this level over the next few years, is in practice only possible in enterprises by the state itself. At the same time, police interests require that the individual working parties are not too small and that they are employed on a comparably narrow area. Allowing for these conditions, it seemed logical from the outset to think of employing the detainees on wasteland cultivation. The moorland areas acquired by the agricultural administration in the Osnabrück government district to the right and left of the Ems [River] strike me as a particularly suitable object for the employment of the detainees.

136. Letter from the Reich Leader of the Labor Service, Konstantin Hierl,[164] to the Prussian Minister President Hermann Göring in Berlin, dated 29 July 1933[165]

We have found that in various concentration camps the political prisoners there are employed on work that belongs to the domain of the Labor Service. Thus we understand that the Oranienburg concentration camp employs its prisoners on track building within the forest. The political prisoners work there under the supervision of several SA men armed with carbines, moreover in areas that are continually accessible to the public. One Chemnitz newspaper recently already described a concentration camp as a labor camp.

This state of affairs is apt, I believe, to damage the idea of the German Labor Service, which is an essential instrument for youth education in the conception of the Führer and Chancellor. The population is unable to see a difference between the work by the political prisoners and the young men who are voluntary members of the Labor Service. As labor service is intended to be an honorable duty, political prisoners should not, in my opinion, be employed on work that the German Labor Service regards as its work on German soil. I ask you therefore to use your influence to ensure that the political prisoners in concentration camps, if they are permitted to work at all, are employed on tasks that correspond to the character of their imprisonment—work in quarries, etc. It would also seem appropriate that political prisoners in concentration camps perform their work where they are not noticed by the public.

137. Minutes of the session of the Small Ministerial Council (Kleiner Ministerrat) on 11 February 1937[166]

Reich Leader ss stated that the employment of prisoners in sizable parties for beet cultivation was entirely possible. Employment in smaller units is not recommended as the available guard personnel would not be sufficient in that case.

138. Sopade (the spd in exile, which collected testimonies from inside Nazi Germany) report on the pattern of work in the Dachau concentration camp, dated May 1937[167]

All prisoners in the camp have to work. [. . .] The working groups are called "Work Commandos." There are workshops for joinery, locksmiths, blacksmiths, tailoring, footwear, a bakery, a butchery, etc. The joinery is the biggest. In it work is done for the military. Furniture for the ss leaders is also made there.

The work leaders in these enterprises are prisoners. The head of the joiner's shop, for instance, is the Communist Ewald Thunig. At one time he was moved out of the joiner's shop and had to be brought back there because after his departure everything got into a muddle. It is said that good specialist workers are not released from Dachau because one does not want to do without them. It is not least for that reason that Thunig, for instance, is still in Dachau. Anyone deported to Dachau has, first of all, to go to the gravel pit. When everything has been checked and when it has been established what he can be used for, he is assigned to a work commando. The prisoners line up in companies on the parade square at 7 o'clock. Then they are put together into the separate work commandos and move off into the enterprises. [. . .] The prisoners prefer working in the economic enterprises rather than in the commandant's office, because there they receive a piece of bread with sausage in the morning and only bread in the afternoon. When working for the commandant's office there is only once a piece of dry bread. Working hours in the summer are from 6 o'clock in the morning until 10 o'clock and from 3 o'clock to 6 o'clock in the evening. In the winter from 7 o'clock to 11:30 and from 1 o'clock to 4:30. As most of the time there are urgent orders, these working hours in the enterprises are kept very irregularly. Many hours of overtime have to be worked, especially in the joiner's shop. Frequently work goes on until 10 o'clock at night. Exploitation of the prisoners is enormous. The scant food they receive does not let them recover their strength, and they are always dead tired when they come home at night. Unlike in the prisons, they receive no money for the work they do. Similarly, food rations are no better or larger for heavy work.

139. Report of the former Dachau inmate Dr. Karl Ludwig Schecher on the economic enterprises in Dachau before the war[168]

The economic enterprises were a large-scale enterprise of the ss for the exploitation of the labor force, the inmates. They had developed from the economic installations necessary for a large camp [. . .] such as bakery, butchery, tailor's shop, footwear shop and saddler's shop, as well as a large joiner's shop with an attached small locksmith's shop. The main figure of the economic enterprises was the then ss *Oberführer* Pohl, a former paymaster in the navy. The economic enterprises had initially been started up with state money, then with funds from the Reich Treasury and progressively developed from enterprises for the needs of the camp into general "economic" enterprises designed to earn money for the money chests of the ss, which in fact they earned. The joiner's shop in particular rapidly became a large-scale enterprise, where bunks, lockers, tables and stools were produced, some of them in serial production, for the equipment of concentration camps and barracks. Production was probably relatively cheap as no wages were paid at the time for the work of the inmates by the economic enterprises.

140. Minute of the Reich leadership of the NSDAP regarding the construction of brickworks in Buchenwald, dated 15 June 1938[169]

Gruppenführer Pohl commented on this: The creation of the brickworks is neither an ss matter nor a matter of the Party or the state. The reason for establishing the brickworks is that employment has to be found for the number of concentration camp inmates, which has risen very substantially with the *Anschluss* of Austria. The foundation of the works goes back to a directive of the Führer issued on the occasion of a conference of the Führer with the Reichsführer ss and the architect Speer. By way of explanation *Gruppenführer* Pohl added that the architect Speer needed some 2 billion bricks annually, whereas industry has so far met only 18% of this requirement by its annual output. The fulfillment of this task, with unused labor, will therefore simultaneously provide a counterpoise to industry. However, these inmates (in Dachau their number has lately risen from 2,000 to 7,000) will be employed not only in this works but also in a further work yet to be established in Sachsenhausen. The inmates are moreover to be employed in 3 major granite quarries (Ostmark and Bavarian Forest) in order to produce building material for the constructions of the Reich there too.

141. Letter from the Chief of Administration of the ss, Oswald Pohl, to the City of Hamburg's treasurer, dated 13 September 1938[170]

On 3.9.38 the *Reichsführung* of the ss bought a few plots in the Hamburg state territory under the cover name "German Earth and Stone Works Ltd." These plots are situated in Neuengamme and are recorded in the Neuengamme land register, Folio 41. Altogether they amount to 506,053.07 square meters. The plot used to belong to a Hamburg consortium. On the plot there is a brickworks that had been shut down many years ago. This alone was the reason why the *Reichsführung* ss acquired the plot. Within the framework of major economic projects, which have been ongoing for about a year, we intend to bring this brickworks into production again at an early date, to modernize it and perhaps to enlarge it on a not inconsiderable scale. The raw material there (clay), as our scientific experimental stations have established, is quite excellent. Resumption of production will take place within the initiative to find employment for the very numerous layabouts in our concentration camps, a task that, as is well known, is one of my duties. We intend to produce there first-rate brick goods at a reasonable cost. I believe that this fact will not be without interest to yourself and the Hamburg building authorities. [. . .] I am passing this information on to you today in order to ask you not to make any difficulties in approving our purchasing contract.

142. Letter of ss *Oberführer* Hans Krebs to Heinrich Himmler, regarding the employment of concentration camp inmates, dated 19 November 1938[171]

Reich Leader ss,

On my journey home from the festivities of 9 November[172] I had a fairly lengthy conversation about the concentration camps with ss *Brigadeführer* von Grawitz,[173] the acting President of the German Red Cross. Comrade Grawitz pointed out that his observations in the concentration camps had shown that, for all the necessary harshness of detention, these political prisoners were actually in the best of health, while many decent German workers have to work in health-damaging enterprises and often die a premature death. I was reminded in this conversation of the fact that in the radium mines in Joachimsthal in the Ore Mountains (Sudetenland) our poor Sudeten German radium miners mostly die a premature death in their fortieth year due to the radium emanations of the ore. I pointed out the injustice of this. [. . .] I would like, quite briefly, to suggest to you the idea of examining what possibilities there are for employing such major criminals, who have to be excluded from the community for life, in these radium mines.

143. Reply from Karl Wolff[174] to ss *Oberführer* Hans Krebs, dated 15 December 1938[175]

Dear Party comrade Krebs,

Your letter of 19.11.1938 was submitted to the Reichsführer ss on his vacation. He has instructed me to thank you very much for your lines and to inform you that he considers your suggestion excellent. He asks you to create the possibilities for implementing this plan in collaboration with the Chief of the Administration Office of the ss, ss *Gruppenführer* Pohl, Berlin W 50, Gaisbergstr. 21, and with the leader of the Death's Head *Standarten* and concentration camps, ss *Gruppenführer* Eicke, Oranienburg nr. Berlin.

The Reichsführer-ss intends to make the most serious criminals available to the radium mines. However, if they have behaved well for 3 years and worked well he wishes to give them the opportunity of returning to the people's community. I ask you for your comment whether the period of 3 years is too short and what term you would consider appropriate.

144. Internal Reichsbank report regarding a credit application by the ss, dated 22 August 1939[176]

The ss has created various economic enterprises in order to employ detainees from the concentration camps (mainly security confined detainees) as laborers for tasks of the Four-Year Plan. [. . .] The brickworks in Weimar is already in production, but is being further extended. The Hamburg works will go into production in November of this year, initially only to supply its own requirements for the further development of the plant. The brickworks in Oranienburg will probably not be ready for full production for another year or two. The two granite works have already been in operation for a year, but are not yet entirely completed.

The granite plant in Flossenbürg already shows a surplus of some RM 70,000 over the first 5 months of 1939, whereas Mauthausen, because of the extensive construction and development work there, has not so far achieved a surplus. The brickworks, on the other hand, are not yet yielding any income as they are still in the construction or reconstruction stage. [. . .] The brickworks are designed for the dry-pressing method. This method, unlike the widespread wet-pressing method, is thought to have the advantage of not impairing the health of the workers, but it has the drawback that the cost of manufacturing the bricks is 50% higher. Nevertheless, the capital invested so far in the brick enterprises should not be regarded as a bad investment because the various facilities can be used for the production of high-value stones (clinker, clinker slabs) and because the shortcomings of the dry-pressing process were discovered in good time, i.e. in the stage of the construction of the plant.[177] In the further development of the plant, provision is now to be made only for the wet-pressing process. [. . .] In Oranienburg it was found—something the management had already drawn attention to—that the large factory building as well as various subsidiary buildings were already fully constructed, whereas the clay pit is still relatively poorly developed and the firing experiments of the Oranienburg clay are not yet completed. It should be pointed out that the clay pit is about 8 km from the factory and that the clay has to be ferried there by vehicles. In the front part of the building 4 large tunnel furnaces have been installed in the assumption that the Oranienburg clay would permit manufacture of valuable bricks by the dry-pressing method. This hope has not yet, according to the present experts, come true. It is, however, believed that the furnaces will be able to be used in future if a certain percentage of Hamburg clay (of particularly high quality) is added to the Oranienburg clay. [. . .]

The labor available to the enterprise gives rise to only slight costs for the firm, as most of them are prisoners, mainly detainees in security confinement[178] (at present about 4,000). Admittedly, a certain core (3–400) of trained workers is needed alongside them, to train the prisoners and guard them and to do especially qualified work. The daily wage for the prisoners is RM 0.50 and is payable to the Reich. [. . .] The performance of the prisoners is said to fluctuate between 15 and 50% of the normal performance of a skilled worker. The peculiarity of work with prisoners results in occasional interruptions which do not always ensure continuous operation. Operation must sometimes be suspended when prisoners try to escape or if the guard personnel is used for other purposes, in the quarries, also in fog. [. . .] The costs of the guard units are borne by the Reich; the costs for fencing the enterprise (barbed wire fences, walls), on the other hand, have to be met by the enterprise for the time being.

THREE

Running the Camps

The Camp ss's origins were in Dachau, the first ss camp. In 1933 recruitment of officials was haphazard—the professional corps of ss guards was still a long way off—but most of the men were united by hatred of the left and Jews. Many of them also had a background in political violence. As Nazi Party veterans, they had fought in the political battles of the late Weimar Republic. Some had also seen active service at the front line in World War I, while others had made their formative experiences in radical right-wing paramilitary organizations.[1]

Once appointed Dachau commandant in the summer of 1933, Eicke soon began to create a distinct corps of ss guards. Yet he faced many challenges. Initially, the Camp ss units were formally subordinated to the regional commanders of the regular ss. Also, the Camp ss had to report to the central ss administration. These arrangements were a regular source of friction between Eicke and the regular ss, reinforcing his conviction that the ss in the camps had to become more independent. After he was appointed Inspector of the Concentration Camps in 1934, Eicke's vision of a distinct Camp ss—as a special corps for the protection of the state (Staatsschutzkorps)—received a new impetus. The ss units who guarded the camps came to be known as ss guard units (Wachverbände), led by Eicke, who no longer had to report to regional ss units. Eicke was backed by Himmler, and a different title for Eicke soon followed, reflecting the guard units' new menacing name: Death's Head Units. In April 1936, therefore, Himmler appointed Eicke leader of the Death's Head Units. From 1937 the Death's Head Units were divided into three regiments (*Standarten*), each based at one of the major ss camps (Dachau, Sachsenhausen, and Buchenwald) and financed from the Reich budget, as Himmler and Eicke were keen to establish a distinct armed force under ss control.[2]

In fact, once the structure of the ss camp system was in place by

1937, Eicke's interests shifted more and more toward consolidating and extending the Death's Head Units, which he wanted to develop as an ss military force amid increasing Nazi preparations for war. On 17 August 1938 Hitler formalized the status of the Death's Head Units as a separate armed force in a secret decree, declaring that "the ss Death's Head Units are neither part of the Wehrmacht nor of the police. They are a standing army of the ss for the solution of special tasks of a police nature."[3] Hitler's decree as well as Himmler's keen support gave a further boost to the Death's Head Units, which increased from 2,546 men in December 1935 to 9,172 in December 1938 and rapidly further in 1939.[4] Here were the foundations of the Waffen-ss, which would commit countless atrocities during the war.[5]

Under Eicke's control and direction, discipline and terror in the camps became somewhat more standardized and guard duty became more militarized. As part of this process, Eicke also streamlined the administrative structure of the remaining camps, following his Dachau model.[6] For example, the Camp ss was formally divided into commandant staff personnel (*Kommandanturstab*) and the guard troop (*Wachtruppe*). The latter was not normally allowed to enter the camps; its main role was to patrol the camp perimeter and guard prisoner work commandos outside the camp compound, and members of the guard units consequently often had less direct contact with prisoners.[7] What really held the system together were not its bureaucratized structure or Eicke's written rules but the close personal relations, particularly among senior ss men, which were based on a shared ideological commitment to the ss cause.[8] All in all, there emerged in the 1930s a professional corps of ss guards and officers, most of whom had volunteered to serve in this pioneer force as self-proclaimed "political soldiers."

The commandant staff was the "true power and administrative headquarters of the camp."[9] From the mid-1930s, each camp consisted of five departments dedicated to specific tasks. Each department was headed by an ss officer, ensuring the smooth operation of the camps. Overall authority lay with the commandant. Below the commandant, arguably the most important department was the "protective custody camp," headed by an ss officer known as *Schutzhaftlagerführer* (protective custody camp leader), effectively the commandant's deputy. An immensely powerful figure who did much to shape the overall atmosphere in the camp, he was in charge of the prisoners and the ss *Rapport-*, *Arbeitseinsatz-*, and *Blockführer*. These ss officials—a rather small group of mostly NCOs—were responsible for supervising the everyday life of prisoners, overseeing prisoners' roll calls, work details, and the prisoners' huts, with blocks of up to 250 prisoners. Each camp also had an administrative office and a medical office, headed by an ss doctor. Supposedly in charge of the prisoners' health, doctors were often involved in abuses and also helped to cover up murders as "suicides." Finally, there was the political section, staffed by Gestapo officials who compiled regular reports on prisoners' conduct for the Gestapo's attention. The political section's staff often brutally interrogated prisoners upon arrival and also during their imprisonment.[10]

In the overwhelming majority, the Death's Head Units consisted of ordinary ss soldiers and NCOs, most of them in the guard troop. According to official ss figures, there were 6,476 regular men and 1,571 NCOs in the Death's Head Units on 31 December 1938.[11] Altogether they were predominantly lower middle class and very young, with an average age of 20.7 years in 1938. Above the regular troops and NCOs stood the ss *Führer*: at the end of 1938 there were only 437 such ss officers in the Death's Head Units, a mere 5.2 percent altogether.[12] These men often made their career in the camps, and a distinct network of Camp ss officers emerged, characterized by patronage, personal connections, corruption, and the common aim to destroy supposed opponents and social outsiders.[13] All in all, Eicke saw himself and his men as a corps of soldiers fighting the political enemy behind the barbed wire of the concentration camp.

3.1. Theodor Eicke and the Concentration Camps

Before 1933, few would have believed that Theodor Eicke, born in 1892 in the then German province of Alsace into a lower-middle-class family, would become one of the most feared men in Germany. Leaving school without a diploma in 1909, he signed up for the army. During World War I he served as a paymaster. Like many who later joined the Nazi Party, he was deeply embittered by Germany's defeat, for which he blamed the left and the Jews.[14] After attempts to obtain a degree failed, he became a police informer until he was dismissed in 1920. He did not find a permanent job until 1923, when he began work for the I. G. Farben chemical factory in Ludwigshafen in the Palatinate, a position he held until he began full-time service with the ss in 1932 (fueled by his hatred for the Weimar Republic, he had joined the Nazi Party and the sa in 1928, and the ss in 1930). Eicke soon rose through the ranks and became a *Sturmführer*. In 1932 he escaped to Italy after he had been convicted by a German court of planning bomb attacks directed against the Weimar Republic's institutions. A fugitive from justice, securely set up in Fascist Italy, Eicke ran a camp for Nazi refugees from Austria.

In February 1933 Eicke returned to Germany, hoping to find a role in the new Nazi regime. Yet the foul-tempered, bullish, and aggressive Eicke quickly found himself locked into a major power struggle with the Nazi *Gauleiter* of the Palatinate. In the end, Eicke was arrested and admitted for observation to a psychiatric hospital in Würzburg. Locked up, a desperate Eicke wrote several pleading letters to Himmler and asked him for help. Before long, in June 1933, Himmler relented and gave Eicke another chance to make his mark in the nascent Third Reich: he appointed him commandant of Dachau. From this point his career took a meteoric rise, and Eicke would shape the concentration system until 1939 and beyond, implementing the Nazi policy of terror and exclusion.[15]

One of Eicke's first major actions outside Bavaria, as we have seen, was the taking over of the Lichtenburg camp in 1934 and the removal of the civil servants nominally in charge (147). Full of contempt for any bureaucratic regulations, which he saw as a potential obstacle for radical Nazi politics, Eicke insisted that the Camp ss must act like political soldiers, not civil servants or prison guards, and act in blind obedience to the Führer (**148**). He often lectured his men about Nazi ideology and insisted that they must treat all inmates harshly; otherwise these dangerous enemies of the state would fight back and destroy Germany (**145**).

Rudolf Höß, later the first commandant of Auschwitz, got his first taste of the concentration camps under Eicke at Dachau in 1934, as he later recorded in his memoirs, written soon after the war in Polish captivity (**145**). Many of the men in the Camp ss worshipped Eicke. Höß, too, was full of admiration for Eicke's unrelenting ideological zeal and his extreme severity toward prisoners. Eicke also insisted on comradely relations among ss leaders and men and socialized with rank-and-file guards, who could allegedly always approach him directly, bypassing their immediate superiors.[16]

Apart from extreme drill, one of Eicke's initiation rites for new recruits left a particularly profound impression on them: he forced them to witness the flogging of prisoners (**173**).[17] Eicke's belief in strict discipline was so strong that he even locked up some wayward ss guards as prisoners if they had violated his tough regulations, soon extended from Dachau to all remaining camps (**157**). In 1933 and 1934 Eicke also passed extremely harsh disciplinary regulations for camp prisoners, initially at Dachau and Esterwegen, and then elsewhere in the camp system. These regulations stipulated severe punishments, including the death penalty, for prisoners who violated the rules (**149** and **150**). Unconditional discipline and order, as reflected in these formal regulations, were to replace the arbitrary violence of the early camps—at least on paper.

Officially, only the camp commandant, not individual guards, had the power to order disciplinary punishments. For the most severe sanction—flogging—confirmation from the Inspectorate in Berlin was required. Eicke had created this bureaucratic apparatus to safeguard individual ss guards against prosecution by the judiciary.[18] In exceptional cases he even fired individual ss guards who had abused prisoners without official orders (**158**) to appease the judiciary and to prevent entirely arbitrary brutality. At the same time, there was always an acceptance among ss leaders of the open violence of the Camp ss. Eicke tolerated and even encouraged the abuse of prisoners as long as it did not cause any problems for the ss's reputation (150). Like his mentor Heinrich Himmler, Eicke was a micromanager. He personally intervened in all matters, even the most trivial ones, and issued numerous orders to all members of the Camp ss (146). Of particular importance were his personnel decisions, as he played a key role in recruiting a corps of committed Camp ss officers loyal to him (145).[19] All this reinforced the ss's self-perception of being an elitist yet comradely order with a distinct martial and masculine identity.

Eicke was always keen to gain wider recognition and praise for his part in the development of the camp system and the Death's Head Units. Without his personal sacrifices for the Nazi cause, he lamented in a 1936 letter, the camps and their ss units would not exist (152). Eicke's position was strengthened by his close relationship with Himmler, who clearly admired his loyal and tough paladin (160). In 1938 Himmler entrusted Eicke with the "reeducation" of ss men who had violated the strict ss rules in a special platoon of the Sachsenhausen Camp ss. ss men in this so-called Education Platoon (Erziehungssturm) soon became notorious among the prisoners for their brutal behavior (161). Eicke remained formally in charge of the concentration camps until November 1939, when Richard Glücks, his former deputy, took over, initially without changing the basic structures of the concentration camp system established under Eicke (154).[20] During the war Eicke commanded the ss Death's Head Division, notorious for its atrocities against enemy soldiers and civilians, in France and the Soviet Union, until he died in an airplane crash in early 1943 in Ukraine.[21]

DOCUMENTS

145. From the notes of Rudolf Höß, written in November 1946 in Cracow prison[22]

He [Theodor Eicke] is to be seen as the real creator of the concentration camps [. . .]. He was also the person who gave the concentration camps their form and appearance. In 1933 the Reich Leader ss lifts him from the general ss and makes him *Standartenführer* at the

Dachau concentration camp following the dismissal of two [*sic*] incompetent predecessors.

Eicke immediately gets down to reshaping the camp in line with his ideas. Eicke is a rigid old Nazi from the "period of the struggle." All his doings are based on the idea: National Socialism has seized power for itself at the cost of heavy sacrifices and after a long struggle: the task now is to unify this power against all enemies of this new state. That is how he also sees the concentration camps. To him the inmates are always enemies of the state, who have to be kept locked up, treated harshly and, in the event of resistance, annihilated.

In this spirit he teaches and educates his ss leaders. [. . .] Inmates are handled severely and harshly. The least offense is punished by him with flogging. He has the flogging performed before the assembled guard personnel—at least 2 companies—in order, as he puts it, to make the men hard. The recruits, in particular, are made to watch the floggings regularly. The Alpha and Omega of all of Eicke's teachings is: out there, beyond the wire, the enemy is lurking: he is watching all your doings in order to profit from your weaknesses. Do not therefore display any weakness, show the enemies of the state your teeth. Anyone showing even the least pity for these enemies of the state has to disappear from our ranks. I can only use hard ss men, ready for anything, there is no place for softies among us!

Eicke also does not tolerate any arbitrariness. The inmates are to be treated harshly but justly. He alone can order punishments. He organizes surveillance in the protective custody camp and thus has it in his hand. Gradually he subdivided the whole concentration camp and gave it the form that was subsequently applied to all concentration camps. He turned the guard troop into a hard, rough team that really guards but is also quick with the rifle if an enemy of the state attempts to escape. Even the slightest offense in guarding is punished incredibly hard by Eicke. Yet his men love him and call him "Papa Eicke." In the evening he sits among them in their canteen or in their quarters. Talks to them in their language, listens to their troubles and worries, teaches and educates them into what *he* needs—rough, hard men who shrink from nothing if he gives the order!

Every order given has to be implemented, even the hardest—this is what he demands and preaches at every instruction. And these instructions hit home, enter their flesh and blood. These guards of Eicke's period as commandant of Dachau are the later protective custody camp leaders, *Rapport* leaders and other leading functionaries of subsequent camps. They have never forgotten being molded by Eicke! [. . .]

In 1934 he becomes the first Inspector of Concentration Camps. Initially he controls matters from Dachau, then he moves to Berlin in order to be near to the Reich Leader ss. He now embarks with ardent zeal on reshaping the existing camps of Esterwegen, Sachsenburg, Lichtenburg and Columbia on the Dachau model. Dachau leaders and men are constantly transferred to the other camps in order to bring with them the "Dachau spirit" and to become a little more military and Prussian. The Reich Leader ss gives him a free hand, he knows that he could not entrust the concentration camps to a more "suitable" person. Himmler has repeatedly stated this quite openly, he approved of Eicke's views on the concentration camps and on enemies of the state and completely shared these views. [. . .]

Even as Inspector, Eicke remained true—also later—to his practice of chatting to the guards and lower ranks of the commandant's staff without the presence of their superiors. As a result he gained popularity and the loyalty of the men. [. . .] To the superior officers this practice of Eicke's was not to their liking. For one thing, Eicke learnt everything that happened in the camp, nothing essential remained hidden from him. For another, he was always informed on the behavior of all the ss leaders outside service hours. [. . .] Later he had letter-boxes installed in every camp, which he alone could open, which meant that every man could turn to him directly with requests, complaints and denunciations. He also had confidants among the inmates, who—unidentified—reported to him everything that was worth knowing. [. . .]

Eicke's personal life was very simple and reserved, he had a happy marriage to a very good woman. They had a son and a daughter. He felt uneasy in his grand villa in Oranienburg—generously built for him by Pohl. He would have preferred to stay in his simpler apartment in Frohnau near Berlin.

Eicke was hard—cruelly hard—in his orders and if these orders were not obeyed.

Many an ss man—including a few leaders—were reduced to the

ranks before the assembled men, clothed in inmates' clothes and given 25 lashes. He even bullied his own cousin in this way.

For the bulk of the inmates he has no understanding—they were enemies of the state—although he has taken the side of a few individuals, whom he knew more closely. For his ss men he would do anything—whether only from comradeship or with a purpose in mind I am unable to judge.

Personally he was clean and untouchable.

146. Service regulations issued by Theodor Eicke for escort sentries and prisoner guards in Dachau, dated 1 October 1933[23]

The sole duty of the escort sentries is the guarding of the prisoners. They focus their attention on their behavior during work. Lazy prisoners are to be made to work. Any maltreatment or chicanery, however, is strictly forbidden. If a prisoner is conspicuously negligent or lazy in his work, or if he answers cheekily, the post will establish his name. At the end of his spell of duty he then makes his report. Self-help means a lack of discipline. If the prisoners are to have respect for the sentry, then the ss man has to be a leading example to the prisoner. While a prisoner has to do hard physical work, the ss man as a sentry should not be permitted to stand around in a lazy manner, lean against something, shift his rifle to his back or put his hand on the muzzle. A sentry behaves in a ridiculous and unsoldierly manner if he avoids rain, seeks cover under trees or wall projections and watches the working prisoners from that position. The ss man has to display pride and dignity and by his soldierly example to show the Communists and bigwigs that he is the exponent of the Third Reich. Addressing with *Du* equals fraternization.[24] It is humiliating for a Death's Head bearer to be made a messenger by Bolsheviks and bigwigs. This kind of person is not impressed by words, but by the example of action. An ss man who will not submit to this compulsion of self-education had better leave the camp [. . .].

If a prisoner attempts to escape, *he is to be fired on without warning call.* A sentry who, in the execution of his duty, has shot an escaping prisoner dead will go unpunished [. . .]. If a party of prisoners mutinies or revolts, then they are fired on by every sentry on duty. Warning shots are forbidden as a matter of principle.

147. Report by Theodor Eicke regarding his takeover of the Lichtenburg camp, dated 2 June 1934[25]

(1) On 28.5.34 I took over the Lichtenburg concentration camp under my own leadership. State of the troops, in terms of mood and discipline, very good. State of the civilian camp administration corrupt and lazy.

(2) On 29.5., upon my own initiative, I arrested the former administration director Faust [of Lichtenburg] and had him taken to the Secret State Police office Berlin. Reason: corruption [. . .], behavior dangerous to the state.[26] Reich Leader ss has already ordered protective custody arrest for Faust. Since mid-March 1934 no accounts have been kept, abt. 3½ thousand Reichsmark are not at present accounted for. The remaining reasons can only be communicated by word of mouth.

(3) The authority of the camp command is safeguarded in all directions. For the consolidation of this authority it is urgently necessary for 2 ss leaders to be placed at my side. At the moment I am the only ss man here with leader rank.

148. Theodor Eicke's Commandant's Order 1/34 for the Lichtenburg concentration camp, issued 2 June 1934[27]

We are the exponents of the National Socialist revolution and the most loyal pillars of the state created by us. The development of the state is still at its beginning; the revolutionary élan of the ss and its esprit de corps must not be watered down by the fact that they want to re-educate us into prison warders. We shall never become officials, but remain men of action and the black assault force. Officials become comfortable, fat and old. We, as fighters, remain healthy and alive. No ss leader will become an official, but must remain a soldier and leader.[28] In the time to come we shall be needed as well as our merciless spirit of attack. We rally round our Führer and, whenever the interest of the Movement requires it, we must act. Alongside the laws of the state there is for us the firm and unwritten law of personal action for Führer and Movement. This action goes all the way to the final outcome. As officials we are tied to the dead letter of the law, as political soldiers and fighters we act according to our revolutionary principles wherever the Führer and the Movement are in danger. We are therefore here not for our own sakes, or for our livelihood, but solely and exclusively for our Movement and our fatherland. Anyone therefore who does not wish to be a 100% ss man, had better depart voluntarily and seek employment as a salaried policeman. We do not look at status or origin, but solely and exclusively on the kind of fellow you are and whether your heart is in the right place. [. . .] There is no room for unclean elements in this elite force.

As the responsible camp commandant I will do all I can to strengthen loyalty and comradeship in the force and to mend any tears or cracks in the foundations. Until now your superiors were officials and a corrupt director, from now on soldiers will be in charge of you, for better or worse. Together we will place stone upon stone until completion, but cast aside bad stones as worthless. I am ready to listen at any time to the youngest comrade and will stand up for any comrade if he proves an open and honest character. In service there is only merciless severity and hardness; outside service hours there is heartwarming comradeship.

149. Special camp order issued by Theodor Eicke for the Esterwegen camp, dated 1 August 1934[29]

Purpose

It is left to every protective custody detainee to reflect on why he got to the concentration camp. Here he will be given an opportunity to change his inner attitude to nation and fatherland in favor of a people's community on a National Socialist basis or else, if the individual prefers, to die for the dirty Second or Third Jewish International of a Marx or Lenin. [. . .]

Order and discipline

Regardless of origin, status or occupation the prisoners are, without exception, in a subordinate position. Whether old or young, everyone has to get used to military discipline and order from the very first day on. All ss men, right up to the commandant of the concentration camp, are the superiors of the prisoners; their orders are to be followed at once and without argument. [. . .]

Salute

In order to promote discipline, the prisoners are obliged to give a military salute to all ss members. If a prisoner is addressed by an ss man, he has to adopt a military stance. On the march, salutes are performed by turning of the head. In front of ss leaders, from *Sturmführer* upward, the salute is given on the order of the ss man leading the squad by the command "Eyes right," concluded by "Eyes front." At the same time caps are to be taken off. If a superior officer enters a workplace, the head cover is not removed: the prisoners continue their work undisturbed. Reports are made by the leader of the escort sentries and by the foreman of the prisoners.

If prisoners' quarters are entered by a superior officer, the prisoner closest to him has to draw attention to this by shouting "Attention!" The senior room prisoner reports the number present, those in the room stand to attention.

Salutes are given as a matter of principle if a superior officer enters the camp; they are not given if he walks along the sentry path outside the wire fence. [. . .]

Duty to work

The prisoners, without exception, are obliged to do physical work. Status, occupation and origin are of no concern. Anyone refusing to work, evading work or, for the purpose of doing nothing, feigning physical weaknesses or sickness, is regarded as *incorrigible* and is made to answer for himself. Working hours in the camp are laid down, exclusively, by the camp commandant. Beginning and end of working time is announced by horn signals or the workshop bell.

If the requirements of the camp so demand, work can be done at any time outside the established working hours and on Sundays and holidays with the approval of the commandant.

Prisoners may be granted a bonus for working on the moor, with the approval of the commandant. [. . .]

Behavior in the camp

Yelling, shouting and overly loud calling are forbidden in the camp.

Huts and quarters may only be entered and exited by the prescribed entrances. Anyone who climbs through a hut window by day or night, gets on hut roofs without instruction, throws stones over the camp wall, leaves his hut during the night—between last post and reveille—will be fired on *without warning*. The same consequences have to be expected by a prisoner who, without permission or instruction, enters the neutral zone bounded by pickets.

Crowding near the wire obstacles by the picket boundary is forbidden. Disregard of this prohibition will result in fire with live ammunition. Orders by the camp sentries are to be obeyed instantly; if necessary an order may be lent emphasis with the firearm. [. . .]

Camp doctor

The camp doctor exists only for the sick, not for the work-shy. Prisoners trying to avoid work by unfounded or prissy sick-reporting are detailed to the "penal work" section. Anyone asking to see the doctor has to report for examination the same day. Anyone found by the doctor to be capable of work will be given punitive work. Members of the penal work section asking to be seen by the doctor without good reason will be punished according to the disciplinary and penal order. [. . .]

Agitators

Anyone talking politics or making seditious speeches in the camp, at his workplace, in the quarters or at resting places, who arranges to meet with others, meets others or drifts around with them for this purpose, anyone collecting true or untrue reports and photographs of the camp or its installations, receiving them, passing them on, smuggling them out of the camp by secret notes or in any other way, giving them to persons discharged or being transferred to take outside, burying them or concealing them in clothing and other articles, throwing them by means of stones over the camp wall, climbing on roofs and trees, giving signals or light signals, inducing others to escape, giving advice or assistance for escape, will be *treated as an agitator*. [. . .]

Public danger

Anyone offering presents to a sentry, trying to bribe him, glorifying Marxism or some other November party[30] in his presence, making derogatory remarks about the National Socialist people's state and its government, proving recalcitrant, secretly giving information about the camp and its inmates to an outside visitor to the camp, producing, receiving or passing on letters, notes, photographs, or pieces of clothing, caps, cigarette cases suitable as hiding places, will be treated as a danger to the public. [. . .]

Punishments

Crimes, offenses and infringements will be punished in accordance with the disciplinary and penal order for protective custody prisoners.

150. Disciplinary and penal order for the Esterwegen camp, issued by Theodor Eicke on 1 August 1934[31]

Introduction:

Within the framework of the existing camp regulations the following penal regulations have been issued for the maintenance of discipline and order in the Esterwegen concentration camp.

These regulations are binding for all prisoners of the Esterwegen concentration camp from the moment of their arrival to the hour of their release.

Penal executive is in the hands of the camp commandant, who answers personally to the Inspector of Concentration Camps for the observance of the camp regulations issued. The latter is subordinated to the Political Police Commander [Heinrich Himmler] and issues his instructions on his behalf.

Tolerance means weakness. Because of this realization merciless action will be taken whenever the interest of the fatherland requires. The decent misguided fellow German will not be affected by these penal regulations. The political agitators and subversive intellectuals [. . .], however, should know this: Watch out that you are not caught—else we will reach for your throats and silence you according to your own methods.

§ 1.

Punishment of 3 days' strict detention will be imposed on

(1) anyone not immediately getting up from his bunk upon reveille or failing to tidy up his bed or quarters,

(2) anyone at mealtime asking for a second helping, or getting the cook to give him two helpings, without his company leader's permission [. . .]

§ 8

Punishment of 14 days' strict detention with 25 lashes at the beginning and the end is imposed on:

[. . .] anyone who makes derogatory remarks, in letters or other communication, about National Socialist leaders, the state or the government, authorities and institutions, glorifies Marxist or liberalist leaders or November Parties, reports events inside the concentration camp [. . .]

§ 9

Punishment of 21 days' strict detention is imposed on:

anyone removing, deliberately damaging, destroying, wasting or reshaping articles owned by the state, no matter of what kind, or using them for a purpose other than the one prescribed. Apart from the punishment the individual or entire prisoner company will be liable for the total damage. [. . .]

§ 11

Anyone making political or inciting speeches at his work place, in his quarters, in kitchens and workshops, lavatories and rest areas for the purpose of *agitation*, rallies together with others for this purpose, forms cliques or drifts about, collecting, receiving, burying true or false reports for the purpose of enemy atrocity propaganda about the concentration camp or its installations, passing them on to outside visitors or others, smuggling them out of the camp in secret notes or in any other way [. . .] or encouraging others to escape or to commit a crime [. . .] will, according to revolutionary law *be hanged as an agitator!*

§ 12

Anyone attacking a guard or an ss man physically, refusing obedience or, at his workplace, refusing to work, encouraging others to do likewise for the purpose of mutiny, [. . .] [or who] bawls, shouts, agitates or makes speeches on the march or at work *will be shot dead on the spot as a mutineer* or subsequently hanged. [. . .]

§ 19

Detention is executed in a cell with hard bedding, bread and water. Every fourth day the prisoner receives hot food.

Penal work includes hard physical or especially dirty work, performed under special supervision.

Secondary punishments to be considered:

Pack drill, flogging, postal ban, food deprivation, hard bedding, tying to a pole, reprimand and admonition.

All punishments are recorded on file.

Detention and penal work extend protective custody by at least eight weeks; a secondary punishment imposed extends protective custody by at least four weeks. Prisoners kept in solitary confinement are not released within the foreseeable future.

151. Theodor Eicke to the commandant offices of Dachau, Esterwegen, Lichtenburg, Sachsenburg, Columbia-Haus, dated 2 December 1935[32]

Responsibility and camp security

[. . .]

Anyone committing a guard offense during this time [the Christmas and New Year season], getting drunk, culpably exceeding the last post or leaving the force without permission is to be suspended on disciplinary grounds at once. I will mercilessly remove the person concerned from the force. Anyone wearing the Death's Head as a symbol stands at the place of his duty until death relieves him. [. . .]

Other matters

A year of work is drawing to its close. In retrospect we realize that in hard fulfillment of duty we have grown by implementing the task put to us by the Reich Leader ss. Cautiously building, we placed one stone upon another and removed bad stones in good time. The mortar that holds us all together is the ss Death's Head spirit instilled in us. It makes us strong and ensures that disloyalty and unseemliness remain far removed from our corps; for the Death's Head strikes its wearer if ever he deviates from our prescribed course.

We let ourselves be guided by our wish and striving to be the best and most reliable Schutzstaffel.[33] He who joins our ranks enters into comradeship with death; this is symbolized by our badge. We are not expected to show loyalty *enforced* by an oath or blind discipline, because such loyalty will endure in non-dangerous times only. We want, we must, we shall be the dedicated-until-death Schutzstaffel who, when all the rest give up the struggle as lost, carry the flag of freedom through fire-spewing streets at one word of the Führer or his Reich Leader ss and, if need be, die in the attempt. Such self-sacrifice calls for men with buoyancy and enthusiasm, men who, when the Führer demands it, advance defiant of death. Let us test if we have the strength to strive toward such a lofty goal! [. . .] It is necessary, however, on the threshold of the New Year, once more to look at ourselves! Anyone who cannot take upon himself these brutal but, to a Death's Head bearer, indispensable conditions, may walk away from us in peace at the end of the year. Anyone, however, who, hypocritically and with concealed cowardice, believes he must remain in our ranks for the sake of his livelihood, let him know that, at the right time, he will become a victim of his own hypocrisy.

ss leaders and men!

We are standing at the beginning! Keep our ranks pure. Tolerate no softies or weak characters among yourselves; they would bring shame on our corps and, if things got tough, become cowards and traitors. The ss uniform does not make anyone an ss man unless he is filled with fighting spirit and unreserved enthusiasm. This noble Death's Head spirit will, across all hardships and obstacles, weld us together also in our new fighting year and sweep us forward. From it we draw the strength for iron fulfillment of duty and for unreserved battle readiness for the Führer and his idea. Without that spirit we are a hollow, useless deception. Cultivate this esprit de corps, then the Führer can be assured.

But use your special leave for rest and recreation. These are my wishes for the Winter Solstice[34] and for the New Year!

I shall keep my loyalty to you,
keep yours to the Führer!

152. Letter from Theodor Eicke to the Reich Leader ss regarding the Death's Head Units, dated 10 August 1936[35]

The ss Death's Head Units developed from a corrupt guard troop of just under 120 men from Dachau, starting in the autumn of 1934 [1933?]. There were times when no jackets, no boots and no socks were available. Without grumbling the men wore their own things on duty. We were generally regarded as a necessary evil that only cost money; nondescript watchmen behind barbed wire. I virtually had to beg again and again to get the state treasuries to come up with the scant pay for my leaders and men. I myself, as an *Oberführer* in Dachau had a monthly salary of 230 RM and was fortunate because I had the trust of my Reich Leader SS. Initially there was not a round of ammunition, nor a rifle, let alone a machine gun available [. . .]. My men lived in drafty factory buildings. There was poverty and hardship everywhere. Back then these guard units were subordinated to *Oberabschnitt Süd*, which left its worries and troubles to me, but otherwise, unasked, sent me people whom, for some reason or another, they wanted to be rid of in Munich. This contaminated my troops and their mood. I found disloyalty, embezzlement and corruption. Within the space of 4 weeks I had to dismiss about 60 men for these reasons. [. . .]

When I could get no further, the Reich Leader SS granted my proposal and subordinated the entire guard personnel exclusively to me. Now began its undisturbed rise. I got down to the job indefatigably and joyously, educated men to be made sub-leaders and sub-leaders to be made leaders. Common dedication, privation and cordial comradeship created, within a few weeks, an exemplary discipline from which a superb esprit de corps arose. We did not become megalomaniacs because none of us had anything; we quietly did our duty behind the barbed wire and ruthlessly removed from our ranks anyone who displayed the least trace of disloyalty. Thus shaped and educated, the guard contingent grew in the quiet of the concentration camps. Its ideals were loyalty, courage and fulfillment of duty. On 30.6.34[36] an important task came our way. Thanks to a unified leadership the formation remained free of damaging influences. I looked after my men and endeavored to be a model to them. We grew stronger and, with this, my concerns increased. Nuremberg 1935 displayed us to the public for the first time.[37] We passed our test there. No one suspected that most of my men were wearing their own clothes. The corps spirit readily made this sacrifice. The force was being rejuvenated and only muscular figures from 17 to 19 were recruited to its ranks. After the Party Rally of 1935 the Führer gave his signature. For the first time we received a budget as a basis for our livelihood. Immediately after 1 April 1936

Running the Camps

I increased the force from 1,800 to 3,500 men. The newly enrolled recruits are racially the best Germans between 17 and 19; they came with enthusiasm from the Hitler Youth. As for training, we have reached the stage, thanks to an excellent leader corps and good sub-leaders, that in Nuremberg 1936 the ss Death's Head formations can march past the Führer with 2,000 men [. . .].

Ideological schooling is being intensively practiced and expertly led with my *Sturmbannen*. 75% of the men of the ss Death's Head Units today no longer belong to any Church.

Within less than 11 months I have reorganized and extended 5 concentration camps, 4 of which were in the hands of the sa, and created transparent conditions there. A large, modern new concentration camp is at present being established in Sachsenhausen [. . .]. For 20 days each month I am traveling and exhausting myself. My family life until now has come second. I live only to fulfill my duty to my troops that I have come to be fond of.

153. Commandant office Order no. 95 of the Sachsenburg concentration camp, passing on a message issued by Theodor Eicke on 29 April 1936[38]

The present guard rota is a tough test of the character qualities and the reliability of the individual. I am aware that the comrades in ful-fillment of their duties are for days on end tied to the camp and cut off from the world outside. This is due to the present circumstances, in particular to the fact that the units can only gradually be brought up to full budget strength and that twice as much effort must there-fore, for the time being, be demanded of the individual.

In spite of this burden I demand from you that you prove your loy-alty and reliability more than ever and that you do not grumble if ser-vice seems unbearable to you at this moment. I have no use for anyone who can be loyal and reliable only in good times: let him leave before he exposes himself to the disgrace of expulsion.

I am aware of your hardships and am striving every day to re-move them, but this can only be done one step at a time. Remain steadfast and loyal, lest our reputation and reliability suffer dam-age. I hope to be able to effect alleviations soon. Until then prove yourselves to be men and conscientiously do your duty to the Füh-rer and our fatherland.

154. Undated guidelines of the Inspectorate of Concentration Camps from the prewar period regarding "Purpose and structure of concentration camps"[39]

The purpose of the concentration camp is to safeguard all those enemies of the people and the state, *who by their behavior threaten the existence and security of the nation and the state*, who therefore, for security, educational or otherwise preventive reasons, have to be deprived of their personal freedom on the basis of legal provisions.

Such enemies of the people [. . .] are taken into protective custody (or preventive custody) and assigned to a concentration camp. The nature of the detention of these persons is determined by the deportation order of the executing authority. The necessary regulations and instructions have been issued by the Chief of Security Police. Supervision of the concentration camp is carried out by the Inspector of Concentration Camps, who is directly subordinated to the Reich Leader ss and Chief of German Police.

An ss leader runs the concentration camp as responsible camp director. For dealing with his official business the camp director has several ss leaders as section leaders by his side, with the necessary personnel (ss sub-leaders and men) who are answerable to him for the orderly running of their sections.

The members of the concentration camp service perform their service with a sense of duty. They discharge their official duties toward the inmates severely but fairly. Any other unofficial contact with the inmates, even the very slightest, is most strictly prohibited and results in the immediate expulsion from the ss and deportation to a concentration camp.

Topping up of the commandant's staff is done solely from the Death's Head *Standarten*.

Special regulations will be issued in the event of war.

The sections of a concentration camp are:

(1) the commandant's office and the Adjutant's office
(2) the Political Section
(3) the protective custody camp
(4) the administration
(5) the camp doctor

155. Posted Order of the ss Death's Head Units and the Inspectorate of Concentration Camps of 1 March 1937, signed by Theodor Eicke[40]

Atrocity propaganda

The émigré enemy has changed his previous tactics. In the past he publicized alleged brutality by the ss staff and maltreatment. Now he is going over to describing the "degeneration" of individuals, so that every open-minded reader is bound to fall for the skillful presentation of these reports.

Now that the new direction of the attack has been identified, I warn all camp commandants to prevent most rigorously any performance of private work by prisoners in the workshops. We are accused of corruption because *Scharführer* X has had his wife's and his child's shoes resoled in the camp's footwear shop at state expense. Also because furniture for domestic use has been produced in the camp's workshops. *Scharführer* X has had a prisoner fill a bucket with petrol, cover it with a cleaning rag and carry it out through the camp gate. Then he used it to fill up his motorbike. [. . .] I request that the troops and the personnel of the camp commandant be once more instructed about the dangers of corruption; at the same time I refer once more emphatically to the prohibition of filling private orders by prisoners.

Once the attacks have been thoroughly investigated on the spot, I shall impose isolation on all Jews in Dachau.[41] Order to follow.

Maltreatment

On the arrival of a prisoner transport two ss men have dealt out boxes on the ear to two especially cheeky detainees. Much as I have sympathy, as a National Socialist, for such a procedure, I cannot and must not tolerate such behavior or we would run the risk of being described, by the Ministry of the Interior of the German Reich, as incapable of dealing with prisoners. I therefore request you act educationally. Cheekiness must not be punished by the individual but only by the camp commandant. In order to protect the ss against attacks, Reich Leader ss has threatened expulsion for the least maltreatment (box on the ear).

Flogging

When the punishment of flogging is applied, it will suffice in future to have a group of ss as witnesses, instead of a platoon. Such a group has to stand at least 8 meters away; it may be supplemented by members of the commandant's staff. Also, only ss men with at least 2 years' service in the camp may be called upon as witnesses.

156. Posted Order of the ss Death's Head Units and the Inspectorate of Concentration Camps of 4 May 1937, signed by Theodor Eicke[42]

Courtesy

I request that you see to it that in performing the Hitler salute any kind of bowing, even toward ladies, is avoided. We did not bend our spines in the struggle for the victory of the Movement and do not bend them today. Superior officers are to be formally saluted with body erect and arm *fully extended*. The relaxed salute with the arm bent equals an infringement of respect. Even with uncovered head I ask that bowing is avoided as far as possible. The Hitler salute needs no admixture of bourgeois forms.

Recruitment

I refer to the regulations issued. Accordingly only the racially best men are to be enrolled in the ss Death's Head Units. These have to be at least 1.70 m tall and *very young*. If 16-year-old applicants tower considerably above their coevals, they can be enrolled without problem. Applicants with ss service behind them should not have exceeded their 22nd year at the time of enrollment. Older ss applicants and those awaiting army service within a year are only a burden to the ss Death's Head Units. [. . .]

157. Posted Order of the ss Death's Head Units and the Inspectorate of Concentration Camps of 4 June 1937, signed by Theodor Eicke[43]

ss *Oberscharführer* Zeidler in the Sachsenhausen concentration camp has, because of sadistic tastes, beaten a prisoner in a most vile manner. He was reduced to the rank of ss man, permanently expelled from the ss and handed over to the criminal judge. This case is being made known as a warning example. During instruction there should be continuous reference to the consequences of prisoner maltreatment. [. . .] The punishments that a camp commandant can impose on recalcitrant inmates are so harsh and thorough that there is no need for acting on one's own initiative. The reputation of the Schutzstaffel is kept clean in all instances by expulsion of the culprit.

158. Posted Order of the ss Death's Head Units and the Inspectorate of Concentration Camps of 4 June 1937, signed by Theodor Eicke[44]

[. . .] *Expulsions and punishments*

[. . .] *Staffel* candidate Heinle, Ottmar [. . .] I/ss Death's Head Unit
Dishonorable dismissal
Reason: Dealing with inmates, falsification of a Party document, false official information [. . .]

ss *Unterscharführer* Wohlrabe, Willi [. . .] III/ss Death's Head Unit, ss no. 279 467
Reduction to rank to *Rottenführer*
Reason: Violation of duty as guard [. . .]

ss *Oberscharführer* Zeidler, Paul, commandant's office Sachsenhausen, ss no. 16782
Reduction to rank of ss man, permanent exclusion from ss
Reason: Grave maltreatment of prisoners.

159. Posted Order of the Death's Head Units and the Inspectorate of Concentration Camps of 6 July 1937, signed by Theodor Eicke[45]

Reinforcement of ss Death's Head Units

A new era is beginning in the history of the ss Death's Head Units. Their reinforcement and reorganization makes increased demands on the nerves of leaders and sub-leaders. It is not enough to replenish our target figures numerically with people; what matters is that, in the shortest possible time and by overcoming great difficulties, we collect in our ranks a selection of nordically defined men. We can only use the best German blood, even if during that selection we must hurt some individuals. This principle is unassailable and is the guideline of our actions. It guarantees the realization of our aim — to create for the Reich Leader ss and hence for the Führer and the Movement an ss force on which one may rely in all circumstances. What good is the symbol, the Death's Head, if it becomes just a mere decoration on our collars, while we are getting stuck in the beginnings of a ludicrous attempt to re-create a military organization[?] Our actions must be dominated by the determination to turn the noble human material entrusted to us into death-defying fighters, in a tough school and by making ourselves the model, fighters with an attitude that cannot, under any conditions, be severed from us. We must teach the men to forget that little bit of "I," so that, if necessary, they will unreservedly stake their lives and stubbornly do their duty. Unless this Schutzstaffel spirit unreservedly grips every one of us, then our work is pointless and a vacuous game. Leaders and sub-leaders should always remember that our men have come to us with a happy heart, very young, with great enthusiasm and voluntarily. Bright-eyed they see their new surroundings, full of trust in the ss leaders and sub-leaders, who enjoy a good reputation in the public [. . .]. These men were not called up by some defense law: they came *voluntarily* in order to serve the Führer. Following an inner urge, they left their parental home very early in order to let themselves be molded physically and spiritually by the Schutzstaffel. This free will weighs more than the law; it should therefore be gratefully acknowledged and carefully guarded, because from it will come future achievements and deeds. Without that free will there is no obedience, no loyalty, no sense of honor or duty. The heavy responsibility to reshape this free will into soldierly virtues weighs upon the shoulders of those whom destiny has chosen as leaders, teachers and educators and placed before the troops. There they stand, not because of some ranking order but because of their responsibility for which they have passed the test. It is an excellent arrangement that ss leaders are not officials whom the state feeds even if, all their life long, they have run alongside their duties at an officials' trot, merely making legal articles the law of their actions [. . .].

Our strength lies in the maintenance of consistent purity in our own ranks. Softies and unreliable men, who damage the honor and reputation of the Death's Head Units, are, according to well-tried justice, mercilessly removed from our ranks; this applies to leaders and other ranks.

Go now to your work and do not tire.

Our goal forever remains: Germany!

160. Birthday greetings from Theodor Eicke to Heinrich Himmler, dated 6 October 1937[46]

Reich Leader,

On your birthday I wish you from my heart everything that is good, strength and health. God will continue to protect you and bless your intentions for the well-being of our Führer and our fatherland. 5000 leaders and other ranks of three Death's Head *Standarten*, into whose hands your will gave weapons, at today's flag parades venerate their inspired creator and leader.

I have but one aim—to weld together the men entrusted to me in the spirit of the Schutzstaffel, in line with our symbol, into a death-defying fighting force.

Our entire strength belongs to you and thus to the Führer. Fulfillment of duty and loyalty are and remain the morning prayer of the ss Death's Head Units.

Heil Hitler!
Ever your obedient
Eicke.

161. Instruction by Heinrich Himmler regarding the establishment of an Education Platoon at the Sachsenhausen concentration camp, dated 21 July 1938[47]

An Education Platoon is to be set up at the Sachsenhausen concentration camp with immediate effect.

The Education Platoon comprises two sections spatially separated from one another:

(a) Section I (Education Section)
(b) Section II (Correction Section)

Allocation into:

(A) *Section I* (Education Section)
(a) ss men who have been stripped of their rank and have to start again as ss candidates, [. . .]
(d) ss members who, while on guard duty in the concentration camps, committed an offense against guard duty and thereby endanger the camp security [. . .]

(B) *Section II* (Correction Section) [. . .]

(b) members of the ss quartered in barracks in the concentration camps who have any kind of dealings with inmates, smuggling letters, accepting presents or making contact with prisoners or their families in any other way, if they have been expelled from the ss for this offense.

162. Letter by Theodor Eicke to the camp commandants regarding the prisoner amnesty on the occasion of Hitler's fiftieth birthday on 20 April 1939, dated 10 March 1939[48]

The protective custody inmates in concentration camps due to be released this year on the occasion of 20 April 1939 are to be, for the first time, instructed at a short parade on the significance of their readmission to the people's community. This should be done by making the inmates of the separate camps, having completed all release formalities and having put on their civilian clothes, fall in in a secure and suitable room, where the camp commandants in the presence of all the leaders of the camps' commandant staff, as well as the guard squads of the ss Death's Head *Standarten*, will address them. In this address the former inmates should be briefly told that, by their good behavior, they had demonstrated their will to live according to National Socialist principles and had thereby reached the road to freedom. They would be readmitted as members of the German people's community, whereby they would undertake the obligation to work with all their strength and love for the fatherland and cooperate in the building of our great nation.

3.2. The Leaders of the Camp ss

As we have seen, Eicke was keen to shape a distinct network of Camp ss leaders who would implement his vision of the concentration camps. Eicke often tried to handpick ss men as senior camp leaders who had trained at Dachau, a hard course of military-style training as well as ideological schooling. All of the future ss leaders already shared the radical anti-Semitism and hatred of the left, but during their training these beliefs were reinforced, as the men were directly exposed to the "enemy" in the camp.[49] Many senior Camp ss leaders gradually worked their way through the ranks, proving their talent for abuse and torture.

If Eicke liked an ss man, he was determined to have him appointed — even if he had a criminal record, as was the case with Max Koegel, who had been sentenced for fraud in the 1920s (**164**). With Eicke's backing he soon worked his way up to senior positions in the Camp ss. Later, during the war, he was to serve as commandant of the Ravensbrück women's concentration camp as well as the Lublin and Flossenbürg camps.[50] Likewise, Eicke rejected men he saw as unsuitable for the camps. One such case was that of ss *Oberführer* Karl Taus, who had been transferred, like many candidates for senior office within the Camp ss, to the Dachau camp for training in 1938. Taus was too soft for Eicke's taste, so he had him transferred to the regular ss (**171**).[51] Still, Eicke occasionally had to accept men he deemed unsuitable, illustrating the marked gap between Eicke's sense of elitism and the available candidates. This was the case with Karl Künstler, whom Eicke appointed commandant of Flossenbürg in January 1939 after the first commandant, Weiseborn, had died. Eicke appointed Künstler, even though he regarded him as an unreliable alcoholic.[52]

The future commandants found their way into the Camp ss in different ways. Hans Loritz, for example, had been a policeman in the Weimar years. Born in 1895, he served in World War I and found work with the Augsburg police until he was fired for misconduct in 1928. He then worked as a collector for the Augsburg gasworks. Embittered about his unsuccessful career and the Weimar Republic's seeming social and political chaos, he joined the ss in 1930 and the Camp ss in 1934, where he soon distinguished himself as a zealot (170)—leaving a good impression with Eicke, who furthered his career. Loritz served as commandant of several camps. From 1934 until 1936 he was commandant of Esterwegen, before he served as Dachau's commandant until 1939. During the war he was commandant of Sachsenhausen, where he served until 1942, overseeing the systematic mass murder of Soviet prisoners of war.[53]

Another senior ss camp officer was Karl Koch, the notorious commandant of Buchenwald. Born in 1897, he had also served in World War I, during which he was seriously wounded. He later worked for a bank and an insurance company, interrupted by spells of unemployment. He joined the ss in 1931 and soon found his way into the Camp ss, where he served in various camps, including Sachsenburg, Dachau, the Columbia-Haus, and Esterwegen. When Eicke needed someone to head the new Sachsenhausen camp, Koch was his natural choice, as he had already proved himself.[54] In 1937 Koch became commandant of Buchenwald, entrusted by Eicke with establishing this new ss camp. Eicke remained impressed by Koch's radical determination to enforce his will, as his comments in Koch's personnel file reveal (166). Koch, like other senior Camp ss leaders, began to regard the camp as his personal fiefdom. In Buchenwald he forced prisoners to work on his new mansion and to carry out forced labor for him and his wife, Ilse.[55] Koch and other camp commandants regularly issued strict orders to their Camp ss units. These directives allow us a glimpse into their mind-set. Koch, for one, was extremely pedantic and clearly obsessed with his men's discipline. He demanded blind obedience and publicized his punishments of guards who had violated their duties, even telling ss guards what kind of uniform they had to wear while on leave (167).

Like other ss officials, Koch was also a radical anti-Semite who meted out brutal punishments against Jewish prisoners on many occasions. Alongside other Buchenwald ss officers, Koch also stole from Jewish inmates in the wake of the November 1938 pogrom, one of his many brushes with theft and corruption (169).[56] This would eventually prove his undoing. Himmler ordered his officers to act "decently"

at all times. This definition of "decency" was, of course, highly perverted, as Himmler and the ss always pushed for extreme violence
against all supposed enemies. Still, when personal animosities between
Koch and his official ss superior resulted in an internal ss investigation during World War II, the levels of corruption uncovered were
judged excessive, even by ss standards. Koch was detained and eventually executed by an ss firing squad at Buchenwald in April 1945.[57]

DOCUMENTS

163. Curriculum vitae of the Dachau ss *Obertruppführer* (equivalent to *Hauptscharführer*) Max Koegel, dated 27 October 1933[58]

Koegel Max, born 16 October 1895 in Füssen as the fourth son of the
master joiner Andreas and his wife Felizitas Koegel. Attended the primary and further education school. A double orphan at age 12 I became a shepherd on an Alpine pasture. From my 16th to my 19th year
I was a porter on the Zugspitze[59] and, when war broke out, partici-
pated in a Zugführer candidates' course. On 4 August 1914 I joined
the 1st Heavy Cavalry Regiment as a volunteer and on 22 November 1914 went into battle [. . .]. I was wounded 3 times. On 12 January 1919 I left the army and took up service as a District Controller
in Garmisch. In 1922 I bought a shop there, but had to give it up in
1926 because of heavy losses. After that I worked in Vienna and Zurich as a [sales] representative. In 1928 I joined the firm of Haufwer-
ke A.G. as an employee in Füssen. Released on 8 April 1933 at my
own request. Since then with the guard troop in the Dachau concentration camp. Political activity: 1919–22 Völkischer Block, 1922–24
Bund Oberland[60] and since February 1932 in the NSDAP.

164. Letter from the Dachau commandant Theodor Eicke to the Lead-er of the Political Police in Bavaria, Heinrich Himmler, dated 27 No-vember 1933[61]

ss *Obertruppführer* Koegel has commented on the matter in a
report.[62] His report is attached.

In 1926, that is 9 years ago [*sic*], Koegel was sentenced to
9 months' imprisonment for his transgression. The coming
German law does not base itself on bare legal paragraphs, as does

Roman law, but endeavors to lead the lawbreaker to a genuine improvement, or if that cannot be achieved, to render him totally harmless. Koegel committed his transgression not for personal gain but from real economic hardship and we should ask ourselves now whether he should suffer for it all his life, seeing that he has already served his punishment before the law and justice.

As National Socialists we should moreover examine whether Koegel or the corrupt November system is guilty of that incident. After mature reflection one may say that the accursed big-wig-cracy of liberalistic-Marxist hue is solely and exclusively responsible if a fellow German guiltlessly came into conflict with the rigid law of the November system.

What remains incomprehensible is that National Socialists and his *own ss comrades* approve of the measure of a dirty government by still continually calling, today, nine years later "Crucify him!"

The undersigned has had to feel on his own person what it means to be exposed to public opinion. When he was sentenced to 2 years penitentiary,[63] so-called National Socialists likewise gave his tormented wife a wide berth and were not ashamed to call her, publicly, the wife of a criminal. Had my Führer not seized power in Germany I would have remained a convict all my life and would never have been able to hold public office.

I request therefore that a line be drawn at last also under the Koegel affair. He is a man of honor and as an old frontline soldier and fighter for Adolf Hitler worthy to be an ss leader. His achievements and his proven reliability speak in favor of this [. . .]. Dachau is a territory of work, where there is no time for gossiping. Füssen[64] evidently cannot yet free itself of liberalist thinking. I ask that the authorities there be instructed to leave Koegel alone at last.

Finally I request that his promotion to *Sturmbannführer* be supported. I need Koegel for positive work; let Füssen find someone else for the indispensable rubbish.

165. Commandant's Order no. 1 for the Ettersberg[65] concentration camp, issued by Karl Koch on 20 July 1937[66]

The following regulations are issued with immediate effect: after completion of the camp they will perhaps be revoked.

(1) No ss leader may leave the camp without my permission. When a leader's departure is reported, I am to be given the name of his replacement, who cannot then go on leave.

(2) Sunday afternoon is free. On that afternoon individual section leaders can grant leave of absence to individual ss members of their section until 12 midnight within their base [. . .]. However, the sections must always remain manned to such a degree that, in the event of an alarm, the full deployment of the section concerned is guaranteed.

(3) In agreement with me the leader of the guard squad may grant leave of absence to their base to free men and sub-leaders; however, the security of the camp must not be endangered.

(4) I readily acknowledge the hard service of every individual during the construction period and will introduce alleviations to the extent possible for me within the limits set me by the Leader of ss Death's Head Units and Concentration Camps [Eicke]. That is also why leave should be used for recuperation; a person should not return from leave more exhausted than he was prior to leave.

Abuse of alcohol will be punished by me with merciless severity or else I will have the person concerned dismissed. Anyone putting the security of the camp at risk cannot expect me to show consideration to his family.

166. Theodor Eicke's internal report on the Buchenwald commandant Karl Koch, dated 2 August 1937[67]

Assessment:

I. Overall racial picture: *Nordic-Phalian, medium height, slim figure.*

II. 1. Character: *open, calm, determined*

   2. Will: *very energetic and strong*

   3. Sound commonsense: *fully and totally present*
     Knowledge and education: *good average*
     Comprehension: *easy and sure*
     National Socialist ideology: *impeccable*

III. Bearing and behavior: in office and out of office (Special inclinations, weaknesses and faults): *entirely correct and assured, very strict but fair, superior.*

IV. Training record, courses, specialist training: *infantryman, was in the war* [. . .]

V. Degree and training skills:

    1. through service in the old army, the Reichswehr or Police *1933 State [Land] Police, Kassel.*

    2. in ss service: *good (leader of the political stand-by unit, Saxony)*

    3. in athletics: *sa bronze sport badge, silver Reich sport badge*

    4. in teaching: *easy to understand and confident*

VI.Suitability:

    1. *for promotion to ss Standartenführer*

    2. for what official position: *commandant of the Buchenwald concentration camp* [. . .]

Comment by the superior office:

Resolute and circumspect, Koch has assisted me in reconstruction of the Sachsenhausen concentration camp. Indefatigable, he set the camp up in barely 4 months. Since 7 July 1937 he has been working on the establishment of the Buchenwald concentration camp: his energetic action has made it possible to accommodate 1,000 inmates in the new camp after barely 4 weeks' construction time. His achievements are above average.[68]

167. Commandant's Order no. 3 for the Buchenwald concentration camp, issued by Karl Koch on 3 August 1937[69]

[. . .]

(3) Playing the radio is forbidden during service hours.

(4) I forbid the wearing of combined uniform (black-gray).

With double epaulettes, whether jacket or coat, a gray cap is worn in every case [. . .].

(7) The most meticulous cleanliness is to be observed in the camp. Refuse is to be thrown into the containers yet to be put in place by the Administration in order to prevent rats, mice, etc. being attracted by food remains. Other waste, collected for the Four-Year Plan, will likewise be collected in the containers yet to be put in place. The Administration will supply suitable containers.

(8) The duty leader is to be present at every roll call or work assignment for the inmates.

(9) I have punished ss *Scharführer* Gotthold Michael with a simple admonition because he settled service matters directly with the

Effects Administrator of the Sachsenhausen concentration camp, by-passing official channels.

I am punishing SS *Rottenführer* Kurt Kespohl, 26./VII/SS-TV "Thüringen" with 3 times ½ hour practice drill/pack drill because on 29.7.37, while the responsible sentry, he had been reading a book. If the offense is repeated application will be made for his expulsion [. . .]

(12) Attention is drawn to the fact that only the latrines are to be used. Contravention will be punished.

168. Commandant's Order no. 8 for the Buchenwald concentration camp, issued by Karl Koch on 30 August 1937[70]

[. . .]

(3) I have reason to point out that all SS members are forbidden to touch an inmate, or to drill him without authorization. Punishments are imposed only by me personally. Offenses by individuals will not be covered up by me! Also, I can see no reason why prisoners reporting for work or for leaving work are, without any reason, shouted at using swear words. We wish to do our duty strictly but decently, without on the other hand being soft. Hard—fair—if need be annihilating, that is our motto [. . .]

(6) I do not wish to see another SS member, whether on duty or off duty, burying his hands in his trouser pockets. If it is cold, there are gloves for that—but for the time being it is summer.

The inmates, in particular, are to be shown an especially military behavior. The clothes in the guard units should be more uniform, this leaves a lot to be desired: either everyone without collar or else no one. There are to be no SS men on duty without cap and with sleeves rolled up.

169. Report on events in the Buchenwald camp after the November 1938 pogrom, from the indictment of SS investigator Konrad Morgen against Karl Koch, 1944[71]

The major part of the Jews entered the Buchenwald camp with their valuables. Under the strict camp rules an inmate has all his property taken from him. The valuables are to be handed over in the presence of witnesses and to be kept in containers. The inmate has to confirm the valuables surrendered by him on an index card. This regulation was disregarded. The Jews were made to pass along long tables. There they had to throw their valuables into open crates placed there. [. . .] Thus the effects room no longer acquired estimable moneys and valuables, of the whereabouts of which nothing is known. On the subsequent release of Jewish émigrés, World War participants, men married to Aryan women and persons of importance to the economy, these had to sign the following printed declaration:

> Declaration
>
> I hereby declare that I have not surrendered any money, any valuables or any effects in the concentration camp Buchenwald and that nothing of the kind was taken from me. Consequently I have no claims against the Buchenwald concentration camp.

Given the political situation at the time it is understandable that the released Jews raised no objections to this. [. . .]

In addition to the hard physical punishments ss *Standartenführer* Koch was also very fond of operating with fines. The occasions for these were mostly the alleged malicious destruction of some camp object, windowpanes, furniture, lamps, blankets, etc. [. . .]

It happened on various occasions that well-off inmates, who were in the concentration camp for only a short time, offered substantial donations for their release.

170. Submission by Fritz Arnold, a former inmate of the Esterwegen camp to the examining judge at the State [*Land*] Court Oldenburg, dated 18 October 1947[72]

ss *Standartenführer* Loritz assumed control of the camp in mid-July 1934. The man came from Dachau and he did it proud. A beast in human shape, one cannot imagine anything worse. He scarcely dealt with the prisoners in person, but his orders were all the worse. Immediately after his arrival various kinds of instructions were posted in the individual huts; every other word in them was shooting, hanging, etc. The brutality of the guards got worse with each day, the Jews were thrown into the bunkers and there tortured in the most hideous manner, the machine guns rattled from the watchtowers and the bullwhip descended mercilessly on the backs of the prisoners sentenced to flogging. This was how that sadist raved day after day and the burial place by the canal not far from Esterwegen will surely provide a powerful testimony of what was going on in the "hell of Esterwegen" at that time.

171. Internal assessment of ss *Oberführer* Taus by Theodor Eicke in a letter to the Chief of ss Personnel, dated 14 June 1938[73]

ss *Oberführer* Taus, hitherto staff leader under ss *Gruppenführer* Mazuw, was transferred, by order of the Reich Leader ss, first to the Dachau concentration camp, subsequently to the Buchenwald concentration camp, to familiarize himself with camp service.

In the Dachau concentration camp Taus was a total failure. He was thereupon assigned to ss *Standartenführer* Koch, Buchenwald concentration camp. It is now beyond any doubt that Taus has neither the disposition nor the ability to be used as a responsible leader in a concentration camp. [. . .] The creative organizational talent that should be absolutely demanded of a camp commandant is totally lacking in Taus. ss *Oberführer* Taus is incapable of starting up the huge machinery of a prisoner camp on his own; he cannot command and makes his decisions dependent on the opinion of his subordinates. He talks more than he acts. His intervention gives rise to uncertainty and is apt to bring on every kind of danger. Taus lets himself be carried by the flow and does not have the energy to carry out his orders ruthlessly.

In a concentration camp only the best ss leaders can be used today. Service is so rich in responsibility and so dangerous that only individuals truly guided by duty, who entirely set their personality aside and do not know leisure time, can bear the weight of that responsibility. Unless the responsible leader in a concentration camp presents an inspiring example and establishes his authority, the concentration camp very soon develops into a dangerous powder keg which the insidiousness of the criminals attempts to set off almost every day.

3.3. Rank-and-File Guards

Rank-and-file ss men played a major part in the everyday lives of prisoners. Inside the camps, the men serving as *Blockführer* were the masters over up to five prisoner huts. Outside the camps, regular ss sentries patrolled the perimeter and prisoner work details. Relatively little has been written about these rank-and-file guards; sources remain scarce and difficult to locate. Some material is available for Sachsenhausen ss guard units, however, and some of these observations can be applied to the camps more generally. In Sachsenhausen, the majority of ss commandant staff NCOs were in their twenties and came from the lower-middle class. Highly ambitious, most of them had worked themselves up through the ranks after they had initially trained as ordinary sentries in the guard troop. Many had already served in the Nazi movement previously, where they had been exposed to Nazi ideology. Ideology and propaganda also featured prominently after they joined the Camp ss and reinforced in them the belief that the enemy must be destroyed. Many young and relatively uneducated guards happily seized the opportunity to bully older prisoners who were, as was the case with many Jews, often from better-off backgrounds.[74]

Still, the rank-and-file men of the Camp ss were not simply stupid, lazy, and corrupt, as Benedikt Kautsky, a survivor of Dachau, Buchenwald, and Auschwitz, wrote in 1946 (183).[75] Also, there were many ways to the camps, especially the early camps. The ss man Hans Steinbrenner, for example, who became notorious for his crimes in Dachau (see chapter 1), later claimed that he had arrived in the camp in spring of 1933 (as one of the first ss guards) without being told in advance where he would be taken (172).[76] Still, it is clear that later on, many men actively volunteered for service in the Camp ss. New recruits for the guard troop often joined at a very young age (181). If one can trust a 1935 exile newspaper interview with Hans Bächle, an ex-ss guard from the Berlin Columbia-Haus camp, many rank-and-file ss men were somewhat disillusioned about their duties in the camps (177).

Running the Camps

In the mid-1930s a shift occurred among the rank-and-file ss guards as the Camp ss became more militarized in the new Death's Head Units; this is already reflected in a Sachsenburg prisoner's account from 1936 (179). Some orders for the Sachsenburg guard units offer a glimpse into the life of the rank and file. Service in the Camp ss was strict (174), with a severe daily regime that included early-morning exercises (175). ss officers admonished guards to watch dangerous prisoners at all times (176). Overall, guard duty became more regularized as Camp ss leaders applied Eicke's regulations, but there always remained a gulf between these rules and the harsh reality in the camps. As the postwar trial against Richard Bugdalle, a Sachsenhausen ss man, illustrates, the abuse of prisoners by individual guards continued unabated (182). Brutality, torture, and worse were common among rank-and-file guards, as was well known even outside Germany.

DOCUMENTS

172. Interrogation of the former ss *Untersturmführer* Hans Steinbrenner by the State Police Upper Bavaria, dated 19 August 1948[77]

On 16.2.1933 I voluntarily and from inner conviction joined the General ss and the Party. After its seizure of power in March 1933 I served with the ss *Motorsturm* LL/1. Together with other comrades I was drawn upon to reinforce the Munich Protection Police. On 22.3.1933 I was on my way to Ettstrasse to do my service there. On my way there I was stopped in Promenadestrasse and asked to step into a bus already standing there. I explained to Erpsenmüller [an ss official] that I had to go to Ettstrasse, whereupon he replied that, on orders of the *Standartenführer*, all ss men had to board the bus. [. . .] This bus took us to the Schwabing brewery. We did not know at the time what was going on. In that brewery we were joined by several more ss men, in addition weapons and ammunition were handed out. In the bus, but still at the brewery, someone asked who knew the way to the Dachau munitions factory. Presently we drove to Dachau. Having arrived there, our *Standartenführer* Freiherr von Malzen von Bonekau[78] walked through the gate of the munitions factory. In front of that gate stood a sentry of the State [*Land*] Police. When our *Standartenführer* returned he led us into the building that was surrounded by barbed wire.

There he addressed us. The sense of what he said was as follows: "On behalf of the Führer or the Reich Leader SS Himmler we have been ordered here to guard the greatest enemies of the state and criminals. Attempts to escape were to be prevented by our firearms. I hope that no one escapes, even if they have to be shot dead, because the more of these pigs die the better it will be for Germany."

173. From the memoirs of Rudolf Höß about his time in the mid-1930s as a Block and Rapport Leader in the Dachau concentration camp, written 1947[79]

I came to Dachau [in 1934], once more became a recruit with all the joys and woes, and myself became an instructor. The soldiers' life captivated me. But during lessons, during instruction, I heard about the "enemies of the state," of the inmates beyond the wire, about the use of our weapons and the danger of the "enemies of the state," as Eicke, the Inspector of Concentration Camps, called them. I saw the inmates at work, being marched out and marched in. And I heard about them from comrades who had been serving in the camp since 1933. I clearly remember the first flogging that I saw. On Eicke's instruction at least one company of the force had to be present at the execution of this physical punishment. Two inmates who had stolen cigarettes in the canteen had been sentenced to 25 lashes each. The troops had assembled in an open square, with rifles. In the center of it stood the flogging buck. The two inmates were brought along by block leaders. The commandant appeared. Reports were made by the Protective Custody Camp Leader and the senior company commander. The Rapport Leader read out the punishment verdict and the first inmate, a small stocky work-shirker, was made to lie across the buck. Two men from the force held down his head and hands, while two block leaders executed the punishment, alternating blows. The inmate made no sound. Unlike the other, a strong, broad political prisoner. At the very first blow he screamed wildly and tried to tear himself away. He continued screaming to the last blow, even though the commandant repeatedly called on him to be quiet. I was in the front line and was thus compelled to watch the whole proceedings. I say "compelled" because, had I been in a line further back, I would not have watched it. Hot and cold shudders were running down my back

Running the Camps

when the screaming started. Yes, the whole proceedings, from the very start, made me shudder.

174. Special guard troop order of the commander of the guard troop of the Sachsenburg concentration camp, dated 6 December 1934[80]

1. Over the next few days the camp will receive a considerable intake of detainees who have only now been detained for Communist activities. Added to this is the fact that the camp regulations for the detainees have had to be considerably tightened up. In consequence there is the danger that the detainees may try to escape, gang up together, etc.

2. For this reason it has to be pointed out to all men immediately that they must keep their eyes on every detainee and that the existing regulations must absolutely be strictly observed. In particular, sentries and escorts are to be especially warned by the leader of the camp service and by every guard on duty that they must not let any of the detainees handed over to them or to their guard area out of their sight even for a moment.

It is to be pointed out to every [ss] man that the slightest infringement of the regulation will be punished by arrest, in some cases by dismissal.

175. Order no. 13 of the ss Death's Head *Sturmbann* Sachsen (at Sachsenburg camp), dated 17 January 1936[81]

[. . .]

2. Early-morning exercise:

The *Hundertschaften* [ss units of around one hundred men] must regularly perform the early-morning sport set out in the Special *Sturmbann* Order of 3.1.36. Early morning sport serves the loosening of the body as well as its hardening. It is therefore not admissible that a Staff *Scharführer* of the *Hundertschaften* decides not to hold early-morning sport because it is too cold. Early morning sport is canceled only in extremely unfavorable weather, i.e. during heavy snowfall, rain or unusually severe cold.

I have had occasion to notice that during early-morning sport the rear of the column slips into the bushes and there awaits the return of the others in order to close up with them again. In future a platoon commander will form the head of the column and the Staff *Scharführer* will form the end. Only the guard and standby *Hundertschaft* are exempt from early-morning sport for the duration of their period on duty.

176. Special order of the ss Death's Head *Sturmbann* Sachsen (at Sachsenburg camp), dated 12 March 1936[82]

Re: Detainees

1. I have time and again pointed out in my orders that detainees are to be left in the ss quarters as little as possible without supervision. Recently, however, the practice has arisen of detainees again, for hours on end, being left hanging around without supervision in the rooms of the platoon commanders, in the offices, or in the area of the *Hundertschaften*, without any control of what the detainee is actually doing.

Thus it could happen that a detainee, while cleaning an office, is well informed on the pay rates of the men and the same detainee would surely also have had opportunity to read other official papers. This is an irresponsible action both on the part of the *Hundertschaft* leaders and the Staff *Scharführers*, the sub-leaders and every individual man. Everyone should be aware of the damage that a detainee could cause by going abroad with the knowledge thus gained of the camp, of the troops and of the camp's operation, if he there uses his knowledge against us in the émigré press or even, if it comes to it, uses it against the security of the camp.

I am today, for the last time, issuing orders about the activity of detainees within the ss barracks, at the same time pointing out that, in the event of the least failure to obey my order I shall, once and for all, remove all detainees with service duties in the ss barracks, with all these to be done by the troops themselves so that every leader, sub-leader or rank-and-file man will, as in every other barracks, have to serve himself, the troop carrying out all the rough work such as barracks cleaning, window cleaning, toilet cleaning and such like itself. It is therefore in the greatest interest of every man to restrict the presence of the detainees to a minimum and so to prevent [them from] being better informed about the barracks than some ss men.

2. I expect from the *Hundertschaft* leaders that they will take this order as an opportunity to thoroughly point out to their men the dangers that might arise from unsupervised detainees. The *Hundertschaft* leader always bears the responsibility for all rooms assigned to his

Hundertschaft as dayrooms, dormitories, storerooms, offices, etc. It is not enough for him to enter these rooms only every few months for a locker inspection. Only more frequent checks can bring about the changes outlined in Paragraph 1.

177. *Arbeiter-Illustrierte Zeitung*: **Article with the report of a former warder of the Columbia-Haus concentration camp, dated 23 May 1935**[83]

Reports about the Berlin "Columbiahaus" have been repeatedly published, but never before has a report like the one below been published. So far the reports about the special prison of the Gestapo came from its victims, from prisoners tortured in the "Columbiahaus." Here, for the first time we hear one from the other side, from an ss man of the guard troop in the "Tempelhof hell."

It is the *Sturm-Mann* Hans Bächle,[84] an "old fighter," a "well-tested concentration camp guard." From August 1934 to April 1935 he served in the "Columbiahaus," first in the administration, then in the external service and finally in the internal service.

On 20 April 1935 he let the protective custody prisoners Hausmann and Windig, adjutants of the former Silesian *Gauleiter* and *Oberpräsident* Helmuth Brückner,[85] out of their cell and took them "for work" into the basement. The two men had been delivered along with Brückner. Brückner had been arrested because he had wanted to set up an opposition within the NSDAP and was said to have been a follower of Röhm [. . .]. They were old friends of Bächle and persuaded him to free them. They waited in the basement until the coast was clear, then they made their escape. Bächle sat down at the wheel of a car in his black uniform and took the fugitives to Silesia. No one thought of stopping a car with an ss man from the "Columbiahaus" at the wheel, a Gestapo ss man. [. . .] The border patrol detained the three for a while. Then they were allowed to drive to Prague. For a few days they drifted about Prague. Then they continued their journey to Switzerland and Luxembourg. Here is the report of our source who saw Bächle after his arrival in Prague and spoke to him.

Sturm-Mann Hans Bächle, tall, elongated face dominated by an uncontrolled mouth, thick lips and a long chin, shy eyes, broad forehead.

He makes curt replies, often evades. "I continue to be a Nazi," he says, but it does not sound very convincing . . . But was he ever a convinced

Nazi? He claims that he was [. . .]. Seeing him sitting before you, a little sleepy, a little shy . . . it hardly seems credible at the first moment that he had been one of the black guards, the terror of the helpless protective custody prisoners. But this is just it: they are the terror of helpless prisoners. They are heroes for only so long as they are facing unarmed enemies. Strip them of their uniform and they shrink like little fairground pigs when the air escaped from them. Did he have a few human lives on his conscience? He says no. Had he taken part in torture? He says no. Had he been present when prisoners were beaten? He says no. Answering a similar question he says that prisoners were beaten in the "Columbiahaus." That this was customary in the "Columbiahaus." Why were they beaten? "If they behave badly the prisoners are beaten with a riding crop, mostly 15 to 20 lashes, often more" [. . .].

"Morale among the comrades is not very good. Pay is not paid punctually and altogether they are not treated as a force should be treated. Only Hitler's *Leibstandarte* [bodyguard], they are pampered. Naturally. Anyway, in a year's time it will only be Reichswehr [army] people who are in command. That is what all comrades are already saying. Then it will all be over with the ss."

178. Order no. 255 for the ss Death's Head *Sturmbann* Sachsen and the Sachsenburg concentration camp, dated 18 December 1935[86]

Thursday, 19.12.35 at 20:00 this year's Christmas festivity will be held in the dining hall. All members of the Sturmbann have to take part, with the exception of the men on guard duty; for these the festivity takes place on Friday evening. The official on guard duty, however, has to grant leave to the men individually at the beginning of the festivity, so that those concerned can collect their gifts. Dress code for the evening: black cloth suit, long trousers, shaft boots, no cap. Decoration of the hall will be carried out by *Unterscharführer* Kunze.

179. Report of the former Sachsenburg inmate Alfred Richter on the Camp ss, published May 1936[87]

Let us look at the transformations of the ss Special Squad Saxony, which grew out of the Saxon Schutzstaffeln. Especially "well-tried" men were brought in from all over Saxony [. . .].

The "Special Squad Saxony" occupied barracks on the troops'

exercise ground Heller near Dresden and was hurriedly drilled in military fashion by the former Reichswehr[88] sergeant Max Simon. The men had to commit themselves for two years and they were told that they would later be taken over by the police or the judiciary. They would also be able to choose the army. For a few months they were in the Hohenstein protective custody camp as guard personnel, then, in August 1934, they arrived at Sachsenburg.

There they were to take over the concentration camp. Eight days before the official hand-over the then-*Hauptscharführer* Kurtz arrived with a few corporals' units to prepare for the entry of the troops. Even then the contrast to the SA was conspicuous: the SS were smarter fellows, more disciplined and better armed. The SA called its SS comrades "gang of murderers" and—because of the color of the uniform—"damned blacks." The guard troop leader Simon then (on 25 August 1934) told the assembled inmates that the "good times" were now over; he would grind those swine into the dust all right. Ingenious sadists were now arriving. The name "SS Special Squad Saxony" was dropped after a while. Until about March 1935 the SS guard troop was engaged in its development and reinforcement. A barracks was equipped—money no object. After all, prisoners are cheap labor; besides, economies were being made with their food and their clothes. The joiner's shop, the shoemaker's, tailor's, locksmith's, blacksmith's and bookbinding shops were working almost exclusively for the SS. In the business building, next to the garage, a stabling block for horses was created, where 12 riding horses were later kept for the "leaders." [. . .] The armory shop was also enlarged. Service was being made harsher, it was more exhausting and also lasted longer: it smelled more and more of "military."

The gulf between the prisoners and the SS contingent was to be deepened [. . .]. Numerous orders proved that the SS wanted to maintain its attitude of "matter-of-fact superiority" toward the prisoners by deterrent measures. Displayed in all SS quarters was the motto: "SS—your honor is loyalty." The technical equipment of the *Stürme* was excellent. For official business with outside, use was made of telex and police radio. The SS men were trained, first of all, in Pistol 08, Rifle 98 (new model), submachine gun, hand grenade and light machine gun [. . .].

At the beginning of 1935 came unofficial controls by the Reichs-wehr. This made it clear that the function of the guard troop had changed. While until then it had been the ambition of the leaders to train a Gestapo force, this changed with the introduction of general compulsory military service [in 1935]. The designation "ss Guard troop Saxony" was abbreviated to "Guard troop Saxony." Gray uniforms, modeled on the army cut, were introduced, the steel helmets were painted gray.

180. *Neuer Vorwärts*: Article by a former political prisoner of the Lichtenburg concentration camp, dated 14 February 1937[89]

The supposed task of the guard contingents in the concentration camps is to "educate" the detained political opponents and "school" them in the Hitler spirit. One would have thought that they were interested in demonstrating to the prisoners that the National Socialists were morally superior to the Marxists, to the so-called subhumans. I had to live nearly a year in close proximity with 600 ss men; I know them drunk and sober, I know their thinking and actions, I have seen them stealing and cheating, torturing and killing, and I know that they do not care even for an appearance of a model way of life, or an exemplary attitude. It is not prejudice that makes me judge the ss so harshly, but my close personal contact with them, a contact to which I, as an arrest trusty, was compelled in a particular way. [. . .]

A particular characteristic of the guard contingents was their intellectual inferiority and dullness. Many ss leaders and sub-leaders could barely write, let alone do sums or even draft a report. On one occasion the arrest duty officer Ludwig intended to make a penal report on the arrest inmate Fischbock. I was to write the report, but did not do so. When I entered the duty office in the early morning I saw Ludwig with a number of scribbled pieces of paper, "working" on his report. [. . .]

A bad role in the camp was played by the drunkenness of the ss men. Not infrequently their binges — also called "comradeship evenings" — went on until daybreak. Then the guards — especially the two company leaders Ludwig and Hinkelmann — performed their tasks in a drunken state. Such days were difficult for all of us. The reeling men would then call someone a "great rascal," fetched him from his cell and mercilessly chased him back and forth a roughly 50 m long passage in the arrest anteroom until the bullied man collapsed. [. . .]

The conditions here described may testify to the fact that the ss men did not greatly care about their so-called ideals. But they also said quite openly that they were fed up to the back teeth with the "whole mess." During the six months that I worked in the "arrest"[90] I had a better opportunity than most to be with many ss men, to talk to them and to study them [. . .]. I repeatedly heard the complaint that the ss guard troop were "prisoners with rifles." Also, the concentration camp was often called "corruption camp Lichtenburg." [. . .]

Sadism, brutality, corruption, stupidity, emptiness within to the point of being tired of life — that is what the ss in the Lichtenburg camp is like, and it is probably similar throughout the whole Reich.

181. ss memorandum regarding recruitment to the ss Death's Head Units (issued in July 1937)[91]

When are volunteers enlisted in the Death's Head Units?

Anytime until further notice. Subsequently each year in late spring (end April) and autumn (end October). Names can be put down any time.

Who can be enlisted?

1. Applicants who

(a) have German nationality,

(b) can provide evidence of their Aryan origin back to 1800,

(c) are morally, mentally, physically and racially impeccable, ideologically stand on the basis of National Socialism and, alongside their other suitability, have a taste and love for ss service,

(d) have not been sentenced for offenses or crimes, regardless of whether or not the punishment has been served (with the exception of offenses committed in the struggle for the Movement),

(e) are unmarried.

In addition the conditions listed below must be met:

minimum height: naked 172 cm
minimum age: completed 16th year
maximum age: completed 22nd year [. . .]

How long does the applicant have to commit himself for? 4 years!

This includes a probation period of 3 months, during which the applicant, if unsuitable, may at any time be released without notice and without reasons being given [. . .].

Where does one apply?

(a) To the Leader of Death's Head Units and Concentration Camps, Berlin NW 7, Friedrichstraße 129, Block F,
(b) to the Death's Head Units:
   1. SS-TV "Oberbayern," Dachau near Munich,
   2. SS-TV "Brandenburg," Oranienburg near Berlin,
   3. SS-TV "Thüringen," Ettersberg, post Weimar,
(c) to the nearest *Standarte* of the General SS [. . .]

What emoluments do members of the SS Death's Head Units receive?

(a) free lodging, clothing, equipment and military board,
(b) the following pay rates (inclusive of food charges) per month:
   SS Mann (in the first year) RM 65.-
   SS Mann (in the second year) RM 77.-
   SS *Sturmmann* RM 95.-
   SS *Rottenführer* RM 105.-
   SS *Unterscharführer* RM 118.70
   SS *Scharführer* RM 158.53
   SS *Oberscharführer* 181.84
   SS *Hauptscharführer* 186.50

182. Judicial interrogation of the former SS *Blockführer* Richard Bugdalle, dated 19 May 1958[92]

At the beginning of 1933 after the Seizure of Power I joined the Waffen-SS [*sic*]. Just then I was without a job. In the SS I was trained in infantry service. In 1937 I was already an *Unterscharführer* and was assigned to the Sachsenhausen concentration camp. The reason was that after recovering from a head influenza I was no longer suitable for sub-leader service with the troop. I was too excitable and snapped too easily at the SS men under my command. But I never struck any subordinate, although on one occasion I came close to it—that was during drill service. I no longer know any further details. For that reason I was several times criticized by my superiors. [. . .] The fact is that I was asked by my company commander if I wanted to apply for service in a concentration camp—to which I said yes. At that time I had no idea whatsoever of my official duties. I came to Sachsenhausen as a block leader, that was in 1937. I can no longer give a more accurate time. To the objection that this assertion is not credible, I declare that it could have been in the middle of 1937. Rapport leader Campe instructed me in my tasks as block leader. Campe must have been an *Oberscharführer*. In particular I was explained the meaning of the various colored badges that the prisoners had to wear. I had to ensure a strict observance of existing camp regulations. Details of these regulations I no longer know today.

183. Benedikt Kautsky's portrait of ss men in the prewar concentration camps, 1946[93]

Lazy and stupid, cruel and cowardly, undisciplined and corrupt—these are the main characteristics from which the ss leadership has to fabricate the average ss man. The standard product, achieved with the help of psychological and material methods of influencing, served its purpose completely. Even if laziness, indiscipline and corruption did not ensure a frictionless functioning of the apparatus, this did not matter. [. . .] If frictions arose, these were mostly settled at the expense of the inmate. [. . .] But in spite of everything—the type of the prewar ss man offered certain chances to the inmate. The psychological treatment from above was countered by the inmate by his psychological treatment from below. If he remained upright without being cheeky, if he proved himself equal to physical stress without giving the impression of an intellectual, if he proved that he knew the law of the camp, then he had a hope of finding some modus vivendi with the ss, especially in the smaller camps, where inmates and ss knew one another. As a farmer to his domestic animal that he has known a long time, so the ss man only relatively rarely went to the extreme.

Things changed during the final prewar years, when the great "actions" brought masses of new inmates into the camp, especially when maltreatment was linked to opportunities for enriching oneself—as, for instance, during the Rath action in November 1938[94]—or when cruelty was ordered from above.

FOUR

Life and Death in the Camps

Throughout the 1930s a range of daily rituals and everyday patterns emerged in the camps. Yet, the Camp ss were unable and unwilling to control every single aspect of prisoner life. Just as in the early camps, they delegated various supervisory tasks to prisoners (sometimes called Kapos), including cleaning the prisoners' quarters and maintaining discipline inside the prisoner huts. Some of the prisoner functionaries held considerable power over fellow inmates. For example, they helped to assign prisoners to work details and distributed food and other resources. This practice resulted in a hierarchy of prisoners in which some had considerably more power and influence than others.[1] All of this, inevitably, had a profound impact on prisoner relations, discussed in detail in the next chapter.

For the ss the camps were tough institutions where prisoners would be punished and, if possible, "reeducated" through strict discipline and hard labor.[2] Everyday life followed a highly regimented schedule that borrowed from timetables common in German prisons and the army.[3] As in the early camps, there were many other military influences on life in the camps, as the "political soldiers" of the ss applied perverted notions of discipline to terrorize and humiliate inmates.[4] Meanwhile, labor was now compulsory for all inmates. Sick and elderly inmates, in particular, often could not cope with the pace of work and the long hours, especially during the freezing winter months. But there was no letup: punishments for "shirking" work were frequent and severe.

Following the systematization of the camp system under ss control, living conditions in the individual concentration camps began to resemble each other more closely—in contrast to the sharp variations inside the early camps. Prisoners who were transferred from one ss camp to another found the same basic structures in place. Inmates were normally housed in blocks, often consisting of wooden huts, supervised by the senior block prisoner, who was responsible to an ss block leader. Inside the huts, prisoners slept on bunks that had to be kept spick-and-span lest they risk blows from ss guards and Kapos. Reflecting the ss obsession with cleanliness, seen as an important aspect of the prisoners' purported reeducation, prisoners had to spend a great deal of their spare time cleaning their huts.[5]

From the mid-1930s the ss began to introduce prisoner uniforms to replace the rags which many prisoners had had to wear in the early camps. There were washing facilities in most huts, yet often these were very basic and completely inadequate. Hygienic conditions were often poor, particularly in camps set in old buildings such as Lichtenburg and the Berlin Columbia-Haus (190 and 192). In most camps there were no lavatories, just latrines. Illness and disease were widespread, though conditions were not yet lethal. Death rates in the prewar camps were relatively low, at least compared to the war years. However, mortality rates started to rise in the final years before the outbreak of war.

As the camp system expanded in the late 1930s, with more and more prisoners arriving in the camps, living conditions deteriorated further. The camps were already filled to capacity following the raids against social outsiders in the spring and summer of 1938, when many thousands of Jewish prisoners arrived in Dachau, Buchenwald, and Sachsenhausen in the wake of the November pogrom. In Buchenwald a special new compound was built, consisting of five primitive huts without heating and running water. This "little camp" for the Jews arrested in the pogrom's aftermath was separated from the main camp by barbed wire. There were only two latrines for several thousand prisoners, resulting in terrible hygienic conditions.[6] In fact, in the aftermath of the 1938 pogrom, more prisoners died in the camps than ever before. In October 1938 the Dachau camp authorities recorded 8 deaths. In November 1938 53 deaths were registered, and in December, 90; the vast majority of the dead were Jews.[7] Meanwhile, death rates were also on the rise in camps with few Jewish prisoners. Deaths were particularly frequent in the new Mauthausen camp. Here at least 114 prisoners died in the first six months of 1939 amid dreadful work in the camp's notorious quarries; this was a staggering number, as there were on average only about 1,300 inmates in Mauthausen at that time.[8] As the war approached, then, the camp system changed and took on a more lethal character.

Life and Death in the Camps

4.1. Daily Rituals and General Conditions

While daily rituals had often differed in the early camps, there emerged over the course of the 1930s a more common pattern across the ss camp system.[9] Nonetheless, some unmistakable traditions had originated in the early camps. Admission was still the first ritual all prisoners had to undergo upon arrival. Paul Martin Neurath, a political prisoner of Dachau and Buchenwald after the annexation of Austria, later described the first day in the camp in a sociological study in which he tried to give an objective description of life in the camp (195). Neurath also identified some behavioral patterns that were typical of camp life. For example, prisoners soon began to use a distinct language, a practice also common in other total institutions such as the army or prisons.[10] Other prisoners, by comparison, gave more personal descriptions of their first days in the camp (188), etched into the memories of almost all survivors. Many new arrivals had already gone through other stations of the Nazi terror system: arrest and police interrogation, detention in a police prison, and then transport to the camp. They were frequently in poor physical condition, as they had often not received sufficient food during their prior imprisonment. Transports to the camps were usually by train or by trucks and accompanied by policemen whose behavior seemed harmless to prisoners compared to what followed once they had arrived inside the ss camps.

Upon arrival, prisoners were met by ss guards, driven on by beatings and verbal abuse. Prisoners had to fall in like soldiers and then listen to a "welcoming" speech by a Camp ss leader, who lectured them that they were now concentration camp prisoners with no rights whatsoever. Often such speeches included death threats (187).[11] Prisoners were then escorted to the "political section," where Gestapo officers interrogated them and created a prisoner file. Then they were stripped of their clothes and had to hand over their personal effects. Finally, they were given a prisoner number and uniform. Almost immediately afterward, guards often made prisoners exercise for hours, picking out individual prisoners for particularly severe abuse (187).[12]

At the end of their first day prisoners were led to their huts to meet fellow inmates. New arrivals often only received their first food ration at night. When their first day in the camp ended, prisoners were completely exhausted and in shock. These feelings were exacerbated by the fear of further abuses and the uncertainty of when (and if) they would be released.

A typical day in the camps started very early, sometimes as early as 5 a.m. or even earlier in the summer, and left prisoners with little spare time. After reveille, prisoners always had to rush to get ready. Washing was a difficult endeavor, as there were not enough facilities, and making the beds was obsessively supervised by Kapos; the SS also forced inmates to keep their belongings, such as uniforms, shoes, and crockery, neat and tidy. Inmates then had coffee, typically a disgusting mixture with little resemblance to real coffee. Roll call followed. Here prisoners had to stand at attention until all inmates had been accounted for by various SS officials. Sometimes roll calls, which happened even in heavy rain or extreme cold, took hours (187 and 195). After roll call, work started. Work shifts typically lasted until between 4 and 7 p.m., interrupted only by a brief break for food. Sunday was normally the only free day, although SS officials frequently forced prisoners to work as an additional punishment. Numerous prisoners died of exhaustion, especially toward the late 1930s when the SS began to exploit prisoner labor more systematically (198). After work there followed another roll call for the prisoners, who were by now completely exhausted. SS guards also executed punishments during evening roll call. After roll call, prisoners returned to their huts. Often, while they had been away at work, SS guards had inspected the huts and found imaginary "infractions." Prisoners who had just returned from work and roll call thus frequently had to clean up and make their beds once again. At Dachau, the day ended at around 9 p.m. with lights out. Prisoners were not allowed to leave their huts at night, and guards were instructed to shoot anyone who did so. Even nights did not bring relief. In winter, prisoners were often freezing because huts did not have sufficient heating. Moreover, SS guards regularly woke up prisoners at night, abusing them further.[13] All in all, then, there was never any real rest for the prisoners in the camps.

Life and Death in the Camps

Food was often insufficient and extremely repetitive (190 and 191). Prisoners who were fortunate enough to receive some small sums of money from their relatives outside could still improve their diet by buying extra rations at inflated prices at the camp canteen, ss-run kiosks that sold basic foodstuffs and everyday goods. Prisoners without money tried to swap other items for food or cigarettes. A flourishing barter trade emerged, and some prisoners also shared their extra rations with poor or weak inmates (200). Still, there were sharp socioeconomic differences among the prisoners (199).

If prisoners were sick or if they had been hurt during work they had access to the camp infirmary, at least in theory. Camp infirmaries were supervised by an ss doctor and poorly equipped, often lacking even basic medicines and food. Hygienic conditions across the camps were poor. In Buchenwald, for example, the defective water supply resulted in a typhoid epidemic in late 1938 and early 1939. Prisoners were ignored for weeks by the ss doctors, and countermeasures were taken too late, leaving twelve prisoners dead, according to official ss figures. But these deaths left the ss unimpressed, and hygienic standards did not improve. Before long, Buchenwald had to be placed under quarantine once more following a dysentery outbreak.[14]

With the increasing centralization of the concentration camps, the ss also began to formalize its delegation of tasks to prisoner functionaries. In 1937, for example, a Buchenwald ss officer wrote down the responsibilities of a "block elder," a senior prisoner appointed by the ss. The next chapter will look more closely at who these so-called Kapos were, though some of their powers are illustrated in the present chapter (194, 196, and 201).[15]

DOCUMENTS

184. Service timetable for Tuesday, 7 May 1935, in the Sachsenburg concentration camp[16]

Duty prisoner company leader: ss *Rottenführer* C.
Deputy [. . .]: ss *Unterscharführer* P.

Reveille: 5 o'clock
Coffee: 5:30

Roll call: 6:00
Start of work: 6:05
Breakfast: 8:30
Start of work: 9:00
End of work: 11:30
Lunch: 12:00
Work deployment and start: 13:30
End of work: 17:30
Roll call: 18:00
Lights out: 21:00

185. *Die Neue Weltbühne*: Report by the former Communist Reichstag deputy Hugo Gräf on conditions in the Sachsenburg concentration camp, dated 19 March 1936[17]

The hygienic installations are beyond any description. As three times the number of prisoners had to be accommodated, there are neither tables nor benches in the large prison hall on the fifth floor of the former factory building or in the other two auxiliary accommodation quarters for the prisoners. In consequence one cannot rest properly during the midday break or after conclusion of work. Instead the prisoners sit on the edges of the lower beds—there are three tiers of them—and in this extremely uncomfortable position they eat, tidy up their camp clothes, or write letters. On the pain of severe punishment it is forbidden to lie on the beds or use the beds before bedtime, shortly before nine o'clock in the evening. From eight o'clock in the evening until daybreak no window is to be opened. Of course the hall is filled with intolerable air, the emanations of the wet or sweaty working clothes make breathing a torture.

In the large prisoner hall only four toilets, without flushes, are available. Of course these are not nearly sufficient and many prisoners do not even have a chance to perform their needs in the time between the end of the day's work and the start of work on the following morning. Washing facilities? They are so scant and insufficient that many prisoners are often unable to wash or clean their teeth for a whole week. On Saturday afternoon all prisoners must go under the shower. Showering proceeds so quickly that individual prisoners often have not got enough time even to soap themselves.

Naturally, rigorous economies are applied to food. Fat, butter or margarine have not been available for months; in the evenings the prisoners receive bread and jam. The bread is supplied by a large bakery in Chemnitz: it is specially prepared for the prisoners and almost inedible. Four to five times a week there is a thin potato soup at midday, with entrails chopped into it, this is known as "Sour patches." Legumes, rice, noodles and vegetables were received by us only rarely. [. . .]

Prison clothes are only available for some of the prisoners: old police uniforms and worn drill clothes of the Reichswehr. Many prisoners have had to wear their own clothes for months; given the working methods in the camp these clothes are totally useless after a short time. [. . .]

Since the beginning of 1935 all the protective custody camps in Germany have been run on uniform directives. ss *Obergruppenführer* Eicke, formerly the commandant of the Dachau camp and known for a number of affairs, has been the commander of all protective custody camps. On 1 April 1935 Eicke introduced a camp and penal order valid for all concentration camps. Under the new regulations the protective custody prisoner has significantly fewer rights than a prisoner in a prison or penitentiary. He has no right to complain, he only has duties. The least infringement of duties is brutally punished. On 1 April punishment by flogging was officially introduced. In addition, the penal order envisions tying to the pillory, and, for certain offenses, even execution by shooting or hanging. In recent months the Sachsenburg camp has moreover been surrounded by an electrically charged wire fence.

186. *Internationales Ärztliches Bulletin*: Report of the former prisoner and physician Dr. Valentin on the care of the sick in concentration camps, dated May 1936[18]

Having just escaped the Third Reich I want to report in the *Internationales Ärztliches Bulletin* on what I experienced in 19 difficult months in 5 different Saxon protective custody hells. Naturally I can report only on fragments of my impressions and will, in this report, confine myself to the care of sick protective custody prisoners. [. . .]

The real sickness figures in German concentration camps are exceedingly high. Mental and physical suffering, [. . .] hard work and inadequate food eventually corrode even the most resistant organism. When, at Hohenstein Castle for instance, the camp doctor finally reappeared again after 3 weeks, there were often 200 or 300 prisoners who wished to see him (out of 1,500 prisoners). Among these prisoners was certainly not a single malingerer, but among the remaining 1,200 there were certainly some who would have urgently needed medical advice and help. They did not report because they knew that at least two-thirds of their comrades who, on a cold staircase, were awaiting the Sturmbann doctor would be driven back to their rooms by the SA medical orderly with a rubber truncheon. If a Jew actually reported sick, he could nearly always expect especially hard work or even the bunker.

The SA medical orderlies were brutal and mostly ignorant, absolutely untroubled by the most primitive medical knowledge. That was true also for some of the SA doctors, who frequently acted just as irresponsibly as the medical orderlies. Even the SA and SS leaders had no confidence in them: thus in Sachsenburg they preferred to be treated secretly by the Jewish prisoners Dr. Mannheim and later Dr. Serelmann rather than attending the consultation hour of the notorious SS *Sturmführer* Dr. Gebhard. [. . .] Most calls in the sick bay were after pack drill, which was very frequent in Hohenstein—for Jews at least once a week. The peak of brutality we experienced was after a 12-hour penal sport period on 30 April 1934: 150 comrades, some of them old men and war invalids, were left lying unconscious on the so-called grinding stone. Faced with such mass misery the SA medical orderlies saw no way of helping. Thus those who had collapsed remained lying for hours on end on the square, under a scorching sun, trampled by the prisoners who were continuing their drill. Instead of the medical orderlies the SA leaders carried out resuscitation attempts with the aid of their "dagger of honor" and cold water. [. . .]

Treatment methods were the most primitive imaginable. Whether or not it was appropriate, each patient had, first of all, to sweat. The following incident shows the result of this. A definite case of meningitis was brought to Hohenstein. Again and again he was given a compress. His fever continued to rise. When he was delirious he was eventually taken to the hospital in Pirna, where he later died. Food for the sick in Hohenstein was even worse than generally; there was no bed linen.

Life and Death in the Camps

Urine bottles passed from bed to bed without being cleaned or rinsed for months. Altogether dirt in the sick bay was mountain-high. Isolation of infectious diseases was obviously impossible. As a result colds and barber's itch, etc., spread widely, although this could have been avoided.

"Patient care" in the concentration camps is an important part of the protective custody disgrace in the Third Reich. To fight against it is one of the *tasks of all freedom-loving doctors throughout the world!*

187. Sopade report on the arrival of prisoners at the Esterwegen concentration camp near Papenburg, dated December 1936[19]

Treatment of recently admitted prisoners in Papenburg is inhuman. Even the transportation to the concentration camp in open trucks with excessive security from heavily armed ss in storm and rain is a heavy stress for bodies weakened by hunger and maltreatment. The new arrivals are received with kicks, blows with rifle butts and foul language. Until the reception formalities are completed, over which a lot of time is taken, the new arrivals have to stand for hours in wind and bad weather, only scantily clad. After hours of waiting, during which time no one was allowed to move away, came reception of uniforms. With the prevailing cold—the author of this report was admitted in February—the changing of clothes was not fast enough for the guards and there was more pushing and shoving. Then came a drill in heavy Dutch wooden clogs. This footwear was unfamiliar to all and even old army veterans were scarcely able correctly to implement the orders of the young louts. After an hour's drill the new arrivals were at last allowed to go to their huts and had to "make beds." Needless to say, these were not made well enough for the camp commandant and the job had to be done again and again. Only then did they receive their first food, toward 7 o'clock in the evening.

188. Report of a prisoner on his arrival at the Dachau concentration camp, published in 1936[20]

As I jumped out of the car three ss men pounced on me with the words "Filthy Jewish pig" and started beating me. When I explained to them that I was not a Jew at all, they replied that I was not to speak in the camp and went on beating me. The final result was that I had blue and black eyes and a terrible pain in my head. That same day every one of the 68 men was collected singly and given the so-called "Schlageter celebration,"[21] as the prisoners called it. This Schlageter celebration consisted of every man receiving 25–40 blows with a bullwhip on his bare buttocks. It happened very often that the ss men deliberately made a mistake with the counting and that there were 50 or 60 blows.

189. Report by a former prisoner on the daily pattern in a concentration camp, published in 1936[22]

Waking at 5 o'clock in the morning, at 6 o'clock bad black coffee, at 6:30 labor service without a break until 12 noon. Then food that is no food, but an evil-smelling thick paste that everyone forces down his throat with great revulsion. From 12:30 to 7 o'clock once again work without a break, in the evening there is 50–60 grams of rotten sausage and tea without sugar. At 9 o'clock signal for bedtime and woe to him who is not lying on his sack of straw. He would, without fail, come under the bullwhip.

190. Report by an ss nco in Lichtenburg to the Lichtenburg protective custody camp leader, regarding prisoner rations, dated 21 July 1936[23]

I hereby bring the following report to your notice. After the food provisions for the prisoners were introduced on the initiative of Herr Amtsrat Goerke, I have repeatedly observed in letters written by prisoners to their families that they are hungry, with hints that food should be sent to them. Even though the prisoners know that the sending of food is prohibited.

Careful observation by me shows that the food is insufficient to satisfy the prisoners, in particular the evening meal which usually consists of light diluted soups. Recently there has even been an increase in instances of the prisoners collecting remnants of bread from the waste pit in the yard and taking them to their quarters to eat them there. In response to questioning it has been established that the prisoners do not find their food sufficient and therefore try to satisfy their hunger in this way.

191. Summary of reports by former prisoners on catering in the concentration camps, published in 1936[24]

In view of the invariably heavy work done in the concentration camps and the other physical demands, such as drill, heavy punishments,

Life and Death in the Camps

etc., the question of the prisoners' food is of special importance. After an examination of the reports one has to conclude that the food situation represents another factor worsening the lot of the protective custody prisoners. Food is inadequate in every respect. It is not nourishing and is prepared without flavor.

During 26 months of protective custody in Dachau the prisoner 41F81[25] lost weight from 79 kg to 49 kg. 41F81 is 21 years old and a gardener by occupation. Measured by the work performance expected the food quantity is not sufficient. If we examine the menus of the major camps we will find confirmation of this.

[. . .]

In Sachsenburg the food consists of three slices of bread with jam and coffee substitute in the morning, of totally over-soured soups and porridge at midday—which were inedible—and of three slices with jam and a small piece of cheese or one slice of sausage in the evening. In fact, this bread for supper was only available twice a week, for the rest of the time there was soup. (41HK).[26] The Lichtenburg prisoners receive 30 grams of bones or meat per day, plus in the summer 400 grams of bread and 500 grams in the winter, usually with margarine.

192. Sopade report on conditions in the Berlin Columbia-Haus concentration camp, dated December 1936[27]

A released protective custody prisoner who had passed through many penal institutions reports:

I came to the "Columbiahaus," the old military penal institution. The food was good, treatment "correct," I was no longer beaten. The guards were really young ss men, of 20 to 22 years. But even that "correctness" was nothing but unending torture. When a guard appeared and unlocked the cell—each cell held two men—we had to jump up, stand at attention, very exactly, quite correctly, hands on our trouser seams, stand at attention and make our report: "Beg to report: two company, passage two, occupied by two men. By protective custody prisoner No. —— and protective custody prisoner No. —— who are asking the Herr Wachtmeister for permission to step outside." The guard would give his consent but invariably remained standing in the doorway. So one had to ask again: "Request the Herr Wachtmeister to pass him." And everything went on in so correct a manner. Of course we had to "build our beds." I had been a soldier, I had been in action, I know this drill. But these young louts, who were probably not even able to shake up a straw mattress correctly, were harassing us "quite correctly" with their "make your beds." With matchsticks and other aids we tried to implement the regulation and make our beds painstakingly accurate. Often it was all of no use. Five times a day or more they would pull down our work of art and order us to "build your beds."

Each day we had an hour off. For 25 minutes we did gymnastic exercises, for 35 minutes we stood in a square and were permitted to smoke. It was a colorful mixture of people, some in their own clothes, some in institutional garb, which, however, was worse than in the worst of the war years. People who came into security confinement were made trusties. [. . .] Everyone wore a colored strip on his arms and legs, the One-hundred-and-seventy-fivers[28] a yellow one, the political prisoners a purple one, those who had already served their sentence a red one, those who were going to or coming from a[nother] concentration camp a green one. Only those acquitted wore no stripes.

193. Sopade report on the Lichtenburg concentration camp, dated May 1937[29]

Four times: morning, midday, afternoon and evening we had to fall in for labor service parade. On this occasion the commandant, his adjutant Remmert or the company leaders stood at the exits of the prisoner quarters, urging the prisoners to move faster, driving them back into their cells and sleeping quarters, commanding "at the double," or, if they had slept badly or were still drunk, which often happened, making the prisoners do half an hour's "sport" before starting work. [. . .]

The prisoners came to roll calls from the workshops, from their quarters and from their work locations outside the camp. About 850 men stood in a square in the yard. All access was barred by sentries, some with machine guns. The rapid action platoon of the ss—about 40 men—always marched up for that. Audible to everybody the platoon commander's "Load live ammunition and put at safe" rang out across the yard.

Life and Death in the Camps

194. General instruction of the Buchenwald protective custody camp leader, SS *Obersturmbannführer* Rödl, dated 9 October 1937[30]

Protective custody camp!

General instructions:

1. When an SS leader enters a prisoner quarter, "Attention" is to be called out in a loud voice. The block elder[31] thereupon, in military stance, reports to the most senior entering officer on the strength of his block. If a higher-ranking officer is in the block already, the "Attention" call is dispensed with.

Submission of requests and complaints is forbidden; this must only be done through official channels. Otherwise there is **punishment**.

2. Making a report: If a prisoner has a request to make, official channels are to be used. This starts with the block elder, who passes the report on to Section III. If a prisoner has information to provide on thefts, attempted escapes, sabotage, etc., then he has to report these at once to Section III. If he fails to make this report, he makes himself equally as culpable as the perpetrator.

3. Cleanliness: The block elder has to see to absolute cleanliness within his block [. . .] and has to take the necessary measures on his own responsibility. At 9:00 rooms and beds should be in a clean condition.

4. Parade: Falling in for parade is done noiselessly, swiftly and in military fashion. Talking, turning one's head, etc., is punished. All prisoners stand **at attention** in line.

5. The working tempo is accelerated. **Quick-march is commanded.** Private conversations are forbidden. All reports received will result in most severe punishment. Every punishment is followed by prolongation of detention.

195. First impressions of Paul Martin Neurath[32] upon his delivery to the Dachau concentration camp in 1938, completed in 1943[33]

When a new arrival first enters the concentration camp it looks totally different to him from what he had imagined. He may have thought of it as a kind of super-prison with thick stone walls and vast numbers of dark cells, where he would be given third-degree tortures of the most elaborate kind by black-garbed Gestapo officers to make him confess to his most secret activities and thoughts.

What he actually finds is a kind of military camp. As a rule he is not put into a dark cell or into solitary confinement, but into a bright hut, along with hundreds of fellow prisoners. The ss men, soldiers in field-gray uniform with a skull and crossbones on their cap and collar, beat him without any thoughts of refined torture methods, without asking questions and without being interested in their answers. [. . .] When the prisoner gets to the camp he has either been terribly ill-treated already in the train or he is violently ill-treated as he leaves the freight truck. He is whipped into a frame of mind on the spot that leaves him no chance of systematically observing his surroundings. He is continually harassed and beaten and thus driven through a well-organized routine—undress, take fingerprints, get a number, register, put on prison garb, haircut, etc. Then he has to fall in on the parade ground in rank and file with the other new arrivals, where he is kept standing until, after the evening parade, he is taken to his block that from then on becomes his "home."

196. Undated instruction of the Buchenwald ss regarding the tasks of the senior block prisoner[34]

The senior block prisoner ensures that the camp order and the instructions of the camp leadership are implemented by all prisoners of his block. He is responsible for their implementation, for order and cleanliness, as well as for the furniture in his block. Subordinate to the senior block prisoner is the hut service, assigned to him for the execution of his tasks. The work of the senior block prisoner begins even before general reveille. He sees to it that no one leaves his bed, let alone the block, before reveille and that, at the waking signal, every inmate immediately gets up from his bunk. The self-evident duty of every prisoner to wash himself and his clothes, and to make his bed, is monitored by the senior block prisoner. Under his direction the coffee and the helpings to which the inmates are entitled are distributed. At the first whistle signal for morning parade, about three-quarters of an hour after reveille, he makes his block fall in, convinces himself that no one is left behind in the block and,

Life and Death in the Camps

at the second whistle signal marches them to the parade ground. Marching must be in absolute silence and tidy order. On the parade ground he makes the block halt, dress by the right and count. He makes sure that the number of prisoners which he has already reported to the senior camp prisoner is actually present and then—if his count tallies with the report made to the senior camp prisoner—makes his report to the ss block leader. If his total does not tally with that reported to the office before the parade, he must instantly report this to the senior camp prisoner. On no account must he report to his block leader different figures from those reported to the senior camp prisoner.

Once the parade has been inspected and the command "Work squad fall in" has been given, he goes to the place assigned to him. His tasks during the falling-in and the departure of the work squads are:

Closing off the camp to prevent any work-shy prisoners sneaking back into the camp and there hanging about without working; checking the notice boards; counting service at the desk of the labor service leader, etc. His post is assigned to him by the senior camp prisoner.

Once the work squad has moved off he will, as a rule, go to the scribes' office. There he is told the timetable of his service for the day in question. The possibilities are: service in the kitchen, where the senior block prisoner has to supervise the correct operation of the hut service during the issue of food and helpings, and the return of the cleaned saucepans; service with the paymasters, when he has to ensure the smooth procedure of payout. If assigned to service on the camp roads, he makes sure that no one hangs about in an unauthorized manner between the huts and that the roads are clean and in good order. Before assuming his service he goes to his own block and convinces himself that everything is in order in the block. Beds must have been made impeccably, lockers, day and sleeping quarters, washroom, toilet and anteroom must be clean.

During the day no one except the hut service is permitted in the block. The senior block prisoner is responsible also for the observance of this regulation. When working time is finished, he sees to the handout of the food and to quiet and order during mealtime and free time. He has to concern himself with the orderly receipt of the prisoners' clothing and bed linen and to ensure the smooth exchange of linen in the room. In the event of new arrivals to the block, it is the task of the senior block prisoner to instruct them, familiarize them with the camp order and initiate the filling out of the forms required for new arrivals.

At the evening whistle he has to convince himself that all prisoners are in the block and by lights out (second whistle) he should have counted the occupancy. If a prisoner is missing, he has to report at once to the senior camp prisoner, who sets the rest into motion. The senior block prisoner is also responsible for quiet at night. During that time no one is permitted to leave the block, show himself at a window or turn on the light.

197. Letter of Faybusch Itzkewitsch[35] from the Buchenwald concentration camp to his family, dated 26 November 1938[36]

Because Itzkewitsch is illiterate, written by prisoner Jul. Meyer.

I am a prisoner here.

My address is: protective custody prisoner Faybusch Itzkewitsch No. 1925 Block 11, Weimar, Buchenwald
The following regulations apply to me:

1. I am not allowed to write or receive letters.
2. Receipt of money or parcels is not permitted.
3. Visits or inquiries to the commandant's office are pointless. [. . .]

Dear Horst, I am in good health. Cordial regards from your Papa.

198. Recollections of Adolf Gussak of his detention in the Mauthausen concentration camp, recorded in 1958[37]

I came to Mauthausen on 21 March 1939. Here I first worked in the quarry. We wore very thin clothes and only wooden clogs. As for food, there was watery tea at midday with sausage jelly which contained pieces of ice. If anyone did not keep up with work he had to undress and lie down. Frozen stiff, the bodies were then loaded like stones on vehicles and taken to the camp. There the senior block prisoners had to sort the frozen men by numbers. Then the murdered persons were piled up in the washroom. It happened that some among them were still alive. But it was not taken very seriously, they mostly croaked in the washroom already. In the morning, if the beds were not made with hair-width accuracy, if the check pattern was not entirely straight, there were hard punishments. 25 lashes or two hours under a cold shower. In the quarry we had to carry heavy stones. With them on our backs we had to climb the 180 steps up. The SS beat us. As a result there often was some pushing: everybody wanted to escape the blows. If anyone fell down he was finished off by a bullet in the back of his neck.

199. Account by Paul Martin Neurath on money in the Dachau and Buchenwald concentration camps, completed in 1943[38]

Naturally the prisoners get no wages for the work done in the concentration camp. Any money they have comes from their families, who send it by postal order. The prisoner has this either paid out to him direct, whereby accurate records are kept to ensure no one receives more than the permitted weekly amount, or it is credited to a personal account on which he can draw at predetermined intervals. In Dachau the former method is practiced, in Buchenwald the latter. In Dachau the prisoners are allowed to receive up to 15 Mark per week (65 Mark per month), in Buchenwald 10 Mark every ten days (30 Mark per month). In actual fact only a small portion of the men receive the full permitted amount. Ten or fifteen Mark is quite a lot of money, a skilled worker or office employee earns about 35 to 40 Mark a week. The "Ten-or-fifteen-Mark recipients" are the rich. In Dachau the men buy directly from the canteen, which is in a block on the parade ground. In Buchenwald, where the canteen is outside the fence, every block has its "canteen man," who accepts their orders and money and buys for the whole block. He is part of the hut service. At a specified time all block purchasers come [. . .] to the canteen to do their shopping. As they receive only a fraction of what had been ordered, the meager supplies have to be arbitrarily divided and there are disputes. Profiteers' cartels are established and articles are sold and resold until the end user often pays a multiple of the original price. [. . .]

A person in Dachau who receives 5 Mark a week (70 Pfennig per day) could probably buy the following:

> Sunday: one pack of cigarettes 0.70
> Monday: ½ pound of butter, ½ pound of crackers 0.80
> Tuesday: a tin of fish 0.50
> Wednesday: artificial honey 0.70

Thursday: a few personal items such as soap, shoelaces or tooth-
paste 0.30; cigarettes 0.70
Friday: crackers 0.30
Saturday: fish 0.50
Total: 4.50

That leaves him with about 50 Pfennig, of which he pays 5 to 10
Pfennig as an extra tip for his weekly shave (or even 20 Pfennig if he
has himself shaved by a hut barber).

He may spend the rest on some extraordinary expenses, perhaps
for one of the things that have to be bought illegally (wooden clogs,
belt, "tools" for bed-making, steel wool or sandpaper, etc.). Extraordinary expenses can also include bribes, though these are less common in Dachau than they are in Buchenwald. [. . .]

If a man receives 8 to 10 Mark a week, he can buy additional food
in the canteen and eat it instead of the regular food. Men who have
enough money give away their salted herrings or tripe or any other
less popular food. Bribes also begin to play a greater role from 8 to 10
Mark, as do regularly paid services. A person who receives 15 Mark
a week can afford to pay another person 2 Mark for making his bed
for him, or polishing his shoes or some other regular cleaning task.
In a political block he will perhaps also pay part of his money into a
fund that supports those who receive no money at all.

200. Report of the Lichtenburg prisoner Ludwig Bendix on his purchases for needy prisoners in the mid-1930s, written in the late 1930s[39]

Most of them wanted tobacco when we asked them. With the inadequate camp food I considered it right to provide the people with nu-
tritious stuff, a piece of butter or fat or sausage. I could not and did
not wish to see why the slight amounts of 2 RM a week, which were
in question here, should just be puffed into the air. I therefore made
it the duty of my representative to buy accordingly and tried to make
this particularly palatable to him by increasing the amounts by 30 to
40% if his "budget" could not be balanced otherwise. Later I learnt
to my extreme displeasure that the comrades in question often conducted a lively barter trade, exchanging the foodstuffs given them by
me as presents against tobacco.

Life and Death in the Camps

201. Report by Julius Freund on forced labor in 1939 in the quarry of the Buchenwald concentration camp, published in 1945[40]

26 May 1939 was a day that pushed Quarry Squad No. 2, under the leadership of Kapo Erich, to the edge of desperation. Fog lay on the camp that May, a cold wet morning welcomed us. On parade it was raining so hard that our twill clothes were soon wet through and water collected in our shoes. The wind whipped the rain into our faces. One would have liked to lie down and die to be released from this torture. Steam rose from our wet and cold clothes which clung to our bodies. At the command "Caps off" they all stood motionless, the rain beat down on the bald shaven heads and large drops ran down our necks. Despite fog and rain the command came: "Work squad fall in." Normally we would not move off in such heavy rain and fog because of the danger of escape. Among the columns moving off was also the 200-men-strong group from No. 2 Quarry. They hung their heads, everything had become a matter of indifference to them. There was only the splashing of water in their boots at every step, giving the marching column a strange ringing and singing accompaniment. In that state we received the command "Sing." The command was pointless, no voice and no tune came from the 200 prisoners' throats [. . .]. The command "Sing" was repeated. Again it was pointless, nothing moved. Who could have sung in that miserable condition! It was a demonstration against everything and they had to pay for it heavily. When they got to No. 2 Quarry, the command came: "Except for the stonemasons, everybody halt on the spot!" All prisoners except the stonemasons had to go to the tubs, small tipping tubs running on narrow-gauge rails. Stone blocks weighing 100 to 200 kg were being loaded up. Then the tubs filled with blocks of stone had to be pushed uphill on a zigzag road up to the main road. If any of these tubs had rolled back, there would have been fatal casualties! Back from the road, alongside the empty tubs, we went downhill at a trot. Time and again the malicious question came from the command: "What about the singing?"

To spite us, the rain did not abate. The wetness time and again penetrated to the still warm body, so that cold shivers ran down the backs of the poor prisoners. At last came the longed-for midday break. Instead of half an hour's rest, work recommenced after 15 minutes. All there was was a piece of bread in your bag, and that piece of bread had become entirely wet. Work continued at an even faster pace. The older prisoners could no longer keep up; they had a job to keep on their feet. At 15.30 work should have finished in order to get back to the camp in time for the evening parade. But that hour on 26 May proved the crowning moment of the day. This time two blocks of 4,000 kg each, probably intended for a monument, still had to be loaded on two large tubs. These were the final remains of strength that were spent here. There was no point in cursing or beating [us], [we] were simply finished. The heavy blocks had been dragged right up to the tubs, one could not let go of them, one was begging each other for help. Don't fail now or the block will crush us and some men will be killed! Anxious minutes passed as they were holding the blocks. Just then, like a miracle, there appeared a Communist Kapo with a group of prisoners who by his intervention saved many people from being crushed to death.

4.2. Self-Assertion

Prisoners tried to improve their living conditions as much as possible, within an environment created and dominated by the ss. Many inmates did not submit fully to the ss order. Rather, they struggled to retain some dignity. To be sure, open resistance was very rare, given the prisoners' exposed and isolated position, the overwhelming power of the ss, and the dire sanctions awaiting defiant prisoners.[41] Still, there were many ways in which prisoners tried to preserve some degree of agency. For example, in the scant spare time they had after work, prisoners often engaged in cultural activities, while others even held clandestine political meetings.

Often, historians have seen such activities as acts of resistance, and the issue of prisoners' resistance has long dominated the historiography on life inside the camps, informed by postwar accounts of political prisoners. As a result, the extent of prisoners' self-assertion—perhaps a more useful term—has sometimes been exaggerated. Also, life in the prewar camps was not yet a continuous struggle against death.[42] Focusing on prisoners' attempts to survive the wartime camps, the literature has often ignored the fundamental differences between the wartime camps and the prewar camps, which were not yet places of mass murder. Also, in the prewar camps, inmates always had some hope to be released. The following documents seek to clarify this fundamental difference and add nuance to our understanding of life and death in the prewar camps.[43]

Prisoners organized some activities themselves—such as playing music, singing, reading books assembled in the official camp libraries, playing chess, and having political discussions (202)—which were often a source of encouragement and helped inmates to cling onto the social identity they had developed before their imprisonment.[44] Meanwhile, the ss camp authorities also tried to exploit cultural activities for their own purposes. The ss forced prisoners to listen to official Nazi speeches over the radio, which probably did not leave much of an impression on many of the prisoners. Likewise, prisoners were forced to play music together in camp orchestras and choirs.

Therefore music in the camps had a highly ambiguous role: on the one hand, it was an expression of self-assertion for prisoners; on the other, it was a form of ss domination, such as when ss officers forced inmates to make music during punishments.[45]

Apart from cases of cultural self-expression, a few prisoners dared to challenge the ss openly.[46] Often, this resulted in death. Take the case of Paul Schneider, a Protestant pastor and member of the Confessing Church, an association of Protestant clergymen critical of Nazi attempts to intervene in matters of church doctrine. The Nazi regime began to suppress the Confessing Church from the late 1930s and arrested many of its members, including its leader, Martin Niemöller.[47] Paul Schneider was taken to Buchenwald in November 1937 and regularly looked after prisoners, although the ss made him work in the quarry and tortured him on several occasions. His activities in the camp were particularly irritating for the ss, who had by now forbidden any official church services or clerical visits. In April 1938, Schneider refused to salute a swastika flag in the camp. ss guards beat him and put him in the bunker from where he occasionally gave short sermons to prisoners, leaning out of his cell window. Guards immediately stopped his sermons (204). In July 1939, Schneider finally died in the camp's infirmary, apparently murdered by the ss.[48]

A particularly dangerous form of self-assertion was escape. The chances of success were slim, as camps were surrounded by an electric perimeter fence, supervised by armed guards on watchtowers. Furthermore, punishments were draconian, both for the escapee and for the remaining inmates, who often received collective punishments. When a Dachau prisoner escaped in 1937, he was almost immediately recaptured by the local police, apparently with support from members of the Hitler Youth. Upon his arrival back in the camp, ss guards paraded him across the grounds before he received lashes in front of the assembled prisoners (203). Often, recaptured prisoners were also put into solitary confinement. After their release from the bunker, a *Fluchtpunkt*, a target point, was attached to the back of their uniform. This stark symbol singled out prisoners for particularly harsh treatment by the ss.

Overall, there were relatively few escape attempts in the prewar camps. However, it is impossible to give exact figures because of ss

Life and Death in the Camps

falsifications. For example, according to official ss figures some sixty-seven Buchenwald prisoners were punished between August 1937 and late 1938 because they had tried to flee or helped someone to escape. Yet, these numbers are problematic, because ss guards regularly ordered inmates to approach the perimeter fence, whereupon the ss shot them. Such executions then found their way into the official statistics as "shot while trying to escape" (*auf der Flucht erschossen*), with at least twenty-six such cases in Buchenwald between the camp's official opening in July 1937 and 1 July 1938. Until the end of 1938, just seven Buchenwald prisoners actually managed to escape.[49]

One of the most significant escapes was that of Emil Bargatzki and Peter Forster, two Buchenwald prisoners who ran away from Buchenwald in May 1938. Forster had been accused of trying to escape before, for which the ss had punished him with twenty-five lashes. On 13 May 1938, Forster, a Social Democrat detained in camps on various occasions before his confinement in Buchenwald in 1937, and Bargatzki, a petty criminal in preventive police custody since March 1937, were on a work detail outside the camp, digging a shaft for a sewage works. All of a sudden, Bargatzki and Forster killed the ss guard watching them with a spade and ran away. An orgy of violence soon followed inside the camp. The remaining prisoners were beaten and ss terror increased, on direct orders of camp commandant Koch (206). Meanwhile, a nationwide hunt for Bargatzki and Forster began. For the ss, this case was a good propaganda opportunity. Its journal *Das Schwarze Korps* published an obituary for the dead ss guard, underlining the necessity for the elimination of "subhumans" like Bargatzki and Forster and for the strict application of Nazi terror in the camps to protect the national community (205). Bargatzki was quickly arrested on 22 May 1938 and put before the Weimar Special Court, which sentenced him to death. He was hanged on 4 June in front of the assembled Buchenwald camp by two criminal prisoners on the ss's orders, the first official execution within the concentration camps. Forster, in the meantime, had escaped to Czechoslovakia, where he was arrested. Nazi Germany almost immediately demanded his extradition. An international campaign followed, with demands that Forster must not be extradited as his act had been one of anti-Nazi resistance. At a time of increasing tensions between the Third

Reich and Czechoslovakia over Nazi claims for the Sudetenland, Forster's case thus became entangled in international relations. The Munich agreement of late September 1938, signed by Germany, Britain, France, and Italy, allowed Nazi Germany the annexation of the Sudetenland. As a result, the government of what remained of Czechoslovakia became more cautious and defensive toward its powerful German neighbor. It soon agreed to extradite Forster to the Third Reich. He was put before the Weimar Special Court and sentenced to death, whereupon he too was executed at Buchenwald in December 1938, little more than half a year after his escape from the camp.[50]

DOCUMENTS

202. Report by Benedikt Kautsky on the prisoners' leisure time in the Buchenwald concentration camp, published in 1946[51]

A substantial part of leisure time in Buchenwald was accompanied by the radio. In all the huts loudspeakers were installed, serving mainly the relaying of the orders of the camp leadership to the office, the senior block prisoners, the infirmary, etc., but which were also occasionally connected to the official German stations. Thus we heard the news almost every evening, and on free Sunday afternoons the radio was switched on continually; stopping the radio was regarded and imposed as a bitter punishment. Important speeches, Reichstag meetings, etc., had to be listened to by us. Thus I heard nearly all Hitler's speeches. [. . .]

Such a Sunday afternoon with the permanently switched on radio, however, could also become a pain—in a crowded block, where more than 100 men were chatting, where cooking went on the stove, where people were continually walking in and out, where food was handed out and consumed, where various administrative tasks had to be performed—issue and collection of personal clothing, compilation of the widest variety of lists—and where, last but not least, people were playing, singing or reading. It took strong nerves to concentrate on chess or on your book. Nevertheless entire chess tournaments were held and a large number of books read. I will have to devote a whole paragraph to the Buchenwald *library*, even though I am convinced that to many prisoners it meant not nearly as much as to myself. The running of the library was entirely in the hands of the prisoners—the ss scarcely bothered about the choice of the books to be acquired. The political prisoners, who were in charge of the library, made sure of acquiring good material when they chose the books. When the camp command only made small funds available, they had the excellent idea of requesting the camp command to permit the prisoners to donate money or books for library purposes. Now the prisoners themselves could order the books they wanted. [. . .]

203. Recollections of the Dachau prisoner Alfred Hübsch of the escape of the political prisoner Matthias Neumeyer from Munich in autumn 1937, written c. 1960[52]

The ss, the gendarmerie, the police and even the Hitler Youth were alerted to catch him. Telephone and telegraph were set in motion. Even the frontier guards of Switzerland. Now we—the whole camp—were put on alert and had to march to the parade ground. The ss marched through the gate, the camp commandant Loritz in person. Now came two men in civilian clothes. One had a poster round his neck, saying: "I greet you, I am back again!" The other, the taller one, had the large kettledrum of the ss music corps hanging from his neck and had to beat it ceaselessly. The one with the drum was "Hias" [Neumeyer], as he was called in the camp. The other was a civilian work colleague from Munich-Grosshadern, who had helped him escape. The buck was brought to the middle of the parade ground, Neumeyer was strapped to the buck and whipped. The civilian was taken to the bunker.

204. Report of the second protective custody camp leader in Buchenwald to the commandant's office, regarding the behavior of the Pastor Paul Schneider, dated 2 September 1938[53]

The protective custody prisoner Paul Schneider, born 29.8.97 in Pferdefeld, at present under arrest, displayed unbelievable behavior on 28.8.38. At 6:30 in the morning, during the morning report to me on the strength of the protective custody camp, Sch. suddenly opened the window of his cell, climbed up in his cell until he had sight of the fallen-in prisoners. For about 2 minutes Sch. preached in a loud voice to the prisoners on parade. He took no notice of my order to break off his sermon at once and leave the window. I thereupon ordered the arrest administrator to get Sch. forcibly away from the window. I immediately reported this incident to the camp commandant.

205. *Das Schwarze Korps*: Article about the killing of ss *Rottenführer* Albert Kallweit by the escaping Buchenwald prisoners Peter Forster and Emil Bargatzki, dated 26 May 1938[54]

He died for us!

On 13 May 1938 ss *Rottenführer* Albert Kallweit of the 3rd ss Death's Head *Standarte* "Thüringen," while doing his duty at a lonely post in the Thuringian Forest, fell victim to an insidious, cowardly attack [. . .]. While the German nation is peacefully going about its daily work, the ss man of the Death's Head Unit is permanently in contact with the enemy.

One of these fighters, one who with a fervent heart did his duty for the National Socialist community, was ss *Rottenführer* Albert Kallweit of the 3rd ss Death's Head *Standarte* "Thüringen."

On the morning of 13 May 1938 ss *Rottenführer* Kallweit escorted two prisoners along a lonely path on the edge of the forest. They were on the way to their place of work. With natural calm Kallweit, as often before, walks behind the two prisoners. He does not suspect that the two subhumans in front of him are having murderous thoughts. [. . .] The professional criminal Emil Bargatzki, with thirteen previous convictions, and the recidivist protective custody prisoner Peter Forster, on whose faces Nature has written "Crime," are determined to commit murder. Suddenly they jump the sentry and forcefully strike his head with a spade. Kallweit still manages to jump a few steps away from the path into a field, but before he can use his weapon in self-defense further blows with the spade hit his head. He slumps to the ground. Bone splinters subsequently found at the spot testify to the beastly brutality with which he was struck.

206. Report of the Communist prisoner Ernst Frommhold on the escape of Peter Forster and Emil Bargatzki, written ca. 1945[55]

When the news came that the sentry had been slain, the top leaders of the NSDAP, the ss and the sa appeared in Buchenwald. Among them was ss *Gruppenführer* Eicke. The criminal bloodlust of the commandant Koch was for these gentlemen probably a little too obvious to the public. Therefore, and not because of their kind hearts, they prevented the open murder of 60 innocent prisoners. They knew that many would collapse under rifle butts during the next few days. The slaughter of many was achieved even without specific instructions. For now they contented themselves with the flogging of every fifth man. The *Scharführers* had to go on flogging until late at night. Maybe the camp command thought it too dangerous to keep us standing on the parade ground this night. We were sent to our hut. A depressive atmosphere weighed us down. Surmise of the coming day's events dominated our thoughts. That same evening it had been announced that any smoking was forbidden. The next morning the columns moved off. But in the evening they were dragging many prisoners back on their shoulders. During the next few days it was a matter of course that, along with a lot of wounded, there were a lot of dead. But even these tough days passed.

207. *Pariser Tageszeitung*: Article on the execution of Peter Forster in the Buchenwald concentration camp, dated 25–26 December 1938[56]

A few days ago the news arrived of the execution of Peter Forster, that unfortunate German worker who had succeeded in escaping from the Buchenwald concentration camp and whom the government of the "renewed" Czechoslovakia had extradited to Germany because during his escape, along with his comrade Bargatzk: who shared his fate, he had killed an ss man.

4.3. Violence and Punishment

Violence and punishment were common in the camps. As we saw in chapter 3, Eicke's regulations prescribed severe punishments for their smallest infringement, following strictly prescribed bureaucratized procedures. When an ss guard wanted officially to punish a prisoner (213), he had to report him to his superior, who then had to decide whether to forward the case. Official disciplinary punishments were pronounced by the camp commandant, whose decision was recorded on a form sheet.[57] In the case of flogging, the Inspectorate had to approve the punishment—which it almost always did, apparently.[58]

Official punishments could take various forms, including the removal of mail privileges, reduced food rations, and confinement in a cell. ss guards also had prisoners tied to trees or to wooden posts for several hours, a savage punishment that caused immense pain and even fractures (217).[59] Among the harshest forms of official punishment was solitary confinement in the bunker. Bunkers were bare prison cells, located in a separate prison building within the camp's perimeter. Cells here were unheated, prisoners received little or no food, and guards regularly tortured prisoners, so arrest in the bunker could come perilously close to a death sentence (211). Murders in the bunkers were usually covered up as "suicides" (210 and 212).[60]

Flogging was one of the most common forms of punishment. Prisoners who had been sentenced to this punishment were supposed to receive up to twenty-five lashes by two ss men, usually with a bullwhip or a horsewhip, often in front of the assembled prisoners. The prisoner had to kneel down on a buck and was often forced to count the lashes; otherwise the guards started the beatings all over again. In this way, the number of lashes was at the guards' discretion and far exceeded the official punishment procedures. In Dachau, Egon Zill, a notorious Camp ss leader, ordered his guards (in 1940) to execute "double lashes" (*Doppelschläge*), so a prisoner sentenced to twenty-five lashes would actually receive fifty blows or more.[61] Many prisoners who received lashes had to be taken to the camp's infirmary because they suffered gaping wounds (208).

Life and Death in the Camps

In addition to official punishments, there were of course also the many informal and ad hoc sanctions handed out on a daily basis by Camp ss men, without involvement of their superiors. Individual camp commandants occasionally punished entire blocks of prisoners or even the entire camp, as was the case in April 1938 when Buchenwald commandant Koch ordered that prisoners be deprived of their lunch (215). Meanwhile, ss guards regularly singled out individual prisoners and slowly hounded them to death (212). Torturous exercises—such as marching, jumping, and running in military formation—were another common form of harassment by guards when they wanted to punish prisoners without official sanction (209).[62] ss guards treated prisoners at their discretion. Prisoners had no right to appeal whatsoever.

All in all, these unofficial punishments were an integral part of the ss system of torture. To be sure, Eicke still occasionally issued orders to the commandants, with instructions on how official regulations were to be applied, but such orders often amounted to little more than empty words. By the late 1930s the camps had become places of almost unlimited ss terror.

DOCUMENTS

208. Anonymous report on flogging in the Sachsenburg concentration camp, dated c. 1936[63]

There has always been flogging in the Sachsenburg concentration camp, but more especially since the SA guards were replaced by SS men. Throughout the night the bunkers resounded with the cries of the whipped and maltreated. But the flogging only became official and public since 1 April 1935, the day when the new camp and penal order was introduced. [. . .]

With the introduction of the flogging regulation Sachsenburg received a new commandant, the SS *Obersturmbannführer* Schmidt transferred there from Dachau.[64] Schmidt is a fat, bloated man, whose broad chest barely holds his many orders and decorations. In Sachsenburg he was fairly often under the influence of generously consumed alcohol. The kind of person the new commandant was is best revealed in his maiden speech, made on 22 May 1935 on the occasion of a flogging.

"Prisoners!" he shouted in a squeaky, often croaky voice, "I have had you called together here because among you there are some vile pigs who still do not seem to know why they are actually living in a concentration camp and what new brisk wind now blows in Germany, in the new Germany of our great leader Adolf Hitler. You don't seem to have understood that you are prisoners here or who it is that actually holds the power! *I* hold it, no one except *me*, and I will prove to you that I hold it, right away. I come from Dachau, a much bigger camp than Sachsenburg. There the prisoners made me hard and brutal. Yes, I repeat: they made me hard and brutal! But I saw those fellows off, you can be sure of that, and I will see you off here as well! I will be hard and cruel!" [. . .]

The floggings were staged liked executions. The very first one, on 8 May 1935, when four prisoners were whipped, was typical of the subsequent ones. In the evening of that day the three prisoner companies, after marching into the camp, had to line up in the yard in a square of six men each—2nd company in the middle, 1st and 3rd on the right and left flanks. Two rapid-action contingents of the ss, all with steel helmets, surrounded the prisoners two deep, with rifles loaded and safety catches off. In addition, to nip any attempt of mutiny or disobedience in the bud, heavy machine guns had been put in place. The windows of the main building opposite were crowded with curious ss men, who were off duty but did not want to miss the spectacle of a public flogging. In the ss infirmary even the sick were watching. Standing on their beds they were waiting for things to happen. And happen they did!

On the free side of the square there appeared the three company commanders and the leader of the prisoner department of the camp, *Untersturmführer* Weigel, a particularly vicious fellow who was nicknamed "Uncle." Also to appear were the security officer and the barrack duty officer. All in full dress, i.e. with steel helmet, strapped-on bayonet and revolver. The camp doctor, Dr. Gebhardt, also turned up.

Four prisoners were due to be whipped that day. All four had been sentenced to fourteen days' strict arrest and—before starting their dark-cell detention and also after serving it—they had to receive 25 lashes each, following the camp regulations. The reasons for this inhuman punishment were relatively trivial: in one case for forbidden

Life and Death in the Camps

smoking, with the other three for ridiculing the state government, for repeated refusal to salute and for "disobedience."

After the names of the four delinquents had been called and they had stepped in front of the flogging table, twelve ss men slowly stepped up in single file upon a command, each with a crude cane in his hand. Now they seized the first prisoner [. . .] and held his extremities so he could not move. At the command "Go!" the first ss man got into position, first made a few trial slashes in the air and then struck with full force. The victim's body reared up, his arms and legs tried desperately to tear himself away. In vain! The ss dogs who held him down were stronger than him. After five lashes the first whipper was relieved and a second one continued the flogging with a fresh stick and with fresh strength. The person whipped had to count the lashes in a loud voice. The second man to be whipped was a blond giant of a Czech. Proud and upright he stepped up to the flogging stool and laid over it himself for the whippers. Loud and clear he counted every terrible lash. No moan was to be heard, no cry of pain! This man was not to be humbled by the uniformed hangmen! Erect, he afterward strode off to his bunker. Not he seemed to be the one whipped, but the ss men who trotted after him like bedraggled dogs. [. . .]

Meanwhile there had been plenty of work for the medical orderlies because more than six of the protective custody prisoners who had been made to watch had fainted and had to be carried away. This fainting will be readily understood if one realizes that the hideous execution was performed with such brutality that many of the canes snapped or splintered on the bodies of those whipped. To render this impossible in future the canes were later soaked in water on the camp commandant's orders. For this purpose an oblong tin box was specially constructed in the camp workshop and the hut service had to ensure, by adding water to it, that the flogging tools remained supple and usable.

209. Sopade report on the prisoner drills in the Lichtenburg concentration camp, dated December 1936[65]

"Sport" was an object of fear. Young and old, healthy and sick had to line up for it. In February 1936 the camp commandant Reich[66] instructed the company commander Bräuning—one of the notorious torturers in the camp: "Make sport with 2 Company, so they crawl back to their cells on their bellies." This intention was and always remained the guiding principle and all "exercises" were designed for that purpose. 50 or more knee bends with arms stretched out in front, at a frighteningly slow pace; in a crouch, hands folded in front of the knees, jumping around the yard—an exercise that is prohibited in the army; push-ups on the ground continually raising and lowering the body; ceaseless falling in with ever changing directions and fronts. Lie down—Up! Lie down— Up! At the double, march, march. These are a few of the varieties of body gymnastics that were to make us "crawl back to our cells on our bellies." Woe betide him whose physical condition was not equal to these demands.

210. Report of the former Dachau inmate Hans Behrend on the murder of Edgar Loewenstein, written in April 1947[67]

On 16/2/1937, in the morning shortly after the beginning of work, the camp commandant Baranowski,[68] the *Rapportführer* Hoess[69] and the *Sturmführer* Schober appeared at the work place of the "Scharnagl" squad that consisted mostly of Jews who had been brought to Dachau a few days earlier from the concentration camps Lichtenburg, Sachsenburg and Sachsenhausen. Under their direction began a terrible terror on the part of the present lower ranks of ss. I was working as a scribe in the first room of Hut No. 6, which bordered directly on the work area. I observed how my fellow inmate Edgar Loewenstein was desperately trying to get out of the pond that was being filled up with earth. This was not an exceptional scene then, because the ss and Kapos amused themselves every day by throwing "lazy" prisoners into the water. I do not know who had thrown Loewenstein into the pond, but the incident was also observed by my fellow prisoners Heinz Eschen, Albert Bruckner and Hugo Federmann, who were standing next to me.

Soon afterward Max Simon, or it could have been Theodor Weill—I no longer clearly remember which of these two fellow prisoners—appeared in the room and drew our attention to the fact that ss *Hauptscharführer* Vincenz Schoettl, the block commander of No. 6 Block, was drilling Loewenstein in the fifth room, which was then not occupied. Heinz Eschen[70] moved to the back, but I did not move out of the hut all morning.

Suddenly the door connecting Room 1 and Room 2 opened and Loewenstein entered, soaked through head to toe and filthy, a torn-off part of his braces round his neck and desperately asked to be given a piece of rope. Heinz Eschen, grasping the danger of the situation and with the hope against hope of saving him, took him by the arm and made for the clothes store in order to get him fresh clothes. No sooner had Eschen and Loewenstein left the hut than the ss block leaders Schoettl and Spatzenegger entered through the inner door, simultaneously, in great excitement, yelling "Where is Loewenstein?" To our answer they screamed "He must have gone mad" and rushed to the clothes store, from where, according to Eschen's statement, they once more chased Loewenstein to the empty Room No. 5 in No. 6 Hut. Shortly afterward some fellow prisoners called into the hut from outside that Loewenstein had disappeared and should be searched for. Eschen searched throughout the sixth block and eventually found Loewenstein in the toilet between No. 4 and No. 5 Rooms, hanged. He straightaway hurried to the "Jourhaus" to inform the camp administration of Loewenstein's "suicide." I used the brief span of time to see what had happened. Because of the shortage of time and my understandable inner excitement I was unable to collect any detailed impressions. Immediately afterward the camp commandants Loritz, Baranowski and the *Rapportführer* Hoess appeared on the scene and the toilet with the corpse still suspended had to be nailed up by Eschen until, later in the evening during the roll call, after inspection by a judicial commission, the body was removed by ss medical orderlies.

Subsequent scene-of-crime inspection of the toilet revealed that plaster had crumbled down from the sidewall and that the lavatory pan was damaged. One did not have to be a trained crime officer to realize that this was not a case of suicide but of murder, and that the victim had either offered resistance or had subsequently tried to free himself from his position. Anyone who had known Loewenstein would know that he would have never had the energy to top himself; nor had there been any reason for it, since he had worse things behind him. [. . .] The murder was carried out by the ss men Schoettl and Spatzenegger. Given the discipline in the ss it may be regarded as certain that they had acted on the orders of their superiors. These would have been Loritz, Baranowski and Hoess, who were at least accessories;

after all, at the scene of the crime they must have made the same observations as I had. The same is true of the judicial commission which, nevertheless, released the body for burial.

211. Sopade report on the bunkers in the Dachau concentration camp, dated May 1937[71]

At present there are two kinds of bunkers in Dachau: so-called penal bunkers and isolated bunkers. The penal bunkers are windowless, about 2½ m wide and 3 m long. They contain a wooden bunk. In the middle of the floor an iron ring is anchored to which the prisoner is chained by one foot. The floor is concrete. The isolated bunkers have a window above the door to the passage. Half-light enters from the passage. In the room there is a stool, a bunk and steam heating. The floor is wooden. The cells are clean. At the moment there are about 25 isolated bunkers. One of the bunker guards is the notorious SS man Kannschuster [sic].[72] When he is drunk—which happens often—he takes pleasure in letting loose his big fierce dog into the penal bunkers. He opens the bunker door and sets his dog on the prisoners, who cannot evade it because they are chained up. The dog attacks the prisoners, jumps up at them and tears their clothes off their backs.

212. *Neuer Vorwärts*: Article on the murder of Max Sachs in the Sachsenburg concentration camp, dated 6 June 1937[73]

A former inmate of the Sachsenburg concentration camp, who left Germany a short time ago, has sent us the following eyewitness account of the murder of our comrade Max Sachs in September 1935. [. . .]

On his delivery to the Sachsenburg concentration camp Dr. Max Sachs was assigned to the 3rd prisoner company. In this company I was prisoner sergeant. Sachs had already suffered much ill-treatment in Dresden [. . .]. From the moment of his arrival Sachs was the object of maltreatment by every SS man, all the more so as the SS men realized that Dr. Sachs had been a journalist of the "Dresdner Volkszeitung."[74] In reply to a question by *Rottenführer* Gersch whether he still remembered this or that article in "Volkszeitung," Dr. Sachs stated that, according to his experience in detention so far, there had been a lot of truth in those articles. This remark impressed all the political prisoners.

The result was that Dr. Sachs was immediately taken to the arrest cell in the guardhouse. I brought him a few things to his arrest cell. The guard told me: "He doesn't need a towel any longer, he'll soon be able to dry himself with his skin." I could hear that Sachs was being maltreated in his cell and was moaning. For midday parade Sachs, being no longer able to walk, was loaded on a wheelbarrow and pushed to the parade ground by several prisoners. There he was first sworn at in the most obscene manner by *Standartenführer* Schmidt, the camp commandant. Then Sachs was assigned to the manure squad.[75] This squad also contained a number of criminals who obeyed the instructions of the ss guards in every respect. I had occasion to watch Dr. Sachs at his work and have to say that he was giving it his best effort. But again and again his work was described as "inadequate." There was a hail of kicks and rifle-butt blows. In this the ss man Michael particularly distinguished himself.

After the evening parade Dr. Sachs was again brought, or more correctly, dragged, to the arrest cell. As I had made a temporary quarter for myself in the guard room, I was able to see that Sachs had to kneel in his cell, his hands folded behind his neck. On my second appearance in the guard room I saw that Sachs had fallen over through weakness and was being spat at and sworn at by the ss men. Every other word referred to his former function. When I handed out the evening meal, Sachs was lying unconscious in his cell, with water having been poured over him. On the following morning Sachs was again dragged to the parade ground. All political prisoners felt genuine pity for him as it was obvious that Sachs was at the end of his strength. We surmised that he would be the next candidate for death. On that morning Sachs was first brought to the drill ground. There were two large piles of stone there (sharp broken granite), 8 to 10 m high. Supporting himself on his elbows he was made to crawl up and down them [. . .]. When Sachs could crawl no more, [. . .] he was introduced to the prisoners standing around as a "recalcitrant person." Then he was again assigned to the manure squad, i.e. dragged and pushed there. There he had to carry manure and when he collapsed next to the manure tub an ss man pushed his face into the manure. The victim was pulled up and when he could no longer stand he was put in the full manure tub. The prisoners had to spray him with ice-cold water. I was able, with other colleagues, to watch all this from the library. I [. . .] walked over to the prisoners' toilet that was alongside the manure pit. Sachs was lying on the ground totally exhausted and I could hear him softly begging, with a rattle in his throat, that they should shoot him. *Standartenführer* Schmidt, who came up to him, laughed sneeringly, kicked Sachs with his boot and said: "You'll get that anyway—but not until I say so. Meanwhile you're getting twenty-five [lashes]—for refusing to work. I have already applied for approval by telegraph." (The approval came from *Gruppenführer* Eicke) [. . .]

The torments continued for a few more days. Sachs's final day began like this: In my prisoner quarters there happened to be a prisoner called Endesfelder. Following my instructions I demanded that he leave my room as he belonged to another company. The prisoner, however, stated that he was there on orders of the guards so as to give Sachs a bath. Thereupon the prisoners Bundesmann, Endesfelder, Weißbach and a few others whose names I no longer know, criminals and some of them former SA members, went to the arrest cell to get Sachs. In order to watch the proceedings in their entirety I went to the prisoner washroom on the third floor. Sachs was lying entirely naked on a bed frame and, accompanied by the laughter of the guards, was being worked on with a scrubbing brush. The duty guard was *Unterscharführer* Count von Einsiedel, his deputy *Rottenführer* Gersch and SS man Dietrich. I could see that Sachs was producing green stools; in my opinion he had internal injuries. This observation was confirmed by others. After half an hour Sachs was dragged through the room. What happened next probably led to Sachs's early death. The prisoners Bundesmann and Endesfelder seized Sachs by his legs and dragged him down the stairs so that Sachs hit each iron-coated step with his head. He had a rattle in his throat and groaned. Von Einsiedel and Gersch walked behind, smiling. [. . .] The following morning Sachs was to have been given a bath by prisoners, in a bath tub. [. . .] They had thrown Sachs into the tub and run ice-cold water on him. This was to result in the desired "heart attack." Sachs was next placed on a flat cart. On this occasion I was able to do the dead man a final service by closing his broken eyes. An old blanket was thrown over him and prisoners, under escort,

Life and Death in the Camps

had to take the dead man to the Frankenberg cemetery. In the camp it was put about that Sachs had died of a heart attack. This kind of death, however, was familiar to every prisoner as there had been several such heart attacks not long before. A few prisoners who were unable to refrain from remarks about this sad case were put immediately under arrest.

213. Note of the protective custody camp leader of Buchenwald, ss *Obersturmbannführer* Rödl, regarding the prisoner Werner S., who was suspected of having tried to escape, dated 14 October 1937[76]

Protective custody prisoner No. 1788 Werner S. was punished in Sachsenburg [where he had previously been held] with twice 14 days strict arrest and 25 lashings for cheekiness and circumvention of official channels. There is suspicion that S. wanted to hide in order to disappear at a favorable moment as the light had already been turned off. I request punishment of the protective custody prisoner Werner S.

214. Report by the former Buchenwald prisoner Willy Apel on acts of violence by Buchenwald ss men in October 1937, written in 1945[77]

There were still no toilet facilities in camp and no washrooms. Great latrine trenches were dug, about 25 feet long, 12 feet wide, and 12 feet deep. Once two boards were nailed across them, the toilets were finished. On each of these boards sat ten to fifteen men. From behind came ss Sergeants Abraham and Zöllner, both with large truncheons. They beat the prisoners with the truncheons until they fell into the trenches. Ten prisoners drowned in excrement. Woe to him who dared to aid those calling for help. He ran the danger of being beaten to death himself.

215. Punishment order of the Buchenwald commandant Koch, dated 29 April 1938[78]

In the gardening section there have been repeated thefts lately by prisoners of planted red and white radishes and chives. I therefore punish the whole camp by *withdrawal of the midday meal on 1 May 1938.* The punishment is to be announced to the prisoners at midday on Sunday after they have fallen in for parade.

216. Recollections of the political prisoner Anton B. of inmates being tied to a post in Sachsenhausen, published in 1949[79]

An even worse method of punishment was tying to a post. Twelve iron tubes had been sunk in the ground in a circle and into one of them a pole was inserted, about 1.80 m high. A cross-beam was fitted to the post, making a cross. To this cross the prisoner was tied while standing on a stool. When the prisoner was tied up the stool was pulled away, so that the prisoner only touched the ground with the tips of his toes. The whole weight of the body thus hung on the cross. If the prisoner tried to alleviate his position when it had become unbearable, the cross would turn with him. Most of them fainted within some 20 minutes. At the center stood the *Scharführer*, who poured a jug or a bucket full of water over the prisoner to revive him again. This hanging lasted for an hour, from 12 noon to 1 o'clock. When the prisoner was eventually released, he collapsed like a sack because he was unable to move even a finger. Moreover, the prisoner had to go back to work straightaway. The pain was so bad that it was still felt six months later.

217. Recollections of the Dachau prisoner Dr. Maximilian Reich of the camp punishments in 1938, written in 1939, revised in 1956[80]

The following camp punishments existed officially, regardless of the continually parallel excesses of unbridled bestiality already mentioned:

Gateway standing: In the evening, from the end of the roll call (abt. 6 o'clock) until the onset of darkness or bedtime (8 o'clock) the poor devil had to stand face to the wall, motionless, throughout 4–6 weeks, but sometimes for an unlimited period. That may seem easy, but before forming such a judgment one should try it out on oneself. For the prisoners, dead tired as they were from their heavy compulsory labor, the effort of standing motionless at attention—something one does not expect even the best trained troops to do for more than a brief time—was real torture. It often happened that here or there one man in the line of those standing at the gateway fainted and collapsed. What happened to such a delinquent depended entirely on the mood of the duty ss man. Accordingly, a fainted man either had a bucket of cold water emptied over him or else was revived with a hard kick. If this kind of first aid was unsuccessful, the unconscious man was left lying where he was until the command "Dismiss" was given and he was brought to his hut by his exhausted comrades. Gateway standing was the mildest of the camp punishments.

Penal labor: was another, just about bearable, form of punishment. It meant that one had to work for an additional hour after the others returned from their compulsory labor in the evening. Penal labor was for two to eight months. It meant the loss of any other free time. One therefore had to work also on Saturday afternoons and on Sunday. This meant the loss of the only recreation and pleasure that existed in the camp—the opportunity to meet other comrades. This psychological torture was the core of the punishment and far more difficult to bear than the physical overexertion. The penal work people were in a terrible mental state and one can understand their, and their comrades', pure joy when the end of penal labor was announced by the block scribe.

Pack drill: a collective punishment imposed not on individuals but on the entire occupancy of a room or even a whole hut. It is imposed when a block leader is not satisfied with the overall orderliness in his section. The punishment could be tolerable or beastly, depending solely on the degree of mercilessness of the ss man entrusted with the supervision. Pack drill was also done after return from work. It consisted of running at the double and the "Up—down" so popular as the private amusement of the ss. There was no limit to the inventiveness of the ss guard: he could order any exercise he chose for as long as he pleased, with the result that the 1–2 hours of pack drill sometimes had a very bad end especially for the elderly or ailing inmates.

Of medieval inhumanity were the two most feared punishments, "the tree" (tying up) and "Twenty-five" [lashes, i.e., flogging]. Only very few survived such punishments without permanent damage to their organism. For many the consequence of such torture was permanent ailment and for some it was death.

Tying to the "tree": In camp parlance the stake to which one was tied was called the tree. The victim's hands were tied behind his back and pulled upward by chains until only the tips of the tortured inmate's feet touched the ground. This terrible position they had to endure for 1–2 hours. [. . .] Anyone who saw these human wrecks dragging themselves to their hut, reeling, with badly swollen wrists after this torture cannot but be filled with insatiable hatred of the ss torturers. To crown this shameful procedure the victims of the torture had to drag the "tree," a kind of gallows, to its storage place themselves. [. . .]

218. Recollections of Rudolf Wunderlich of unofficial punishments in Sachsenhausen in the spring of 1939, written in 1944[81]

It was sometime during the first few days of April 1939, I was employed in the Construction Squad Neubau-IKL (Inspectorate Concentration Camp) on earthworks, loading tubs and then, with 3 men, pushing the tubs up uneven ground from the building pit. A miserable struggle. Suddenly we heard that the "Grayhound," as the prisoners called Beerbaum [an ss *Unterscharführer*], was with the squad. After a short while he acquainted himself with tub pushing. My tub was his victim. Even during loading there was a hail of blows with a shovel or a spade handle. This continued while we were pushing the tub uphill. Although the foreman helped us, it was too slow for Beerbaum. B. was waiting for us at the tip. While one drove the tubs back into the pit, I and the other prisoner had to go with Beerbaum. Suddenly our squad commander, a certain *Unterscharführer* Ett[l]inger [. . .] was also present. We now had to go into the basement of the new building. There I, as the first man, had to lie across a few building blocks and Beerbaum struck out furiously. He hit my thighs and my ass and twice the small of my back. I had to count with him. At the eighth stroke I began to scream. Nevertheless Beerbaum continued to hit me. I must have received 15–18 strokes. Then it was the other man's turn. Although he screamed soon, he also received 10–12 strokes. Ett[l]inger did nothing and said nothing. After that Beerbaum chased us back to our tub.

Life and Death in the Camps

FIVE

Prisoner Groups

Just as the camp system never stood still, the inmate population also underwent important transformations throughout the 1930s. During the mid-1930s, the Nazi regime used the camps mainly as instruments for the repression of political opposition. Despite the fact that most prisoners had been released by 1934, there were still arrests and re-arrests, although in smaller numbers compared with 1933. But in the late 1930s, amid a marked intensification of persecution, social outsiders began to outnumber political prisoners. By October 1938, one historian estimates, so-called asocials made up 70 percent of the camps' population.[1] Yet we know relatively little about these prisoners. Sources are sparse because social outsiders rarely wrote memoirs—unlike political prisoners, in whose contemporary and postwar accounts such outsiders are often portrayed very negatively, at least partly reflecting wider social and moral stereotypes and prejudices against them. Political prisoners resented having to live side by side with beggars or criminals, and also often suspected them as traitors and informers (**219, 225** and **231**). Much has been written about tensions between political and criminal prisoners, culminating in a ferocious and never-ending battle between the two prisoner groups. Yet was this really true? Were criminal prisoners really as brutal as the ss? Was there no solidarity between political prisoners and social outsiders? And were prisoners whom the ss classified as criminal really serious offenders? Without exploring the fate of prisoners classified as criminal and asocial in more depth, it will be impossible fully to resolve these questions; previously unpublished documents shed some new light on the fate of these long-ignored inmates (**233**).

In some camps, such as Sachsenhausen, Communist prisoners took a dominant position among the prisoner population, occupying key positions open to prisoner functionaries (**225**). In Buchenwald matters were more complex. Here, the ss initially appointed a few criminal inmates as senior Kapos, yet political prisoners managed to gain the upper hand. In general, there was much debate among Communist prisoners as to whether they should take over key roles that inevitably involved some collaboration with the ss. The Communists' key aim was to preserve solidarity with fellow Communist prisoners and to maintain some underground political activity. These prisoners were usually highly disciplined and had considerable organizational skills, following years of political agitation during the Weimar Republic and clandestine resistance in the early period of the Third Reich. They knew the daily rituals of life behind bars and had some experience in negotiating the perilous relationship with the guards. In fact, some political prisoners had earlier acted as trusties (*Kalfaktoren*) in prisons, something of a precedent for the Kapo system. Also, a number of them were skilled workers, which is why the ss often preferred them as Kapos on work details. Needless to say, the ss men hated Communist prisoners, but they still often preferred to negotiate with non-Jewish political prisoners rather than so-called asocial or Jewish inmates who were, in their eyes, racially inferior.[2]

5.1. Prisoner Categories

Camp prisoners came from many different social backgrounds. Left-wing political prisoners were overwhelmingly from the working class, while prisoners classified as criminals and asocials were social outcasts, dismissed even by members of the working-class as the *Lumpenprole-tariat*.[3] There were also middle-class prisoners, especially among German Jews and liberal or conservative politicians. One historian claims that these social backgrounds did not matter much inside the camps because all inmates "had been torn from their social situations."[4] To some extent, this observation is true, as all inmates had to face the harsh reality of imprisonment under ss domination. Yet prisoners' social backgrounds did have a crucial bearing on life in the camps. Some bourgeois prisoners found it difficult to integrate themselves with the working-class prisoners, for political or other reasons. Furthermore, ss guards frequently singled out educated middle-class prisoners, especially if they were Jewish, for abuse and maltreatment.[5] Middle-class prisoners often had access to money from their relatives, which could make their life inside the camp slightly more tolerable. Moreover, life was sometimes easier for at least some prisoners who had relevant skills, such as those with administrative experience relevant for the few desirable positions as Kapos in the camp's bureaucracy.

Some survivors described the community of inmates as a "prisoner society" (*Häftlingsgesellschaft*), a term subsequently criticized by others. It is probably a moot point to argue over the terminology here. What is clear is that prisoners did not choose to live with each other; they were forced together by the ss.[6] It was the ss, too, who gradually formalized a distinct scheme to classify prisoner groups. Early on, the classification of prisoners still varied from one camp to another. At Esterwegen, for example, so-called criminals had to wear blue trousers and jackets whose back was marked with the abbreviation "BV" (*Berufsverbrecher*) in yellow, while at Sachsenhausen, criminal prisoners had to wear a green piece of fabric sewn to their uniforms. It was only in 1937 and 1938 that the ss standardized the classification of prisoners across all camps. Upon admission, each prisoner was placed into a prisoner category and given a triangular badge. Political prisoners had to wear a red triangle, criminals a green one, homosexual men a pink one, Jehovah's Witnesses a purple one, and asocials a black or, rarely, a brown one. Jews had to wear an additional yellow Star of David under their classification triangle.[7] These visual markers helped to cement a hierarchy of prisoners along the lines of Nazi ideology (**219**).

Prisoner classifications also influenced where inmates were placed inside the camps. In the mid-1930s, at Dachau and elsewhere, individual prisoner huts often housed prisoners from one particular grouping together: there were separate "companies" for political prisoners, Jews, social outsiders, and so-called second-time-rounders. The latter were mainly Communist and Social Democratic prisoners who had been rearrested following an earlier stint in a camp. They received particularly harsh treatment on Himmler's direct orders.[8]

Prisoners were also divided by the posts they held, with so-called Kapos in particularly influential positions. As we saw, each "company" was led by a "senior block prisoner," an inmate entrusted by the ss with the maintaining of discipline and cleanliness inside the hut. There was also a senior prisoner, or *Lagerältester*, in each camp, appointed by the ss and acting as the go-between between the prisoners and the ss. Other prisoner functionaries were in charge of admitting prisoners to the camp's infirmary and could use their powers to provide some injured or sick inmates with food or medicine. Prisoner functionaries also played key roles in the camps' administration, where they could influence the assignment of prisoners into work details, sometimes a matter of life and death as working conditions deteriorated sharply in the late 1930s.[9]

DOCUMENTS

219. Eugen Kogon's description of prisoner categories, first published in 1946[10]

Who belonged in a concentration camp, in the view of the Gestapo?[11] Primarily four groups of people: political opponents; members of "inferior races"; criminals; and "shiftless elements" (called "asocial" by the Germans). [. . .] The Jews were the target of Nazi bloodlust from the very outset. They were divided up among all the prisoner categories—political prisoners, criminals, shiftless elements, etc.—although they remained segregated in special huts—which exposed them constantly to a heightened danger of annihilation—and usually had to be content with the most menial jobs. [. . .]

The Gestapo had definite ideas as to who was to be classified as a criminal. It distinguished first of all "prisoners in limited-term preventive custody" [. . .], who had served several sentences before. The initials of the German term (BV) also stand for "professional criminal," and that is the designation by which these prisoners were generally known. [. . .] In some camps they managed to secure a dominant position, temporarily or permanently, which they ruthlessly exploited against the other prisoners. There was an everlasting struggle for power between them and the political prisoners, sometimes open, sometimes underground. The outcome of such struggles varied widely. Many SS officers preferred to deal with the convicts, sometimes to the exclusion of all other categories, and assigned them to all the important prisoner functions. [. . .]

Related to the convicts, though far more innocent in character, were the so-called shiftless elements. This was a blanket designation of the Gestapo for vagrants, touts, pickpockets, tinhorn gamblers, alcoholics, pimps, deadbeat fathers, and the like. But in this group there were also men whose only offense was that they had shown up late for work once or twice, had stayed away from work or changed their job without authority, had spoken harshly to their Nazi servants, or had earned their living as gigolos. [. . .] These shiftless elements were a very mixed group and had no marked effect on the character of the camp, though they brought with them many undesirable practices from their former lives. The other prisoners regarded them as shiftless and unreliable [. . .].

The political prisoners too were a motley crew. Beyond doubt the majority were members of the anti-Nazi parties and persons of like mind. But always a certain proportion were former Nazi Party members guilty of some party infraction and veterans accused of anything from petty thievery to desertion. [. . .]

Opposition to the Nazi regime from moral and especially religious motives was regarded in the same light as political opposition. This involved principally clergymen of all the great denominations and members of the religious sect known as Jehovah's Witnesses. [. . .]

In addition to these main categories of prisoners, the ss made a number of other distinctions. Of these the homosexuals deserve special mention. This group had a very heterogeneous composition. It included individuals of real value, in addition to large numbers of criminals and especially blackmailers. This made the position of the group as a whole very precarious [. . .]. Homosexual practices were actually very widespread in the camps. The prisoners, however, ostracized only those whom the ss marked with the pink triangle.

The fate of homosexuals in the concentration camps can only be described as ghastly. They were often segregated in special huts and work details. Such segregation offered ample opportunities for unscrupulous elements in positions of power to engage in extortion and maltreatment. Until the fall of 1938 homosexuals at Buchenwald were divided up among the huts occupied by political prisoners. [. . .] In October 1938 they were transferred to the penal company in a body and had to slave in the quarry. This consigned them to the lowest caste in the camp during the most difficult years. [. . .]

All prisoner categories in the concentration camps had to wear prescribed markings sewn to their clothing—a serial number and colored triangles, affixed to the left breast and the right trouser leg. [. . .] Red was the color denoting political prisoners. Second offenders, so-called recidivists, wore a stripe of the same color above the upper edge of the triangle. Criminals wore a green triangle [. . .]. Jehovah's Witnesses wore purple; "shiftless elements" black; homosexuals, pink. During certain periods the Gypsies and the shiftless picked up in certain special campaigns wore a brown triangle.

Jews, in addition to the markings listed above, wore a yellow triangle under the classification triangle. The yellow triangle pointed up, the other down, forming the six-pointed Star of David. [. . .] Prisoners suspected of making plans for escaping had a red-and-white target sewn or painted onto chest and back. The ss even devised a special marking for the feebleminded—an armband with the German word *Blöd*. Sometimes these unfortunates also had to wear a sign around their necks: "I am a moron!" [. . .]

It must be emphasized that the markings as such offered no assurance that the prisoners actually belonged to the designated classification.

Time and again the greens, or criminals, included men with whom it was possible to work—who showed staunch loyalty, indeed—whereas many a red, or political prisoner, should of rights have worn the green triangle. Reclassifications did occasionally take place, with varying degrees of justification.

220. Sopade report on the organization of the prisoners in the Dachau concentration camp, dated May 1937[12]

Every 54 men are a "room." Previously a room was called a corporalship. Its leader is a prisoner called the "senior room prisoner." Five rooms or corporalships are grouped together as a "block." Previously this was called a "company." Each block is accommodated in a hut of its own. The complete block therefore has 270 men. Each block is headed by a "senior block prisoner," likewise a prisoner. The senior block prisoner is subordinated to the "block leader," an SS man, usually of the rank of a *Scharführer* or *Oberscharführer*. The superior of the *Scharführer* is the *Rapportführer*, who is an SS *Sturmführer*. Next up is the prison camp leader with the rank of a *Standartenführer*. The prison camp together with the camp for the SS constitutes the "Dachau camp." The Dachau camp in its entirety is subject to a "camp commandant," who holds the rank of an SS *Oberführer*. [. . .]

In Dachau there are 9 blocks or companies. They are accommodated in different huts. We now present a description of these blocks:

I Company: This accommodates the so-called "second-time-rounders," i.e. all political protective custody prisoners who had been in Dachau once before and who, because of some offense, or often just because of suspicion, have been brought in for a second time. The second-time-rounders company is one of the saddest chapters in Dachau. It was only set up in the third year after Hitler's seizure of power and has by today become the core of the camp. The point is that the second-time-rounders are in a concentration camp within the concentration camp. According to fairly accurate estimates they number 190 to 200 men. They are entirely cut off from the other prisoners. No camp inmate is permitted to have contact with them. Their hut in the camp is surrounded by a solid fence. [. . .] One only sees these prisoners when they are marched to their place of work. They are assigned to the worst and hardest work. [. . .] The second-time-rounders' company is regarded in the camp as hell. The prisoners, who are mostly kept in their hut, look very ill. Their faces are marked by their strict detention. They are almost exclusively former political functionaries. They are accused of not having given up their activities against the regime in spite of the promises they have had to make during their first stay in Dachau. The mood of these prisoners is more depressed than in the rest of the camp. They are greatly pitied by the rest of the Dachau prisoners.

II Company: This is where the asocial elements are. Mostly people who have shirked their social obligations: beggars, drunkards, etc. They are the only ones who know how long they will be in Dachau, because they have been sentenced.[13] [. . .] On average an asocial person stays in Dachau for six months. If he is brought in for a second time he has to stay for a year, in the event of a third time, 2 years.[14] The asocials also include numerous criminals with previous convictions. The asocials usually feel superior to the political prisoners. There are hardly any relations between the two groups.

III Company: This consists of political protective custody prisoners exclusively. The company numbers 270 men. They are drawn upon for labor service and are used according to their occupations.

IV Company: This too consists of political prisoners exclusively, but mostly of those who have been in Dachau for a long time. This company also includes almost all the prominent personalities, such as the former Social Democratic Minister President of Braunschweig, Jasper.[15] Jasper is still being harassed a great deal. He was told: "So long as there is a decent worker in Dachau, you won't get out." He is made to do earth-moving work.

V Company: Likewise political prisoners.

VI Company: Jewish company. It contains about 100 men, all of them Jews. Now it is intended to move all the Jews in protective custody in the Reich to Dachau. Transports already arrived in February and March. The Jews are treated very badly. They are exposed to great chicanery. They are being constantly shown that they are despised and regarded as lower creatures. All Jews, regardless of what profession they had outside, are used for gravel work. They have to do heavy labor and are treated ruthlessly. Among the prisoners, too, there are many who despise the Jews. The camp command treats the

Jewish prisoners in the vilest manner. Pack drill is the order of the day. Frequently the Jewish company, like the second-time-rounders, is cut off from the other prisoners. Sometimes, to go even further, they are simply locked up in their hut. Thus, on one occasion they were totally locked up for 3 months. The doors to the hut were nailed up, the windowpanes were painted over. Only when the food was brought in was there some ventilation. In consequence the air in the hut was so bad that prisoners often fainted. As they were not allowed out, skin rashes appeared and other diseases. The lockup took place in the months of June to September 1936 and again from February to April 1937. The Jews are subdivided into three categories: political Jews, race defilers, Jewish émigrés.

VII Company: This consists of 3 corporalships or rooms of political prisoners; the fourth room contains the Aryan émigrés, the fifth contains those detained for offenses against § 175 [homosexuals]. The so-called one-hundred-and-seventy-fivers are only used for gravel work along with the Jews.

VIII Company: The first two corporalships contain political prisoners. This is the so-called reception company. Every person arriving in Dachau is first assigned to this company. Here he remains until he is assigned to one of the other companies. In consequence these two rooms are mostly not full. The third corporalship contains former penal prisoners, for the most part repeatedly convicted criminals, who have been sentenced to security confinement. The fourth and fifth corporalship also contains people sentenced to security confinement, but they are mixed here with asocial inmates who would really belong to II Company but are accommodated here because II Company is usually overfull.

The *last company*, which is not really regarded as a full company, contains the disabled and the sick. It also includes the former Reichstag deputy Kurt Schumacher.[16] They are accommodated in Hut X. This hut also contains the canteen and the library. The disabled are used for lighter work, such as help in the library, darning socks, kitchen service, etc., provided they are not in the infirmary and incapable of any work.

Marking of prisoners: All prisoners are marked by colored strips of material on their clothes according to the section they belong to.

The strips are 5 to 8 cm wide. Two are sewn to the trousers below the knee, two on the arms below the elbow and one on the back. [. . .]

Political prisoners: red strips, vertical on the back.

Forced labor [so-called asocials]: blue strips and across.

§ 175: red strips with black dots.

Second-time-rounders: red strips and across.

Security confinement: green strips and across.

Political Jews: red strips with yellow dots.

Jewish émigrés: red strips with blue dots.

Race defilers: yellow strips with red dots.

Bible researchers: red strips with . . . [*sic*] dots and across.

Aryan émigrés: blue strips and across the back.

5.2. Political Prisoners

German Communists made up a large number of all political prisoners throughout the 1930s, reflecting the Nazi obsession with the danger of Bolshevism. Although repression had reached its climax already in 1933, the Nazis continued to crack down on Communists. Social Democrats were also arrested in large numbers. In all, many thousands of left-wing activists were taken into protective custody between 1934 and 1936.[17] Apart from left-wing activists, the ss classified many other people as political prisoners, including some members of the Nazi Party who had fallen out of favor for one reason or another. One member of this small group was Anton Lehner, a Nazi Party veteran, apparently admitted to Dachau on Hitler's orders because of his alcoholism (226).

Political prisoners often engaged in some forms of clandestine resistance, reflected not least in camp songs. One example is the Sachsenhausen Song, composed by Communist prisoners in 1937. If all prisoners stuck together, ran the message, then they could endure.[18] However, because existing sources are rather biased, it is hard to evaluate the true extent of political activities within the camps. There are official Nazi sources, such as Rudolf Diel's report on Communist activity within the camps, which had good reasons to exaggerate the extent of these activities to justify radical measures against Communists (221). Apart from official Nazi documents, Communist sources also have to be read with some care. These accounts often report tightly organized Communist underground resistance groups in the camps. Take the case of the *Gegen-Angriff*, an exile Communist newspaper, which declared in a November 1934 article that Communist prisoners had celebrated the anniversary of the Russian Revolution in the Börgermoor camp in spite of Nazi repression (223). A story like this may well have been embellished for effect to reassure fellow Communists in Germany and abroad that there really was extensive organized Communist resistance in the camps.

Equally, post-1945 Communist accounts exaggerated such activities in the camps to lend credibility and legitimacy to the East German dictatorship.[19] After the forced merger of the East German Social Democrats with the dominant Communists in 1946 into the Socialist Unity Party (SED), East German accounts often stressed the alleged alliance between Communist and Social Democratic prisoners in the concentration camps, as did some leftist accounts written in the West (231).[20] In reality, matters were more complex, just as they had been in the early camps. Communist and Social Democratic inmates agreed that the Nazis were their common enemy, and prisoners from both groups sometimes worked together; yet they also still blamed each other for helping the Nazis into power in 1933.

Beyond that, solidarity among left-wing inmates took many different forms. It was often about practical help. When Walter Poller, a Social Democratic newspaper editor, arrived at Buchenwald in 1938, he immediately received better treatment than others, thanks to help from fellow political prisoners. The prisoners in charge of handing out uniforms gave him much better clothes and shoes than they gave to asocial prisoners who had arrived at the same time. Poller was also assigned a bed in a political prisoners' hut and soon found work as a scribe in the camp's infirmary, where, in turn, he would later help injured or ill political prisoners. Senior political prisoners also gave new arrivals like Poller vital advice about the rules of the camp and told them how to deal with ss guards (230).[21]

Prominent prisoners were particularly vulnerable, as they had been in the early camps. One of the victims was the pacifist Carl von Ossietzky, arrested on 28 February 1933 and later taken to the Esterwegen concentration camp, where ss guards tortured him so badly that he almost died. Following an international campaign, the Nazis released him from the camp in May 1936, although he remained in police custody in a Berlin hospital. Ossietzky was awarded the Nobel Peace Prize in November 1936, but the Nazis forbade him to travel to Oslo to accept it, and Ossietzky was awarded the prize in absentia. A broken and sick man, he died in 1938 (222).[22]

Another prominent political prisoner was Hans Litten, a lawyer with far-left sympathies. In the Weimar Republic Litten had been a brilliant anti-Nazi political lawyer. In 1931 he cross-examined Hitler in a high-profile trial that turned out to be highly embarrassing for the Nazi Party. Soon after they had captured power in Germany, the Nazis exacted brutal revenge. Arrested the day after the Reichstag fire, Litten, whose father was of Jewish descent, was taken to a number of early camps. Meanwhile, Litten's mother, well connected in conservative circles, lobbied for her son's release. All her pleas were rejected, allegedly on the direct order of Hitler, who is said to have harbored great resentment toward Litten. On 5 February 1938, weak and frail, Litten was found hanged in one of the latrines of the Dachau camp. According to an investigation by the German judicial authorities, he had committed suicide.[23] His mother, however, believed that her son had been murdered by the ss.[24] Whatever the truth, it is clear that Litten died of ss torture and abuse (228).

Within the group of political prisoners, Jehovah's Witnesses made up a special contingent. Banned by individual German states as early as 1933 (a national ban followed in 1935), many Jehovah's Witnesses, both men and women, were dragged into the concentration camps from the mid-1930s onward. The ss classified Jehovah's Witnesses as a separate group of prisoners. By 1937/38 they made up more than 10 percent of the overall population of the men's concentration camps and an even larger group in the women's camps: here, at times 40 percent and more of the inmates were Jehovah's Witnesses.[25] Despite strict ss orders to stop proselytizing and practicing their faith, Jehovah's Witnesses continued with these activities in the camps, for instance holding secret Bible meetings. The ss responded with brutal abuse (229), singling them out already upon arrival. At Dachau the ss isolated them from other prisoners in a separate hut and tormented them relentlessly. This took many forms, from open violence to constant ridicule: for example, one day in 1937 or 1938, Dachau ss guards forced a Jehovah's Witness to stand on a sand heap and made him shout "I am the greatest idiot of the twentieth century."[26]

The ss even tried to force Jehovah's Witnesses to renounce their faith. To this end, the ss forbade them to send or receive any mail in 1938, placing a huge strain on the prisoners and their families. In 1939 the ss partly lifted this ban, but Witnesses were still restricted to one letter of twenty-five words per month. Correspondents received a postcard from the ss, informing them that the restrictions were in place because the Witness had not renounced his faith.[27] At Dachau the ss also limited the food to Witnesses. Meanwhile, in Sachsenhausen the notorious ss officer Gustav Sorge ordered prisoners to bury a Jehovah's Witness up to his neck and then made other prisoners defecate on his head.[28] Despite all this abuse and humiliation, most Witnesses were undeterred and did not renounce their faith.[29]

DOCUMENTS

221. Letter from Rudolf Diels (Prussian Secret State Police office) to the Prussian district administrators regarding Communist propaganda among protective custody prisoners, dated 24 May 1933[30]

I attach a pamphlet which, under the title "Fanal," organ of the proletarian protective custody prisoners in Gollnow,[31] has been circulated among the protective custody prisoners. This pamphlet is of a clearly subversive Communist character, proving that even in protective custody the KPD functionaries are leaving nothing untried to rebuild their smashed Party apparatus and are developing a lively propaganda for the Communist ideas. I request all heads of prisons, concentration camps. etc., that contain police protective custody prisoners, to draw attention to the danger of renewed Communist agitation and to initiate suitable surveillance and control measures.

222. Report of a fellow prisoner on Carl von Ossietzky's detention in the Esterwegen concentration camp in spring 1934, published in 1937[32]

Work in the moor was very hard. Ossietzky also worked in the moor for some time. [. . .] Thus it came about that I was the leader of the potato squad. On one occasion I succeeded in getting Carl into that squad. That was during the initial period in Papenburg. This glory lasted for three weeks. This squad was of course better than work in the moor. It always only set out an hour later, one had contact with the civilian population and thus had something to eat. One day when I made my report at the camp gate "Eight men for potato fetching," the commandant and the *Lagermeister* [a senior camp official] suddenly stand by the gate. "Who are they?" he shouted. "Ossietzky?" "Who gave that order?" The *Lagermeister* immediately pounced on me with a dark red face and screamed at me. I did not move. But my Carl was sent back into the moor.

Prisoner Groups

223. *Der Gegen-Angriff*: Article about the commemoration of the October Revolution in the Börgermoor concentration camp, dated 7 November 1934[33]

The comrades were returning from the moor. The floor shook under the noisy wooden clogs. Everyone pushes into the hut. [. . .] "Quiet, friends, we now have time before the evening parade. For certain reasons we must make good use of the time. No one leaves the hut! We have made sure there won't be any unexpected disturbance." [. . .] "Comrades," after a long time this familiar word is heard, addressing everybody. "Comrades, today is the 16th anniversary of the Soviet Union! On one-sixth of the globe the workers' and peasants' power is holding sway. [. . .] We too, comrades, remain fighters for a German Soviet power, for the defense of the Soviet Union. Long live the rule of workers and peasants!" [. . .]

On the following morning the sand squad is pushing the tubs across the snow-covered moor. From a distance the sentries, by their little fire, rifles by their feet, are watching the platoon. "Hermann, yesterday in our Hut 7 [. . .]" "Yes, Jupp, in our Hut 5 also" — "and in our Hut 3, too!" "Boys, it worked out in all ten huts. We are growing and we are stronger than they with their weapons and barbed wire. We shall be the victors of tomorrow!"

224. Text of the "Sachsenhausen Song," composed by the Communist prisoners Karl Wloch, Bernhard Bästlein, and Karl Fischer in 1937[34]

We march along with steady step,
defying need and sorrow;
and marching with us is the hope
of freedom and tomorrow.

What lies behind us is the past,
we won't drag it along;
the future needs a real man,
to it we sing our song.

From Esterwegen we set out,
away from moor and mud,
and Sachsenhausen was soon reached,
the gates were once more shut.[35]

Behind barbed wire is our work,
our backs are sore from bending,
we're turning hard, we're turning tough,
our work is never ending.

A lot arrive but no one leaves,
the years just slip away,
before the camp is fully built
we will be old and gray.

Life lures beyond the wire fence:
it tempts us with its wonders,
the thought makes our throats go dry
and our minds will wander.

We march along with steady step,
defying need and sorrow;
and marching with us is the hope
of freedom and tomorrow.

225. Report by the Communist Harry Naujoks on the underground political leadership in the Sachsenhausen concentration camp and on relations between the criminal and political prisoners, published in 1987[36]

The natural political cell of the prisoners was usually their shared table in the block. This offered the opportunity to speak, as well as providing support and help whenever a personal crisis had to be mastered. It encouraged the individual to take part in the solution of any problems of the day. It involved them in discussions of political and moral problems. Based on the community at table, the senior block prisoner exercised an authority recognized as a rule by everybody. Conflicts resulting from living together in a very small space and from the consequences of ss terror could be kept within limits and any bad behavior by individual fellow prisoners could mostly be settled within the block. Of course this was more difficult if the senior block prisoner and the foreman were behaving in a non-comradely manner or if they yielded to ss pressure. However, provision of work, mutual help, observation of the ss and their intentions could not be a matter for the block functionaries alone. Collection of political and other information and its passing on to a qualified prisoner authority would facilitate generalizations and conclusions by the prisoners. Rapid decisions could only be taken centrally. An urgent need therefore was the creation of an illegal leadership that enjoyed the respect and trust of the anti-fascist prisoners and which would not be obvious to the ss.

Among the political prisoners the Communists were the strongest group: it excelled by its closed ranks and solidarity, by its fundamental and consistent opposition to the Nazis, by its experience and theoretical knowledge. Most of them had been imprisoned for years. Right from the beginning they had looked for opportunities, by legal and illegal work, to defend the interests of the prisoners and to act against the intentions of the Nazis. Whenever the administration or the Gestapo succeeded in breaking up a resistance group, a new circle would become active again soon afterward. [. . .] Many non-Communist prisoners who had experienced the solidarity and resistance activity of the Communists became our followers: Social Democrats, SAP and KPÖ people,[37] trade unionists, as well as bourgeois people and intellectuals who had not belonged to a political organization before. Whoever came, came of his own free will. Any pressure to join such a group ran counter to the laws of illegality. [. . .]

At the beginning of 1937 the barbed wire which until then had separated the camp from the parade ground was removed. The strict separation between the "red" and the "green" side of the camp was also no longer rigorously observed and disappeared completely in the course of time. Whereas the two major prisoner groups had only previously met during work, there were now no longer any obstacles in their free time. Soon, however, problems arose that, with the stronger growth of the non-political groups, gained in importance for the pattern of camp life.

As part of a campaign which extended throughout the Reich, some 300 so-called "BV men" [professional criminals] arrived in Sachsenhausen in mid-March 1937. [. . .] A strange mix of society was coming into the camp. There were some who had a criminal record but who had since worked for years without committing an offense. With few exceptions they had been opportunist thieves and cheats. Some had engaged in arguments with Nazi functionaries or had somehow made themselves unpopular or had been involved in acts of violence by the ss or sa. Others came into camp as "criminals" for slander or breach of peace. A number of Jews were also brought in with the designation "BV." They had previous sentences because, when Jewish shops were raided, they had resisted the looters, or for failure to observe the "name regulation,"[38] or for infringing the regulation on the "employment of Aryan domestic servants,"[39] or for so-called revilement if, for instance, they could not get out of the way of a Nazi demonstration and, when the Swastika flag was carried past them, only had the choice between saluting it with a raised arm or being beaten up.

One purpose pursued by the Gestapo and SS with these mass arrests of persons with previous convictions or suspected persons was the criminalization of protective custody prisoners in the eyes of the public. The various descriptions of the reasons for their arrest were to help in marking all opponents of Nazism as criminals. The fascists were hoping to make those Germans who had become insecure because of the terror to turn away from their persecuted fellow citizens. For the camps the Gestapo and SS created the variety of prisoner categories in order to divide the prisoners and prevent a united stance by them.

These 300 new ones were all categorized by the SS as BV men (with green markers). Many of them had been induced by social circumstances to "acquire" things occasionally by crooked means. But these people were also inclined to form an alliance with power. Snatched from their accustomed lives, they were overrun in the concentration camps by the blind and furious terror of the SS; most of them were seized by panic during their very first hours. They were soon prepared to submit to everything that the SS demanded of them in order to ensure their survival.

Many greens who came from a simple or petit bourgeois background [. . .] found real satisfaction at being on an equal level, in the camp, with prominent politicians, scientists, artists and lawyers. In many cases hatred of those they regarded as "better" led to an atmosphere in which the different prisoner categories could be played against one another.

For the political prisoners a clear relationship with the BV men became a decisive question that was much discussed. Essentially we reached agreement, albeit with occasional reverses. Our attitude to the green ones was generally governed by the fact that these people were also victims of Nazism. Often not even a Nazi court of law had found a law under which they could be sentenced. [. . .] For us political prisoners, our relations of prisoners with one another were determined solely by the individual's behavior to the camp's ss. Of course there were also criminal prisoners who consistently supported the ss. Between those prisoners and their guards relations soon arose which, in the course of time, led to genuine comradeship. [. . .]

As a result of our united front we political prisoners represented a force that was capable, in a conflict with the green ones, of coming out on top. Our conviction that the Nazis would not be at the helm forever gave a ray of hope also to the others and contributed to their growing confidence in us. [. . .] To the majority of the greens our sense of solidarity was something unfamiliar. Anti-fascist comradeship or political conviction meant little to them. Among them each person was first of all fighting for his own place in the life of the camp.

226. Letter from Heinrich Himmler to Anton Lehner, a National Socialist prisoner in Dachau, dated 18 May 1937[40]

My dear Lehner Toni,

Of course you will be released. The date I must still reserve to myself. When you are released I shall also find a job for you. But I will release you only when I have convinced myself that you are totally abstaining from alcohol, which over the years, to the horror of your family and yourself, time and again became your master so that, on many occasions, you presented a picture unworthy of an old National Socialist. Your punishment was not imposed by the Führer in order to hurt you, but in order to divert you, at long last, from a road that would certainly have brought you and your family to the abyss.

227. Report by Herbert Vogel, ss *Sturmmann* in the Buchenwald concentration camp, on a Communist prisoner, dated 18 September 1937[41]

The protective custody prisoner F., Ernst, brought in on 18.9.1937 [. . .] lied to me when I took his personal details. When I asked him if he had ever been in Russia, he replied with a resolute "No." When I had pointed out to F. that he would be punished if he made a false statement and when he was about to sign the personal information sheet, he admitted that he had been in Russia in 1929–1930. As an excuse he thought that this information would be disadvantageous for him.

228. *Neuer Vorwärts*: Article on Hans Litten, dated 19 December 1937[42]

The attorney Hans Litten has also been one of the prisoners of the German concentration camps since their establishment. He is neither a Social Democrat nor a Communist,[43] though in several political trials he served justice against the National Socialists. In the spring of 1931, for instance, he took part in a trial in which National Socialist terrorists were sentenced to terms of penitentiary. The fact that Hitler appeared as a witness in that trial and, cornered by his questions, played a somewhat unhappy role, became Litten's misfortune. On the day following the Nazi arson in the Reichstag he was arrested. Fellow prisoners since released have testified that he had to bear the most horrendous maltreatment. Litten twice attempted suicide. He also suffered an injury recently that, according to official information, is due to an accident at work and is said to be now "almost fully healed."

229. Report by the Jehovah's Witness Arthur Winkler on his detention in the Esterwegen concentration camp, published in 1938[44]

I, the undersigned, was a prisoner in the Esterwegen concentration camp in East Frisia, Germany. My reports are based on personal experiences, and in part on what I saw, heard, and personally encountered. The Gestapo brought me to the camp sketched above, because I am a Jehovah's Witness. Merely the fact that I am a Witness and believe in God's word, gave the Gestapo adequate justification to bring me to this camp. Initially I was brought before an investigative judge; he acquitted and released me, stating: "I do not know what the Gestapo will do with you now." The Gestapo rearrested me two days later. [. . .] The Jehovah's Witnesses are the daily targets for every kind of persecution, terror, and brutality. Using the previously mentioned methods, an attempt was made to force them to disavow their belief in their God Jehovah and his Word, the Bible. They did not receive any Bibles, on principle, in the camp; nor are Bibles given out to prisoners anymore. Attempts were made, with every possible and impossible means, to force them to sign a sworn statement, declaring that they no longer want to be Witnesses, that they will never again resume contact and association with the Witnesses, and that they will no longer read any literature from the Witnesses. In order to ridicule them in front of other prisoners, Witnesses are called "paradise birds," "heaven clowns," "Jesus grasper," and also occasionally they are called "Jehovah." Those who do not capitulate and remain unwavering in their faith are forced to wear a yellow band below the knee, a blatant symbol of identification and to show they were assigned to a punishment company. In the opinion of the ss, the Witnesses were the worst traitors, incorrigible, and the scum of humankind. The brutality mentioned in issue no. 370[45] are not the only ones [*sic*] committed against Witnesses. The report leader Tarré attacked a number of Witnesses in the prisoner bathhouse. They were forced to undress and Tarré personally sprayed them with squirts of ice-cold water. Cold water under special atmospheric pressure was squirted on their sex organs and at their abdomen. During this maltreatment, they were constantly asked whether they still wanted to remain a Witness and they were threatened with the continuation of these measures unless they renounced their faith. Since no one abandoned their beliefs, he continued this sadism until the victims were completely exhausted.

230. Report of the Social Democrat Walter Poller on his arrival in Buchenwald in December 1938, published in 1946[46]

We came to the prisoners' clothing room. Stacked on shelves there are many uniforms, underwear, boots, etc. Prisoners are employed here: they are looking relatively good and clean. Nearly all of them are wearing the red "triangle." We new arrivals are first sorted by them. Over here the politicals who are to wear the red triangle, over there the work-shy and asocial ones for the black triangle, the Bible researchers for the purple one, the criminals for the green one, the homosexuals for the pink one. The Jews receive a yellow one in addition to their colored one: this they have to cross with their colored triangle to make a Star of David. Nearly every prisoner behind the table first asks me what color I have. Next to me stands a "Black." He gets conspicuously worse clothes than me. At the boots issue I first get a pair of "worn-out" boots. As the prisoner is about to hand them over to me, he asks: "Political?" and when I say Yes, he gets me a better pair of boots. Only we politicals are asked whether we have brought along a pullover or a woolen cardigan. Whoever has not got one receives such an item of clothing—but not any of the other prisoner categories.

By now it is clear to me that there is some organization behind this. For a moment I was naive enough to assume that the camp command is behind it, but the next moment I thought the idea absurd and totally in contrast to everything that I have experienced so far, so that I am ashamed of myself. How much more probable, for a thousand good reasons and a thousand-fold experiences, is the assumption that some political organization must still exist even in the camp. [. . .]

When fallen in on the parade ground we have to stand to attention on the command of a prisoner, then a short prisoner emerges from the shadows who lets us stand at ease. He is wearing a thick dark military greatcoat and has an armlet with some lettering that I cannot decipher in the twilight. He then treats us to a somewhat bombastic speech. He tells us how to behave. Inside the camp we would be largely unmolested. Entering huts other than one's own was prohibited. We had to work diligently, until we drop. Any orders by the hut service, the senior block prisoner, the Kapos, the camp supervisors and the senior camp prisoner had to be obeyed instantly and without contradiction. Above all, there must be no attempt to escape—which would be nonsense here anyway. In that event fire would be opened at once and the whole camp would suffer for it. Anyone with a problem could turn to him. If he could help, he would. But anyone not obeying would get it in the neck. He could not possibly enumerate all the punishments that were a daily occurrence in the camp. He could tell us just one thing: there was nothing in the camp that was impossible—all the way to hanging [. . .].

231. Report by the former prisoner Hans Schwarz on the political activity in the German concentration camps, July 1945[47]

When the National Socialists set up the first German concentration camps in 1933—they were Dachau and Oranienburg—[the inmates] were without exception the old functionaries and the most active members of the German opposition parties. These political prisoners were conscious of their task and they fulfilled their duty to the end, often to their death. In the first few years of the German concentration camps informers and accomplices of the ss were probably rare phenomena.

However, this changed immediately when the ss realized that they might easily break the inflexible will of those prisoners by infiltrating numerous asocial and criminal elements among the political prisoners and thereby eliminating the unity of interests, will and action among the political prisoners. From 1937 onward an increasing number of criminal and asocial elements were brought into the camp.

During the first few years the political prisoners also held all positions in the camp, such as senior camp prisoner, camp scribe, senior block prisoner and senior room prisoner, Kapos and foremen, etc. During those years maltreatment, torture and atrocities by prisoners against prisoners were rare, as they were all united by the common idea of a common hatred of Nazism. No special political activity was therefore necessary. The running of the camp, self-administration among the prisoners, political schooling and information were a unity.

This picture changed considerably in the years after 1937. In several camps the ss and the camp command first appointed professional criminals, who were available for anything, as Kapos and in some cases also as senior block or senior room prisoners. At exactly the same time as the appointment of these professional criminals began a wave of informing, of black marketeering and corruption, of the most cruel maltreatment all the way to the killing of one's own comrades in the German concentration camps. At that time the political prisoners' lives are no longer safe from their fellow prisoners. They are compelled to organize in groups of their own, to maintain their cadres, in order to be able to perform their task of working for the interests of their fellow prisoners. The political prisoners therefore had to fight for every position in the camp, such as senior block prisoner, Kapo, etc., since the ss were only too willing to grant favors to anyone who would work for them. These professional criminals and—let us state it clearly and openly—individual demoralized "political prisoners" were prepared in exchange for cigarettes [. . .] or to save their lives to participate in anything that the ss demanded of them. Thus a political leadership of the prisoners gradually crystallized, which of course had to be hidden from the eyes of the camp command. This political leadership that had to be kept strictly secret, as punishment of death was unhesitatingly carried out by the ss camp command for any activity within the concentration camps, had to build up an apparatus that could not be wrecked at one blow by the Gestapo or the camp command.

This apparatus made use of the influential positions in the camp by filling these posts with truly responsible political prisoners and by dealing with any differences by education and enlightenment or, where other means did not work, by physical force. Thus, in the camps where the political prisoners held the leading positions narcs and informers were rendered harmless by every available means. With the result that spying and informing rapidly ceased [. . .]. Our comrades as Kapos and foremen, despite the orders of the ss, ensured that maltreatments by ss men and civilian ss workers were, often at the risk of their own lives, prevented.

5.3. Social Outsiders

Historians have only begun recently to explore the fate of so-called asocial and criminal prisoners in the camps, but even this new scholarship can tell us relatively little about their backgrounds or their treatment inside, though it is clear that they were often severely abused (38).[48] As we have seen, various party and state institutions had begun to use the camps to repress social outsiders already in 1933. This practice continued throughout the 1930s. The Bavarian authorities, for instance, continued to transfer workhouse inmates, including beggars and vagrants, from the overcrowded Rebdorf workhouse, set in a small Bavarian town, to Dachau. Welfare authorities elsewhere also transferred some workhouse inmates as well as welfare recipients to camps. Indeed, it became increasingly common for the authorities to dump alleged asocial elements in concentration camps. Initially, workhouse inmates were often only held there for a short while, but before long they could be transferred to the camps for well over one year.[49] Of course, detention in a concentration camp was just one among many instruments used by the welfare and police authorities; others included handing over individuals to courts and, of course, detaining them in state welfare institutions, where conditions were sometimes approaching those inside the concentration camps.[50]

There were many links between the different institutions of confinement in the Third Reich. In Bavaria, for example, welfare and police offices could send certain men deemed "asocial" to the Herzogsägmühle Central Ramblers' Hostel. Conditions in the hostel were tough. Among the detainees were long-term unemployed men, alcoholics, the homeless, vagrants, and Gypsies. All inmates were screened to identify those who would have to be excluded more permanently from society. Those classed as recalcitrant or unreformable were regularly admitted to Dachau, where they were classified as asocial. Any resistance to the welfare authorities could be punished severely. If an inmate ran away, for example, he could be transferred to Dachau immediately after his recapture.[51]

Among the social outsiders caught up in the Nazi web of terror was Willy S., a twenty-five-year-old man from Dresden, who had run away from Herzogsägmühle several times because of the unbearable conditions. On 7 February 1938 the welfare authorities finally transferred him to Dachau. S. appealed in vain. He would spend the rest of his life at Dachau, where he died on 31 October 1941 (236).[52]

Another case was that of an allegedly work-shy man from Garmisch-Partenkirchen, site of the 1936 Winter Olympics.[53] The local Nazi welfare office there requested his transfer to the Dachau camp in fall 1936 and applied to the Dachau camp authorities for his admission, also requesting that the man be castrated. The Dachau camp doctor declined to admit him, but the camp commandant overrode this decision and the man was transferred to Dachau (233).

A similar fate befell Georg B., a thirty-three-year-old builder from Ausgburg. B. had long been known to the local welfare and police authorities. A medical report classified him as a typical asocial. His parents, it said, had been alcoholics, too, confirming the Nazis' unshakable belief in hereditary degeneracy. To make matters worse, B. also had a string of criminal offenses. The report concluded that B. should not be allowed to remain in a social housing project on the outskirts of Augsburg, which should be reserved for Aryan families with children. In May 1937 the Augsburg welfare authorities finally had enough of him and requested his transfer to Dachau. Here, the camp doctor demanded B.'s sterilization, which had to be approved by a Hereditary Health Court, set up by the Nazis in 1933–34 to decide on applications for sterilization.[54]

Such cases were not exceptional. A number of concentration camp inmates, classified as congenitally ill, were sterilized. Others were castrated. One month in the summer of 1938, for example, at least two prisoners underwent this surgery inside Buchenwald infirmary itself (237).[55] Here were graphic examples of the Nazi policy of cleansing the German body politic, implemented by close collaboration between the ss, the medical profession, welfare authorities, and ss police.

Some homosexual men were also admitted to the camps, as we have seen.[56] Inside, they were treated with extreme severity by ss officials like Rudolf Höß, who allegedly tried to "cure" them of their homosexuality (239).[57] Not all homosexual men in the prewar camps

254

wore the pink triangle; some wore the green triangle as the ss classified them as criminals for violating paragraph 175 of the German
criminal code. This rather confused classification—typical of ss efforts to divide prisoners into distinct groups—makes it hard to estimate numbers of homosexual prisoners. In Dachau, it seems, there
were just under six hundred homosexual prisoners between 1933 and
1945. Most of those arrested before 1936 were released after a year
or two, while those arrested from 1937 onward were usually not released and often died in the camps. This pattern undoubtedly reflects
the general radicalization of Nazi policies toward social outsiders.[58]

After so-called asocials, criminals made up the largest contingent
of social outsiders in the concentration camps.[59] Taken to the camps
since 1933 (16), their numbers rose in the late 1930s.[60] Once inside,
they were by no means always favored by the ss, as some political
prisoners later claimed. On the contrary, ss officials subjected criminal prisoners to brutal welcoming ceremonies, just as they did other new arrivals (240). For the Nazis and the criminal police, who ordered the transfer to the concentration camps, alleged habitual and
professional criminals threatened the very fabric of the Third Reich.
They were seen as a moral, social, political, and biological menace
to the people's community—a picture frequently at odds with reality, as many suspects were just petty criminals, with numerous minor convictions for theft or fraud. Only few of them, it seems, were
guilty of serious offenses, such as robbery or homicide, as the punishment of such crimes remained the domain of the judiciary (and
regular prisons). Many hundreds of Jews were arrested as criminals,
too, simply because of violations of the ever more draconian anti-
Semitic legislation.

One such criminal prisoner was Josef K., a thirty-year-old lathe
turner from Vienna. He was arrested on 14 June 1938 by the Vienna
criminal police amid the "Work-Shy Reich" raids and taken to Dachau,
from where he was transferred to the new Flossenbürg camp alongside
other criminal prisoners on 1 July 1938.[61] K. had long been known to
the police. His criminal record included a six-week sentence for handling stolen goods and an eight-month sentence for attempted burglary. On 30 November 1938 the Flossenbürg commandant, following a central ss rule that the camp authorities had to report regularly

on each prisoner's conduct, wrote a negative report, and K.'s release was declined (241). He was eventually set free on 20 April 1939 after the commandant claimed that his behavior had improved under the impact of hard labor and the harsh realities of life in the camp. K. was forced to sign a declaration that he would not disclose any details of his imprisonment.[62] By no means all criminal prisoners were released, however, especially after the beginning of World War II.

Criminal prisoners were, of course, subject not only to ss terror but also to the judiciary. Take the case of Leopold K., a forty-six-year-old worker from Vienna. Arrested in Vienna on 15 June 1938, he was taken to Dachau and then to Flossenbürg, on the same transport as Josef K. A petty thief who had served several prison sentences, he still had an outstanding conviction by a court in Krems on the Danube for attempted theft. Soon after his arrest, the Krems court wrote to the Flossenbürg camp to request K.'s transfer to a state prison where he would serve his sentence. Remarkably, the ss agreed to this and many similar requests (242).[63] K. was transferred to the Straubing penitentiary in Lower Bavaria, returning to Flossenbürg after he had served his sentence. He was finally released in February 1941.[64]

DOCUMENTS

232. Letter of the Bavarian Ministry of the Interior to the Ministry of Finance regarding the campaign against the "mischief of begging and work-shyness," dated 17 August 1934[65]

The drive against the mischief of begging and vagabondage, which had assumed a downright alarming scale last year, resulted last autumn, following the week of struggle against begging throughout the whole Reich,[66] in extraordinary success. This contributed substantially to a raising of the population's morale and inducing them to make great efforts for the Winter Aid Scheme.[67] One consequence of the drive against begging was, admittedly, an overcrowding of the workhouse in Rebdorf, as a thorough action against the relevant strata of the population was, and still is, possible and successful only by confinement in a workhouse. All other means, especially that of short-term punishment, have failed. My attempts to enlarge the Rebdorf workhouse through the building of extensions, in particular a camp of huts, in order to provide room for a major number of prisoners, were unfortunately unsuccessful as, in the budgetary discussions, the funds could not be made available. There was therefore no other way than resorting to the Dachau concentration camp for the provisional accommodation of the work-shy prisoners and placing a major number of prisoners—now over 500—there.

Admittedly, the camp administration has demanded a sum of 1 M per day per head for the accommodation of each prisoner, deducted from the budget of the workhouses. I shall not be able to concede this rate. The budget that was laid down on the basis of a figure of 1,000 prisoners—including 200 females in Aichach[68]—only amounts to a sum of 90 Pfennig.

Developments have made it necessary for new strict instructions to be issued for the drive against the resurging mischief of begging. It may be expected that the total of prisoners in the course of this year will greatly exceed 1,000 heads, as this figure, if Dachau is included, has already long been surpassed.

The total of prisoners is expected, in the course of this year, to reach at least an average of 1,200 heads. This means, given the approved budgetary funds, a sum of only 77 Pfennig per head of prisoners. As, according to the data announced at the budgetary discussions, the requirement for food in the camp amounts to 60 to 70 Pfennig per head per day, I shall not be able to pay more than that to the Dachau camp budget from the workhouse budget. As for their clothes, the workhouse inmates so far transferred to Dachau at the request of the camp administration have brought these along from Rebdorf anyway. The rest of the expenses will have to be met from the Reich's contributions to protective custody.

I am informing you of this in advance and will be grateful for your comment.

233. Letter of the NS People's Welfare, District Head Garmisch-Partenkirchen to the Dachau concentration camp, dated 12 September 1936[69]

We have an asocial element here that requires acceptance into your camp. However, the man is an invalid with severe testicular tumor, residue of a stroke, disturbed balance and speech disorder. He refuses to submit to an operation that, in the view of the district physician, would make the asocial person fit for work.

I request information on whether we can successfully continue proceedings for his admission to your place. It might be possible in this way for the asocial element to be improved. Above all, it would certainly make it possible for the operation to be carried out under the pressure of circumstances.

Heil Hitler!
The District Office Head

ss Station physician, Dachau concentration camp
[Handwritten note]
Unfortunately one cannot force anybody to undergo an operation. The protective custody detainee, unless—as may be assumed—he is altogether unsuitable for admission, would certainly be assigned here to the invalids' company. Admission must therefore, from a medical point of view, be refused.

234. Reply of the Dachau concentration camp to the Garmisch-Partenkirchen District Head of ns People's Welfare, dated 22 September 1936[70]

With reference to your letter of 12.9.36 I can inform you that there are no concerns here regarding the delivery of your asocial element to the Dachau concentration camp [. . .]. A condition, however, is that you will meet the relevant costs, i.e. RM 1.20 per day for accommodation. In addition, in the event of the operation in question being performed, you would also have to assume the hospital and operation costs.

Following his delivery to us every attempt would be made to induce the man to undergo the operation, because otherwise he would be almost unsuitable for involvement in a productive work process. In this case he could only be drawn upon for light work, which of course would not hold out a promise of enduring improvement to the same extent as in a healthy person.

235. Letter from the Dachau camp doctor to the Municipal Health Office Augsburg regarding the sterilization of Georg B., dated 19 August 1937[71]

An application for the sterilization of B., Georg because of serious alcoholism was made by me today and will be directed to the Hereditary Health Court Munich, competent for the camp. The papers concerning drinker care[72] have been returned directly [to this court].

236. Application by the Central Ramblers' Hostel Herzogsägmühle to the District Office Schongau for the deportation of Willy S. to Dachau, dated 3 February 1938[73]

Hereby we request the District Office Schongau to be good enough to deport S. to the Dachau concentration camp for his education. We are making this request for the following reasons [. . .]. It was impossible to get S. to do any work either by kindness or unkindness. He invariably unlawfully left the work assigned to him and had to be searched for every time. His favorite place was where work had been finished but food not yet issued. He was rebellious and recalcitrant to foremen, house leaders and superiors. [. . .] On 1.1.38 S. secretly escaped from the hostel. By this behavior he grossly violated his work task. [. . .] S.'s whole behavior has to be described as asocial and dangerous to the community to the highest degree. He repeatedly and grossly violated the work assigned to him. It is urgently necessary to protect the people's community from such a person and to deport S. for some time to the Dachau concentration camp.

237. From the monthly report of the SS doctor in the Buchenwald concentration camp, dated 8 June 1938[74]

During the month under review 4 sterilizations were performed at the Weimar municipal hospital. In the operation room of the prisoners' infirmary 2 castrations were carried out. The new operation room in the prisoners' infirmary meets the requirements of sterile operating. Sterilization and castration applications are continually dealt with or have been confirmed. The entire body of prisoners is being schematically examined for possible sterilization or castration applications.

238. From the verdict of the State Court Stade on the former Buchenwald SS *Oberscharführer* Otto Hop, dated 25 January 1972[75]

During his introductory period the accused proved himself satisfactory within the meaning of his superior officers so that the independent leadership of Block 26 and later also of Block 25 was soon afterward entrusted to him. Both blocks were then occupied by so-called

ASR (work-shy, Reich) prisoners. As an outward distinguishing mark these prisoners wore a black triangle on their striped garb. [. . .] Soon after assuming his activity as a block leader the accused developed into a feared and brutal thug whom the prisoners avoided whenever possible. He frequently beat the prisoners for trifling or freely invented reasons, not only with his fists but also maltreating them with cudgels or by kicking.

239. Notes by Rudolf Höß on homosexual prisoners, written 1947[76]

The homosexuals had already become a problem in Dachau, even though numerically they were unimportant compared to Sachsenhausen. The commandant and the protective custody camp leader believed that it would be best to distribute them about the camp among all the rooms. I held the opposite view because I knew them sufficiently from penitentiary.[77] It did not take long before reports were coming in from all blocks about homosexual intercourse. Punishments made no difference whatever. The epidemic spread. — At my suggestion the homosexuals were now all put together. They were given a senior room prisoner who knew how to deal with them. And they were put to work separately from the other prisoners. Thus for a long time they pulled the road roller. [. . .] At one stroke the epidemic was over.

240. Report by the political prisoner Alfred Hübsch on the arrival of criminal prisoners at the Dachau concentration camp in 1937, written ca. 1960[78]

Reception of these unfortunates [professional criminals] was a very special pleasure for the "Staf" [*Standartenführer* Baranowski]. With biting irony he gave them the customary "instructions." He began something like this:

Listen up, you filth! Do you know where you are? — Yes? — No, you don't know? Well then, I'll explain it to you. You are not in a prison and you are not in a penitentiary either. No. You are in a concentration camp. That means you are in an educational camp! You are to be educated here — and we'll educate you all right. You may rely on that, you stinking swine! — You will be given useful work here. Anyone not performing it to our satisfaction will be helped by us. We have our methods! You'll get to know them. There's no loafing about here and let no one believe he can run away. No one escapes from here. The sentries have instructions to shoot without warning at any attempt to escape. And we have here the elite of the SS!—our boys are very good shots. You can rely on that. But if someone slips through nevertheless, he won't get far. Our search service goes into action at once and woe unto him who is brought back! He'll get something on his a...hole! Well, that's what I wanted to say to you.—Dismissed!

241. Letter of the commandant of the Flossenbürg concentration camp to the Reich Criminal Police Office regarding the preventive police custody prisoner Josef K., dated 30 November 1938[79]

The BV[80] detainee Josef K., born [...]08 in Vienna, was delivered to the Dachau concentration camp on 15.6.38 and transferred to the Floßenbürg concentration camp on 1.7.38.

His behavior and work performance at present are *still* bad.

K. is lazy and sluggish at work and has to be constantly criticized.

At this time I decline his release.

242. Letter of the Flossenbürg concentration camp commandant to the Straubing penitentiary regarding the transfer of the preventive police custody detainee Leopold K., dated 3 August 1939[81]

The preventive custody detainee Leopold K. [...] was today, at the request of the Provincial [*Land*] Court Krems, transferred by mass transport to the Straubing penitentiary.

While he is serving his sentence care is to be taken to make it impossible for him to make contact with other detainees. He is not allowed to send any mail, nor to receive any; this [mail] is to be sent to the postal censorship office of the concentration camp. He must not be drawn upon for work outside the penitentiary because, as an inmate of a concentration camp, he is at all times under suspicion of trying to escape. When he has served his sentence I request that he is immediately transferred back by mass transport.

In particular I point out that he must not receive any visits, not even from a lawyer.

Preventive police custody is merely suspended by this transfer. Lifting of preventive police custody and release of the detainee are decided by the Reich Criminal Police Office in Berlin.

5.4. Jews

Jews made up only a small percentage of the prewar camps' overall population, probably not more than between 5 and 10 percent before the November 1938 pogrom. Yet the treatment of Jews was always particularly harsh, hardly surprising given the ss's virulent anti-Semitism. Indeed, some historians have seen the prewar concentration camps as a testing ground for the regime's anti-Jewish policy. In the camps the ss could more or less treat Jews at their discretion, especially from the mid-1930s when legal investigations of camp atrocities petered out. Jewish prisoners came from different social, political, and religious backgrounds. Jews in the camps could be anything from left-wing political activists to bourgeois politicians, cattle dealers to businessmen, secular to orthodox. There was, therefore, relatively little cohesion among Jewish prisoners, at least initially. For the inmates, these differences were often profound. For the ss, by contrast, they did not matter much: for them, all Jews were on the lowest rung of prisoners.[82]

As soon as they arrived in the concentration camps, Jews were subjected to the full repertory of ss terror. Take the case of a Jewish man who reported from exile in August 1936 on what he had experienced at the Esterwegen camp. Like tens of thousands of other German Jews, he had left Nazi Germany in 1933 to look for a better life for his family and himself abroad, safe from state-sponsored anti-Semitism. He went to Paris and established a business that soon folded under the impact of the economic depression. With no future in France, he returned to Germany to find work, leaving his family behind in France. The Nazi authorities soon caught up with him and took him to Esterwegen for "instructive custody," along with other Jewish refugees who returned to Germany.[83] At Esterwegen the man was subjected to the worst imaginable treatment by the ss and even considered suicide. Anti-Semitic bullying by young ss guards was rife. Until his imprisonment the man had seen himself as a German national who, like many other Jews, had fought in the German army in World War I.[84] Released after six months, he left Germany as quickly as he could (243).

Jewish prisoners were often housed in so-called Jewish blocks. In Dachau the camp authorities even temporarily isolated Jewish prisoners more than once in a hut with boarded-up windows as a punishment for foreign and exile "atrocity propaganda," allegedly the result of a Jewish world conspiracy. The prisoners were allowed to leave the huts only briefly each day.[85] ss guards also regularly mocked the Jewish religion. On Yom Kippur, the highest Jewish holiday, Dachau ss men in 1937 deliberately forced Jewish prisoners to carry out senseless labor (244). Jews were also often held longer than other prisoners because commandants' reports on Jews were negative in the extreme. In addition, releases of Jewish prisoners were regularly suspended altogether on Himmler's personal orders. In November 1937, for instance, Himmler temporarily banned any releases of Jews from Dachau because of foreign "atrocity stories" (245). A ban on releases, the ss assumed in its paranoid belief in a Jewish world conspiracy, might stop Jewish journalists abroad from publishing more critical stories about the camps.

Anti-Semitic atrocities inside the camps escalated further in the late 1930s, as prisoner numbers continued to rise: during the "Work-Shy Reich" raids of 1938, at least twenty-five hundred Jews were taken to the camps. The police had often arrested them under the pretext of minor violations of anti-Jewish legislation. Inside the camps, living conditions deteriorated sharply (246).[86] Throughout the 1930s, Jews in the camps almost always appear to have suffered the highest death rate of all prisoner groups.

In the wake of the November 1938 pogrom, as we have seen, around twenty-six thousand Jewish men, from all ages and backgrounds, were taken to the concentration camps in Dachau, Sachsenhausen, and Buchenwald.[87] The mass arrests had been carried out in mid-November by the Gestapo, aided by local policemen. In major towns with large Jewish populations, such as Frankfurt am Main and Breslau, Jews were taken to collection points from which they were bussed to the train station, sometimes after an agonizing wait of several days. Eventually, special trains took them to the camps, guarded by armed guards, sometimes officers. Deliberately, as a means of humiliation and abuse, no food was provided for prisoners on their long journey. When the prisoners arrived, ss men made them assemble at the station, where they beat them and often issued death threats. The way to the camp was accompanied by further violence.

Once inside the camp, the Jews arrested after the pogrom had to undergo the typical initiation ritual, followed by daily roll calls, excessive drill exercises, and often also exhausting labor, such as in feared construction work of the new brickworks in Sachsenhausen (**248**).[88] Jewish prisoners in the camps often tried to help the new arrivals get over the first days inside (**249**), as did some of the other inmates. Still, conditions in the overcrowded camps were dreadful and many Jewish prisoners were also systematically robbed by the ss (**169**). Scores of them were brutally murdered.[89]

Most Jewish prisoners were released a few weeks or months after the pogrom.[90] Before they were released, the ss terrorized the Jewish prisoners one last time and made them wait for hours by the camp gate. Prisoners were subjected to an intimidating interrogation at the political section and threatened with immediate re-arrest and death if they told anyone about their experiences in the camp (**249**).[91]

DOCUMENTS

243. Report of a Jewish re-immigrant on his experiences in the Esterwegen concentration camp, written in August 1936[92]

Conditions in Germany had compelled me to leave my homeland. As it seemed out of the question that, given the nature of my past activity I would ever have an opportunity to work in my old occupation, I went to Paris with my family in 1933. I had some funds and so I succeeded in establishing my own small enterprise. Unfortunately the initial success I achieved could not be maintained. The crisis that descended on France[93] shook my business so hard that I eventually had no alternative but to go into liquidation. Chance seemed to help me. An opportunity arose for me to accept a good position in a large enterprise in Germany. I had never concerned myself with political problems and had not bothered about politics in Paris either. As with most refugees, the struggle for my existence displaced all other issues. I therefore had no hesitation in accepting this position. After all, I had to provide for a largish family. I was also guided by the thought that I did not wish to become a burden to anyone in a foreign country while I still had some assets in Germany. I therefore went first to my hometown and reported to the police. From there I went to my new place of work to assume my post. I had left my family in France, intending to let them follow me later. On 6 December I was arrested in my office. I was taken to prison and spent 10 days there in solitary confinement. I was told nothing about the reason for my arrest. The arrest was performed by the Secret State Police. A record was taken down that included the reason for my emigration to France and the reason for my return. They wanted from me detailed information about my activity in Paris, in particular whether I had belonged to any political organizations and whether I had drawn any subsidy. In the interrogation I was told that the order for my arrest had come from Berlin because I was a re-immigrant.

I was treated well in prison. But I noticed that the prisoners were segregated by religion. There were letters on the cells. Mine bore a "J" (Jew), others bore a "K" (Catholic).

Along with two other arrested Jews I was taken to the railway in a special prison van. The other two were likewise so-called re-immigrants. [. . .] The transport by railway took several days and was mostly by night. New prisoners joined the transport frequently. [. . .] Sometimes on the way we spent the night in police prisons. The time of suffering began when the prisoner transport was handed over by the police to the ss in Papenburg. [. . .] The 26 prisoners boarded a large transport vehicle; they also included some recidivist penitentiary criminals. While we were still on our journey the ss escorts endeavored to intimidate the prisoners. The fact that the prisoners were addressed with "Du" [the intimate form of address in German] we calmly accepted. But we were horrified by the blows they administered to us and by the verbal abuse. "Are there any Jewish swine among you?" we were asked when the vehicle had begun to move.

The arrival in the Esterwegen concentration camp near Papenburg was in military style. As we debussed the sentries at the camp gate asked for the exact names of the prisoners. "Who is a Jew?" That question was heard immediately. I was asked: "Why are you here?" —I answered: "I don't know." "Where are you from?" I replied "From Berlin." A box on the ear was the counter-retort. "What are you? You are a Jordan paddler." As an old soldier I knew that the wisest thing was to say Yes and Amen to everything. I therefore replied in military posture: "I am a Jordan paddler."

Even before registration in the office there came a command: "Who wants to be shot dead?" I was in such a desperate mood that, as the only one, I stepped forward from my rank and called out loud: "Me!" I was led out of the office building to a path that ran round the huts and was strewn with white gravel. It is called the "death path" because whoever takes it can be shot dead instantly because access is forbidden. But I didn't know any of that at the time. After a few minutes I was allowed to return without anything happening. I had been prepared for anything. For on entering the reception building I had read a notice: "The commandant decides over life and death!" [. . .] During registration in the office your personal details are recorded. A civilian police official takes part in this. Only after the recording of our personal details were we presented to the camp commandant. He welcomed us with the words: *From today you are leaving human society.* Anyone who lies will be whipped."

After this welcome our clothes and utensils were taken from us and we received prison clothes. Then our hair was shorn. Then we were taken to the bunker, a dark cell, where we had to do gymnastic exercises. Those of us who were worn out were instantly whipped and left lying. Then we were told to shovel sand in the yard into a big push-cart and to push this gadget across the entire yard, which of course only a few succeeded in doing. We had not received any food since the early morning.

Only after these "welcome ceremonies" were we assigned to the individual huts. The senior hut prisoner received us. At half past six in the evening there was a parade in the yard. There was a command: "One of the new Jews step forward."

I stepped forward and was commanded: "Go to the bunker and bring out the buck." This buck is used for flogging. In front of all the prisoners the condemned man is beaten with a bullwhip. Nothing happened that evening. But I witnessed these terrible floggings often enough.

Throughout our entire stay in the camp we were employed on work in the moor. We were rightly called the "moor soldiers." [. . .] During work in the moor various prisoners were "shot while trying to escape." [. . .]

I have to point out that the Jews in the camp—during my time there were over 30 Jewish prisoners—were treated especially badly. They were never given a so-called "dodge job." At roll call there were continual anti-Semitic insults.

Myself, I managed to survive those six months. Anyone who, like myself, had been in the front line for 4 years in the World War, had learnt to survive privations. The fact that I had been on active service, that I became a reserve officer, that I had earned the Iron Cross II and I class meant nothing to the 18-year-old lads who guarded us. When, during physical harassment I repeatedly pointed out that [. . .] I had been 4 years on active service, I had to accept the answer: "You're lying." And when I mentioned my E.K.I [Iron Cross first class] they said: "You probably stole that."

These young men, who had been detailed to guard the inmates in a concentration camp, seem to have odd ideas about Jews. How often have I been asked: "How is it that you are physically so strong?" My answer: "I did sport in my youth" caused great astonishment. One day when, during work in the moor, I came to a ditch the sentry suddenly commanded: "Throw the Jew in the water." "Yessir, Herr *Wachtmeister*, I can swim!" — "What? The Jew can swim? Jump in, Jew!" In this way I had an involuntary refreshing bath. The sentries were greatly surprised when they saw that I was a good swimmer.

The ss guards are given reading matter on the Jewish question. As far as I was able to establish, also a special edition of the Talmud. A very popular subject of discussion was this: "Surely you know the Talmud?" — "No. Among us Jews only special scholars know it!" — "You're lying. Surely you are guided by it. The Talmud allows you to defile little girls." — Especially typical was also a conversation I had with one of the sentries who showed a tendency to be more objective. "Isn't it strange that you Jews are so hated?" he said to me one day. "I used to have Jewish friends in the past, but not until now did I know what Vampires you are!" I tried to explain a little, difficult though this was in my situation. [. . .] These prejudices seem to be ineradicable. [. . .]

There is no norm for release. It is always ordered from outside, though the camp commandant can try to stop it. Nor is there any time limitation for one's stay in the camp. I have known cases when prisoners who were to be detained for 3 months were still in the camp when I was released after 6 months. During release your weight is falsified.

Prisoner Groups

On arrival one is weighed without clothes, but on discharge one is weighed with them.

I ultimately owe my release from the concentration camp to the fact that I declared myself ready never to enter Germany again.

244. Report of the prisoner Hugo Burkhard, a German Jew, on Yom Kippur in Dachau in 1937, published in 1967[94]

It was September 1937 in Dachau. A Saturday that began with the familiar Munich "streaming rain." In the kitchen, when we collected our coffee, our block was greeted with especial friendliness by the ss, differently from usual, and we were unable at first to explain to ourselves the reason for it. Until 2 ss men came up to us and said: "Today we will be friendly toward you because you Jews have your Day of Atonement, your greatest holiday, and therefore the ss want to atone themselves with you today." We had not thought about our holiday at all as we lived in Dachau beyond time, as we were not permitted to practice any religious functions and because to us one day was very much like another. The ss had allowed themselves a tasteless joke with us, which of course we accepted with an embarrassed and uncertain smile and an aching heart. When I collected my coffee I could not yet surmise that this announced atonement would bring us great and dangerous chicanery. We were marched—as always—to the shouting of the ss to our place of work in pouring rain [. . .]. When we arrived at our place of work to dig gravel and sand and to move it away in iron tipping tubs, we had to remove our top clothes immediately even though it continued to pour with rain.

245. Report of the commandant's office of the Dachau concentration camp on the Jewish prisoner Leo L., dated 2 April 1938[95]

Behavior report!

On the émigré Jew L. Leo
born 18.12.82 in Mainz
In the camp since 30.10.37 last assessment 24.1.38 refused.

Assessment

Behavior: bad
Political attitude: Jew

Work performance: bad

Camp punishments: none

According to the instruction from Reich Leader ss and Chief of the German Police of 12.11.37, letter No. 3632/37, suspension of release until further notice is imposed on all Jews in the Dachau concentration camp because of atrocity stories.

The Camp Commandant of Dachau concentration camp

Signed: Loritz

ss *Oberführer*

246. From the report of the Amsterdam Jewish Central Information Office on the situation of Jews in Germany, July 1938[96]

It is not certain how many Jews have been dragged into the Buchenwald concentration camp. *It is, however, certain that the treatment of the prisoners there is very bad.* Police who deliver the prisoners to the camp or collect them from there are not allowed inside—that speaks for itself.

On their very first roll call after arrival the prisoners are told that in Buchenwald they are not in a penitentiary, nor in a prison because there they would be treated humanely—but not here. This is entirely in line with the facts. They are also told that *they would have to remain in the camp all their lives* unless they emigrated immediately. A few of those arrested, who were able to prove their immediate emigration, were released, but others were not. Indeed cases have become known of Jews being brought into the camp who had been just about to emigrate and already held foreign visas.

The people have to fall in as early as 4 o'clock in the morning, the first roll call is at 6 o'clock, then begins the drill. *Work is very hard.* The prisoners have to drag stones, which is hard enough for people used to physical labor—but how much more so for people who had mostly only done mental work all their lives. No distinction is made between old and young people. This unbelievably hard work has been expected even from *men over 60* or indeed *over 70*.

Similarly there is no consideration for the sick. The supervisors delight in tormenting the poor inmates; for instance they deliberately trip them up and if they fall down under the heavy weight of stones they are even punished. Anyone collapsing during work, which of course occurs frequently, is treated with a rifle butt until he gets up again. It has become known that one man lying on the ground, unable to get up again, asked the supervisor to shoot him. The answer was: "*Well, go to the fence, you Jewish pig.*" The man summoned his last bit of strength and went off in the direction of the fence and was *instantly shot*. It is said that prisoners repeatedly ran in the direction of the electrically charged wire fence in order to be shot. This is followed by the laconic announcement: "*Shot while trying to escape.*"

Work in the camp is not only hard, driving many prisoners to such acts of desperation, but it also lasts for nearly the whole day. Not until 12 o'clock is there a break of 40 minutes. Then work continues until 6 o'clock. After that there is two hours' drill. Only after the evening roll call is there a free hour, when one is allowed to talk. At 9 o'clock is lights out.

Accommodation of the many prisoners in the camp is totally inadequate. *There are 440–460 people in a single hut*, many of them roughing it on the floor.

The Jews are made to work together; alongside them there are "Aryans" locked up, chiefly asocial elements, Gypsies, etc. Each group of Jews has an Aryan prisoner as a supervisor. Unless this man does a lot of beating himself, he'll get beaten. So he does it. [. . .]

The prisoners are allowed to receive and send mail twice a month. Naturally, the letters are dictated and have to be written on prescribed paper. The inmates are allowed to have a little money sent to them, with which they can buy cigarettes, etc. [. . .] The first letters coming from the camp asked that emigration should be arranged as quickly as possible. That was the only way to shorten detention time.

It is obvious that many people cannot survive this kind of work physically nor, quite apart from maltreatment, psychologically. Little wonder *that there are many deaths*. Their families suddenly receive the information that they can collect an urn. The cause of death is never revealed, nor can it be established anymore because the bodies are cremated. Thus a family hardly ever learns anything about the dreadful sudden end of a father, son or brother.

247. Notes by the political prisoner Alfred Hübsch about the mass transport of Jews to Dachau in November 1938, written ca. 1960[97]

Everything was happening in a rush. In the early morning of 10 November 1938 we learned that an attempt had been made in Paris on the life of the German attaché, Freiherr vom Rath. It was said Rath had been murdered by a Jew called Herschel Grünspan.[98] [. . .] Before we could learn further details through the *Völkischer Beobachter*, through *Das Schwarze Korps* or through Julius Streicher's agitation rag *Der Stürmer*, the first special trains, packed with thousands of Jews, were already arriving on the industrial track. [. . .] The first arrived. Long before they could be registered, the second lot arrived. Watches and jewelry had to be surrendered to the ss. That the latter did very well for themselves is obvious. Already the next trains were arriving. Masses and masses. The men were standing in rows of ten. Initially outside the gate, then, as further trains were coming in and night was falling, they were made to stand in rows of ten along the parade ground by the security ditch. They stood there day and night. The searchlights circled throughout the night. The scribes wrote day and night. They were granted additional food that was brought over to them. They wrote and wrote . . . Several blocks had been prepared to receive the masses. A huge tent had also been erected for that purpose. When 100 had been registered, shaved, bathed and had their hair cut, an ss *Unterführer* [an ss NCO] took them to the blocks, by day and by night. In two days and nights approximately 10,000 Jews were registered and assigned. [. . .] As the clothes store had long used up its stock of prisoner clothes, the new arrivals were allowed to keep their pre-arrest clothes. This was very much to their advantage because a great many were thus able to smuggle major amounts of money into the camp. Also, in view of these masses, the ss did not have enough time to search their clothes thoroughly! Anyway, they had done very well with the prisoners' valuables. [. . .] In the evening we, standing off to the side, heard lamenting cries of "Water! Water!" Yet it was cool and damp, so that we were freezing, but we remained standing. [. . .] And yet, and yet: a few daring ones tried to get through to them with a bucket of water and one of our beakers. [. . .] It is worth noting that all Jews were wearing identification marks from their transport.

Everyone still had a luggage label with a number hanging from their jacket. Moreover, a stamp had been applied to their upper arm and face. So they were all stamped like cattle for slaughter.

248. Report by a German Jew on Sachsenhausen after the November 1938 pogrom, written in late 1938[99]

Worst affected of all were those who had to do service at the brickworks, in road construction and in the [ss] settlement. Even the march there and back of often 1,000 prisoners to outside work was made a torment by the rifle-butt blows of the escort personnel. The scenes which occurred, especially at the brickworks, were of a cruelty that almost defies description. The main targets during the initial period were evidently people who, because of their previous education, did not appear suitable for physical work. Rabbis, academics and other intellectuals were quite incredibly harassed by foremen and guards. [. . .] The attitude of the guards varied. Even among them there were sections that tried to proceed humanely and caringly. Likewise the great majority of foremen were decent people, especially if not supervised and controlled by sadistic ss men. Most of them even tried, as far as they could, to lighten the other prisoners' lives. Considerable consideration and solidarity could be expected especially from the political prisoners, but also from those labeled "professional criminals."

249. Report by a Jewish doctor from Frankfurt am Main on his detention in Buchenwald after the November pogrom, written in 1939[100]

The train moved to Weimar without a stop; there we were unloaded and already we felt a different wind blowing as we passed from the hands of the police into those of the ss (the so-called troop for special duties). Here we were lined up in an underpass, very tightly, the first rank quite close to the wall. If anyone was not standing correctly or if he moved there would be some blows.

Then we were loaded into transport vehicles and if things were not fast enough there was some more blows. [. . .] After a journey of about 10 km we arrived at the gate of the Buchenwald concentration camp at about 2 o'clock. Debussing had to be very fast; if it wasn't fast enough there were blows. Not knowing that in the camp one was not allowed to keep a hat on, I had, like most of the others, kept mine on, but it was knocked off, along with my spectacles, by one of the ss men forming a double line. Admittedly, when I did not find it myself, he picked it up for me. Then we moved at the double across the assembly ground of the camp, with those who were too slow being again spurred on by blows with sticks. Here we were again divided into columns, with a helping hand, and our personal details were recorded. Everyone received a number printed on a piece of canvas and we were informed that loss of this number would, along with other deadly or hellish punishments, be punished initially with 25 lashes.

We then came to a hut, where we were received by Viennese prisoners who had been there for a few months and who were acting as kind of hosts. [. . .] They calmed the new arrivals and initiated them into the usages and customs of the camp. They held something like a special position as the camp administration gave them a degree of freedom in organization. They immediately informed us that it was of course absolutely necessary for a certain discipline to be observed in a camp, also with regard to their instructions. We should not be surprised that they, if the guard personnel were nearby, would sometimes shout and curse us terribly, and at times even pretend to strike us. But that would all be play-acting, so the ss men should not think that they were not treating us correctly. [. . .]

On the day after our arrival, or rather on the same morning, we were lined up outside about 6 o'clock. The bulk of one's activity consisted of standing about. In between one's hair was shorn and personal details were again taken down. Not until 6.30 in the evening did we actually get our first food, a soup with fish, very good in itself. Altogether the food we received was perfectly good. This meant that from 7.30 in the morning of 10 November until 6.30 the following evening I had not eaten or drunk anything. Thirst and the irregularity of food and of the timetable were what we suffered from most. In the morning there was no coffee, the first meal was sometimes at 10 and sometimes at 12 noon; sometimes the meals followed closely one after another and sometimes at great intervals. This was due, in my opinion, to the fact the organization simply could not keep pace with the sudden arrival of some 10,000 people. [. . .]

In the camp we were accommodated in large wooden huts. Initially there were three such huts. Over the next few days two new huts were added at record speed. Each of these huts was for 2,000 men. They had four-tier bunks, wooden planks on top of each other; one lay on them without any straw and without blankets. All one had for covering oneself was what one happened to have brought along—in my case a thin overcoat. For heating our hut had a small iron stove, in other huts there was none. One lay so close together one could hardly move, really like sardines in a tin. One never changed or took off one's clothes, one was covered up to one's knees with a thick crust of clay and one could not wash. As an old soldier I could more or less cope with all that. In the war we also sometimes did not wash or undress for weeks on end and we were also covered in dirt. But that time it was honorable dirt and one knew what one was doing it for. Nor was one then treated like cattle. Our accommodation was such that we always felt that we were cattle locked into a dirty cowshed. Also the manner in which we were, after roll call, driven into our huts was entirely the manner in which cattle are driven into their sheds, moreover always with the prospect of receiving a blow with the riding crop from any ss men happening to be standing nearby if, as is natural given the large crowd, things did not go fast enough. [. . .] Any human dignity one possesses has to be pocketed in the camp. Needless to say, one is addressed by "Du," the official address being "The Jew such-and-such." If an ss man, mostly a *Scharführer*, asks who one is and one answers, he would say: "You used to cheat the Aryans, you Jewish pig" etc., and one had to keep silent. Words like Jewish pig were the order of the day. Woe to him who is driven to protest. I have repeatedly watched a flogging of 25 lashes, on one occasion even 40–50 lashes. A buck is ready at all times: the person concerned is laid across it and there receives 25 extremely violent lashes with the bullwhip. [. . .] The so-called Kapos acted as assistant supervisors; they were prisoners too, some of them had been there for years. They were all Aryan. [. . .] While some of them were very friendly and decent, as long as there was no ss man about—if some were nearby, there was of course constant shouting and indecent swearing, shoving and hitting, but often only pretend—other Kapos were decidedly rough and sadistic toward the prisoners. Strangely enough—I often wondered about that—the so-called habitual criminals [. . .] were, on average, much more good-natured than the political prisoners. Whether they wanted to ingratiate themselves I don't know. But one can't generalize. There were decent people also among the political prisoners and tormentors among the criminals. [. . .] It was quite unexpected by me when, in the morning of the eighth day, the loudspeaker suddenly announced: "The Jew Dr. X from Y with all his belongings (i.e. my summer overcoat) to the gate." After waiting for a while, during which time some 20 people had assembled there, we were taken by a Kapo to be shaved; he whispered to me that we would be released. My speedy release after only 8 days was due to the fact that I was already in the middle of my preparations for emigration and that there was a letter from a highly placed foreign diplomat that he would give me a visa for his country at any time. This last day is a day I shall never forget, a day that profoundly shook me. The scribe who once more took my personal details, the young Viennese boys who shaved us, the workers we encountered, the guard of the infirmary, where we were once more quickly examined to make sure we bore on our bodies no traces of any punishment — they all whispered to us: "You lucky devils!" Here we slipped, unnoticed, a few cigarettes we happened to have in our pockets to another [prisoner], there a piece of bread to a starved worker. But the feeling that we were leaving, while the others had been inside for weeks, months and years and we could not take them with us, was terrible.

As we were subsequently taken to the gate we passed the parade ground where our comrades were just eating. They waved to us and called out softly: "Auf Wiedersehen!" No one was jealous, but it was as difficult for us, who were leaving, as it was for them. But before we were released we had to stand for another 4–5 hours in a cutting wind and in damp weather, directly under the main watchtower. And as an ss man was doing sentry duty just then, who wanted to show off, we were not allowed to move without him calling down some vulgar remark and a threat. [. . .] Finally we were taken to the "political section," where we signed a statement that we had neither seen nor experienced any maltreatment, etc., etc. "And if you tell any atrocity fairy tales, you'll be arrested again immediately and you'll never get out of the camp again. If you tell any tales abroad, you realize that we have our spies everywhere and you'll be 'dealt with.' You probably know what this means."

5.5. Women

Women were in some ways "supplementary" to the camp system, at least in the prewar years.[101] Still, the regime also locked up women in concentration camps, right from the start.Women were admitted to the camps for broadly similar reasons as men, but in much smaller numbers, and generally housed separately from men. The first central Nazi camp for the detention of female protective custody prisoners was Moringen near Northeim. Moringen was a Prussian workhouse, holding only 150 inmates by the time the Nazis had come to power. Its director, Hugo Krack, a Prussian bureaucrat, was keen to fill its empty cells with political prisoners to create some extra revenue for the workhouse. Soon, male prisoners began to arrive, and a round of arrests and releases began. Initially guarded by the police, backed up by ss and sA men acting as auxiliary police, the ss was in charge from August until November 1933, when the men's camp was closed down. In June 1933 the first female inmates arrived, and soon, in October 1933, Moringen became the central Prussian concentration camp for women (250), led by Hugo Krack, who had earlier distanced himself from the brutal ss treatment in the men's camp. On average ninety female prisoners were held at any one time, guarded inside by members of the local National Socialist women's association. Initially under the auspices of the Prussian Ministry of the Interior, Moringen operated as the national German concentration camp for women from 1936, though it was still outside the Inspectorate of the Concentration Camps' direct control. Moringen continued to be run and guarded by civilians rather than by the ss.[102]

Women detained in Moringen came from many different backgrounds. Often they were left-wing political activists, especially Communists such as Centa Beimler, Hans Beimler's wife, or women taken into protective custody for criticizing the regime. This was the case with Frieda K., whom the Halle Gestapo admitted to Moringen in 1934 (251). Other prisoners included Jehovah's Witnesses, probably the largest prisoner group at Moringen and soon housed in a separate room. As anti-Jewish persecution increased, more Jewish women were detained in the camp, too. Some were accused of violating the Nuremberg racial laws, but most were so-called returning émigrés, such as Frieda Sherwood-Schweitzer (252). Other prisoners admitted to the camp included women who had had abortions, illegal under the German criminal code, and women detained as asocial and criminal, including prostitutes. In these cases, local welfare and police authorities had some leeway whether to send prostitutes to Moringen or to leave them to the judiciary or welfare authorities (253).[103]

Inside Moringen, conditions were better than in the men's camps at the time. Gabriele Herz, a Jewish middle-class woman arrested as a returning émigré in 1936 (she came back to the Third Reich from Italy, having explored the possibility of starting a new life there), and held at Moringen in 1936 and 1937, later remembered that living conditions were somewhat better than at the Berlin Alexanderplatz police headquarters where she had been temporarily held after her arrest. But Moringen was still a harsh penal institution, modeled on rules common in prisons and workhouses. Days were strictly regulated, and common punishments included the removal of mail privileges and solitary confinement (254).[104] Women were housed in large dormitories, food was scarce, and work was obligatory. Prisoners had to sew and wash clothes, for example, and in the summer they sometimes worked under guard in the fields outside (255).[105]

By late 1937 Moringen had become too small for the growing number of female prisoners. In December the ss began to establish Lichtenburg as the central concentration camp for women, after its male prisoners had been transferred to the new Buchenwald camp (257).[106] Inside Lichtenburg, a medieval castle, conditions were much tougher than at Moringen. Prisoners were housed in cold and damp rooms, and they were guarded by women selected and trained by the ss (256), equipped with guard dogs and truncheons.[107] Discipline was strict, and sanctions included flogging (though not officially).[108] The prisoner population changed, too. Following the raids against social outsiders in 1938, so-called asocials and alleged criminals made up a large number of the new arrivals. As in the men's camps, the treatment of prisoners reflected their standing within the regime's racial hierarchy, with Jewish women at the very bottom.[109]

By 1938 the ss was already planning to build a new ss camp for women that could be expanded as the ss expected to arrest more people in the run-up to war. Lichtenburg was therefore only a temporary solution. The ss soon replaced it with Ravensbrück north of Berlin, opened in May 1939, a hut camp mainly built by male prisoners from Sachsenhausen.[110] On 27 May 1939, according to an official statistic, Ravensbrück held some 970 female prisoners and numbers quickly rose further, prompting the ss to build new huts to increase the camp's capacity. Discipline was severe from the outset. Special arrest cells were built on the camp's grounds, following a specific request to Eicke by the later commandant, Max Koegel (258).[111] Ravensbrück's perimeter was guarded by ss men. Inside the camp, prisoners were supervised by female guards. Some had already served at Lichtenburg, while others signed up after they had seen advertisements in the local paper (259). While not formal members of the ss, they belonged to the ss's retinue and were subject to its disciplinary codes. New guards received some short basic training at Ravensbrück that reinforced the basic ss rules regarding prisoners.[112] The ss also introduced a formal system of prisoner functionaries, which had not been as extensive in Lichtenburg. Overall, conditions were even tougher than they had been at Lichtenburg, deteriorating further as more and more women were arrested after the outbreak of war, and Ravensbrück gradually developed into a site of lethal slave labor, murder, and mass death.

DOCUMENTS

250. Express letter from the Potsdam district administrator to the State [*Land*] Councilors and Police Presidents in Brandenburg, Eberswalde, and Rathenow regarding protective custody for women, dated 28 October 1933[113]

By Order of the [Prussian] Minister of the Interior all *female* protective custody detainees within the district are to be transported, with appropriate police escort *as soon as possible* to the detention camp Moringen, District Northeim, Government District Hildesheim with timely notification of the Workhouse director there. I request that the completed deportation and the number of the transferred female prisoners be reported to me *by 3 November 1933.*

251. Report of the Gestapo Halle to the Gestapo office in Berlin regarding Frieda K., dated 19 November 1934[114]

On 16.11.34 Frieda S., née K., married, born in Wörmlitz, resident in Rottelsdorf, district Eisleben, was taken into protective custody for disparagement of the [Nazi] Movement. When [a local Nazi party official] appeared on 30.10.34 to request membership card and Party badge according to correct procedure, Frau S. began to insult the Party and its institutions in a vicious manner. When her husband was looking for the Party badge, she exclaimed: "Where did you put that piece of shit? So that this scum leaves us alone. And add the rags while you're at it, or else I'll burn them in the boiler!" (Meaning the brown shirt.) She further said: "Best thing would be to take the revolver and shoot the whole gang down!" Expressions such as "riff-raff, louts, etc." were used. She also said: "Quick, so that none of that gang steps into my house again" and "If my husband is kicked out from the Party for theft, then all Party members in Rottelsdorf should be thrown out because they were all thieving!"

Considering the exceedingly vicious insulting of the National Socialist Movement we request—unless the Court issues a warrant of arrest—that Frau S. is assigned to the Moringen concentration camp. Presentation to the judge will follow shortly.

252. Report by Frieda Sherwood-Schweitzer on her detention in Moringen in 1935, written in 1955[115]

In 1934 I traveled to Berlin on a visit and, without reporting my departure, emigrated to Italy for a year. [. . .] In 1935 I returned to Halberstadt, where I was then, suspecting nothing, immediately summoned to the police for interrogation. This was followed by several more interrogations when I was, each time, taken to the police station by two officers, which of course, in a small town, attracted much attention. The Gestapo in Magdeburg was not satisfied with any evidence, which was supplied also by our personal friend, President Kämpfert, as well as the Police President of the town of H[alberstadt].

From March until May 1935 I therefore had to report to the police in H[alberstadt] every day. Until, at the beginning of May, the first imprisonment followed. [. . .] A few days later I was let out again, with interrogation and fingerprinting like a serious criminal, and now I was taken under escort, with iron chains on my hands, by police car to the railway station. Of course I didn't know where I was being taken as we could not see out. I ended up in the women's prison in Hanover, where I spent about 8 days under similar conditions, except with rather better food [. . .]. Next, approximately on 15 May 1935, I was taken by the same kind of transport, under supervision, to the Moringen/Solling concentration camp. After a lot of investigations and interrogations we were then detailed to work. I shared my dormitory with the other so-called émigrés from every country. We slept on straw and had to fetch this and arrange it ourselves. And of course clean everything. Repeatedly, as a punishment, I had to pick up the straw by hand from the floor, piece by piece. Of course I no longer remember details of the brutality of the punishments. The worst for me, the thing that ruined my health for life, was that, weak though I was, I had to do heavy work and carry especially heavy loads. The result was a total collapse. I crashed on the staircase with a kettle that was almost too heavy to lift and damaged a bone in my back—which unfortunately was only established very much later by X-ray pictures. This detention was moreover made harder for us psychologically because we had to read and reread all political books, Hitler's history (*Mein Kampf*) and talk about them. We were not allowed to hear other news on the radio. Several times we had foreign inspectors, of course everything was magnificent then, the food especially good and "a lot" of extras; it was all the more bitter before and after. We had the first high officers of the Nazi Party come to inspect us, their tone alone could have killed, let alone the treatment. Every time they found that we were still too well off, telling us to just wait and see what else was going to happen to us.

253. Decision of the Police Directorate Bremen regarding the transfer of Minna K. into police security detention (*polizeiliche Ordnungshaft*) in the Moringen concentration camp, dated 23 November 1935[116]

Minna K., née A., born [. . .] in Lutterberg, resident in Bremen [. . .], is to be taken into police security detention.

Reasons:

K. has worked for many years as a professional prostitute. For this reason she was first punished in 1909. A series of further punishments for the same reason were imposed on her in subsequent years right up to the present. K. has also been repeatedly punished for theft, always in connection with sexual intercourse, as well as for fraud, being sentenced most recently on 19 November 1934 to 8 months' imprisonment for repeated recidivist theft; she served this sentence. Because of her behavior, which considerably disturbs public order, police conditions were imposed on K. on 28 July 1934; it was explained to her that roaming on public streets and squares, as well as in public establishments, was forbidden and that all women who habitually practice immorality as a livelihood have to be resident in the controlled street and that, if she offended against these conditions, she could be taken into police security detention. K. thereupon declared on record that she would not practice professional prostitution and wished to remain decent. However, K. repeatedly violated the conditions imposed on her. She was frequently found at night in establishments of largely questionable reputation. On 3 December 1934 she received the first warning, but imposition of security detention was not decided upon at this time. Already on 14 January 1935, however, she was again found attending various establishments at night along with unknown men, evidently with the intention of enticing men into committing sexual intercourse. In view of her recent warning K. was, by decision of 15 January 1935, taken into police security detention for a duration of 4 weeks, which she duly served. Following this, K. served the abovementioned imprisonment of 8 months. In spite of her warning, her police security detention and her penal detention—measures intended to have a deterrent effect on K.—she was again, on 20 November 1935, found wandering about, having been released from penal detention on 11 October 1935. She drifted about at night in inebriated condition in various establishments and was evidently out to capture men again. When she was interrogated several hours after her sobering up, she still smelled very strongly of alcohol [. . .].

By her behavior K. has shown that she continues to a considerable degree to represent a danger to public order. The efforts of the police to keep the town's streets and establishments clean in a moral respect are being frustrated by K. Moreover, she endangers other fellow Germans, especially juveniles, by her immoral roaming about and by her presence in establishments. K.'s behavior therefore represents a rebellion against the National Socialist government, which, in accord with the will of the Party, is endeavoring to bring about the moral recovery of our nation. It is therefore necessary to take K. into custody in order thus to remove the danger she represents to other fellow Germans.

254. Report by Gabriele Herz, a German Jewish returning émigré, on her first days in the Moringen concentration camp in October 1936[117]

The "Jews' Hall" to which the command from Madam Chief Warder Berns consigned me nearly two weeks ago is a small space that offers its five occupants only very limited domestic facilities. A long, unfinished table, four stools, one chair, five narrow blue cubbyholes mounted on the wall for soap, toothbrush, and towel compose all of the "furniture." Our few belongings are stored in cartons, cardboard boxes, and suitcases, stacked up under the table for lack of any other storage space. The only window faces the courtyard and is, of course, fitted with iron bars.

Adjoining this room is the "Great Hall," with its approximately eighty women, and beyond that lies the "Bavaria Hall," with its seventeen inmates, and the infirmary [. . .]. We are considered political prisoners and are kept strictly separate from the criminal prisoners, who occupy the ground floor. Unlike us, these criminals must perform manual labor. They have to wear the black institutional uniform whereas we can keep our own clothes, and any contact with the "blacks" is strictly forbidden. I have quickly made friends with my four sisters in misfortune in the Jews' Hall. Frau Herta Kronau was the only one to keep a guarded attitude at first; over three years of imprisonment have made her distrustful. But it was well worth the effort to win her over. Herta is one of the most intelligent and most cultured women in the camp, and once you have gained her trust, she reveals herself to be accessible and warmhearted. Now age forty-three, she has worked as a commercial artist in her youth, as a nurse during the World War, and later as a social worker in the welfare system [. . .]. She had joined the Communist movement early on and was quickly promoted to a leadership position. [. . .]

Radical-left convictions are responsible for Ilse Lipinski being here as well. Endowed with wit, a quick mind, and a good command of several fields of knowledge, she used to work in a public library in Berlin. [. . .] [T]he oldish Fräulein Gertrud Mannheim [. . .] gets on our nerves with her many questions and well-intentioned bits of advice. Like me, she is a "remigrant," a returning émigré. She had spent some time with her brother in Danzig, that thoroughly German city that the Nazis are trying, quite rightly, to get returned to the Reich. Nonetheless, the Gestapo determined that, for a Jew, Danzig counts as abroad, and thus did poor Fräulein Mannheim find herself confronted, upon her return to Berlin, with the surprising fact that she had "emigrated and immigrated back again," an offense whose consequences she is now to ponder here in Moringen.

"Racial disgrace," that utterly vile mixture of hatred, meanness and exterminatory intent concocted by the Nazis, was the downfall of the youngest among us, the lovely Anni Reiner. She had been engaged to an Aryan, but the planned wedding was rendered impossible by the Nuremberg Race Laws. But however draconian the law, the groom would not part with his bride-to-be. Entirely understandable: Anni, with her sweet face, her merry blue eyes and her curly blond hair, truly is a feast for the eyes. [. . .]

What surprises me most is the absence of meaningful activity. I asked my companions about this: "Now this is called an 'instructional camp,' but so far I haven't been able to detect the slightest trace of any kind of instruction whatsoever. I know we have to have the *Völkischer Beobachter* (the Nazis' official paper) read aloud to us every day, and we're supposed to pay attention and accept it uncritically. But that's it."

255. Sopade report on the Moringen camp, dated May 1937[118]

The Moringen women's concentration camp accommodated 134 women at the end of 1936. The prisoners suffer terribly from lack of space. The narrow rooms in which they are accommodated do not permit any proper ventilation and were only inadequately heated during the winter. The individual quarters are designated by the women as Prussian quarter, Bible researcher, Jewish and Bavarian quarters according to whether they hold women from Bavaria, Prussia or Jewesses.

Food is worse than in the transfer prisons and consists every day of one-pot meals without any variety. In the summer many women were used for hard work in the fields, for which they received a small improvement to their food. Many women were unable to do that work in their undernourished condition and collapsed in a faint in the fields or had heart attacks.

The old Bible researchers give a lot of trouble to the women supervisors. They do not give the Hitler salute, nor do they let themselves be kept from their worship.

As a particular piece of chicanery prostitutes of the worst kind have lately been mixed among the camp's political inmates: they are to spy on their fellow prisoners. This measure is felt to be especially oppressive by everybody.

256. Recollections of the Communist Lina Haag of her arrival in Lichtenburg concentration camp in 1937, written in 1944[119]

We were taken to the Lichtenburg. Lichtenburg is the old fortress of Torgau, a massive medieval fortress with many towers, large courtyards, dark dungeons and endless halls, a frightening gigantic edifice with powerful walls, not a serene castle but the ideal concentration camp. [. . .]

In one of the inner yards we are lined up. About 30 women, politicals, Jewesses, criminals, prostitutes and Bible researchers. Women constables of the ss circle around us like gray wolves. This is the first time I see this ideal type of German woman. Some have empty faces, others brutal ones, the mean lines around the mouth are shared by all of them. They stride about the yard with long paces and flowing gray capes, their voices of command ring out across the yard, the big Alsatians that they have with them pull alarmingly on their leashes. [. . .] Across the cobblestones we are taken in front of the commandant's office, where we have to memorize the instructions posted on the notice board—a long list of prohibitions, the house rules, the laws of inhumanity.

257. Letter from the Gestapo Würzburg to the local district offices regarding the closure of the Moringen camp, dated 2 April 1938[120]

The Secret State Police office in Berlin in a telex of 29.3.1938 announced that all female protective custody prisoners have been transferred from the Moringen concentration camp to the Lichtenburg concentration camp. Inquiries about female protective custody prisoners are therefore no longer to be directed to the Moringen concentration camp, but to the Lichtenburg concentration camp via the State Police office Würzburg.

258. Application by the deputy director of Lichtenburg Max Koegel to Theodor Eicke regarding the establishment of arrest cells in the new Ravensbrück camp, dated 14 March 1939[121]

I have established that in the new Ravensbrück women's concentration camp, which is to go into operation shortly, there are no arrest cells in place or envisioned.

In the Lichtenburg camp there are prisoners who, on the Gestapa's instructions, are to be kept in solitary confinement. It is moreover impossible to maintain order in the camp if the defiance of those hysterical women cannot be broken by strict arrest, since no other harsh punishments may be applied in the women's camp. [. . .] I therefore request that, within the protective custody camp, a cell block with 30 to 40 cells be constructed.

259. Recollections of Erika Buchmann of the women SS supervisors in Ravensbrück, published in 1959[122]

The prisoners brought quite a number of women SS supervisors with them from the Lichtenburg. These women had sought employment on the strength of advertisements seeking "women to supervise work-shy women." They worked under good economic conditions. After they were hired—they had to prove their "pure Aryan" origins—they were instructed that Communists, Socialists and other enemies of National Socialism were "subhuman," and that women from the eastern countries, Gypsies and Jewesses were "racially inferior" and that they and the criminal prisoners were to be treated with extreme harshness.

SIX

The Camps and the Public

The Nazi regime was keen to control the representation of the camps both to the German public and to people abroad. Nazi propaganda about the concentration camps—in newspapers and magazines, at public rallies, and on the radio—reflected their changing function and purpose and was present in many different ways through the 1930s. Most Germans had heard of the concentration camps, contrary to their self-exculpatory protestations after 1945. Popular reactions to the camps varied greatly, though the success or failure of Nazi propaganda is notoriously difficult to assess. As Germans were unable to express their opinions freely, it is hard to reach firm conclusions about what ordinary people thought about the regime generally and the camps in particular.[1] However, it is clear that the Nazi propaganda image did not fully dominate popular discourse. Despite censorship and attempts to quell rumors about the realities of life and death in the camps, the Nazis could never fully control what people knew. As in 1933, there were still contacts between the camps and the surrounding local population, ranging from business links to personal relations, all of them allowing glimpses into the not-so-secret world of the camps. What is more, many released prisoners continued to relate their experiences to others, despite the dangers involved.

Popular concern with the concentration camps did not stop at the German borders. Already in 1933, many foreign newspapers critical of the Nazi regime ran regular reports on atrocities in the camps, as did German exile publications. Such publicity continued for the rest of the 1930s, much to the chagrin of the German authorities. News of critical reports often reached Berlin, as German diplomatic missions abroad regularly submitted details about foreign newspaper articles about the camps, provoking attempts to counter this so-called atrocity propaganda. One way of doing so was to arrange staged visits of foreign journalists and other delegations, with the camps prepared in meticulous detail. This resulted in some more positive foreign reports about the camps—portrayed as places where Communist agitators and asocial elements were justly locked up—which reflected not only the ss propaganda strategy but also broader political sympathies across the European right as a whole in the 1930s.

6.1. The Camps in Nazi Propaganda

Few regimes spent as much time and effort on propaganda as the Third Reich. The Nazis, above all Joseph Goebbels, Reich Minister of the newly founded Ministry for Popular Enlightenment and Propaganda, firmly believed that terror alone would not win over the Germans who did not yet support the regime. As Goebbels said in his first press conference as propaganda minister on 15 March 1933, only days after the Reichstag elections where the Nazis and their far-right allies, the DNVP, had received just under 52 percent of the vote, the Nazi regime would "not be content with 52 per cent behind it and with terrorizing the remaining 48 per cent."[2]

Nazi propaganda took various forms, including the use of modern media such as film and radio. It was most effective where it built on existing beliefs and attitudes.[3] German newspapers, in particular, spread the regime's message about the camps.[4] Newspapers had been brought under the control of the regime soon after the seizure of power. Before long, all journalists had to be members of the Reich Association of the German Press, with Jews and political opponents excluded from membership. Meanwhile, editors had to comply with a law that made them personally responsible for the articles in their newspapers. Furthermore, newspaper content was centrally coordinated and monitored by Reich Press Chief Otto Dietrich.[5] At weekly conferences Dietrich dictated editors a general line that often included precise instructions on what to print and what to omit. In September 1934, for instance, Dietrich told editors how to proceed with the cases of Ernst Torgler and Carl von Ossietzky, two high-profile political prisoners held in camps since 1933 (261). Dietrich's detailed directives reflected the regime's determination to manage public opinion about the camps. In December 1936 Dietrich ordered that reports on incidents within the camps should generally be avoided. However, he added, newspapers could report on individual cases, for instance to mobilize local populations to help capture supposedly dangerous escaped prisoners (271). The message behind this directive was clear: the true scale of Nazi terror in the camps was to be hidden from the

German public.[6] Yet readers could be told that the camps' inmates were dangerous criminals, a message reinforced by an entry on the concentration camps in a widely read 1937 German encyclopedia (272).

In 1933 and 1934, German newspapers were full of reports on the early camps with their tens of thousands of prisoners. After the releases of most inmates and the closure of most early camps, the volume of newspaper reports soon began to decline, too. At that time the Nazis were keen to communicate to German readers that they had now secured power. This view was expressed, for example, in an April 1934 interview with Hermann Göring in which he boasted that the Communist opposition had been almost entirely eliminated. Yet, because there was still a latent Communist threat, Göring added, he had ordered "draconian measures."[7]

Meanwhile, the focus of Nazi propaganda on the camps gradually shifted in the mid-1930s from an emphasis of their political role to their new function as places for the exclusion of social and racial outsiders from German society. Such propaganda sometimes had anti-Semitic undertones. In May 1934, for example, German radio broadcast the arrest and transfer to Oranienburg of a Jewish banker who had allegedly slandered Goebbels (260). More often, German papers ran reports on the detention of the so-called work-shy and criminals in the camps. A local Bavarian newspaper, for example, focused on the arrest of work-shy elements at Dachau and stressed the camp's alleged rehabilitative effect (262). The camp's function as a site of social discipline also featured in a 1935 report in a Berlin newspaper. Based upon exaggerated crime figures, it declared that the detention of habitual criminals, allegedly men with extremely long criminal records, had led to a notable reduction in crime rates (264).[8] Along the same lines, the *Illustrierter Beobachter*, a glossy Nazi magazine, published a photo essay on Dachau in December 1936. A new era had begun, the essay insisted, with social outsiders being detained in the camps in large numbers. Inside the camp, the article continued, these inmates were taught strict discipline and order through hard labor. Of course, the article made no direct mention of ss abuses, claiming that all inmates were healthy. Yet there was a sinister reference to prisoners' sterilizations, highlighting the camps' bio-political function (though contrary to the article's propagandistic lies, inmates deemed congenitally ill were forcibly sterilized and did not have any real right to appeal) (270). The increasing significance of the camps as weapons of Nazi racial policy was the subject of another photo essay in the *Illustrierter Beobachter*, reporting on the official visit in 1939 of an Italian racial scientist to Sachsenhausen (273).

Despite the growing focus on the exclusion of outsiders from German society, the regime continued to publicize the camps' function as a political deterrent.[9] Anyone who voiced opposition toward the regime could be detained in protective custody in a concentration camp, ran the message of a January 1936 article in the *Völkischer Beobachter*, the Nazi Party's flagship newspaper with mass circulation. Far from being places of completely arbitrary terror and violence, the article suggested, the camps were so highly regulated that abuses were impossible (266). In a similar vein, a 1936 circular by the Bavarian Political Police, concerned with the public impact of protective custody arrests, urged newspaper editors to publish selected cases, though editors had to seek the police's permission first to ensure that it remained in control of media coverage (267).

The ss also promoted the camps in its own viciously anti-Semitic weekly, *Das Schwarze Korps*, published since 1935 and required reading for ss members (though it also sought a wider readership).[10] Several articles here focused on the ss guards inside the camps and their supposedly selfless and courageous service. A December 1935 article waxed lyrical about storks in the Esterwegen camp, looked after with love by caring ss men (265). Playing to its audience, *Das Schwarze Korps* was also keen to stress the comradely relations among Camp ss men (269) as well as the friendly contacts with local communities (275). In reality, matters were always more complex.[11]

Apart from the domestic impact of reports on the camps, Otto Dietrich and other Nazi leaders remained concerned about foreign reports of crimes in the concentration camps.[12] At Gestapo headquarters, officers collected and filed foreign press reports about the camps.[13] These reports, frequently with graphic descriptions of Nazi abuses, prompted the Gestapo to counter the alleged atrocity propaganda. In March 1935 a senior Gestapo official, possibly Reinhard Heydrich, wrote to the Foreign Ministry, urgently demanding that German diplomats defend the camps against negative reports in the foreign press. In fact, there was no need to worry about the attitude of the increasingly Nazified Foreign Office toward foreign reports about the camps. Reflecting their own concerns over such reports, German diplomats collected several dossiers of press clippings relating to the concentration camps.[14]

A common feature of the Nazi response to foreign criticism was to point the finger at other camps. The claim that it was the British who had invented the concentration camp, not the Nazis, was particularly popular (263). Many Nazis, including Hitler himself in a 1941 speech, made such claims to detract from the horrors of the Nazi camps.[15] However, the British camps of the Boer War, while also known as "concentration camps," were fundamentally different from the Nazi camps. In the Boer War, prisoners were overwhelmingly women and children who were generally free to move around the camp, and deaths resulted from neglect, not from torture or murder.[16]

The Nazis were also keen to highlight supposed abuses in foreign camps in the 1930s, such as those established in Austria. Here, the clerical-authoritarian regime had set up camps for the internment of its political enemies, which remained in operation until the German annexation of Austria in March 1938. These camps were officially known as *Anhaltelager* (internment camps) and not as concentration camps, as the Austrian regime, concerned with its reputation, wanted to avoid any comparisons with the Nazi concentration camps. Nazi propaganda, keen to discredit the Austrian regime amid plans for annexation, portrayed these sites as brutal terror camps where Austrian Nazis were held in conditions much worse than those that prevailed in the Third Reich. In fact, such claims were far from the truth; moreover, the *Anhaltelager* were not exclusively directed against Austrian Nazis, but also against the sizable Communist and Social Democratic opposition.[17]

All in all, the concentration camps never disappeared from the Nazi-controlled public sphere. Himmler summed up the propaganda picture of the camps in a radio broadcast on 29 January 1939, the Day of the German Police, celebrated annually by the ss and police. In it, Himmler railed against the alleged foreign obsession with Nazi camps and presented them as hard but fair, as well as effective instruments of crime control. This broadcast no doubt reassured at least some of his listeners (274).[18]

The Camps and the Public

260. Reich-German radio report of May 1934 on the detention of a German Jew in the Oranienburg concentration camp[19]

The Jewish employee of the *Kommerz- und Privatbank* in Berlin Dr. Jakob Wassermann has been arrested for greatly offensive remarks about Reich Minister Dr. Goebbels, made with cynical impudence and repeated several times. His arrest, made at his place of work, caused considerable satisfaction among the staff, as the outrageous behavior of this Jewish employee had already resulted in unpleasant arguments. He has been taken to the Oranienburg concentration camp, where he will be able to reflect for a longer period on how a guest of the German people should behave in Germany.

261. Instruction to the German press from Reich Press Chief Otto Dietrich, dated 1 September 1934[20]

According to a confidential notice from the Prussian State Ministry the cases of Torgler, Ossietzky[21] and other Marxists still in protective custody will be carefully reexamined in mid-September as to whether they, as is the case with most of the rest of the Marxist prisoners, can be released.

262. *Bayerische Ostmark*: Article on the detention of so-called work-shy elements in Dachau, dated 1 December 1934[22]

By executive Order of the Bavarian State Ministry, dated 16 October and 20 November 1934, the Dachau concentration camp was designated as a labor institution for the accommodation of male persons of at least 18 years of age, and the labor division of the Taufkirchen-on-Vils reformatory as a labor institution for women aged at least 18 years who, though capable of work, have, because of moral offenses, become a burden on public welfare themselves or have allowed family members, for whose maintenance they were responsible, to become a burden on public welfare. Assignment to a camp takes place through the police directorates, town councils and district offices, upon application of the welfare association, for a duration of at least three months up to three years. This provides an opportunity to remind work-shy, slovenly and otherwise uneconomical persons, who avoid work, fathers who leave the care of illegitimate children to welfare, fathers who leave the care of their families to welfare, and women of the same type, of their duties by means of compulsory labor and to direct them toward an orderly way of living. It may be expected that the mere possibility of being assigned produces an educational effect.

263. Letter from the deputy head and inspector of the Gestapo to the Foreign Ministry regarding propaganda about the concentration camps, dated 12 March 1935[23]

In view of the fact that foreign newspapers continue to carry atrocity stories about alleged shortcomings in the German concentration camps or [. . .] that they try to create an atmosphere for the abolition of the camps in Germany, I consider it of urgent importance to stand up energetically to these activities with the cooperation of the Herr Reich Minister for Popular Enlightenment and Propaganda [Goebbels]. It might be a good idea to point out that other countries, too, such as Austria and lately Holland are trying to defend themselves from anti-state activities by the establishment of concentration camps. In this connection it might be especially effective to point to the starvation of thousands of innocent women and children in English concentration camps in the Transvaal during the Boer War, to the tying of insubordinate Indians to the cannon mouths during the crushing of the Indian Rebellion, the shooting of German sailors helplessly swimming in the Baralong incident,[24] and the brutal starving out of German women and children during the British blockade,[25] the notorious Devil's Island of Cayanne,[26] the robbery of the German colonies,[27] the shameful consequences of the Versailles peace treaty and similar disgraceful actions and brutalities. I shall be particularly grateful for early information on what has been initiated in this matter from your end.

264. *Berliner Börsen-Zeitung*: Report on preventive custody police in the concentration camps, dated 24 October 1935[28]

With the seizure of power by National Socialism [. . .] the work of the criminal police in its struggle against crime acquired an entirely

The Camps and the Public

new aspect. A particular success—that can already be unambiguously stated today—has been the measure of so-called preventive custody. In Prussia the permitted maximum of preventive custody detainees has been laid down by decree as 525. At present, however, only 476 professional criminals are affected; these are in the educational camp Esterwegen in the district of Hanover. They include 215 burglars, 144 thieves, 66 impostors and receivers [of stolen goods], 18 murderers and 36 sex criminals.

The list of previous convictions of these prisoners is enormous. It turned out that their offenses total 2,329 years' penitentiary and 2,492 years' prison, i.e. about 5,000 years of custodial punishment.

The professional criminals include a 62-year-old robber with no fewer than 42 previous convictions, who can look back on 20 years and 3 months of penitentiary and 12½ years of prison. A 59-year-old pickpocket with 22 previous convictions has served 26 years and 1 month of penitentiary and 1 year and 1 month of prison. Another, a burglar with 18 previous convictions has served roughly 26 years of penitentiary and the list of previous convictions of a 60-year-old thief and robber shows a record figure of 28 years and 7 months of penitentiary.

One has but to read these figures to realize how urgent the need was for measures that would protect the people's community from these incorrigibles. In underworld circles the institution of preventive custody has from the start caused general panic and produced its desired effect.

While this measure has greatly contributed to reducing the number of criminal offenses substantially, a new Order of the Minister President [Göring] moreover authorizes the criminal police to impose certain obligations on criminals at liberty and thereby to control them permanently. Such measures are e.g. prohibition of the use of vehicles, of the change of domicile without police permission, prohibition of the use of certain establishments, prohibition of leaving one's residence at night. The accurate observation of these restrictions is closely monitored by the criminal police at irregular times of the day and night. In Prussia such restrictions have at present been imposed on 740 criminals. In the case of 220 further persons, such measures have been revoked again because of impeccable behavior. Declining figures of individual crimes provide a clear picture of the effect of these measures. Whereas in March 1932 there were 479 cases of housebreaking in Berlin, by March 1934 this figure had declined to 214 and in March 1935 to 167. Breaking and entering of shops declined from 706 in March 1932 to 179 in March 1935. Breaking and entering of offices and businesses declined from 117 to 30 over the same period. The effect is especially conspicuous with bicycle thefts. In March 1932 there were 1,101 cases, in the same month in 1934 there were only 521 and this year only 486. [. . .] It is also interesting that so-called real automobile thefts and the moving of the vehicles abroad have almost completely stopped. Admittedly, automobiles are still occasionally stolen, but almost exclusively for the purpose of joyriding or for stealing their contents.

265. *Das Schwarze Korps*: Article on storks in the Dachau and Esterwegen concentration camps, dated 12 December 1935[29]

On the suggestion of the Reich Leader ss the Dachau and Esterwegen concentration camps experienced a welcome enrichment of their "overall population" by the accommodation of young storks. To prevent the extinction of these popular animals, which are both useful and well-loved by children, preparations for the reception and care of these birds were made in the camps with special attention. [. . .] Their favorite spot was the drill yard. There, unfazed by loud commands, they strutted solemnly between the ranks of the practicing ss men. They seemed to know that their interest was mutual; so far no ss man has failed to enjoy the birds' behavior and flying attempts in his free time. [. . .] Thus it happened that a friendship developed between the men and the birds that found an expression also in deeds. A few "expert" ss men tried to provide a white color to two birds with a strikingly gray plumage by repeated washing with *Persil*. However, the birds did not turn white as their mates because their color was genuine.

One day one of their pupils broke his beak. The camp doctor proved his skill by applying a splint and after 8 days the beak was again sound and capable of use. [. . .]

Gradually autumn approached and with it the time when storks are in the habit of seeking warmer climes. Storks from the wider neighborhood of the camp arrived to make "close contact" with the camp storks and they jointly prepared for their long journey. At the end of August our feathered camp inmates, along with other storks, embarked on their journey to the south. Let us hope that the birds, whom we have come to like, will return next year. They are certain of a joyful reception.

266. *Völkischer Beobachter*: Article on the importance and tasks of the Gestapo, dated 22 January 1936[30]

On the basis of the results of its observations the Secret State Police takes the necessary preventive police measures against the enemies of the state. The most effective preventive measure is undoubtedly the deprivation of freedom, applied in the form of "protective custody" whenever there is a risk that the free activity of the person concerned could endanger the safety of the state in some way or other. Application of protective custody is regulated by directives of the Reich and Prussian Minister of the Interior and by a special custody examination procedure of the Secret State Police to ensure that—as far as the task of the preventive struggle against enemies of the state permits—there are adequate guarantees against abuse of protective custody. Whereas short-term protective custody is served in police and local court prisons, the concentration camps, which are under the authority of the Secret State Police, accommodate those protective custody prisoners who have to be taken away from the public for a lengthier period. The main core of the inmates of the concentration camps are those Communist and Marxist functionaries who, as experience shows, would immediately resume their struggle against the state if set free.

267. Circular of the Bavarian Political Police regarding press publications on protective custody, dated 28 January 1936[31]

Various newspapers have lately carried reports on protective custody arrests. On state police grounds and to ensure an undisturbed execution of police measures the publication of protective custody arrests in the press is to be avoided on principle in the future. In cases when the publication of a protective custody arrest seems desirable on grounds of expediency or as a deterrent example, the approval of the Bavarian Political Police is to be obtained without exception. Receipt of such approval may only be waived in cases when publication is initiated officially. In these cases a copy is to be submitted to the Bavarian Political Police—Press Department. Editorial offices of relevant newspapers and periodicals within your area of competence are to be suitably informed and, to avoid vigorous police procedure in the event of contravention, to be urged to observe the instruction meticulously.

268. *Das Schwarze Korps*: Article on the concentration camps and their inmates, dated 13 February 1936[32]

When the foreign press runs out of puff in its smear campaign against Germany—and this has been happening ever more often and in ever shorter intervals over the past few months—it reaches for the worn-out story that evidently seems to have the greatest pull: the "atrocities in the German concentration camps." The number of concentration camps has shrunk down to a few which, according to the sworn statements of Jewish émigrés, are holding the intellectual elite of the German Reich. The atrocity story manufacturers use the concentration camps just as sensationalist novelists use the Wild West and the gold rush towns like Sacramento and Santa Fiffi, along with trap-doors, back stairs, automatic firing devices and mysterious Chinamen and whatever else is an indispensable requisite, which, when we read about it in bed at night, makes our hair stand on end and makes us draw up our feet to our stomach. [. . .] They [the prisoners] are a collection of race defilers, rapists, sexual deviants and habitual criminals who have spent the major part of their lives behind penitentiary walls, as well as other individuals who, by their behavior, have placed themselves beyond the people's community and who, only three years ago, were pampered as "victims of bourgeois society" by psychoanalysts and crime attorneys. The foreign press was already able to report a lot about these "victims of brutal arbitrariness," and a lot more besides that has come only to its ears and not to those of a single person in the German Reich. In spite of their sharp ears they carefully overlooked, and therefore also kept from their press, the fact that numerous former political opponents were released from concentration camps at Christmas and that they received gifts of clothes, food and a sum of money from *Gauleiter* Streicher.[33]

They don't want to know about any of this abroad. Nor do our neighbor nations learn what these brothers in spirit look like, those "noblemen of German civilization and culture" who alone are the guarantors of peace in Europe. With our native courtesy we authorize the foreign press to reprint these pictures free of charge, our only condition being that they let their readers vote whether they would like to have these "martyrs of their convictions," so close to the hearts of the émigrés, as their guests—or perhaps rather not.

We make a present of them to any country that is anxious to acquire a rich collection of especially valuable specimens of notorious criminals and avowed enemies of any order.

269. *Das Schwarze Korps*: Article about sport competitions of the ss Death's Head Units, dated 3 September 1936[34]

The phrase "Sour weeks, cheerful celebrations" applies especially to the ss Death's Head Units. Rarely is there an opportunity for cheerful and carefree celebration in a circle of comrades; it is never possible to assemble all the men of a *Sturmbann* at the same time because some of the men are on duty. The holding of sport competitions within III ss Death's Head *Sturmbann* "Sachsen" therefore did not mean festive days for the men, but initially just an addition to their service.[35] Alongside guard duty and general training, work over the past few weeks—as everywhere in the ss—was focused on the Reich Party Rally. As the sport competitions were not to be held under the "cannons" of the *Sturmbann*, but tested the performance of the individual "hundreds," the spare hours of the last 14 days had to be used to discover which of them was the best [. . .]. In the course of the [final] day there arrived the *Kreisleiter* [a Nazi Party district leader] from Flöha and the neighboring mayor as well as further guests of honor, such as all the concentration camp commandants and leaders of the ss Death's Head Units. ss *Gruppenführer* Eicke and the Saxon Minister of the Interior ss *Brigadeführer* Dr. Fritsch had also insisted on being the guests of III ss-tv "Sachsen" [. . .]. Before the communal coffee break a Roman chariot race was held by the "hundreds," the inventive costumes of the various participants meeting with lively applause. The evening united the guests and all leaders and men—except those on guard duty—in a comradeship party. Food and drink were provided and so was entertainment. ss *Gruppenführer* Eicke, the commander of the Death's Head Units, who had been expected in the afternoon, arrived in the evening and, as always, the ss *Sturmbann* "Sachsen" spent a relaxed evening with its *Gruppenführer*.

270. *Illustrierter Beobachter*: Article on the Dachau concentration camp, dated 3 December 1936[36]

These are no longer the political inmates of 1933, of whom only a small percentage is still in the camp while the rest have long since been released, but for the most part a selection of asocial elements, recidivist political muddle-heads, vagabonds, work-shy persons and drunkards who have been placed under compulsory labor according to § 20 of the Reich Welfare Act, émigrés and Jewish parasites on the nation, offenders against morality of every kind and a group of professional criminals on whom preventive police custody has been imposed. They have all been deprived of every field of activity for their base instincts: work alone is open to them, work which many of them have shunned all their lives.

On our walk through the camp we often encounter the typical face of the born criminal; by way of contrast the camp itself is marked by exemplary and strictly planned order. Military discipline and punctuality, painstaking cleanliness and the ornament of meticulous work on all things are the outstanding features of the whole camp; their maintenance is unwaveringly carried out by the camp command, with the ss guard personnel setting a fine example themselves. [. . .]

There is many an inmate from totally wrecked social circumstances who has never in his life received such good and regular food, who has never been able to lay his head on a pillow every night as he does here, in the Dachau concentration camp. There is many a man who would gladly exchange a stay abroad, especially in the Soviet paradise, with a German concentration camp rather than return there. In the camp he comes to know the value of orderly human life and if there is a spark of humanity left in him he will surely get on to the right path and prefer work to the hardships of life as a vagabond.

The inmates' state of health is excellent. The regular lifestyle, good nourishing food and regular sleep, regulated work and rest breaks, the absence of any kind of dissipation and alcoholic excesses, have played their part. On the other hand, things are different regarding

The Camps and the Public

the inmates' hereditary health. The hereditary biological symptoms of some inmates occasionally compels the camp doctor to make an application for the sterilization or even castration in accordance with the Law on the Prevention of Offspring with Hereditary Diseases. If the application is granted after careful examination, the inmate still has the right of appeal, with a conscientious decision being made for the well-being of the whole nation.

Discipline in the camp is strict and the service of the ss on this lonely outpost, keeping guard in the service of the people's community, is hard. The most sacred values of the nation are at stake in this tough setting, but very few think of this when the conversation is about the Dachau concentration camp, because they don't know it. That is why the *Illustrierter Beobachter* thought it appropriate, with a series of pictures, to present a useful insight into the camp which, primarily, wishes to be an educational institution for the simplest basic rules of human coexistence.

271. Instruction by the Reich Press Chief Otto Dietrich to the German press regarding reports on the concentration camps, dated 11 December 1936[37]

Reports on incidents in concentration camps are undesirable as such reports are apt to trigger damaging effects at home and abroad. The heads of state [*Land*] offices have been instructed in individual cases, e.g. when several professional criminals have escaped from a concentration camp and a major search is being organized, to publish local reports, which are not however to be taken over by the Reich press.

272. *Neuer Brockhaus*: Dictionary entry under "Concentration Camp," 1937[38]

Concentration camp: 1) during a war a camp for the detention of civilian prisoners or of troops that have crossed into neutral territory; 2) in the German Reich an accommodation camp supervised and guarded by the police, where persons are temporarily detained so they do not endanger the government's constructive work after the 1933 National Socialist revolution. These [prisoners] are followers of Bolshevism, which National Socialism regards as the mortal enemy of all European culture, or else persons who have proved themselves politically rootless or dangerous [. . .], or who have committed treason against the National Socialist constructive work and the people's community. They are formed into groups and made to perform useful work. Most concentration camps were dissolved after the calming of conditions.

273. *Illustrierter Beobachter*: Article about the visit of an Italian racial scientist to Sachsenhausen, dated 5 January 1939[39]

The head of the Racial Policy Office in the Italian Ministry for National Culture, Professor Landra, is visiting the Sachsenhausen concentration camp on the occasion of his visit to Germany. The inmates' physiognomies show that they are asocial elements that positively demand isolation. The Jewish criminal types compared to the open features of the men of the *Leibstandarte*[40] [. . .] convey to the Italian visitor a lasting impression of Germany's racial policy aims.

274. Broadcast speech by the Reich Leader ss and Chief of the German Police Heinrich Himmler on 29 January 1939, the Day of the German Police[41]

Allow me on this occasion to say a very frank word about the concentration camps. I know how mendaciously and foolishly this institution is being written about, spoken about and blasphemed, especially abroad. Certainly, like any other deprivation of freedom, the concentration camp is a harsh and strict measure. Hard labor that forges new values, a regulated lifestyle, an unprecedented cleanliness in accommodation and personal hygiene, sound food, strict but fair treatment, guidance to learn to work again and to acquire new craftsmen's skills — these are the methods of education. The slogan that stands above these camps is: There is a path to freedom. Its milestones are: obedience, diligence, honesty, orderliness, cleanliness, sobriety, truthfulness, readiness to make sacrifices and love of the fatherland. I find it strange that the Western democracies, where concentration camps are a downright time-honored institution, with the only exception that — in contrast to the German camps — freedom-loving nationalists are imprisoned there, concern themselves most of all with the problem of the German camps. Surely this is due only to forgetfulness, which can be fairly easily remedied.[42] Moreover, it can be stated without any doubt that in many of these countries, richly blessed as they are both with the earth's treasures and with unemployed, the unemployed and indeed also a large section of those in work, cannot eat their fill as the criminals do in the German concentration camps.

At any rate one result of this rigorous procedure against criminality is that the total number of criminal offenses has again declined last year by a further 7%. We know that the isolation of bad elements as well as the isolation of political functionaries who stubbornly deny the greatness and the well-being of the nation represent only the smaller part of the work of the police. The new German police knows that its greater task lies in positive education, in winning people over for individual cooperation and the trust of the public.

275. *Thüringer Gauzeitung*: Article on the summer festival organized by the Buchenwald ss for the people of Weimar, dated 22 August 1939[43]

It was truly a summer festival! The sun was fiercely scorching the lawns as the first visitors arrived toward four o'clock. The commanders and men of the 3rd ss Death's Head *Standarte* had come along with their families, friends and acquaintances in order to experience a festival of joy after long and hard service. Everyone had contributed something to make this festival beautiful. Three huge dance platforms and another for the music had been erected. A large number of funfair games shooting alleys and sausage stands framed the large festival square. Everywhere there was sizzling and steam. Two huge oxen were being roasted on the spit—whose mouth wouldn't water at the sight? Over it all stood slender pine trees with festive garlands; together with the children's colored balloons and the colorful dresses of the women and girls they provided a radiant picture of life affirmation.

6.2. Foreign Views on the Camps

Reports on the concentration camps, the Nazi regime's flagship instrument of terror, appeared in many exile and foreign publications and gave readers insights into the realities of life in the camps. Some foreign papers eventually found their way to Germany, as did exile publications. While the circulation of the latter was a criminal offense, many foreign newspapers remained openly on sale at major railway station kiosks until the outbreak of World War II, and some Germans, albeit only a small educated minority, could read foreign reports on the Nazi regime. British and American newspapers, as well as newspapers published in other countries, ran stories about the camps throughout the 1930s amid their reporting of political events in the Third Reich. However, foreign correspondents often toned down their reports to comply with Nazi regulations; otherwise they would have risked expulsion from Nazi Germany or the banning of their newspapers in Germany.[44]

German authorities carefully managed visits of foreigners to the camps, just as they had done in 1933, and also banned some critical journalists from visiting the camps altogether. In spite of these restrictions, however, critical reports on the camps continued to appear in the foreign press. Some foreign journalists drew their information from exile publication or spoke to released prisoners, many of whom escaped abroad. At the center of British and American reports on the camps was the fate of prominent political prisoners such as Ernst Heilmann, Carl von Ossietzky, or Hans Litten. The *New York Times*, perhaps the United States' most influential newspaper, ran more than seventy stories by U.S. foreign correspondents on the concentration camps between 1933 and 1939.[45] The *New York Times* reports also described the increasing Nazi use of the camps as a weapon of anti-Jewish policy. Articles appeared on the detention of Jews who had re-emigrated to Germany and those whom the Nazis accused of "race defilement." There were also stories about the mass arrests of Jews in the wake of the 1938 pogrom.[46] One 1937 photo essay in the *New York Times Magazine* reprinted Nazi propaganda photographs from the 1936 report in the *Illustrierter Beobachter* mentioned above (270).[47] Although the report did not use the pictures approvingly, its overall tone was fairly neutral. Context was crucial here, as it was published not long after the Berlin Olympics, when some American journalists, duped by Nazi propaganda and the short letup of open public displays of anti-Semitism during the Olympics, believed that Nazi Germany had become a more humane place to live.[48]

British reports in *The Times*, the British political establishment's paper, also continued to draw attention to the Nazi camps.[49] Some articles were surprisingly detailed. A 1935 report, for example, offered a thorough account of the camps and their inmate groups, questioned the moral and legal bases of the concentration camps, and demanded their closure (277). This report was forwarded by the German ambassador, Leopold von Hoesch, a conservative career diplomat, to the German Foreign Office. In his accompanying memorandum, Hoesch cautiously implied that the concentration camps were an international embarrassment for Nazi Germany (278).[50]

Other articles in *The Times* focused on prominent political prisoners, just as papers in the United States did. From 1938, many articles concentrated on the fate of the protestant pastor Martin Niemöller (1892–1984), a leading figure in the Confessing Church. In the late 1930s the regime cracked down on the Confessing Church, and Niemöller, as one of its more prominent figures, was arrested in 1937, as were several hundred other pastors. The case of Niemöller, a submarine captain in World War I, attracted considerable international attention and galvanized a vocal campaign for his release. In the early spring of 1938 he was put on trial before a Berlin special court, which acquitted him of all serious charges. When he was released on 2 March 1938, foreign reporters were expecting him outside the court.[51] As Goebbels triumphantly recorded in his diaries, the Nazis duped foreign journalists who had been waiting for Niemöller outside the main entrance.[52] Gestapo officers, acting on Hitler's direct orders, led Niemöller through the court's side entrance and took him to Sachsenhausen, where he was kept in solitary confinement. Still, news of his arrest quickly leaked abroad and proved embarrassing for the Nazis, given that Niemöller had been cleared of all serious charges.[53] Held at Sachsenhausen as Hitler's personal prisoner he was assigned relatively easy work, but he was often abused by ss guards.[54]

Altogether, reports in *The Times* were often rather matter-of-fact (282), while reports in some other British papers, such as the liberal *Manchester Guardian*, were more openly critical of the Nazi regime and the camps. The *Guardian* even published a list of Dachau prisoners who had been murdered between the spring of 1933 and the spring of 1935.[55] In 1936 a member of the prestigious Athenaeum gentlemen's club, a Mr. Weigall, wrote a letter to the *Guardian*'s editor about his visit to Dachau at Himmler's personal invitation. Clearly, this visit had been carefully controlled by the ss, leading the author to claim that the camp "was a well-run and well-managed institution." His letter was a response to a recent article with graphic detail about the harsh treatment of Dachau prisoners, in turn prompting the article's author, a special correspondent, to write a stern rebuke of Weigall's naive and misleading letter (281).

Many visitors to the camps were deceived—or wanted to be deceived—by Nazi propaganda. When official delegations visited the camps, the ss put on a show to divert visitors' attention from the prisoners' suffering. Preparations for official visits were excruciating for the prisoners, as they had to stick to the ss script on the day of the official visit and clean the camps and the huts to pretend that they were being treated well.[56] Typically, ss officials led visitors around selected areas to impress them with the camp's order, cleanliness, and discipline. Visitors were also presented with some handpicked prisoners. Often, these were criminals whose imprisonment seemed more reasonable to foreign visitors than the detention of the Nazis' political opponents.

One of the most famous official visits took place in October 1935 when a delegation of the International Committee of the Red Cross (ICRC), led by Carl J. Burckhardt (1891–1974), a distinguished Swiss historian and diplomat, visited Dachau, Lichtenburg, and Esterwegen. The Nazis permitted the Red Cross this visit because it had helped to improve living conditions for Austrian Nazis in Austrian *Anhaltelager* in 1934. After his visit to the camps, Burckhardt wrote a confidential report for the attention of the International Committee of the Red Cross, filed in November 1935. Burckhardt made some critical remarks but overall paints a rather ambivalent picture of the camps (279). Decades later, Burckhardt offered a rather different account of his activities in his memoirs. In addition to his official report, Burckhardt insisted, he had also compiled a longer, more critical report condemning the camps. Allegedly, he had this report forwarded to Hitler, who read it. This version is doubtful. Had they really received a highly critical report of the camps in 1935, Nazi leaders would hardly have invited the ICRC back for another official inspection of the Dachau camp in 1938.[57]

Apart from official visits and foreign newspapers, the Nazi regime was also monitoring exile newspapers' reports on the camps, despite their fairly small circulation. Often edited by Social Democrats and Communists who had escaped from the Third Reich, these papers regularly ran reports on the camps that were graphic in the extreme.[58] In December 1934, for example, the *Pariser Tageblatt*, edited by Georg Bernhard, a German Jewish liberal politician and journalist, published a report of a released Dachau prisoner on the Nazi practice of covering up murders (276).[59] Such reports by former prisoners still offer valuable insights into the camps.[60] Eyewitness accounts of released prisoners also informed a pamphlet on Nazi terror that the British government published in 1940 after Nazi Germany had launched World War II (283).

DOCUMENTS

276. *Pariser Tageblatt*: Report by a released inmate on murders in the Dachau concentration camp, dated 20 December 1934[61]

I remember a whole string of cowardly murders of protective custody prisoners, all of them committed by the Steinbrenner group[62] and camouflaged in camp reports and press reports as "Shot while trying to escape" or as "Suicide in his cell." Throughout the time that I was in Dachau only one single protective custody prisoner, Hutzelmann from Nuremberg, took his own life, worn down by the frightful tortures and in despair over the daily humiliations. All the other comrades were murdered, beaten to death, trampled to death or shot dead. I can list 23 names off by heart of anti-fascist freedom fighters, whose unparalleled heroism and courageous steadfastness, committed world-view, and belief in a free Germany enabled them to hold out unbroken to their painful end without betraying a comrade.

277. *The Times*: Report on the German camps, dated 24 January 1935[63]

The German Government and the German people find it difficult to realize how deep an injury is being done to their country's cause by the continued existence of the concentration camps. The secrecy with which they have been shrouded has intensified the damage. In all foreign countries the story of the mental and physical tortures which took place in the earlier days of these camps is only too well known; in Germany it is still largely unknown or disbelieved. To-day, on the other hand, the great diminution in the numbers interned and the efforts of the Government to "humanize" conditions behind the barbed wire are largely unknown outside Germany [. . .]. This would not, of course, mean that the National Socialist Government would be abandoning the use of the "strong hand" against its political opponents. It must be remembered that by far the greater part of such action is being exercised to-day through continual arrests, long imprisonment during inquiries, and finally trial before an ordinary court, or the new *Volksgericht*.[64] The number of men and women in prison, awaiting trial, is enormous; group trials, in different towns, are taking place daily, and all prisons are overcrowded by the political prisoners. All this, however, is under the forms of law, even if the law itself is being stretched beyond due measure to fit the new "national mentality."

Politicals and Criminals

The men in the concentration camps, on the other hand, are outside all legal protection. They are detained at will—often the personal will of one or two prominent people. They can employ no defender and they have no guarantee and no remedy against an irresponsible outrage on spirit or body which their black-uniformed guards may choose to inflict. It is a relief to know that so many have been released, though this is little consolation to the man who has been interned for 18 months and who sees the gates open only to let others out. It is ground for thankfulness to learn that in some cases excesses by the guards have been punished[65] and that physical torture has been forbidden: but it remains true that a cruel officer can find slower and subtler ways of breaking a human spirit.

Of the position to-day one must speak with some reserve, owing to frequent changes and the lack of official information, but the following sketch can be relied upon as generally accurate.

The inhabitants of the camps are known as *Schutzhäftlinge*, men who have been arrested for the protection of the State, because they are suspected of having opinions which might lead them into injurious activity, even though there is no evidence that would justify a charge of treason. The number of women in *Schutzhaft* to-day is quite small. Among them are said to be two girls who recently placed flowers on Rosa Luxemburg's grave. The number of men in the camps may be estimated at about 2,000. Besides these there are a number of *Schutzhäftlinge* detained in various prisons, probably not more than 1,000 in all.

In many of the camps these political prisoners are outnumbered by convicted criminals or companies of the special class of habitual criminals who are also confined there for the general protection of society. The two sections, politicals and criminals, are usually kept apart, though in some cases they have lived and worked together. One of the deepest sources of indignation among the friends of an interned man, who may be of the highest personal character, is that he must be kept in the same category and under the same conditions as some of the worst law-breakers.

Conditions of Life

It is also difficult to be up to date with regard to conditions within the camps. Efforts from headquarters to repress brutality have already been indicated. Conditions of life, however, remain hard enough, and the somewhat hypocritical pretense that the camps were reasonably comfortable places of physical and moral training, open to the inspection of any foreigner, has been abandoned. Permits to visit are no longer obtainable, and every one knows that the threat of "K.L."—the popular contraction for *Konzentrationslager*—is meant to be a very unpleasant one. Since last summer visits from relatives or friends have been forbidden, except for a few special permits, and the prisoners may receive no parcels. There is sometimes, however, a camp canteen at which those who have any money may buy some supplement to the rough and monotonous daily food.

There are apparently only seven or eight "camps" (the name often applies to an old prison, or other building) still in use in the whole of Germany. [. . .] It is also well known that many of the interned are not Communists, or even Socialists, but are members of the Deutsch National Party,[66] wearers of brown or black uniform whose loyalty is suspect,[67] and a few Jews, pacifists, Bible students [. . .].

The more recent arrivals in the camps are sent for specific periods, sometimes of a few months, often of a few weeks only. This makes the plight of the "old residents" more difficult for them to endure, and for others to understand. Some seem to have been simply forgotten and others are supposed to be detained because of personal enmity in high places. Releases have apparently been made on no fixed principles. The fact that here and there one of the released men has fled over the borders and is now making *Greuelpropaganda* (atrocity propaganda) abroad is used as a reason for retaining others, particularly writers, in confinement. The great bulk of the released men, however, bide quietly at home. They may have good cause for complaint but they keep tight lips, partly no doubt from fear, but partly also from an honorable desire not to spread stories which others might use in a spirit of hate against their Fatherland. Among those who have suffered long internment are now only about 10 or a dozen *Prominenten*, whose hard cases are widely known in other lands as well as in Germany. The Government professes to hold them through fear of their possible activity if released; but their continued internment is probably injuring the Nazi regime far more than any problematical damage which they would do as free men. [. . .]

An announcement by the Leader of the German people that the camps were to be closed forthwith and that the normal instruments of justice were now able to deal with all dangers to the State, would go farther than almost any other act to strengthen his moral position both at home and abroad.

278. Comment by the German ambassador in London, Leopold von Hoesch, on the above *Times* article in a report to the German Foreign Ministry, dated 26 January 1935[68]

"*Times*" of the 24th of this month publishes a lengthy article on the German concentration camps from the pen of an anonymous special

The Camps and the Public

correspondent. [. . .] The article proceeds from the assertion that it is evidently insufficiently realized in Germany what serious damage is being done abroad to the cause of the new Germany by the continuing existence of the camps, but then it is conceded that while within Germany there is still ignorance about the initial shortcomings, abroad the humanization and improvements of conditions that have taken place since are still largely unknown. These alleviations, however, the paper continues, do not prevent the instrument of the concentration camps, because of its faulty basis, i.e. political arbitrariness instead of the law, representing not a strengthening, as intended, but a downright danger to the new Reich. The author then points out that an abolition of this system need not impede the state in any way in its struggle against subversive elements as, in the regular judiciary and the people's courts, it possesses instruments that fully proved their efficacy in this respect by a number of political mass trials recently.

After discussing various details, in the course of which he pays tribute to the extensive reprieves and releases [. . .], while on the other hand alluding to the cases of Heilmann and Litten—whose role in the shaping of public opinion here is known to you from the embassy reports—incidentally without naming names, the article concludes with an appeal to the Führer to reexamine the usefulness of retaining the concentration camps and, if at all possible, in an act of mercy on the occasion of the return of the Saar territory to Germany, to abolish any still existing remnants of this system [. . .].

Of particular interest is the argument, hinted at in the article, that restricting the state's defense against Communist and other subversive elements to proceedings before regular and people's courts, along with the reduction or abolition of concentration camps, would have a substantial effect on opinion over here toward the new Germany. This argument agrees fully with the observation made here continually that although the broadest British circles keep exhibiting a most emphatic interest in protective custody prisoners, as soon as a sentence is passed by a court of law, any participation by responsible and serious elements in intervention attempts in favor of German political prisoners usually come to an end very quickly.

279. Confidential report by Carl Burckhardt, Member of the International Committee of the Red Cross, on his official visit to Dachau, Lichtenburg and Esterwegen camps in October 1935, submitted in November 1935[69]

Between the 19th and 27th of October 1935 I visited three concentration camps in Germany run by the Gestapo (Geheime Staatspolizei), an organization that is part of the black corps of the ss formation led by Reichsführer-ss Himmler. The chief of the Reichsführer ss's Security Head Office is Mr Heydrich, an ss *Gruppenführer*.

1st camp. Lichtenburg close to Prettin, Torgau district.

Visit took place in the company of Mr von Cleve of the German Red Cross and ss *Standartenführer* Tamaschke[70] of the Gestapo's inspectorate of the camps. Around 600 political prisoners and around as many criminal prisoners. 200 homosexuals.

Commandant of the Camp: *Oberführer* Reich of the Adolf Hitler Standarte (absent).

Location of detention: 17th-century castle which served as a prison in the 19th century.

Occupation of the detainees: agricultural work, work in the workshops, kitchen work. Canalization and building lavatories. Baths, installing modern washing facilities. Library containing above all scientific literature, large recreation rooms, well heated for the political prisoners. Dormitories under the roof, without heating. Work together with the criminal prisoners. Prison cells in the cellar, empty during my visit.

Correspondence: 2 letters, 2 postcards to write and receive per week. Censorship. The right to correspond may be withdrawn as a punishment. Possibility of leave up to 8 days in case of death or serious illness in the family.

General remarks: the impossibility for the prisoners to obtain a court judgement or recourse to justice. Complaints: work together with the criminal prisoners. The contagious sick are tended in the same room as those who have had operations etc. (arbitrary sterilizations). Tone among the prisoners: military, without too much severity. Food satisfactory.

The Camps and the Public

2nd camp: Esterwegen, 30 km from the Dutch border, close to the new canal which joins the two rivers: the Hunte and the Ems.

Marshy country, the prisoners are employed above all to improve this and to dig peat.

Commandant ss *Sturmführer* Loritz.[71] Two hut camps. All the installations are hygienic and modern. 1st Camp for the troops. 2nd Camp for the prisoners. The whole surrounded by a guarded wall, in Camp II by a wire fence charged with high-tension electricity. Towers armed with machine guns.

Visit in the company of the same gentlemen as in the previous camp. Around 1,600 prisoners: political prisoners, pederasts, reform prisoners (*Besserungshäftlinge*), ss and sa men; Austrian legionnaires; criminal prisoners.

Tone military, tough, unnecessarily severe — even brutal. Conditions as in the previous camp.

Individual cases:

I. Karl [Carl] von Ossietzky, born 3/10/1889 in Hamburg, intellectual, member of the League for Human Rights. Editor in chief of the *Weltbühne* periodical. Sentenced on 23/11/31 by the Reichsgericht for high treason. (He had protested against rearmament.) His sentence completed, he was arrested when the National Socialist movement came to power.[72] Interventions on his behalf by the English ambassador, without result. State of the prisoner desperate.

II. Heilmann, member of the Socialist party, former Prussian minister.[73] Arrested in 1933, asked for official verdict.

General remarks: the same as for Lichtenburg

3rd camp: Dachau near Munich.

Around 1,800 prisoners. Commandant ss *Sturmführer* Deubel.[74] Location formerly an ammunitions factory and barracks. Modern hygienic installations. Same remarks as for the first camp. The prisoners praise the equality of treatment that they are subjected to by the commandant.

General remarks: everybody demands that they receive official verdict and to know the length of their punishment.

280. *Het Volk*: Article by its Berlin correspondent on maltreatment in the concentration camps, dated 26 February 1936[75]

Cases of maltreatment in Germany have no end [. . .]. Here and there the view seems to be held abroad that the treatment, or rather the maltreatment of the political opponents of the Nazi regime is no longer as bad after three years of the Hitler regime as a year ago. The Ministry of Propaganda is doing what it can to spread the opinion abroad that, while one proceeds rigorously against opponents and while one punishes them harshly, everything else is really quite normal. Another fairy tale is the assertion that there is only one concentration camp left in Germany where political opponents are accommodated—Dachau.

This is a lie. There are still quite a number of other concentration camps in Germany, in fact more than one can keep tabs on here. Political prisoners are being taken to concentration camps in districts where no one suspected the existence of a concentration camp. In addition to Dachau, there are camps in Esterwegen, Lichtenburg, Sachsenburg, Heuberg, Oranienburg; moreover, there is a number of less-well-known camps. A number of instances of recent maltreatment have been reported to me from Sachsenburg, which totally refute the idea that things in Germany are now more lenient than before. The leader of all concentration camps, the ss leader Eicke, has introduced "public flogging" in the concentration camps.

281. *Manchester Guardian*: Reader's letter from J. W. Weigall, The Athenaeum, dated 7 April 1936[76]

Last September, on the invitation of Herr Himmler, I visited Dachau. The date of my visit was not prearranged, but I happened to go on a day that *Gruppenführer* Ei[c]ke, the head of all the concentration camps, was visiting there also. I spent the day there and was given the same facilities for inspection as I have received when visiting English prisons, with additional opportunities of questioning the inmates. To me, as to most Englishmen, the whole system of concentration camps is wrong and repugnant, but Dachau, as I saw it, was a well-run and well-managed institution.

The health of the prisoners may be judged by the fact that on the date of my visit among 1,400 inmates there were only four cases in the camp hospital, which I visited. I was struck by the efficiency and humanity of the officers and the discipline maintained over the guards. I saw no signs of or opportunity for unauthorized brutalities. I inspected the punishment book and was informed by *Gruppenführer* Ei[c]ke that no corporal punishment could be inflicted except by order of the camp commandant and confirmed by him. The number of such punishments in the previous six months was very small, not more than in an English prison.

I have no first-hand knowledge of the conditions now existing in other camps, but I find it difficult to believe, especially as I believe the same officers are in charge, that the conditions in Dachau are so totally different from those existing in September [. . .].

Our Special Correspondent writes: —

Mr. Weigall did not, it appears, visit the so-called "bunkers" where prisoners are kept for weeks or months in partial or total darkness and are frequently beaten. It was precisely in the month of September that the Jewish prisoners (including those who were new arrivals as a result of the Nuremberg laws) were victims of particularly severe excesses. (The beatings committed then were not entered in the books of the camp.) Mr. Weigall appears to know nothing of the constant ill-treatment of prisoners in the "Kiesgrube" (gravel pit). He does not say whether the prisoners he spoke to were selected by himself, and whether he could converse with them freely and without supervision. No prisoner in Dachau will say what he knows unless he is sure that the camp authorities will never learn that he has spoken. [. . .] The results of Mr. Weigall's investigation must therefore be regarded as imperfect and unconvincing as compared with the evidence of ill-treatment given in the *Manchester Guardian* and elsewhere, and based on detailed information received from prisoners themselves.

282. *The Times*: Article on the situation in the German concentration camps, dated 8 January 1937[77]

The curiosity displayed by many visitors to Germany last summer with regard to the number of concentration camps and political prisoners in Germany is gratified this week by the *Berlin Weekly*, which, apparently with official approval, provides information on German affairs for English-speaking readers.

The writer of the article states, on the authority of the Ministry of Justice, that there are in Germany to-day only six [*sic*] concentration camps left. In these there are 4,761 prisoners, of whom 3,694 are designated by the authorities as political prisoners. The remaining 1,067 are habitual criminals. The camps, for the most part in Central Germany, are at Dachau, Lichtenburg, Sachsenburg, Sulza, and Moringen. The guard duties are performed by men of the ss, the uniformed National-Socialist guards [. . .].

283. Letter from the British Consul General R. T. Smallbones to Sir George Ogilvie-Forbes, British chargé d'affaires in Berlin, on Jews in the camps following the November pogrom, dated 14 December 1938, published by the British government in 1940[78]

Below the report about the experiences of a Jew, an educated man, who had been in the trenches during the war and had a good business in Frankfurt. His information tallies exactly with what we were told by other people who experienced similar things. [. . .]

Before an inmate was allowed to go, he was first of all examined by the camp doctor; nobody with open wounds was allowed to go. The others were shaved and then sent to the political officer. He warned them not to tell anything about what had happened to them in the camp. If they did, they would have to pay for it bitterly. He added that the party's arm would reach them even if they left Germany, wherever they were. Then the remainders of their effects were returned to them. Most valuables had disappeared and their money had dwindled. They were told that a complaint about this was an accusation against the ss for theft and that such an accusation would be punished with flogging. As a final dirty trick, they were forced to contribute to the Party's *Winterhilfswerk*.[79] Almost everyone who was released had to sign a declaration — under threat of being re-arrested — that he would leave Germany within a given time — usually between four and six weeks.

6.3. The Camps and German Society

Most concentration camps were situated close to inhabited areas. All of the new SS camps, apart from Flossenbürg, were located near larger towns, not least to enable easy access to transport networks (284). Unlike many early camps, however, the new camps were built in areas protected from outside view, preferably close to natural resources such as stone or clay which could be exploited by prisoner labor.[80] For example, the SS set up Buchenwald on the Ettersberg mountain near Weimar, surrounded by a forest with nearby clay resources. And the commandant of Flossenbürg, a camp deliberately set up near stone quarries, specifically requested that the forest around his camp must not be cleared so as to prevent civilians from looking inside the camp (292). In fact, as living conditions within the camps deteriorated in the late 1930s, the SS was increasingly concerned to keep local people at a distance. Mauthausen commandant Albert Sauer, for example, complained to the district governor that the local police had repeatedly failed to disperse crowds watching prisoners use a ferry to cross a river on their way to work (299).[81]

Reciprocal links developed between the camps and their immediate surroundings. One historian has researched these local relationships at Dachau, which provides a good case study. A former base of the armaments industry, Dachau had one of Germany's highest unemployment rates during the Weimar Republic. In fact, as we have seen, the SS set up its first concentration camp on the site of Dachau's disused armaments factory, relying upon the existing infrastructure such as a railway link, power, gas, and sewage facilities. Official links between the SS model camp and the city council soon developed. For example, the Camp SS had to rely on Dachau's registry office to certify deaths. From November 1937, a bus service, used by many SS men and officers, linked the camp with the city center. Moreover, local businesses delivered goods to the camps. Dachau bakers initially brought bread, while builders had helped construct the camp. A brewery delivered beer, and a tobacconist sold some 500,000 cigarettes per month to the SS. Local farmers provided milk and other products. Sensing a good opportunity for business, some merchants tried to ingratiate themselves with ss men by offering gifts to secure contracts (290). However, the ss did not welcome all approaches. For example, ss men were not allowed to deal with local businesspeople regarded as politically unreliable (293). Yet, despite these extensive contacts, the local community did not profit significantly from the camp. Moreover, as the ss was keen to make their camps independent from the local economy, it gradually opened up workshops and received food and drink from ss-run enterprises—all at local businesses' disadvantage.[82]

In addition to business relations, there were also social contacts. ss officers from the camps were welcomed by local dignitaries at many municipal events. In fact, the Dachau and Weimar city authorities at first celebrated the fact that the ss had set up camps in their towns. Regional functionaries such as the Thuringian *Gauleiter* Fritz Sauckel transferred money to the ss, effectively bribes to cultivate good relations, while Weimar's city leaders arranged several parades of the Camp ss through the streets. Some Weimar people visited funfairs organized by the camp ss, such as the one organized in late August 1939, days before the outbreak of World War II (275).[83]

But local contacts with the ss were not straightforward (291). To start with, a sizable number of clandestine left-wing supporters must have been terrified by the presence of the camp, not least because they knew that local activists had been among the first prisoners of the early camps.[84] Reservations about the camps spread far beyond those with oppositional sympathies as ss threats were extended to other nonconformists, with warnings that they faced imprisonment in the concentration camp if they stepped out of line.[85] In Dachau an official declaration warned local residents that they must not approach prisoner work details outside the camp—such as prisoners building a road, accompanied by armed ss guards—lest they risk severe punishment themselves (295). Meanwhile, "respectable" citizens, otherwise sympathetic to the aims of the Nazi regime, were unsettled by the behavior of some Camp ss men, which stood in sharp contrast to the propaganda image of the ss as an honorable elite force of the new Germany. Locally, ss men, particularly rank-and-file guards, soon gained a reputation for their boorish behavior

The Camps and the Public

while on the town (289).[86] There were also some cases of sexual harassment (294). Following complaints from local residents, Dachau commandant Loritz eventually had to issue a directive in July 1937, ordering ss NCOs to patrol Dachau and arrest any drunken ss men. He even sent detachments of ss guards to the railway station every Monday to supervise ss men arriving on the late train from Munich, after a weekend of heavy drinking (289).

All in all, then, relationships between the camps and local communities were rather ambivalent, as the example of Dachau clearly demonstrates. The city authorities and many inhabitants, though certainly not the large number of local Communist and Social Democratic supporters, had initially welcomed the establishment of the camp, which would, they hoped, help get the local economy out of recession. Yet, when the city council began to promote local tourism in the mid-1930s, it was disappointed to realize that most people in Germany and abroad did not associate Dachau with its picturesque old castle but with its new concentration camp, a place of abuse, torture, and murder that still casts a dark shadow decades after the camp's liberation in 1945.[87]

More generally, popular attitudes toward the camps were ambiguous. As we saw previously, people's attitudes were as diverse as general attitudes toward the Nazi regime. There can be little doubt that many Germans bought into the image of the camps that was constructed by Nazi propaganda, and many Germans needed no persuasion that firm action was needed against suspected Bolsheviks, criminals, and other social outsiders. After all, the Nazi promise to destroy the left and restore order had attracted many Germans to the Nazi cause in the first place. Meanwhile, even some left-wing supporters began to accept the camp as a place for the detention of social outsiders.[88]

However, it would be a mistake to assume that the German people as a whole accepted or tolerated the camps.[89] This is already evident from the testimony of released prisoners (297). Of course, the regime tried to ensure that former prisoners would remain silent, threatening them with immediate re-arrest if they talked about the camps (285). In addition, the Gestapo ordered the control and surveillance of released political prisoners.[90]

Despite the high risks involved, some released political prisoners continued their struggle against the Nazis and also disseminated reports of their experiences in the camps, as did other inmates.[91] These reports continued to subvert the propaganda image of the camps. Rumors about atrocities in the camps still circulated among German society, particularly after the mass release of Jewish men arrested in the wake of Kristallnacht in November 1938 (298). Despite the risks involved, one concerned citizen even wrote to Franz von Epp, Reich governor of Bavaria, to complain about the many deaths in Dachau at that time (296). Contrary to Nazi expectations, most Germans had not been enthusiastic about the anti-Semitic excesses of Kristallnacht. On the contrary, many Germans were opposed to this open outburst of destructive anti-Semitic violence, while others were indifferent. Indeed, the public impact of details about the violence within the camps concerned ss officials to such an extent that they refused to release prisoners with torture marks (283 and 301).[92]

Any discussion of the crimes in the concentration camps could be harshly punished by the regime, and anyone who passed on "rumors" could be dealt with by the judiciary under the "malicious attack" legislation brought in by the regime. Those persecuted by the authorities had often made their critical remarks in pubs or other public areas, sometimes under the influence of alcohol. There must have been several hundred legal cases relating to the camps throughout the 1930s.[93] The surviving trial records cast popular knowledge of the camps in a new light, revealing that many ordinary Germans knew what went on inside the camps, often in surprising detail (286). Some people who told stories about the camps were themselves taken into protective custody. Such was the case of Jürgen Jürgensen, a Social Democratic ex-member of the Prussian Diet, who had collected photos and reports from released camp prisoners before offering them to a friend for publication abroad. Jürgensen was arrested on 12 October 1935. Werner Best ordered that he was not to be released until further notice (287).[94]

Courts sometimes acquitted defendants accused of spreading so-called malicious attacks about the camps. This was the case of Werner R., a twenty-five-year-old dental technician from Munich. His colleague Michael S., who had once served in the Dachau Camp ss, repeatedly boasted about his work as a camp guard. These stories

The Camps and the Public

evidently included reports about the abominable treatment of Jews by the ss (300). When Werner R., annoyed about the former ss man's bragging and the fact that he was harassing a female employee, threatened to hit his co-worker, Michael S. denounced him to the Gestapo. S. claimed that R. had told him that an *Autobahn* worker had been taken to Dachau, on Hitler's orders, after complaining about his low wages. Werner R. was eventually put on trial before a Munich court, yet on 30 June he was acquitted due to a lack of evidence.[95] This case clearly illustrates that some people gained highly detailed knowledge of atrocities in the camps, including the abuse of Jews. Yet, knowledge of these atrocities did not necessarily imply consent with Nazi repression. If it is true, as some historians have claimed, that almost all Germans accepted the Nazi dictatorship by the mid-1930s, why did the regime maintain such a diverse and substantial apparatus of repression—which included, among others, the judiciary, the police, the ss, and the concentration camps—to enforce the Nazi vision of a racially pure national community?[96]

DOCUMENTS

284. Report by the political prisoner Eugen Kogon on the concentration camps, published in 1946[97]

As sites for concentration camps, the ss invariably chose inaccessible areas, preferably forests and moors, not too far from the larger cities. This served a dual purpose. The camps were to remain isolated from the outside world, while the ss itself was to retain access to urban amenities. Again, the Nazis and their sympathizers were thus enabled to profit in supplying the camps, while the rest of the population was kept in a state of terror.

285. Sopade report regarding prisoners released from the Dachau concentration camp, dated March 1935[98]

One can't have a conversation with persons released from Dachau. They are so intimidated that they take to their heels when they fear that one wants to talk to them. At best one can hear a very old friend remark: "Sometime later I'll be able to tell you something—you'll be amazed." Under no circumstances can one get more out of them.

286. From the service log of the Reich Minister of Justice, dated 11 October 1935[99]

Senior Prosecutor's Office Munich reports on the criminal trial of Xaver Kiening under the Malicious Gossip Law. The accused, who had twice been in protective custody in Dachau, until March 1935, made remarks about maltreatment in the camp in July of this year. They had, he said, been frequently got from their beds at night and, wearing only their shirts and underpants, had been made to crawl on the ground outside. In winter a hole had been cut in the ice and the protective custody prisoners thrown in. They had then been made to work all day in their wet clothes. During a jocular fight between prisoners the sentries had shot two protective custody inmates dead on the spot.

287. Letter from Dr. Werner Best to Hans-Heinrich Lammers, State Secretary and Chief of the Reich Chancellery, regarding Jürgen Jürgensen, dated 17 December 1935[100]

The former Social Democratic deputy of the Prussian Diet Jürgen Jürgensen [. . .] was taken into protective custody on 12 October 1935 because he spread the rumor that the ss guard personnel are committing the most brutal floggings against the protective custody prisoners in the concentration camps. Jürgensen has stated that he had received these reports from former SPD comrades who were no longer in Germany. He has therefore spread the atrocity stories about Germany, invented in similar form by émigrés, in order to create a mood detrimental to the government. Ever since 1933 Jürgensen has spread such rumors in various places. At the end of August 1935 he has called on the Herr *Oberpräsident* Kube to inform him that flogging continues to be practiced in the most brutal form in the concentration camps. Regarding the Esterwegen concentration camp Jürgensen made the following assertion:

> When new prisoners arrive in this camp, they have to line up in a square. Then some prisoner, who is in the camp already and is due for punishment for some reason or other, is strapped over a buck and whipped. The person whipped has to join in counting every lashing. It is said that a certain Eicke from the Secret State Police in Berlin has to sign the punishment orders that are given in writing.

Jürgensen admits that he has given the same information also to other higher state offices. He claims that he had merely intended to get some alleviations for his Party comrades still in protective custody, such as the former chairman of the Social Democratic group [in the Prussian Diet], Ernst Heilmann. [. . .]

Jürgensen is at present in the Esterwegen concentration camp; he cannot be released for the time being.

288. Commandant's order no. 7, issued by Karl Koch for Buchenwald, dated 24 August 1937[101]

I have regretfully discovered that some members of the ss have contact with girls who are anything but ss-suitable. Here too, only the best is good enough for an ss man. ss men of my staff, in whom I discover such inferiority complexes, will be reported by me for dismissal as they have not yet understood the laws of the *Schutzstaffel* [. . .]

289. Garrison order no. 11/37, issued by Commandant Hans Loritz for the ss garrison Dachau, dated 15 July 1937[102]

The [ss] patrol examines the leave permits of ss *Unterführers* and men in uniform and civilian clothes (insofar as they are recognized as such) who are in taverns or in the street after curfew. Married *Unterführer* not accommodated in barracks, and men of active units, are also to be examined. Drunken ss members in uniform are to be arrested and sent to the Dachau concentration camp.

Owners of taverns complaining about the performance of the patrol are likewise to be reported to me.

Every Monday at 1.21 hours the patrol stands at the Dachau railroad station and reports to me the ss members who time and again cross the track and jump over the railroad barrier [. . .].

I shall see to it that Dachau at long last becomes quiet and that incidents caused by civilians are not always blamed on the ss of the Dachau garrison by fellow citizens not favorably disposed to us.

290. Commandant's Order no. 9 for Buchenwald, dated 6 September 1937[103]

I forbid the so-called "scrounging" from suppliers. Acceptance of gifts is forbidden to ss men (behavior damaging to the ss).

291. From the situation report of the General State Prosecutor in Jena for November 1937[104]

The Buchenwald concentration camp mentioned in my last report continues to grow; at present it accommodates 3,000 men but, as the commandant told me, is to be extended in the course of next year to a strength of 10,000 men [. . .]. It is interesting that the population of Weimar is not at all pleased about the construction of the camp and that the traders are not keen to do business with it. They are glad when a prisoner succeeds in escaping.

292. Letter from Karl Künstler, commandant of Flossenbürg, to ss *Obersturmbannführer* Dr. Walter Salpeter, ss Administration Office, dated 9 March 1939[105]

As I mentioned to you when you were visiting Flossenbürg, I consider it advisable for the forest not to be cleared: 1. even a concentration camp has to adapt to the local landscape, 2. not to provide civilians with a direct view into the protective custody camp. This will be prevented by leaving the forest to remain as it is.

293. Order from Commandant Hans Loritz for the ss garrison Dachau, dated 1 April 1938[106]

With immediate effect I forbid the purchase of milk from Frau Maria Trinkl, Etzenhausen no. 65 (Würmkanal). Frau Trinkl has repeatedly and in the vilest manner offended several ss men who were doing their duty. I have already taken steps through the competent authority for her being taken into protective custody.

This ban applies in particular to those members of the ss who have until now bought milk from Frau Trinkl.

294. Commandant's Order no. 40, issued by Karl Koch for Buchenwald, dated 8 April 1938[107]

A justified complaint has been received from the Head of the Hermann Lietz School in Ettersberg Castle to the effect that ss men have come to the Castle forecourt in the evening, have fooled about with the kitchen maids and have then pursued them into one of the buildings. We have no business in someone else's property and I forbid entering the Castle forecourt altogether as well as the use of the park paths near the Castle after dark.

295. Announcement of the Dachau District Office, dated 15 July 1938[108]

The SS garrison command is at present improving the "camp street" branching off Friedensstrasse and Pollnstrasse. In addition various new buildings will very shortly be constructed there. For this work prisoners of the concentration camp are being used. To prevent these prisoners from escaping the guard personnel have been instructed to make immediate use of their firearms. To avoid any possible danger to persons not concerned, the commandant's office of the concentration camp has declared a danger zone, entry to which is <u>forbidden</u> to all persons who are not resident there or who do not have any official business there. The danger zone begins at the end of Friedensstrasse and Pollnstrasse (Wolf department store) and comprises the whole area of the camp street as far as the road to the Würmmühle and to the Schropper-, Würm-, and Moosstrasse. The danger zone is marked by warning notices pointing out the ban on unnecessary entry and on the consequences of disregarding the ban. Offenders, quite apart from the danger of being injured, may, under certain circumstances, have to expect immediate arrest and criminal prosecution.

296. Anonymous letter to the Reich governor in Bavaria, General Franz Ritter von Epp, dated 16 November 1938[109]

Your Excellency!

My desperate reflection on whether any help could be found for what has been going on here for a number of days has finally called a name and a title into my mind—or rather two titles: Franz Ritter von Epp, General of Infantry (retd.), Reich governor in Bavaria [. . .]. Does Your Excellency know that among the men who have been taken to Dachau there are holders of high war decorations and war disabled? And that in Dachau, at least until a short time ago, flogging and ill-treatment were practiced?—But Your Excellency probably does not know that during the night of Sunday to Monday (or Monday to Tuesday) 4 or 5 dead bodies were transported out of Dachau. Whether this kind of thing also happened before or after, I do not know [. . .]. I also know that—contrary to Dr. Goebbels's assertions—among the persecuted and robbed there are many people who have already made all preparations for emigration, have received entry permits to foreign states, but have waited in vain for weeks for their passports. I know that the demanded billion has been paid or is fully guaranteed, the atonement for the murder [. . .].[110] And that in spite of this payment the men are being kept back in the concentration camps.

297. Report of a Jewish doctor from Frankfurt am Main on his release from the Buchenwald concentration camp after the November pogrom, written in January 1939[111]

An ss *Scharführer* brought us through the forest to the camp boundary, where he released us with the wish: "Don't get pissed!" We wandered to the neighboring village, about 2.5 km distant, where the landlord in the tavern and his wife first served us lots of coffee, soda water and bread and cheese. The people seemed to know what one needs when one comes down from the top. I had not eaten since the preceding evening. The people were friendly, decent, no questions about the camp. The three elderly villagers who were drinking beer in the tavern were also silent but not unfriendly. In automobiles ordered to come up we then rode down to Weimar and, filthy as we were, with a crust of clay covering us up to our knees, we then traveled to Frankfurt by the scheduled express train. Nobody on the train made any remark about this dirty party that boarded the train. They knew what the dirt meant on passengers who boarded at Weimar and looked like that.

A gentleman who returned [from Buchenwald] a few days later, told me that, when he boarded the train, an Aryan lady got up and offered him her seat. To his reaction that surely he could not accept that, she said: "This is the least that I can do for you!" Such remarks should not go unnoticed, any more than the cordial pleasure of many Aryans, especially the simple people, when they saw one again.

Two lessons we have learnt from our stay in the concentration camp: Make every effort to get out those who are still in Germany, or in the camp, and second, to tell oneself in every situation: Anything is better than the concentration camp!

298. From Ruth Andreas-Friedrich's diary, entry of 16 January 1939[112]

Gradually they are all returning.[113] Those from Buchenwald and those from Sachsenhausen. With a bald skull and eyes full of pain. [. . .] Some have one thing to relate, others another. In Sachsenhausen one was allowed to work. But one was freezing and punishments were harsh. In Buchenwald near Weimar work was forbidden. A single latrine for hundreds of people. The first seven days there were called "murder week." Bad food, gastric flu, diarrhea. People were writhing in spasm. Fall in to fall out [. . .]. Departure to the Beyond. [. . .] Within seven days several hundred people died in Buchenwald. Beaten to death, shot dead, hunted to death.

299. Complaint by the Mauthausen commandant Albert Sauer to the *Bezirkshauptmannschaft* Perg, dated 18 January 1939[114]

For about 10 days prisoners have been taken to a distant construction site (Ebelsberg near Linz) from the Mauthausen concentration camp. The prisoners have to use the ferry in Mauthausen every day at 7 o'clock in the morning and at 4 o'clock in the afternoon. This convoy, especially in the afternoon, attracts some 30 to 40 curious spectators at the Mauthausen ferry every day. The Mauthausen gendarmerie station, whose duty it would have been to disperse such disorder, has not so far considered it necessary to intervene, even though they were aware of the situation. [. . .]

It is pointed out that in case of any incident (attempted escape by prisoners) use will be made of firearms without any consideration. If civilians are injured as a result, the Mauthausen gendarmerie station will be held responsible.

300. Interrogation of the dental technician Michael S., a former Dachau SS man, by the State Police Office Munich, dated 14 June 1939[115]

I admit that shortly after my joining D. [his boss], I spoke to my colleagues in the workshop about the Dachau concentration camp. It is correct that I described the position of the Dachau concentration camp and its fence. In this connection I also mentioned that at the corners of the surrounding fence of the Dachau concentration camp there are guard towers with heavy machine guns. I also said that, in my opinion, escape from the Dachau concentration camp is now impossible.

I also said that I learned in a Dachau tavern that a protective custody prisoner escaped in 1933. The prisoner, I was told, had placed heavy blankets over the electrically charged barbed-wire fence within the camp and had thus got away. The escaped prisoner had then sent a card from Prague to the administration of the Dachau concentration camp, saying: "You can all kiss my ass." I further related that the accommodation quarters of the ss in the Dachau concentration camp are diagonally across the road. [. . .] I recall that I told my colleagues at work that if anyone arrives in the camp with a fat belly, he loses it in an astonishingly short period. I did not tell my colleagues at work that during morning sport, when running, prisoners who cannot keep up get their behinds kicked until they collapse, or that, if a Jew reports for the doctor, he is not seen at all and that many a Jew has died as a result. What is correct is that I told them that prisoners, when they return [from labor], sometimes cannot keep up and therefore receive kicks from their fellow prisoners. I also said that among the protective custody prisoners one prisoner is designated foreman and that this relationship has resulted in friction among the protective custody prisoners [. . .]. I did not intend to spread any atrocity stories with my accounts of the Dachau concentration camp or cause unrest among the population. I believed that my work colleagues would keep my descriptions of the Dachau concentration camp to themselves. I repeat that I only related matters about the Dachau concentration camp that are universally known among the Dachau population and can be heard in every tavern.

301. Report of the second *Rapportführer* of Buchenwald, dated 22 June 1939[116]

The prisoner Jew W. was to be released on 20.6.39. As it was the time of the evening roll call, I got the foreman of the clothes store to send W. to the quarters to have him seen by the doctor. I next immediately phoned the prisoners' infirmary and ordered the medical orderly P. to have W. examined. [. . .] As the doctor was no longer in the infirmary, the examination was carried out by the orderly P. Shortly afterward P. phoned me to say that W. was not fit for release as he had been flogged a few days previously. As such prisoners are not allowed to be released, I made W. report to his block again immediately.

TIMELINE

1933

30 January	Hitler appointed Reich Chancellor by Reich President Paul von Hindenburg.
27 February	Reichstag fire.
28 February	Decree for the Protection of People and State, or Reichstag Fire Decree, abolishing basic constitutional rights and providing "legal" basis for detention without trial (protective custody).
5 March	Reichstag elections: a vote held in an atmosphere of terror sees the Nazi Party poll 43.9 percent.
21 March	Opening of SA camp at Oranienburg, a small town just north of Berlin.
22 March	Opening of SS camp in Dachau, outside Munich.
23 March	Enabling Act, passed by the German Reichstag with 444 votes to 94.
1 April	Organized nationwide boycott of Jewish businesses.
1 April	Heinrich Himmler officially appointed commander of Bavarian Political Police.
28 April	Secret State Police Office (Gestapa) in Prussia officially set up, headed by Rudolf Diels.
14 July	Official ban on all political parties except for the NSDAP.
14 July	Law for the compulsory sterilization of the so-called hereditarily ill.
September	Mass police arrests of beggars and the homeless.
13 November	Prussian decree for preventive police custody of professional criminals in camps.
24 November	National law for the indefinite security confinement of habitual criminals in state prisons.

1934

January	Non-Aggression Pact between Germany and Poland.
20 April	Himmler appointed as Inspector of Prussian Gestapo.
24 April	Establishment of the *Volksgerichtshof* (People's Court).
30 June	Start of violent purge of the SA, which sees execution of SA leader Ernst Röhm on 1 July.
4 July	Theodor Eicke officially appointed as Inspector of the Concentration Camps and Leader of SS Guard Troops.
July	Oranienburg concentration camp closed down by SS.
2 August	Death of Hindenburg; Hitler names himself Führer and Reich Chancellor.
10 December	Inspectorate of the Concentration Camps (IKL) established in Berlin.

1935

13 January	Saar plebiscite: vote in favor of incorporation into the German Reich.
16 March	Reintroduction of military conscription.
Summer	Only five remaining SS concentration camps in German Reich, holding no more than 4,000 prisoners.
15 September	Passing of Nuremberg Laws (Nazi racial legislation).

1936

7 March	Remilitarization of the Rhineland.
17 June	Himmler appointed Chief of the German Police by Hitler.
12 July	Arrival of first prisoners at new Sachsenhausen concentration camp in Oranienburg.
1 August	Opening of the Olympic Games in Berlin.

1937

March	Mass arrests of some 2,000 so-called professional and habitual criminals.
15 July	First prisoners arrive at new Buchenwald concentration camp near Weimar.

Timeline

| 14 December | Reich decree on preventive police custody for so-called criminals and asocials. |
| 15 December | First transport of female prisoners from Moringen to Lichtenburg, designated as the new central ss concentration camp for women. |

1938

13 March	*Anschluss* of Austria.
April	Mass arrests of nearly 2,000 allegedly work-shy men, imprisoned in Buchenwald.
29 April	ss establishes German Earth and Stone Works company, supplying building materials by exploiting camp prisoner labor.
3 May	First prisoners arrive at the new Flossenbürg concentration camp in Bavaria.
June	Action Work-Shy Reich sees mass arrests of so-called asocials with some 10,000 men taken to concentration camps.
8 August	First prisoners arrive at new Mauthausen concentration camp in occupied Austria.
29–30 Sept.	Munich Conference
1 October	German occupation of the Sudetenland.
October	Mass expulsion of Polish Jews from Germany.
9–10 Nov.	Regime-orchestrated anti-Semitic pogrom. Afterward some 26,000 Jewish men temporarily imprisoned in Dachau, Buchenwald, and Sachsenhausen concentration camps.

1939

| March | Invasion of Czechoslovakia by German troops; set up Bohemia and Moravia as so-called Reich Protectorate |
| May | Female prisoners arrive from Lichtenburg at new Ravensbrück concentration camp for women in northern Germany; after the closure of Lichtenburg, there are now six official ss concentration camps in German Reich. |

22 May	Pact of Steel between Germany and Italy.
23 August	Non-aggression Pact between Germany and the Soviet Union.
1 September	German invasion of Poland, leading to World War II.

Daily Inmate Numbers in ss Concentration Camps, 1935–1939

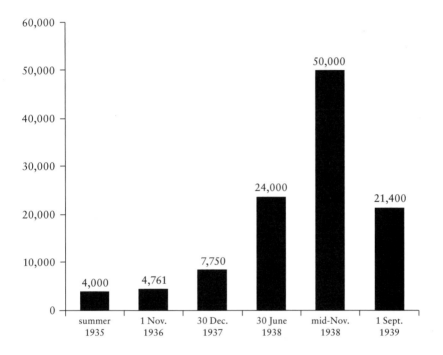

This chart shows daily averages of inmates in ss concentration camps from 1935 to 1939. The figures for 1935, 1937, and 1938 are estimates; see Wachsmann, "Dynamics of Destruction," 33.

ss Ranks and Equivalents in the Wehrmacht and the U.S. Army

Commissioned Officer Ranks

SS RANK	WEHRMACHT RANK	U.S. ARMY RANK
Reichsführer-ss		
(Reich Leader ss)		
	Generalfeldmarschall	General of the Army
ss Oberstgruppenführer	Generaloberst	General
ss Obergruppenführer	General	Lieutenant General
ss Gruppenführer	Generalleutnant	Major General
ss Brigadeführer	Generalmajor	Brigadier General
ss Oberführer		
ss Standartenführer	Oberst	Colonel
ss Obersturmbannführer	Oberstleutnant	Lieutenant Colonel
ss Sturmbannführer	Major	Major
ss Hauptsturmführer	Hauptmann	Captain
ss Obersturmführer	Oberleutnant	1st Lieutenant
ss Untersturmführer	Leutnant	2nd Lieutenant

Noncommissioned Officer Ranks

SS RANK	WEHRMACHT RANK	U.S. ARMY RANK
ss Sturmscharführer	Stabsfeldwebel	Sergeant Major
ss Hauptscharführer	Oberfeldwebel	Master Sergeant
ss Oberscharführer	Feldwebel	Sergeant 1st Class
ss Scharführer	Unterfeldwebel	Staff Sergeant
ss Unterscharführer	Unteroffizier	Sergeant
ss Rottenführer	Obergefreiter	Corporal
ss Sturmmann	Gefreiter	
ss Oberschütze	Oberschütze	Private 1st Class
ss Schütze	Schütze	Private

NOTES

Abbreviations

BA	Bundesarchiv
BAB	Bundesarchiv Berlin
BayHStA	Bayerisches Hauptstaatsarchiv, Munich
BDC	Berlin Document Centre
FZH	Forschungsstelle für Zeitgeschichte, Hamburg
GStA	Geheimes Staatsarchiv Preußischer Kulturbesitz, Berlin-Dahlem
HStA	Hauptstaatsarchiv
IfZ	Institut für Zeitgeschichte, Munich
IMT	*International Military Tribunal*
ITS	International Tracing Service, Bad Arolsen
ND	Nuremberg trials document
PRO	National Archives (formerly Public Record Office), Kew
StA	Staatsarchiv
USHMM	United States Holocaust Memorial Museum, Washington DC
WL	Wiener Library, London

Introduction

1. For the first reports about concentration camps after liberation, see Abzug, *Inside the Vicious Heart.*

2. Arendt, *Origins of Totalitarianism*, 438.

3. For a survey of recent work, see Wachsmann, "Looking into the Abyss."

4. For the development of the camp system during World War II, see Wachsmann, "Dynamics of Destruction," 26–36. Unless otherwise indicated, all references to inmate numbers in concentration camps come from this article. For the number of dead in Auschwitz, see Długoborski and Piper, *Auschwitz, 1940–1945*, 3:230.

5. Arendt, *Origins of Totalitarianism*, 453; Kogon, *Theory and Practice of Hell*, 28–29.

6. Tuchel, *Konzentrationslager*; Drobisch and Wieland, *System der NS-Konzentrationslager.* Both of these monographs offer much detail on the development

of the prewar camps and have been indispensable for this volume. For studies of individual camps, see Benz and Distel, *Terror ohne System*; Benz and Distel, *Herrschaft und Gewalt*; Benz and Distel, *Instrumentarium der Macht*.

7. Some of these questions are highlighted in the individual contributions to Caplan and Wachsmann, *Concentration Camps in Nazi Germany*.

8. Caplan, "Political Detention," 26.

9. On Hitler's appointment, see Turner, *Hitler's Thirty Days to Power*. On the fall of the Weimar Republic, see Blasius, *Weimars Ende*.

10. Evans, "Coercion and Consent in Nazi Germany."

11. When writing about the Third Reich, one has to reflect on the problems of Nazi language. Many historians demonstrate their distance by placing quotation marks around all Nazi terms. We decided against this practice because of its effect on readability. Instead, we frequently use terminology as it was common during the Third Reich. This does not mean, of course, that we accept Nazi terminology. For this approach, see Evans, *Coming of the Third Reich*, xxxii–xxxiii. More generally on Nazi language, see Klemperer, *Language of the Third Reich*.

12. Tuchel, *Konzentrationslager*, 96–100.

13. For the quotation see Gellately, "Social Outsiders," 57. For a critique of Gellately's approach, see Eley, "Hitler's Silent Majority?," 553–61.

14. Still indispensable on the Nazi capture of power is Broszat, *Der Staat Hitlers*.

15. On early camps in Berlin, see Mayer–von Götz, *Terror im Zentrum*, 19.

16. See Baganz, *Erziehung*, 58–61.

17. Broszat, "Nationalsozialistische Konzentrationslager," 337, 347.

18. For examples see Markus Kienle, "Das Konzentrationslager Heuberg," 44; Baganz, *Erziehung*, 108–13. More generally, see Tuchel, *Konzentrationslager*, 38–41.

19. Tuchel, *Konzentrationslager*, 42–45.

20. The term "early camps" was coined by Orth; see *System der nationalsozialistischen Konzentrationslager*, 23–26.

21. See, e.g., Wohlfeld, "Konzentrationslager Nohra in Thüringen."

22. For the most detailed account of developments in Prussia, see Tuchel, *Konzentrationslager*, 60–89. See also Drobisch and Wieland, *System der NS-Konzentrationslager*, 66; Lüerssen, "'Moorsoldaten' in Esterwegen, Börgermoor, Neusustrum."

23. See document 22. For the prisoner figures, see Tuchel, *Konzentrationslager*, 155.

24. On Himmler's rise, see Longerich, *Heinrich Himmler*, 158–79.

25. Tuchel, *Konzentrationslager*, 319.

26. See Endlich, "Die Lichtenburg, 1933–1939," 35–39.

27. See Tuchel, *Inspektion der Konzentrationslager*, 28–29.

28. Tuchel, *Konzentrationslager*, 162, 209–10.

29. For these figures, see Drobisch and Wieland, *System der NS-Konzentrationslager*, 134, 203.

30. For Dachau inmate figures, see Tuchel, *Konzentrationslager*, 155; Drobisch and Wieland, *System der NS-Konzentrationslager*, 288.

31. For the legal apparatus and its prisons in prewar Nazi Germany, see Wachsmann, *Hitler's Prisons*, 65–188; for the figures, see pp. 113, 185, 393.

32. Gruchmann, *Justiz im Dritten Reich*, 345–79, 545–72, 632–45. See also Drobisch and Wieland, *System der NS-Konzentrationslager*, 136.

33. See chapter 2 for further details.

34. For a discussion of this term, see Kershaw, "'Cumulative Radicalisation.'"

35. For the figures, see Drobisch and Wieland, *System der NS-Konzentrationslager*, 203.

36. Wohlfeld, "Im Hotel 'Zum Großherzog.'"

37. Orth, "Concentration Camp Personnel"; Morsch, "Formation and Construction," 101, 170–71; Drobisch and Wieland, *System der NS-Konzentrationslager*, 257.

38. See appendix A. For the Buchenwald figures, see Mahn- und Gedenkstätte Buchenwald, *Buchenwald*, 698.

39. For the first prisoners arriving in the new camps, see Maršálek, *Geschichte des Konzentrationslagers Mauthausen*, 109–10; Skriebeleit, "Flossenbürg—Stammlager," 22–23; Strebel, *KZ Ravensbrück*, 103–7.

40. For Nazi radicalization during the late 1930s, see Kershaw, *Hitler*, 1–230. More generally, see also Evans, *The Third Reich in Power*.

41. See Drobisch and Wieland, *System der NS-Konzentrationslager*, 252–53, 280–81; Tuchel and Schattenfroh, *Zentrale des Terrors*, 126–29; Zámečník, *Das war Dachau*, 99–102.

42. Longerich, *Politik der Vernichtung*, 164; Ayaß, "Gemeinschaftsfremde," 134–35; Schleunes, *Twisted Road to Auschwitz*, 227–29.

43. Evans, *The Third Reich in Power*, 580–92; Longerich, *Politik der Vernichtung*, 190–226.

44. More generally, see Pingel, *Häftlinge unter SS-Herrschaft*, 91–96.

45. Wildt, "Violence against Jews in Germany," 204–8; Kropat, "Reichskristallnacht," 141; Evans, *The Third Reich in Power*, 599.

46. Occasionally, there were still mass releases, reminiscent of the early camps. For example, several thousand prisoners were released in the spring of 1939 on the occasion of Hitler's fiftieth birthday; see Drobisch and Wieland, *System der NS-Konzentrationslager*, 308–9.

47. Ayaß, *"Asoziale" im Nationalsozialismus*, 19–49.

48. See document 16. More generally, see Wachsmann, "The Policy of Exclusion."

49. See document 23.

50. Endlich, "Die Lichtenburg, 1933–1939," 32.

51. Wagner, *Volksgemeinschaft ohne Verbrecher*, 254–98; Ayaß, *"Asoziale" im Nationalsozialismus*, 140–65.

52. For the figures, see Drobisch and Wieland, *System der NS-Konzentrationslager*, 288.

53. See appendix A; see also Caplan, "Political Detention," 39.

54. Wachsmann, "Dynamics of Destruction," 26–32.

55. Caplan, "Political Detention." On the legacy of the prewar camps on the camps of the Holocaust, see Goeschel and Wachsmann, "Before Auschwitz."

56. For the former approach, see Aly et al., *Die Verfolgung und Ermordung der europäischen Juden*. For the latter, see Noakes and Pridham, *Nazism*.

57. Unless otherwise noted, any emphasis—such as italics or underlined text—comes from the original document.

58. See www.camps.bbk.ac.uk for some photographs from the prewar camps, as well as further links.

1. The Early Camps, 1933–1934

1. Königseder, "Die Entwicklung des KZ-Systems," 30. On the Nohra camp see Wohlfeld, "Konzentrationslager Nohra in Thüringen."

2. For a survey of the early camps, see also White, "Introduction to the Early Camps."

3. Mommsen, "Der Reichstagsbrand und seine politischen Folgen," 390. See also Raithel and Strenge, "Die Reichstagsbrandverordnung."

4. For background see Evans, *Coming of the Third Reich*, 328–49.

5. Caplan, "Political Detention," 27.

6. Schneider, "Das Ermächtigungsgesetz vom 24. März 1933."

7. For this estimate, see Wachsmann, "Dynamics of Destruction," 18.

8. Caplan, "Political Detention," 23; Tuchel, *Konzentrationslager*, 107.

9. Noakes and Pridham, *Nazism*, 1:170.

10. Drobisch and Wieland, *System der NS-Konzentrationslager*, 42, 135, 140.

11. For the argument that the camps were improvised see also Broszat, "Nationalsozialistische Konzentrationslager," 323.

12. For a survey of the different early camps see Benz and Distel, *Der Ort des Terrors*, II:17–230. On Oranienburg, see Dörner, "Ein KZ in der Mitte der Stadt."

13. For the figure, see Drobisch and Wieland, *System der NS-Konzentrationslager*, 45.

14. Diercks, "Fuhlsbüttel," 266–72.

15. Goeschel and Wachsmann, "Before Auschwitz," 530–31.

16. Patel, *Soldiers of Labor*, 41–63; Caplan, "Political Detention," 32–33.

17. On the opening of Dachau see Zámečník, "Das frühe Konzentrationslager Dachau."

18. On Hilmar Wäckerle (1899–1941), see Tuchel, "Die Kommandanten des KZ Dachau," 331–33.

19. On legal investigations of deaths in Dachau see StA München, Staatsanwaltschaften 7014. More generally see Goeschel, "Suicide in Nazi Concentration Camps." On background see Tuchel, *Konzentrationslager*, 125–26.

20. Richardi, *Schule der Gewalt*, 48–87; Orth, *Konzentrationslager-SS*, 127–32. On Eicke, see section 3.1.

21. Knoch, "Emslandlager."

22. On the Bredow camp see Rudorff, "Stettin-Bredow."

23. For this paragraph, Caplan, "Political Detention," 35–36; Tuchel, *Konzentrationslager*, 60–89.

24. BAB, R 58/264, Bl. 16, Heydrich's comment of 25 January 1934. On Heydrich, see Gerwarth, *Hitler's Hangman.*

25. For background see Wagner, *Volksgemeinschaft ohne Verbrecher*, 199.

26. Caplan, "Political Detention," 37; see also Herbert, "Von der Gegnerbekämpfung zur 'rassischen Generalprävention,'" 61.

27. This list was attached to Epp's letter to the Bavarian Minister President. See Drobisch and Wieland, *System der NS-Konzentrationslager*, 103–5; Tuchel, *Konzentrationslager*, 155–56.

28. The *Völkischer Beobachter* was the Nazi Party's national newspaper. Printed in Jäckel and Kuhn, *Hitler*, 347–48.

29. "Keine Sabotage des Volkswillens mehr! Ins Reichskabinett gehören Männer, die das Vertrauen der Nation besitzen," *Völkischer Beobachter*, Reichsausgabe, 11 August 1932.

30. On 9 August 1932 the Papen government had passed an Emergency Decree stipulating capital punishment for politically motivated murder. See Bessel, "The Potempa Murder."

31. A reference to the German revolution of November 1918.

32. *Reichsgesetzblatt* 1, no. 17 (1933): 83.

33. Quoted in Wohlfeld, "Konzentrationslager Nohra in Thüringen," 110.

34. "Ein Konzentrationslager für politische Gefangene: In der Nähe von Dachau," *Münchner Neueste Nachrichten*, 21 March 1933.

35. The Reichsbanner was a republican paramilitary force in the Weimar Republic affiliated with the SPD.

36. The derogatory Nazi term for the Social Democrats.

37. This decree was signed by State Secretary Ludwig Grauert (1891–1964), State Secretary since 11 April 1933 in the Prussian Ministry of the Interior. Reprinted in Michaelis and Schraepler, *Ursachen und Folgen*, 9:363–64.

38. Dr. Werner Best (1903–89) was a jurist and influential SS and police leader. See Herbert, *Best*.

39. On Osthofen see H.-G. Meyer and Roth, "Osthofen."

40. Hessisches StA Darmstadt, G 24 Generalstaatsanwaltschaft, no. 360, Bl. 38–39.

41. *Der Prozess gegen die Hauptkriegsverbrecher*, XXXVI, ND-922-D, 6–10.

42. StA München, Staatsanwaltschaften 7014, Bl. 14–15.

43. *Der Prozess gegen die Hauptkriegsverbrecher*, ND-926-D, 42–43. Hans Frank (1900–1946), a Nazi lawyer, was Bavarian Minister of Justice in 1933. As Governor-General of the Nazi-occupied Polish General Government from 1939 to 1945, he became notorious for his role in the Holocaust. See Housden, *Hans Frank*.

44. Quoted in Diehl-Thiele, *Partei und Staat im Dritten Reich*, 95.

45. BAB, R 43 II/398, Bl. 92.

46. Printed in Timpke, *Dokumente zur Gleichschaltung*, 248–49. Max Lahts, a trained plumber, was appointed acting president of the Hamburg prison administration in 1933. He was officially in charge of the Fuhlsbüttel prison and the new concentration camp founded on this site on 4 September 1933. In reality, the new camp was dominated by the Nazi *Gauleiter* of Hamburg, Karl Kaufmann (see next note). See Diercks, "Fuhlsbüttel," 271. On Lahts see Bajohr, *Parvenüs und Profiteure*, 26.

47. Karl Kaufmann (1900–1969) was the Nazi *Gauleiter* of Hamburg since 1928 and was appointed Reich governor of Hamburg in 1933. For this and some other biographical information, see Klee, *Personenlexikon zum Dritten Reich*.

48. GStA, I. HA, Rep. 77, Nr. 484, Bl. 152–54.

49. GStA, I. HA, Rep. 77, Nr. 484, Bl. 153.

50. BAB, R 3001/21469, Bl. 6–10.

51. Erich and Franz Saß had been well-known burglars in Weimar Berlin, infamous for evading prosecution. For the Nazis and the criminal police, they were emblematic habitual criminals. See Wagner, *Volksgemeinschaft ohne Verbrecher*, 172–79.

52. *Der Prozess gegen die Hauptkriegsverbrecher*, ND-926-D, XXXVI, 47–48. Adolf Wagner (1890–1944) was the Nazi *Gauleiter* of Munich since 1929 and was appointed Bavarian Minister of the Interior in 1933.

53. "Entlassungen aus Konzentrationslagern," *Deutscher Reichsanzeiger und Preußischer Staatsanzeiger*, 9 December 1933.

54. This is a reference to the rigged Reichstag elections of 12 November 1933. Only Nazi candidates stood. Camp prisoners were allowed to vote. See Drobisch and Wieland, *System der NS-Konzentrationslager*, 136.

55. A reference to Göring's role as head of the Prussian political police, recently turned into an independent branch of the state administration.

56. BAB, R 58/264, Bl. 16.

57. StA München, Justizvollzugsanstalten no. 40, Bl. 32.

58. Printed in Kosthorst and Walter, *Konzentrations- und Strafgefangenenlager im Emsland*, 65–66. Rudolf Diels (1900–1957) had been appointed in April 1933 as the first head of the new Gestapa in Prussia.

59. BayHStA, Staatskanzlei 6299/1, Bl. 174–77. Reinhard Heydrich forwarded Epp's letter to the Reich Chancellery on 18 April 1934; see BAB, R 43 II/398, Bl. 133–38. Reich governors (*Reichsstatthalter*) were appointed by Hitler and oversaw individual German states (*Länder*).

60. So-called special courts (*Sondergerichte*) were increasingly set up by the legal authorities from the spring of 1933, initially to punish cases of alleged criticism of the new rulers. Later on, the courts expanded their remit.

61. BayHStA, Staatskanzlei 6299/1, Bl. 132–41. According to Tuchel, *Konzentrationslager*, 303, Himmler drafted this letter.

62. That is, Epp's office.

63. BAB, R 3001/25032, Bl. 19–21.

64. On early camps in Berlin see Mayer–von Götz, *Terror im Zentrum*.

65. See the various essays in Benz and Distel, *Terror ohne System*; Benz and Distel, *Herrschaft und Gewalt*; and Benz and Distel, *Instrumentarium der Macht*.

66. Zámečník, "Das frühe KZ Dachau," 28–29.

67. See Drobisch and Wieland, *System der NS-Konzentrationslager*, 106–31.

68. Diercks, "Fuhlsbüttel," 272–74.

69. Matthäus, "Verfolgung, Ausbeutung, Vernichtung."

70. On Kemna see Meckl, "Wuppertal-Kemna," 222.

71. Fackler, *Des Lagers Stimme*; Drobisch and Wieland, *System der NS-Konzentrationslager*, 155–58; Zámečník, "Das frühe KZ Dachau," 29.

72. USHMM, RG.11.001 M.20/Reel 91, Fond 1367, Opis 2, Folder 33.

73. See Mayer, "Berlin-Kreuzberg (Hedemannstr.)."

74. Seger, *Oranienburg*, 27–31. Gerhart Seger (1896–1967), a Social Democrat Reichstag deputy, had been arrested in March 1933 and managed to flee in December 1933 from the Oranienburg camp.

75. Werner Schäfer was the Oranienburg camp's first commandant.

76. Carl Severing (1875–1952) was the Social Democrat Prussian Minister of the Interior until 1932.

77. Hans Stahlkopf (1903–35) was an SA guard who had joined the Nazi Party in 1930.

78. Ernst Heilmann (1881–1940), a leading SPD politician, was arrested in 1933 and killed in the Buchenwald camp in 1940.

79. The Czechoslovakian national was a longtime member of the Social Democrat Party.

80. Rubner, "Dachau im Sommer 1933," 56–57.

81. Otto Braun (1872–1955), a SPD politician, was Prussian Minister President, with a few interruptions, from 1920 until July 1932.

82. Albert Grzesinski (1879–1947), a SPD politician, had served as Prussian Minister of the Interior from 1926 to 1930.

83. Philipp Scheidemann (1865–1939), SPD politician, was famous for proclaiming the German Republic on 9 November 1918.

84. Wilhelm Marx (1863–1946) was the leader of the German Center Party, the popular Catholic party, which was dissolved in 1933, and had also served as Reich Chancellor during the Weimar Republic (1923–24 and 1926–28).

85. Ullstein was a leading liberal Jewish-owned publishing house. Georg Bernhard (1875–1944), a left-liberal journalist, emigrated in 1933 and founded the *Pariser Tageblatt*.

86. Walther Rathenau (1867–1922) was a German-Jewish industrialist. Foreign Minister in 1922, he was assassinated by right-wing terrorists. Matthias Erzberger (1875–1921), a German politician of the Catholic Center Party, signed the armistice in November 1918 and was assassinated by right-wing terrorists in 1921. Gustav Stresemann (1878–1929), a national-liberal politician, was Foreign Minister from 1923 to 1929 and Reich Chancellor in 1923.

87. WL, P.III.h.No.280. Alfred Benjamin (1911–42), a bank clerk from Düsseldorf, was a member of the KPD. Arrested in March 1933 in Düsseldorf, he was transferred to the Esterwegen camp in August 1933. See Lüerssen, "'Wir sind die Moorsoldaten,'" 241.

88. Printed in Jürgens, *Fritz Solmitz*, 85–87. Solmitz (1893–1933) hid these notes, written on cigarette paper, in his watch, which was handed over to his widow in late 1933 after his death.

89. The Marinesturm was an SA unit; some of its men were used for guarding prisoners at Fuhlsbüttel.

90. See 13.

91. WL, P.II.c.No.607. Weinmann wrote his report for the Amsterdam Comite voor Joodsche Vluchtlingen.

92. Ecker, "Die Hölle Dachau," 15, 40, 44. Ecker, a functionary of the Bavarian SPD, was arrested in the spring of 1933 and released from Dachau in January 1934.

93. Both prisoners, Wilhelm Franz (who had worked in the camp's post room) and Dr. Delvin Katz, had apparently been strangled by the SS in the Dachau bunker; see Zámečník, *Das war Dachau*, 43–46.

94. Hans Steinbrenner (1905–64) was among the first SS guards stationed in Dachau. He was convicted of murder after World War II and sentenced to lifelong imprisonment in a penitentiary. For Steinbrenner see also 33 and 172.

95. Langhoff, *Moorsoldaten*, 175–95. Wolfgang Langhoff (1901–66) was a noted theater actor and director. He was arrested in 1933 and detained first at Börgermoor and then at Lichtenburg. Released in 1934, he fled to Switzerland in June 1934.

96. For a brief survey see Drobisch and Wieland, *System der NS-Konzentrationslager*, 100–105. On prisoners more generally see Pingel, *Häftlinge unter SS-Herrschaft*.

97. On women in the camps, see section 5.5. See also Distel, "Frauen in nationalsozialistischen Konzentrationslagern," 195–96.

98. On Gotteszell see Rudorff, "Gotteszell"; on Brauweiler see Wißkirchen, "Brauweiler," 70–73.

99. Following the forced merger of the SPD and the KPD in East Germany in 1946, many East German accounts tended to downplay the tensions between the SPD and the KPD in the early camps and instead highlighted the alleged working-class solidarity. This tendency is still evident in Drobisch and Wieland, *System der NS-Konzentrationslager*, though it was published after the fall of the Iron Curtain.

100. Wagner, *Volksgemeinschaft ohne Verbrecher*, 198–203. See also more generally Terhorst, *Polizeiliche planmäßige Überwachung und polizeiliche Vorbeugungshaft im Dritten Reich*.

101. See Evans, "Social Outsiders in German History."

102. Beimler, *Im Mörderlager Dachau*, 34–35. Hans Beimler (1895–1936), a Communist Reichstag deputy, was detained in April 1933 and escaped from Dachau in May 1933. He died in the Spanish Civil War.

103. Seger, *Oranienburg*, 39.

104. See 47 in section 1.4.

105. *Der Gegen-Angriff*, 24 February 1934. Nico Rost (1896–1967), a Dutch writer and Communist activist, was held for three weeks in Oranienburg in early 1933. *Der Gegen-Angriff* was an exile Communist newspaper, published in Paris. See Grunewald, "Kritik und politischer Kampf." On Rost, see also Laqueur, *Schreiben im KZ*, 134–39. Rost later returned to Nazi camps. Arrested in Belgium in 1942, he was imprisoned in Dachau between the summer of 1944 and the spring of 1945. See his memoir *Goethe in Dachau*.

106. Mühsam, *Der Leidensweg Erich Mühsams*, 26. Kreszentia Mühsam,

also known as Zenzl (1884–1962), was the wife of Erich Mühsam (1878–1934), a writer and anarchist of Jewish descent who was murdered in the Oranienburg camp in July 1934. See Hirte, *Erich Mühsam*.

107. Abraham, "Juda verrecke," here 153–54. Max Abraham was a preacher in Rathenow near Berlin. He was arrested after an argument with a stormtrooper in Berlin in June 1933. See http://www.autorenlexikon-emsland.de/max_abraham.htm, last accessed 29 April 2009.

108. Langhoff, *Moorsoldaten*, 294–97.

109. This is a reference to an ss guard.

110. This is a reference to the Weimar Republic.

111. Ecker, "Die Hölle Dachau," 45.

112. These military terms denoted units of prisoners.

113. Drobisch, "Zeitgenössische Berichte über Nazikonzentrationslager."

114. Kramer and Horne, *German Atrocities*.

115. IfZ, Fa 199/29, Bl. 51–52: Konzentrationslager Oranienburg, Kommandant to Reichskanzler, 24 March 1934, and Oberregierungsrat Dr. Meerwald to Kommandant des Konzentrationslagers, 3 April 1934.

116. "Life in a Nazi Camp: A Farm Student's Experience," *The Times*, 19 September 1933.

117. Dörner, "Das Konzentrationslager Oranienburg und die Justiz"; see also Dörner, *"Heimtücke,"* 255–75.

118. Steinbacher, *Dachau*, 93–100, 137–44.

119. Stokes, "Das oldenburgische Konzentrationslager," 198–99.

120. Gellately, *Backing Hitler*, 52.

121. Dillon, "'We'll meet again in Dachau!.'"

122. Steinbacher, *Dachau*, 181.

123. Evans, *Coming of the Third Reich*, 333–34, 348–49.

124. For this suggestion, see Gellately, *Backing Hitler*, 60.

125. Johe, "Das deutsche Volk und die Konzentrationslager," 334–35.

126. Printed in Krause-Vilmar, "Das Konzentrationslager Breitenau," 472–74.

127. *Berliner Illustrirte Zeitung*, 30 April 1933.

128. The *Amper-Bote* was a local newspaper. Printed in Comité International de Dachau, *Konzentrationslager Dachau*, 44.

129. BAB, NS 4 SA/18, Bl. 54.

130. BAB, NS 4 SA/18, Bl. 33.

131. Tausk, *Breslauer Tagebuch*, 82–83. Walter Tausk (1890–1941), a salesman and writer from Breslau, died in the Kovno ghetto in 1941. Our thanks to Paul Moore for sharing this document with us.

132. Hermann Lüdemann (1880–1959) was a Social Democratic District Governor of Lower Silesia from 1928 to 1932.

133. Edmund Heines (1897–1934), a leading SA official, was appointed Breslau Police President in 1933.

134. On the Dürrgoy camp, see Rudorff, "Breslau-Dürrgoy."

135. BAB, NS 4 SA/18, Bl. 60–62.

136. IfZ Fa 199/29, Bl. 8–10. Louise Ebert was the widow of Friedrich Ebert (1871–1925), a Social Democrat leader and the Weimar Republic's first Reich President (1919–25).

137. Friedrich Ebert (1894–1979), also known as Fritz Ebert, was the son of Friedrich Ebert (see note 136).

138. They died in action in World War I.

139. Ebert Jr. was detained in various concentration camps and released in late 1933.

140. Politisches Archiv des Auswärtigen Amts, Botschaft Washington 1127. See Conze et al., *Das Amt und die Vergangenheit*, 25–73.

141. In the typescript, the following words are deleted: "or have led parasitic lives. The schooling given them is severe, but its sole purpose is to instill a proper regard for what has since 1918 been trampled in the dust: the Fatherland and Germanism."

142. "Konzentrationslager: Eine notwendige Frage und ihre befriedigende Lösung," in NS-*Nachrichten für den Kreis Niederbarnim*, 19 August 1933, copy in BAB, NS 4 SA/18. This clipping from a local Nazi newspaper is annotated with the order "file immediately."

143. "Gegen störende Einmischungen in Schutzhaftsachen," *Deutscher Reichsanzeiger und Preußischer Staatsanzeiger*, 26 August 1933.

144. Sbosny and Schabrod, *Widerstand in Solingen*, 52.

145. *Braunbuch über Reichstagsbrand und Hitler-Terror*, 287. The *Braunbuch* was first published by a group of Communist exiles in Paris in August 1933 and contained several inaccuracies. See Rabinbach, "Staging Antifascism." On the Sonnenburg camp see Nürnberg, "Außenstelle des Berliner Polizeipräsidiums."

146. Carl von Ossietzky (1889–1938) was a German pacifist, author, and Nobel Peace Laureate.

147. Landesarchiv Berlin, A Rep. 339, Nr. 702, Bl. 334–36. Willi P., a former member of the KPD (who had apparently never been detained in Oranienburg), was sentenced to one year in prison for his remarks.

148. Marinus van der Lubbe (1909–34), a Dutch anarchist, was sentenced to death for setting the Reichstag on fire.

149. *The Times*, 29 September 1933. Levy, a German Jew, was a lawyer from Potsdam.

150. *The Times*, 4 October 1933.

151. See "Life in a Nazi Camp: A Farm Student's Experience," *The Times*,

19 September 1933. This article was written by a young non-Jewish agricultural student who was taken to Oranienburg in June 1933. After his release in August 1933, he fled to Switzerland.

152. Favre, "Wir können vielleicht die Schlafräume besichtigen." This report was probably only broadcast abroad.

153. *Völkischer Beobachter* (Berliner Ausgabe), 4 October 1933.

154. PRO, FO 371/16704. Our thanks to Dr. Eckard Michels for sharing this document with us.

155. Reprinted in Stadtarchiv, KZ-*Kemna 1933–1934*, 14.

156. Reprinted in Stadtarchiv, KZ-*Kemna 1933–1934*, 14.

157. Schäfer, *Konzentrationslager Oranienburg*, 23–25, 239–40. The *Anti-Braunbuch* was published in response to the *Braunbuch* (see 52).

158. Printed in Comité International de Dachau, *Konzentrationslager Dachau*, 86.

159. *Berliner Lokal-Anzeiger*, 25 November 1933.

160. The senior ss officer Kurt Daluege (1897–1946) led the police department in the Prussian Ministry of Interior from the spring of 1933. In 1936 he became head of the German order police. He was executed in Prague after World War II for his crimes as acting Reich Protector of Bohemia and Moravia in 1942 and 1943. See Wilhelm, *Die Polizei im NS-Staat*, 198.

161. Printed in Stadtarchiv, KZ-*Kemna 1933–1934*, 20.

162. Kent, *I Married a German*, 253–54. Our thanks to Paul Moore for drawing our attention to this source.

163. *Berliner Börsen-Zeitung*, 6 January 1934.

164. Politisches Archiv des Auswärtigen Amts, Berlin, R 99574 Organisation der Konzentrationsläger. On the Kuhberg camp see Lechner, "Das Konzentrationslager Oberer Kuhberg in Ulm."

2. The ss Concentration Camp System

1. Tuchel, *Konzentrationslager*, 346–47; Hensle, "Die Verrechtlichung des Unrechts."

2. See Endlich, "Die Lichtenburg, 1933–1939," 35–39.

3. On the Dachau killings see Gritschneder, *"Der Führer hat Sie zum Tode verurteilt,"* 32–37.

4. See Drobisch and Wieland, *System der NS-Konzentrationslager*, 189–91.

5. In Esterwegen new regulations were introduced on 1 August 1934; in Sachsenburg on 1 April 1935; Lüerssen, "'Moorsoldaten in Esterwegen, Börgermoor, Neusustrum,'" 183; Baganz, *Erziehung*, 266. On the organizational structure implemented by Eicke see Morsch, "Organisations- und Verwaltungsstruktur der Konzentrationslager."

6. *Völkischer Beobachter*, 22/23 April 1934; for Bavarian numbers see Drobisch and Wieland, *System der NS-Konzentrationslager*, 139.

7. Tuchel, *Konzentrationslager*, 307–8.

8. Wachsmann, *Hitler's Prisons*, 114–17.

9. Caplan, Introduction, 12.

10. Tuchel, *Konzentrationslager*, 308; Herbert, "Von der Gegnerbekämpfung zur 'rassischen Generalprävention,'" 72–73. See also doc. **114** below.

11. Gruchmann, *Justiz im Dritten Reich*, 632–58.

12. Longerich, *Heinrich Himmler*, 158–79.

13. Dörner, "Ein KZ in der Mitte der Stadt," 137; Tuchel, *Konzentrationslager*, 184–87.

14. Tuchel, *Konzentrationslager*, 210–11, 293.

15. Broszat, "Nationalsozialistische Konzentrationslager," 352–53; Tuchel, *Konzentrationslager*, 307–15, 324–25; Baganz, *Erziehung*, 289–92.

16. See Gruchmann, *Justiz im Dritten Reich*, 345–67; Goeschel, "Suicide in Nazi Concentration Camps," 645.

17. For the implementation of this wave of arrests by Reinhard Heydrich, effectively in charge of the Gestapo, see BAB, R 58/264, Bl. 142, 29 July 1935. More generally, see Tuchel, *Konzentrationslager*, 311.

18. On the speech, see Tuchel, *Konzentrationslager*, 1.

19. Stein, "Buchenwald—Stammlager."

20. Morsch, "Formation and Construction."

21. Zámečník,"Dachau-Stammlager," 245–47.

22. Skriebeleit, "Flossenbürg—Stammlager."

23. Freund and Perz, "Mauthausen—Stammlager."

24. Papen, *Ein von Papen spricht*, 25–28. Felix von Papen was a relative of Franz von Papen (1879–1969), Reich Chancellor in 1932 and vice-chancellor under Hitler in 1933–34. He was imprisoned at Oranienburg in 1933–34.

25. According to Tuchel, *Konzentrationslager*, 184, it was a police unit.

26. Quoted in Burkhardt, *Tanz mal Jude!*, 97.

27. IfZ, Fa 183, Bl. 8, 19–21.

28. GStA, I. HA, Rep. 90 Annex P, Nr. 104, Bl. 100. The Society of Friends, also known as Quakers, is a movement of Christian dissenters who have long been active in promoting human rights. On the Quakers' campaigns against the concentration camps, see Schmitt, *Quakers and Nazis*.

29. BAB, R 3001/21265, Bl. 37.

30. BAB, R 58/264, Bl. 140.

31. The order was conveyed to Heydrich by Himmler's adjutant. Printed in Tuchel, *Konzentrationslager*, 311.

32. Oswald Pohl (1892–1951), after 1942 Chief of the SS Economic and

Administrative Main Office (WVHA), was executed in 1951 for war crimes. See Tuchel, *Konzentrationslager*, 385. On Pohl, see also Kaienburg, *Die Wirtschaft der SS*, 106–8; Schulte, *Zwangsarbeit und Vernichtung*, 32–45.

33. Printed in Michaelis and Schraepler, *Ursachen und Folgen*, 9:380, citing GStA, Rep. 77, no. 31.

34. HStA Düsseldorf, RW 58/43825, Bl. 4. The decree is marked "Geheime Reichssache!"

35. Similar letters were sent to state police offices across Germany. HStA Düsseldorf, RW 58/43825, Bl. 5–7. The decree is marked "Geheime Reichssache." Also printed in Nationale Mahn- und Gedenkstätte Buchenwald, *Konzentrationslager Buchenwald*, 47.

36. A small left-wing socialist party, the Socialist Workers' Party of Germany.

37. Jehovah's Witnesses.

38. BAB, NS 19/4003, Bl. 3–52, here Bl. 8–12, 19–24. The *Staatsräte* were appointed by the Prussian Minister President Hermann Göring and had no formal powers.

39. Meaning the Nazi movement.

40. This sentence was later deleted from the manuscript, probably by Himmler himself.

41. BAB, R 58/264, Bl. 202.

42. A reference to the regular Gestapo review of individual prisoners' suitability for release.

43. *Reichsgesetzblatt*, 17 June 1936, 487–88.

44. Printed in Tuchel, *Inspektion der Konzentrationslager*, 45–47, citing Brandenburgisches Landeshauptarchiv, Rep. 2 A, III Forsten, Nr. 16238.

45. Politisches Archiv des Auswärtigen Amts, Berlin, Gesandtschaft Bern 1449.

46. *Der Prozeß gegen die Hauptkriegsverbrecher*, ND-1992 (A)-PS, XXIX, 206–34, here 217–22. The 1937 publication of Himmler's speech was marked "for the Wehrmacht's official use only."

47. Dr. Arthur Gütt (1891–1949), a leading Nazi doctor and proponent of racial hygiene. He was one of the major figures behind the 1933 sterilization laws. See Noakes, "Nazism and Eugenics."

48. The Nazi Party daily newspaper.

49. See his March 1936 speech above (78).

50. The Nazi Party's charity organization.

51. Corporal punishment was allowed in Prussian penitentiaries for men until the end of World War I; but in contrast to the excesses inside the concentration camps, it had been used very rarely in the last decades before it was outlawed. See Wachsmann, *Hitler's Prisons*, 23, 409 (n.18).

52. BAB, R 58/264, Bl. 281.

53. Returning émigrés sent to concentration camps.

54. BAB, R 2/24006.

55. Archiv Dachau, 37518. On Hübsch, a Communist prisoner, see ITS/ARCH/KL Flossenbürg Individuelle Unterlagen, Fragebogen für Insassen der Konzentrationslager, 12 July 1945. Born in 1899, he was arrested in 1936 for trespassing illegally into France. He was imprisoned from February 1936 until liberation.

56. StA Chemnitz, Bestand 30044 Amtshauptmannschaft Flöha Nr. 2393, Bl. 77. Our thanks to Dr. Carina Baganz for sharing this document with us.

57. Printed in Nationale Mahn- und Gedenkstätte Buchenwald, *Buchenwald*, 67–68.

58. Jakob Weiseborn (1892–1939) had joined the SS in 1931 and served in several concentration camps from December 1934. Following a spell as a senior officer in Buchenwald, he was appointed in May 1938 as the first Flossenbürg commandant. See Tuchel, "Kommandanten des Konzentrationslagers Flossenbürg," 201–6.

59. Printed in Stein, *Konzentrationslager Buchenwald*, 29. In the end, the camp came to be called Buchenwald.

60. Fritz Sauckel (1894–1946) was *Gauleiter* from 1927 and Reich governor of Thuringia from 1933.

61. Printed in Drobisch and Wieland, *System der NS-Konzentrationslager 1933–1939*, 255.

62. Botz, *Wien vom "Anschluß" zum Krieg*, 256–57, citing Wiener Stadt- und Landesarchiv, Magistratsdirektion 1849/38.

63. Gostner, *1000 Tage im KZ*, 84–86.

64. The infamous *Todesstiege*, or death steps.

65. Printed in KZ-Gedenkstätte Flossenbürg, *Concentration Camp Flossenbürg*, 9.

66. BAB, NS 19/4004, Bl. 278–94, here Bl. 293–94. The original document is erroneously dated 1938.

67. Milton, "'Jehovah's Witnesses as Forgotten Victims,'" 146; Fahrenberg and Hördler, "Lichtenburg," 172. For the 20 August 1937 order to arrest Jehovah's Witnesses after their release from prison or their acquittal, see IfZ, Fa 183/1, Bl. 382–83.

68. Longerich, *Politik der Vernichtung*, 102–11.

69. Longerich, *Politik der Vernichtung*, 56–57, 67–69.

70. Caplan, Introduction, 8–10.

71. Longerich, *Politik der Vernichtung*, 118–65.

72. Matthäus, "Verfolgung, Ausbeutung, Vernichtung."

73. For an excellent account of the pogrom, see Steinweis, *Kristallnacht 1938*.

74. See for example Düsseldorf Gestapo to Krefeld Gestapo office, 15 November 1938, printed in Faust, *Die "Kristallnacht" im Rheinland*, 142.

75. For numbers see Orth, *System der nationalsozialistischen Konzentrationslager*, 51–52; Zámečník, "Dachau-Stammlager," 252–53; Schüler-Springorum, "Masseneinweisungen in Kozentrationslager," 161.

76. For some examples, see Wildt, "Violence against Jews in Germany," 204–5.

77. See Wachsmann, "The Policy of Exclusion," 133–37.

78. BayHStA, MInn 72644, Bericht über das Ergebnis der Razzia in der Nacht vom 20. auf 21. Oktober 1934, 27 October 1934; see also BayHStA, MInn 72644, Polizeidirektion Nürnberg-Fürth an das Staatsministerium des Innern, 26 October 1934. More generally, see Knoll, "Homosexuelle Häftlinge im KZ Dachau."

79. Forty-eight of these prisoners were released on 5 November 1934. See BayHStA MA 106697, Lagebericht der Polizeidirektion München, 6 December 1934.

80. On homosexuals in the Third Reich see generally Evans, *The Third Reich in Power*, 529–35; Lautmann, Grikschat and Schmidt, "Der rosa Winkel in den nationalsozialistischen Konzentrationslagern," 332–33; Giles, "The Institutionalization of Homosexual Panic"; Jellonnek, *Homosexuelle unter dem Hakenkreuz*, 113, 327.

81. IfZ, Fa 119/1, Bl. 92–93.

82. The Moringen women's concentration camp and the Dachau concentration camp for men. See IfZ, Fa 119/1, Bl. 101–2: Bayerische Politische Polizei an alle Polizeidirektionen. Betreff: Maßnahmen gegen zurückkehrende Emigranten, 21 March 1935.

83. BAB, R 58/264, Bl. 162.

84. ITS Bad Arolsen/ARCH/HIST/KL Dachau 4 (200), Bl. 17.

85. IfZ, MA 311, Bl. 53–54. Also printed in B. F. Smith and Peterson, *Heinrich Himmler*, 97–98. There is no evidence that any gay SS men were shot in the prewar camps.

86. BAB, R 3001/21469, Bl. 45–48.

87. IfZ, Dc 17.02., Reichssicherheitshauptamt—Amt V, *Sammlung der ergangenen Erlasse*, Bl. 46–47. The decree was secret until 18 November 1938.

88. BAB, NS 19/1542, Bl. 2.

89. Hans Pfundtner (1881–1945) was State Secretary in the Reich Ministry of the Interior.

90. Adolf Eichmann (1906–62), an SS officer, was from the autumn of 1938 in charge of the Central Agency for Jewish Emigration in Vienna. Notorious for his central role in the Nazi Final Solution during the war, he was executed after public trial in Israel in 1962. On Eichmann, see Cesarani, *Eichmann*, 61–75.

91. USHMM, RG-11.001 M.01/Reel 4, Fond 500, Opis 1, Folder 261.

92. IfZ, Fa 183/1, Bl. 407–9.

93. Printed in Ayaß, *"Gemeinschaftsfremde,"* 135–36.

94. Printed in Ayaß, *"Gemeinschaftsfremde,"* 138.

95. Österreichisches StA, Vienna, Bestand Historikerkommission, RGVA 500/1/261. Our thanks to Dr. Susanne Heim for sharing this document with us.

96. A reference to Hitler's appointment as Reich Chancellor on 30 January 1933.

97. Fröhlich, *Die Tagebücher von Joseph Goebbels,* 6:181.

98. *Der Prozess gegen die Hauptkriegsverbrecher,* XXV, ND-374-PS. Heinrich Müller (1900–presumed dead in 1945) was a leading Gestapo official.

99. *Der Prozess gegen die Hauptkriegsverbrecher,* XXV, ND-374-PS.

100. IfZ, Fa 183/1, Bl. 6–7.

101. See, e.g., Aly, *Hitlers Volksstaat,* 27.

102. For background see Wachsmann, "The Policy of Exclusion."

103. For the legal apparatus and its prisons in prewar Nazi Germany, see Wachsmann, *Hitler's Prisons,* 65–188; for the figure see 393.

104. Broszat, "Nationalsozialistische Konzentrationslager," 378–86.

105. Evans, *The Third Reich in Power,* 72–80; Tuchel, *Konzentrationslager,* 315.

106. Tuchel, *Konzentrationslager,* 308.

107. *Der Prozeß gegen die Hauptkriegsverbrecher,* XXXVI, 783-PS, 784-PS, 785-PS, 786-PS, 787-PS, 788-PS. See also Gruchmann, *Justiz im Dritten Reich,* 369–74; Zarusky, "Juristische Aufarbeitung der KZ-Verbrechen."

108. Rudorff, "Misshandlung und Erpressung mit System," 64–67.

109. Gruchmann, *Justiz im Dritten Reich,* 345–79, 545–72, 632–45.

110. Goeschel, "Suicide in Nazi Concentration Camps," 643.

111. Tuchel, *Konzentrationslager,* 315; see also Gruchmann, *Justiz im Dritten Reich,* 564–73.

112. Cf. Gruchmann, *Justiz im Dritten Reich.*

113. Marxen, "Strafjustiz im Nationalsozialismus"; McElligott, "'Sentencing towards the Führer?,'" 154.

114. Gruchmann, *Justiz im Dritten Reich,* 324–36.

115. Wachsmann, *Hitler's Prisons,* 175–83.

116. Wachsmann, *Hitler's Prisons,* 180.

117. Broszat, "Nationalsozialistischen Konzentrationslager," 376–77. More generally, see Herbert, *Best.*

118. Tuchel, *Konzentrationslager,* 212–18.

119. Tuchel, *Konzentrationslager,* 274–79.

120. GStA, I. HA, Rep. 84a, Nr. 54826, Bl. 45–48.

121. The Soviet secret police.

122. GStA, I. HA, Rep. 84a, Nr. 54826, Bl. 144–47.

123. GStA, I. HA, Rep. 84a, Nr. 54826, Bl. 11–26.

124. Fritz-Karl Engel was born in 1898 and served as a decorated volunteer in World War I. After the war he ran a small business in the Ruhr valley and was involved in violent clashes with the Belgian occupation forces, leading to his imprisonment in Belgian jails. He joined the NSDAP in 1925 and the SS in 1929. See GStA, I. HA, Rep. 84a, Nr. 54826, Bl. 20–21.

125. This is a reference to abuses in the Berlin Columbia-Haus camp.

126. Wilhelm Brückner (1884–1954) was Hitler's adjutant.

127. Rudolf Hess (1894–1987) was Hitler's deputy.

128. BAB, NS 19/3576, Bl. 1–2.

129. GStA, I. HA, Rep. 90P, Nr. 104, Bl. 149–53.

130. There is no evidence that these SS men—Dr. Hoffmann, Fritz Pleines, and Gustav Fink—were shot because of their participation in atrocities in the Bredow camp. For the murders, see Rudorff, "Misshandlung und Erpressung," 66.

131. BAB, R 3001/21467, Bl. 104–5.

132. BAB, R 58/264, Bl. 152; copy in BAB, R 3001/21467, Bl. 45.

133. GStA, I. HA Rep. 90P, Nr. 104, Bl. 167–70. Bernhard Lichtenberg (1875–1943), a Catholic priest in Berlin, opposed the Nazi regime and was sentenced to prison in 1942. He later died while on his way to Dachau.

134. Friedrich Husemann (1873–1935), SPD politician, was shot in April 1935 "while trying to escape" from Esterwegen; he died in hospital.

135. BAB, R 58/264, Bl. 155.

136. A new national court set up in 1934 to suppress political opposition.

137. GStA, I. HA Rep. 90 P, Nr. 104, Bl. 172–77. See 118.

138. BAB, R 3001/21467, Bl. 185.

139. *Der Prozeß gegen die Hauptkriegsverbrecher*, XXVI, ND-786-PS.

140. Otto Meißner (1880–1953) was State Secretary in the Presidential Chancellery.

141. Philipp Bouhler (1899–1945) was Chief of Hitler's personal chancellery since 1934. He was later in charge of the euthanasia program.

142. Martin Mutschmann (1879–1947) was since 1933 Reich governor in Saxony; from 1935 he was also Minister President.

143. Hans Tesmer, *Regierungsrat* in the Gestapa, "Die Schutzhaft und ihre rechtlichen Grundlagen," *Deutsches Recht,* 7/8, 15 April 1936. Excerpt in BAB, R 58/264, Bl. 254–59.

144. Karl Elgas (1900–1985) was a Communist Reichstag deputy from 1932 until 1933. After serving his sentence in Luckau, he was transferred to the Lichtenburg camp and finally to the Sachsenhausen camp, from where he was released in late 1939. Brandenburgisches Landeshauptarchiv, Pr. Br. Rep. 29, Zuchthaus Luckau, no. 414.

145. BAB, NS 19/1925, Bl. 1.

146. BAB, NS 4/SA 14, Bl. 19.

147. S., a Communist with a string of previous convictions, had criticized the Third Reich in a pub while drunk in November 1935 (BAB, NS 4/SA 14, Bl. 10–11). He returned to Sachsenhausen in February 1937, after serving his judicial sentence.

148. BAB, R 3001/21437, Bl. 60–61.

149. Based on the Law against Habitual Criminals of 24 November 1933, several thousand inmates were indefinitely held in state prisons.

150. BAB, NS 4/SA 14, Bl. 23. See note 126 above.

151. BAB, R 3001/25087, Bl. 96–97.

152. BAB, NS 19/1542, Bl. 3–4.

153. BAB, R 3001/21437, Bl. 152.

154. BAB, NS 4 BU/31, Bl. 14.

155. BAB, NS 4/alt/FL 59, quoted in Tuchel, *Konzentrationslager*, 277.

156. BAB, R 3001/21467, Bl. 316–17.

157. For labor, discipline, and the camps, see Caplan, "Political Detention," 31–33. On senseless labor in the concentration camps, see Sofsky, *Die Ordnung des Terrors*, 220–21.

158. Jaskot, *The Architecture of Oppression*.

159. Kaienburg, "Sachsenhausen—Stammlager," 24–25; Stein, "Buchenwald—Stammlager," 306–7. See also Kaienburg, *Die Wirtschaft der SS*, 603–95.

160. Garbe, "Neuengamme—Stammlager," 315.

161. On the Four-Year Plan see Tooze, *The Wages of Destruction*, 219–30. On the camps' deterrent effect, see Evans, *The Third Reich in Power*, 88–89.

162. Kaienburg, *Die Wirtschaft der SS*, 25; Schulte, *Zwangsarbeit und Vernichtung*, 125.

163. Printed in Kosthorst and Walter, *Konzentrations- und Strafgefangenenlager im Emsland*, 59–61.

164. Konstantin Hierl (1875–1955), in 1933 State Secretary in the Reich Labor Ministry, was in charge of the Reich Labor Service throughout the Nazi period.

165. GStA, I. HA, Rep. 90P, no. 104, Bl. 29–30.

166. IfZ, Fa 199/20, Bl. 24. The *Kleiner Ministerrat* met occasionally after Hitler had ceased to call regular Reich cabinet meetings.

167. Behnken, *Deutschland-Berichte der Sopade*, 4:686–87.

168. Archiv Dachau, 7566, Bl. 74. On Schecher, see ITS/ARCH/KL Dachau Individuelle Unterlagen. Schecher (1883–?), a lawyer, was held at Dachau from November 1935 until April 1945.

169. BAB, NS 1/547, Bl. 4–6.

170. Printed in Johe, *Neuengamme*, 50–51.

171. BAB, NS 19/1151, Bl. 2. Hans Krebs (1888–1947) was a Nazi activist from the Sudeten territory, which was annexed by Nazi Germany in fall 1938.

172. This is the anniversary of the failed Nazi beerhall putsch of 1923, one of the most important days for the Nazis, with annual celebrations in Munich.

173. Ernst Robert Grawitz (1899–1945) had been appointed in 1935 as Reich Doctor ss, the highest rank for a physician in the ss Medical Service. In 1937 he effectively took over the German Red Cross. See Hahn, *Grawitz, Genzken, Gebhardt*.

174. Karl Wolff (1900–1984) was the head of the personal staff of the Reichsführer-ss.

175. BAB, NS 19/1151, Bl. 3.

176. BAB, NS 3/1532, Bl. 1–9.

177. This was an excuse to cover up the failure of the Sachsenhausen brickworks. See Kaienburg, *Die Wirtschaft der ss*, 655.

178. As previously in this document, the author mistakenly uses the term "security confined" (Sicherungsverwahrte) here. In all likelihood, he meant to refer instead to concentration camp prisoners in "preventive police custody."

3. Running the Camps

1. See Orth, "Bewachung," 131–32; on early Dachau ss units see Dillon, "'We'll meet again in Dachau.'"

2. Koehl, *The Black Corps*, 130–35. On the emergence of the Camp ss see also Broszat, "Nationalsozialistische Konzentrationslager," 368–78; Tuchel, *Inspektion der Konzentrationslager*, 48–49; Orth, "Bewachung," 127.

3. BAB, NS 19/1652, Bl. 5–15: Geheime Kommandosache. Der Führer und Reichskanzler, 17 August 1938. On this decree, see Sydnor, *Soldiers of Destruction*, 32.

4. *Statistisches Jahrbuch der Schutzstaffel der* NSDAP (1937), 51, and (1938), 83; on Himmler's view of the Death's Head Units, see BAB, NS 19/4004, Bl. 278–94: Rede des Reichsführers-ss bei der Gruppenführerbesprechung in München der ss-Standarte Deutschland am 8. November 1937; see also Orth, "Bewachung," 127.

5. Wegner, *Hitlers politische Soldaten*. See also Leleu, *La Waffen-ss*.

6. Sydnor, *Soldiers of Destruction*, 20–24; on the Dachau model, see Tuchel, *Konzentrationslager*, 141–53; for a further exploration of Eicke's administrative structure, see Orth, *Konzentrationslager-ss*, 33–51.

7. Orth, "Bewachung," 127.

8. Orth, "Bewachung," 131–37.

9. Orth, "Concentration Camp Personnel," 45.

10. Orth, *Konzentrationslager-ss*, 38–49.

11. *Statistisches Jahrbuch der Schutzstaffel der* NSDAP (1938), 87.

12. *Statistisches Jahrbuch der Schutzstaffel der* NSDAP (1937), 52, and (1938), 87; Segev, *Soldiers of Evil*, 127–28.

13. Orth, *Konzentrationslager-SS*, 127–52.

14. On the origins of the Nazi movement, see Fritzsche, "The NSDAP, 1919–1934."

15. On Eicke's biography see Tuchel, *Konzentrationslager*, 128–41; for Eicke's letters to Himmler see Friedman, *Der Personal-Akt des SS-Obergruppenfuehrers Eicke.* More documents on Eicke can be found in his personnel file, see BAB (ehem. BDC), SSO, Eicke, Theodor, 17.10.1892.

16. Segev, *Soldiers of Evil,* 136.

17. On initiation rites see Orth, *Konzentrationslager-SS,* 129–32.

18. Evans, *The Third Reich in Power,* 82–3.

19. Orth, *Konzentrationslager-SS,* 127–52.

20. Tuchel, *Konzentrationslager,* 339.

21. Tuchel, *Inspektion der Konzentrationslager,* 32–3.

22. IfZ, F 13/6, Bl. 369–82. These extracts are not reprinted in the standard edition of Höß's memoirs; see Broszat, *Kommandant in Auschwitz.* Höß (1900–1947), awaiting the death sentence for his crimes in Auschwitz, was keen to stress Eicke's indispensable role in the development and operation of the camps in order to downplay the responsibility of other SS officers, including himself, for what had happened in the camps. Höß was executed on 16 April 1947.

23. BAB, R 3001/21167, Bl. 62–69, also quoted in Tuchel, *Konzentrationslager,* 144–45, 150; on background, see 144–51.

24. "Du" is the familiar German form of address.

25. BAB (ehem. BDC), SSO, Eicke, Theodor, 17.10.1892.

26. The accusations against this man were later found to be without substance. See Tuchel, "Theodor Eicke im Konzentrationslager Lichtenburg," 64.

27. BAB (ehem. BDC), SSO, Eicke, Theodor, 17.10.1892. On Eicke's takeover of Lichtenburg, see Endlich, "Die Lichtenburg, 1933–1939," 153.

28. An attack on the previous director of the Lichtenburg camp, a civil servant.

29. USHMM, RG-11.001 M.20, Reel 91, Fond 1367, Opis 2, Folder 19. For background see Knoch, "Emslandlager," 541.

30. A reference to left-wing and liberal parties, whom the Nazis blamed for the German defeat in 1918.

31. USHMM, RG-11.001 M.20, Reel 91, Fond 1367, Opis 2, Folder 19.

32. BAB, NS 31/372, Bl. 1–5.

33. The full name of the SS; roughly translated as "protection squad."

34. A Nazi pagan festival to be celebrated instead of Christmas.

35. BAB, NS 19/1925, Bl. 1–9. On this letter, see Tuchel, *Konzentrationslager,* 212–13.

36. A reference to the Röhm purge.

37. A reference to the Nazi Party rallies, held annually in Nuremberg.

38. BA Berlin-Hoppegarten, KL u. Hafta Sachsenburg 2, Bl. 191.

39. BAB, NS 3/291, Bl. 1–2.

40. BAB, NS 31/372, Bl. 31–32.

41. See section 5.4.

42. BAB, NS 31/372, Bl. 46.

43. BAB, NS 31/372, Bl. 70.

44. BAB, NS 31/372, Bl. 69.

45. BAB, NS 31/372, Bl. 73–74.

46. BAB (ehem. BDC), SSO, Eicke, Theodor, 17.10.1892.

47. IfZ, Fa 127/1, Bl. 113–14.

48. IfZ, Fa 170, Bl. 1.

49. Orth, *Konzentrationslager-SS*, 127–32.

50. Tuchel, *Konzentrationslager*, 380. Koegel was found dead in June 1946 in American captivity.

51. Orth, *Konzentrationslager-SS*, 133–34.

52. Tuchel, "Kommandanten des Konzentrationslagers Flossenbürg." See also Skriebeleit, "Flossenbürg-Stammlager," 27–8.

53. Loritz was fired in 1942 for financial irregularities and became a senior SS leader in Norway. Like many leading Nazis, he committed suicide in Allied captivity, in January 1946. See Riedel, "A 'Political Soldier' and 'Practitioner of Violence.'" On suicides within the SS leadership in 1945, see Goeschel, *Suicide in Nazi Germany*, 152.

54. Eschebach, "Karl Otto Koch."

55. For Ilse Koch, who was sentenced to life in 1951 for her part in abuses in Buchenwald, see Przyrembel, "Transfixed by an Image."

56. Stein, *Konzentrationslager Buchenwald*, 111–15. On Koch, see also Wickert, "The Formation of the SS."

57. Bajohr, *Parvenüs und Profiteure*, 93–4.

58. Printed in Friedlander and Milton, *Archives of the Holocaust*, XI/2, 436.

59. At nearly three thousand meters, the Zugspitze is Germany's highest mountain, located in the Bavarian Alps.

60. Two far-right paramilitary organizations in the Weimar Republic.

61. Printed in Friedlander and Milton, *Archives of the Holocaust*, XI/2, 437–38.

62. "The matter" is rumors about his conviction for fraud. In 1922 he had opened a souvenir shop in Bavaria, which went bankrupt in 1926. Koegel was convicted for this fraudulent bankruptcy.

63. A reference to Eicke's own conviction.

64. Koegel's Bavarian hometown.

65. In his second commandant's order of 28 July 1937, Koch ordered that the Ettersberg concentration camp was now to be known as Buchenwald concentration camp; BAB, NS 4 BU/33.

66. BAB, NS 4 BU/33.

67. BAB (ehem. BDC), SSO, Koch, Karl, 2.8.1897. The italicized sections were added on Eicke's orders with a typewriter.

68. This part was added by Eicke in handwriting.

69. BAB, NS 4 BU/33.

70. BAB, NS 4 BU/33.

71. NO-2366, Bl. 20–25 (copy in IfZ). Konrad Morgen (1909–82) was an SS officer and jurist. On Koch's trial see Orth, *Konzentrationslager-SS*, 189–91.

72. StA Oldenburg, Best. 140-5, Nr. 1221, Bl 308–9. Our thanks to Dirk Riedel for sharing this document with us.

73. BAB (ehem. BDC), SSO, Taus, Karl, 24.9.93.

74. See the brief survey in Morsch, "Formation and Construction," 172–77; see also Segev, *Soldiers of Evil*, 127–8; Orth, "Bewachung," 132. For the SS members of the Sachsenhausen command staff, see now also the extensive study by Riedle, *Die Angehörigen des Kommandanturstabs*.

75. For a similar view, see Drobisch and Wieland, *System der NS-Konzentrationslager*, 95–99.

76. For Steinbrenner, see also Dillon, "'We'll meet again in Dachau,'" 546–48.

77. Archiv Dachau, 6454.

78. A mistake in the original. SS *Oberführer* Erasmus Freiherr von Malsen-Ponickau was in charge of the Munich auxiliary police since 20 March 1933. See Drobisch and Wieland, *System der NS-Konzentrationslager*, 51.

79. Broszat, *Kommandant in Auschwitz*, 53–55.

80. ITS/ARCH/HIST/KL Sachsenburg 1, Bl. 5.

81. ITS/ARCH/HIST/KL Sachsenburg 1, Bl. 138.

82. ITS/ARCH/HIST/KL Sachsenburg 1, Bl. 212.

83. "'Ich war Wächter im Gestapo-Gefängnis Columbiahaus!' Das Geständnis eines SS-Manns," in *Arbeiter-Illustrierte Zeitung*, 23 May 1935, reprinted in Schilde and Tuchel, *Columbia-Haus*, 58–61. This interview with Bächle, who had helped two prisoners to escape to Czechoslovakia, may have been embellished for effect by this exile newspaper.

84. On Bächle see Schilde, "Columbia-Haus," 60. Bächle joined the Nazi Party in 1931 and began to serve in the Camp SS in 1934.

85. Helmuth Brückner (1896–1954), *Gauleiter* of Silesia and SA-*Gruppenführer*, was expelled from his offices in 1934 in the aftermath of the Röhm purge.

86. ITS/HIST/SACH—Sachsenburg Ordner 1. Our thanks to Stefan Hördler for sharing this document with us.

87. Richter, "Wandlungen in der SS."

88. The name of the Germany army during the Weimar Republic.

89. "Die 'Elite der Nation': ss-Wachtgruppe im Konzentrationslager Lichtenburg," *Neuer Vorwärts*, 14 February 1937. The *Neuer Vorwärts* was a Social Democratic exile newspaper.

90. A reference to the bunker.

91. IfZ, Fa 127/1. Bl. 1–2.

92. Archiv Sachsenhausen JD5/2; copies of Staatsanwaltschaft Muenchen 1 Ks 1/59 verb. mit 1 Ks 3/59 (Bugdalle, Richard), Bd. II, Bl. 65–68. Richard Bugdalle (1907–82), an ss official in various camps, was arrested in 1957 and sentenced to life for murder in 1960 in Munich.

93. Kautsky, *Teufel und Verdammte*, 98–99. Benedikt Kautsky (1894–1960), an Austrian left-wing economist of Jewish descent, was arrested in 1938 and imprisoned in various camps until liberation in 1945.

94. A reference to the Kristallnacht pogrom of November 1938.

4. Life and Death in the Camps

1. Obenaus, "Der Kampf um das tägliche Brot."

2. Pingel, *Häftlinge unter ss-Herrschaft*, 75.

3. On prisons see Wachsmann, *Hitler's Prisons*, 23–24, 31–33. ·

4. On military "exercises" see Springmann, "'Sport machen.'"

5. Drobisch and Wieland, *System der ns-Konzentrationslager*, 209.

6. Stein, *Konzentrationslager Buchenwald*, 111–15.

7. Archive Dachau, Häflingsdatenbank. Our thanks to Albert Knoll for these figures.

8. Maršálek, *Geschichte des Konzentrationslagers Mauthausen*, 123, 146.

9. Drobisch and Wieland, *System der ns-Konzentrationslager*, 205–16, 290–310.

10. On language see Pingel, "Social Life in an Unsocial Environment," 70–72. On Neurath see Fleck, Müller and Stehr, "Nachwort."

11. See also Pingel, *Häftlinge unter ss-Herrschaft*, 46–47.

12. See Springmann, "'Sport machen.'"

13. On daily rituals, see Pingel, *Häftlinge unter ss-Herrschaft*, 48–49. On Dachau, see Zámečník, "Dachau-Stammlager," 239–41. More generally, see also Drobisch and Wieland, *System der ns-Konzentrationslager*, 294–98.

14. For Buchenwald, see Stein, *Konzentrationslager Buchenwald*, 91–92.

15. See also Pingel, *Häftlinge unter ss-Herrschaft*, 56–60.

16. BAB, NS 4 BU/vorl. 1, Bl. 31.

17. Gräf, "Prügelstrafe." The *Neue Weltbühne* was an exile publication. On this article's background see Baganz, *Erziehung*, 205. Hugo Gräf (1892–1958), a Communist activist, was taken to Sachsenburg in 1934. Released in 1935, he escaped to Prague and then to Britain.

18. Valentin, "Die Krankenversorgung im Konzentrationslager." Our thanks to Dr. Susanne Heim for sharing this document with us.

19. Behnken, *Deutschland-Berichte der Sopade*, 3:1609.

20. Union für Recht und Freiheit, *Der Strafvollzug im III. Reich*, 17.

21. For the Nazis, Albert Leo Schlageter (1894–1923) was a martyr. He had been executed by the French in 1923 for sabotage. For background see Baird, *To Die for Germany*, 13–40.

22. Union für Recht und Freiheit, *Der Strafvollzug im Dritten Reich*, 35.

23. BAB, NS 4 LI/1, Bl. 9.

24. Union für Recht und Freiheit, *Der Strafvollzug im III. Reich*, 35–36.

25. A code added by the editors of this 1936 exile publication to protect the prisoner's identity.

26. Ditto.

27. Behnken, *Deutschland-Berichte der Sopade*, 3:1618.

28. § 175 of the German criminal code made sex between men a criminal offense.

29. Behnken, *Deutschland-Berichte der Sopade*, 4:701–2.

30. BAB, NS 4 BU/31, Bl. 20. This decree was circulated to all prisoner blocks. Arthur Rödl (1898–1945) had been camp compound leader at Buchenwald since August 1937.

31. A prisoner.

32. Neurath (1911–2001), an Austrian sociologist of Jewish descent, was arrested after the annexation of Austria and taken to Dachau and then to Buchenwald. Released in May 1939, he immigrated to the United States via Sweden. He first wrote his account of the camps in the early 1940s, resulting in a PhD thesis at Columbia University.

33. Neurath, *Die Gesellschaft des Terrors*, 30–31.

34. BAB, NS 4 BU/102.

35. Itzkewitsch, a Russian Jew who had settled in Germany after World War I, was taken to Buchenwald on 10 November 1938 after serving a prison term for "race defilement" (his long-term relationship with a German woman became a criminal offense after the promulgation of the 1935 Nuremberg Laws). In July 1941 he was transported from Buchenwald to the Sonnenstein "euthanasia" killing center; for background see Stein, "Juden im Konzentrationslager Buchenwald," 100–107.

36. Printed in Stein, *Konzentrationslager Buchenwald*, 77. Most of the text was already printed on the form, with handwritten additions by J. Meyer.

37. WL, P.III.h.No.794. Gussak was imprisoned as an Austrian Gypsy.

38. Neurath, *Die Gesellschaft des Terrors*, 71–75.

39. Leo Baeck Institute Berlin, JMB MF 425, vol. 4, 67. Ludwig Bendix (1877–

1954), a German Jewish liberal lawyer, was imprisoned several times in prisons and concentration camps between 1933 and 1937. He emigrated to Palestine in 1937. Our thanks to Kim Wünschmann for sharing this document with us.

40. J. Freund, *O Buchenwald!*, 134–35. On the memoirs of Freund, an Austrian prisoner, see Drobisch and Wieland, *System der NS-Konzentrationslager*, 332. He apparently wrote his report in exile in the summer of 1939.

41. For a general survey of resistance in the Third Reich, see Kershaw, *The Nazi Dictatorship*, 183–217.

42. Cf. Garbe, "Selbstbehauptung und Widerstand," 243.

43. For a survey of self-assertion and resistance in the camps, see Garbe, "Selbstbehauptung und Widerstand."

44. Pingel, *Häftlinge unter SS-Herrschaft*, 10; Daxelmüller, "Kulturelle Formen und Aktivitäten." On the Dachau library see Seela, "Die Lagerbücherei im Konzentrationslager Dachau."

45. Fackler, *Des Lagers Stimme*.

46. On political prisoners' resistance, see section 5.1.

47. On Niemöller see chapter 6. For a survey of the Confessing Church see Greschat, "Kirche und Widerstand gegen den Nationalsozialismus." For a survey in English see Steigmann-Gall, "Religion and the Churches," 153–62.

48. Drobisch and Wieland, *System der NS-Konzentrationslager*, 303, 307–8, 325, 331; Stein, *Konzentrationslager Buchenwald*, 65, 93, 130–31.

49. Röll, *Sozialdemokraten im Konzentrationslager Buchenwald*, 62–64. See also for details on the *Fluchtpunkt*.

50. Röll, *Sozialdemokraten im Konzentrationslager Buchenwald*, 64–82.

51. Kautsky, *Teufel und Verdammte*, 222–24.

52. Archiv Dachau, 37.518, Bl. 7.

53. Printed in Nationale Mahn- und Gedenkstätte Buchenwald, *Konzentrationslager Buchenwald*, 85.

54. *Das Schwarze Korps*, 26 May 1938. See Himmler's letter to Reich Minister of Justice Gürtner of 16 May 1938 in chapter 2 (130).

55. Archiv Buchenwald 31/450.

56. "Der Leidensweg des Peter Forster," *Pariser Tageszeitung*, 25/26 December 1938. This was an exile newspaper.

57. For a copy of a form sheet, see IfZ, Fa 183, Bl. 26–27, Strafverfügung!, undated.

58. See also chapter 3.

59. Zámečník, "Dachau-Stammlager," 249–50.

60. Goeschel, "Suicide in Nazi Concentration Camps."

61. Zámečník, "Dachau-Stammlager," 250. On Zill, see Orth, "Egon Zill."

62. Drobisch and Wieland, *System der NS-Konzentrationslager*, 210–13.

63. WL, P.III.h.No.569.

64. Bernhard Schmidt (1890–1960) was commandant of Sachsenburg since 1 April 1935. See Baganz, *Erziehung*, 263.

65. Behnken, *Deutschland-Berichte der Sopade*, 3:1630.

66. Otto Reich (1891–1955) was commandant of Lichtenburg in 1935 and 1936. See Tuchel, *Konzentrationslager*, 386–7.

67. Archiv Dachau, 1118. Loewenstein, a German Jew, had been arrested at the German-Swiss border in 1936 and was transferred to Dachau as a remigrant. A loner, he was bullied relentlessly by SS men.

68. A mistake. Hermann Baranowski (1884–1940) was not commandant of Dachau, but camp compound leader. See Tuchel, *Konzentrationslager*, 371.

69. Rudolf Höß, see above.

70. Heinz Eschen (1909–1938) was Kapo of the Jews' block in Dachau. He allegedly committed suicide on 30 January 1938, following gruesome SS torture. See Jahnke, "Heinz Eschen."

71. Behnken, *Deutschland-Berichte der Sopade*, 4:691.

72. The Dachau bunker administrator (*Arrestverwalter*) Johann Kantschuster (1897–?) could not be traced after 1945 and was declared dead; our thanks to Andreas Eichmüller (IfZ) for this information.

73. "Mord im Lager Sachsenburg," *Neuer Vorwärts*, 6 June 1937. Dr. Max Sachs (1883–1935) was a Jewish Socialist activist and journalist. See Baganz, *Erziehung*, 274–75.

74. A Social Democratic newspaper.

75. Jews were often assigned this humiliating work. See Stein, "Buchenwald-Stammlager," 315.

76. BAB, NS 4 BU/101. Arthur Rödl (1898–1945?) was camp compound leader at Buchenwald from 1937 until 1941. See Tuchel, *Konzentrationslager*, 199, 390.

77. Printed in Hackett, *The Buchenwald Report*, 154.

78. Printed in Stein, *Konzentrationslager Buchenwald*, 105.

79. Archiv Sachsenhausen, D 30/8/2A.

80. WL, P.III.h.No.1058, ch. IX, 2–4. Maximilian Reich (1882–1952) was a prominent sports journalist from Vienna. He was arrested in March 1938 and taken to Dachau on 1 April 1938 alongside 150 prominent Austrians. For background see Neugebauer, "Der erste Österreichertransport in das KZ Dachau," 196–97.

81. Hohmann and Wieland, *Konzentrationslager Sachsenhausen bei Oranienburg*, 13. Rudolf Wunderlich (1912–1988) was a Communist activist. Briefly

arrested in 1933, he was imprisoned at Sachsenhausen from March 1939 until his escape in June 1944.

5. Prisoner Groups

1. Eberle, "Häftlingskategorien und Kennzeichnungen," 97.

2. Hartewig, "Wolf unter Wölfen?" On context, see also Niethammer, *Der "gesäuberte" Antifaschismus*, 33–41.

3. See Evans, *The German Underworld*.

4. Pätzold, "Häftlingsgesellschaft," 114.

5. Pingel, "Social Life in an Unsocial Environment."

6. Pätzold, "Häftlingsgesellschaft," 110.

7. Eberle, "Häftlingskategorien und Kennzeichnungen," 92–99.

8. See chapter 2, **79**.

9. Pätzold, "Häftlingsgesellschaft," 117–23.

10. Kogon, *Theory and Practice of Hell*, 30–37. The word "barrack" has been changed to "hut," in keeping with the other documents. Eugen Kogon (1903–87) was detained at Buchenwald as a political prisoner from 1939 to 1945. See Wachsmann, "Introduction," xi–xxi.

11. The criminal police also admitted prisoners to the camps.

12. Behnken, *Deutschland-Berichte der Sopade*, 4:683–86.

13. This claim is not true.

14. Again, this claim is not correct.

15. Heinrich Jasper (1875–1945), SPD politician, was in custody in Dachau from 1933 to 1939, and was re-arrested in July 1944. He is said to have died in the Bergen-Belsen camp.

16. Kurt Schumacher (1895–1952), SPD politician, was held in various camps, including Dachau, 1933–43 and 1944–45.

17. Drobisch and Wieland, *System der NS-Konzentrationslager*, 199. On Communist resistance in the Third Reich, see Merson, *Communist Resistance in Nazi Germany*. Not all of those who were taken in protective custody ended up in camps, though many did.

18. Fackler, "*Des Lagers Stimme*," 336–38. In many camps prisoners wrote and composed songs that commandants later chose as official anthems for their camps.

19. See generally Niethammer, *Der "gesäuberte" Antifaschismus*.

20. Naujoks, *Mein Leben im KZ Sachsenhausen*, 104.

21. Poller, *Arztschreiber in Buchenwald*. More generally, see Drobisch and Wieland, *System der NS-Konzentrationslager*, 318–22.

22. On Ossietzky, see Sternburg, *"Es ist eine unheimliche Stimmung in Deutschland"*; Kraiker and Suhr, *Ossietzky*.

23. On Litten and his death, see Hett, *Crossing Hitler*.

24. Litten, *Die Hölle sieht Dich an.*

25. Garbe, "Erst verhasst, dann geschätzt," 220.

26. Archiv Dachau 37518, Aufzeichnungen des Alfred Hübsch, p. 5.

27. Garbe, "Erst verhasst, dann geschätzt," 224. For a copy of such a postcard, see ITS/HIST/KL Buchenwald 40, Seite 170R, Kommandantur Konzentrationslager Buchenwald, 1939.

28. Archiv Gedenkstätte Sachsenhausen, J D2/43, Bl. 146–54: Untersuchungsrichter II beim Landgericht Bonn, Vernehmung des Beschuldigten Sorge, 6 May 1957. Sorge (1911–78) admitted this crime and other atrocities at the first Sachsenhausen trial, a Soviet military tribunal held in Berlin in 1947; see Siegel, *Todeslager Sachsenhausen*, 43–44: W. Meyer, "Stalinistischer Schauprozess gegen KZ-Verbrecher?." On Sorge, see Riedle, *Die Angehörigen des Kommandanturstabs*, 163–203.

29. Garbe, "Erst verhasst, dann geschätzt." See also Garbe, *Zwischen Widerstand und Martyrium.*

30. Printed in Drobisch and Wieland, *System der NS-Konzentrationslager*, 153.

31. A prison near Stettin where protective custody prisoners were held in 1933. See Rudorff, "Gollnow."

32. Singer and Burger, *Carl von Ossietzky*, 97–98.

33. *Der Gegen-Angriff*, 7 November 1934.

34. Printed in Naujoks, *Mein Leben im KZ Sachsenhausen*, 51–52.

35. A reference to the 1936 transfer of all remaining Esterwegen prisoners to the new Sachsenhausen camp.

36. Naujoks, *Mein Leben im KZ Sachsenhausen*, 100–101, 52–54. Harry Naujoks (1901–1983), a Communist activist, was arrested in 1933 and held in early camps and prisons. Transferred to Sachsenhausen in 1936, he was appointed senior camp prisoner in 1939. In 1942 he was transferred to Flossenbürg, where he remained until liberation.

37. The Austrian Communist party.

38. Naujoks must be wrong here, as the decree stipulating that all male Jews had to add "Israel" to their first name and all female Jews "Sara" only came into force in January 1939.

39. The 1935 Nuremberg Laws forbade Jews to employ non-Jewish domestic staff.

40. ITS, Individuelle Unterlagen, KL Dachau, Lehner, Toni, Bl. 26, also printed in Heiber, *Reichsführer!*, 47.

41. BAB, NS 4 BU/101. The Political Department forwarded this request to the camp commandant on the same day, asking for F. to be punished.

42. *Neuer Vorwärts*, 19 December 1937.

43. Hans Litten (1903–38) supported the radical left, though he was not a KPD member.

44. Arthur Winkler, "Im Konzentrationslager Esterwegen," *Trost*, February/March 1938; printed in Milton, "Jehovah's Witnesses," 152–9.

45. Presumably of the *Trost* periodical in which the first part of this article appeared.

46. Poller, *Arztschreiber in Buchenwald*, 26–27, 28–29.

47. FZH, 353-1. Hans Schwarz (1904–70), an Austrian socialist, was confined at Dachau and later Neuengamme. After the war he was active in the Hamburg Committee of Former Political Prisoners.

48. See, e.g., Ayaß, *"Asoziale" im Nationalsozialismus*; Schikorra, *Kontinuitäten der Ausgrenzung*; Langhammer, "Die reichsweite Verhaftungsaktion."

49. Eberle, "'Asoziale' und 'Berufsverbrecher,'" 258; Ayass, *"Asotiale" im Nationalsotialismus*, 138–39.

50. Harris, "Role of the Concentration Camps."

51. Archiv Dachau, 26.688, Bekanntmachung des Bezirksamts Schongau, 13 October 1937. On Herzogsägmühle see Eberle, "'Asoziale' und 'Berufsverbrecher,'" 256; Ayass, *"Asotiale im Nationalsotialismus,"* 51–54. More generally on the Nazi persecution of the Gypsies, see Milton, "Gypsies as Social Outsiders in Nazi Germany."

52. Archiv Dachau, 26.907, Landratsamt Schongau, Schutzhaftbefehl, 7 February 1938.

53. In Bavaria the authorities arrested more than a thousand individuals in July 1936, just before the beginning of the Summer Olympics, when the regime was keen to present Germany as a country free of crime and poverty. Those arrested included vagrants, recidivist criminals, and even Communists, whom the Nazis had long accused of being connected to the underworld. More than seven hundred of those arrested were taken to Dachau; see Drobisch and Wieland, *System der NS-Konzentrationslager*, 284.

54. Archiv Dachau, 18.859, Fachärztliches Gutachten der Städtischen Trinkerfürsorge Augsburg, 12 May 1937. See also 235.

55. On the sterilization of camp prisoners, see Hax, "Sterilisierung und Kastration." See more generally Burleigh, *Death and Deliverance*, 43–90.

56. See chapter 2.

57. On homosexual men in the Sachsenhausen camp see Müller and Sternweiler, *Homosexuelle Männer im KZ Sachsenhausen*. See also Pretzel and Roßbach, *Wegen der zu erwartenden hohen Strafe*, 119–68.

58. Knoll, "Homosexuelle Häftlinge im KZ Dachau," 240–41.

59. For a survey of Nazi policies up until 1937, see Wagner, "'Vernichtung der Berufsverbrecher.'" For a more general survey, see Wachsmann, "From Indefinite Confinement to Extermination."

60. See chapter 2, 99.

61. ITS/ARCH/KL Flossenbürg Indiv. Unterlagen Männer, prisoner number 15692.

62. ITS/ARCH/KL Flossenbürg Indiv. Unterlagen Männer, prisoner number 15692, Bl. 12; ITS/ARCH/KL Flossenbürg Indiv. Unterlagen Männer, prisoner number 15692, Bl. 14, Lagerkommandant des KL Flossenbürg to Reichskriminalpolizeiamt, 28 March 1939; ITS/ARCH/KL Flossenbürg Indiv. Unterlagen Männer, prisoner number 15692, Bl. 15, Erklärung, 20 April 1939.

63. On K.'s life see ITS/ARCH/KL Flossenbürg Indiv. Unterlagen Männer, prisoner number 297, Bl. 11, Landgericht Krems to Kommandantur des KL Flossenbürg, 29 May 1939; ITS/ARCH/KL Flossenbürg Indiv. Unterlagen Männer, prisoner number 297, Bl. 12, Kommandantur des KL to Landgericht Krems, 10 June 1939; on similar cases, see Wachsmann, Hitler's Prisons, 175.

64. See ITS/ARCH/KL Flossenbürg Indiv. Unterlagen Männer, prisoner number 297. On similar cases, see Wachsmann, Hitler's Prisons, 175.

65. ITS/ARCH/HIST/KL Dachau 4 (200), Bl. 8.

66. On these raids see Ayaß, "Keiner hat die Bettler vor der Razzia gewarnt," 14.

67. This was one of several nationwide Nazi charity drives.

68. A women's prison and workhouse.

69. ITS/ARCH/HIST/KL Dachau 4 (200), Bl. 57.

70. ITS/ARCH/HIST/KL Dachau 4 (200), Bl. 58.

71. Archiv Dachau 18.864.

72. A division within the local welfare office, policing drinkers.

73. Archiv Dachau 26.907.

74. Printed in Stein, Konzentrationslager Buchenwald, 57.

75. Rüter, de Mildt, et al., Justiz und NS-Verbrechen, 499. The Stade court sentenced Otto Hop (1914–?) to fifteen years in prison as an accessory to murder and several other crimes.

76. Broszat, Kommandant in Auschwitz, 77.

77. Höß had been in the Brandenburg penitentiary from 1924 until 1928 for his part in a political murder. See Wachsmann, Hitler's Prisons, 38–9.

78. Archiv Dachau, 9438, Bl. 11–12.

79. ITS/ARCH/KL Flossenbürg Indiv. Unterlagen Männer, prisoner number 15692, Bl. 18.

80. "Berutsverbrecher," professional criminal.

81. ITS/ARCH/KL Flossenbürg Indiv. Unterlagen Männer, Bl. 18.

82. Wünschmann, "Cementing the Enemy Category"; Matthäus, "Verfolgung, Ausbeutung, Vernichtung," 66.

83. See chapter 2.

84. On Jewish life in Nazi Germany, see Kaplan, Between Dignity and Despair. See also Friedländer, Nazi Germany and the Jews, vol. 1, The Years of Persecution.

85. Drobisch and Wieland, *System der NS-Konzentrationslager*, 301.

86. Matthäus, "Verfolgung, Ausbeutung, Vernichtung," 74.

87. For a survey, see Benz, "Mitglieder der Häftlingsgesellschaft auf Zeit."

88. Pollmeier, "Die Verhaftungen nach dem November-Pogrom 1938," 176–77.

89. Matthäus, "Verfolgung, Ausbeutung, Vernichtung," 75–77.

90. Wildt, "Violence against Jews in Germany," 204–8; Kropat, "*Reichskristallnacht*," 141.

91. See also Behnken, *Deutschland-Berichte der Sopade*, 5:1346.

92. WL, P.III.h.No. 684.

93. A reference to the Great Depression, which hit France later (but longer) than other countries.

94. Burkhardt, *Tanz mal Jude!*, 98–99.

95. WL, 1041/2.

96. WL, 066-WL-1625, Bl. 11–13.

97. Archiv Dachau, no. 9438, Bl. 114–17.

98. The correct spelling is Herschel Grynzspan (1921–?), the assassin of Ernst vom Rath. See chapter 2.

99. WL, B. 323, 5–6. For a collection of eyewitness accounts of the November pogrom see Barkow, Gross, and Lenarz, *Novemberpogrom 1938*, 485–654.

100. WL, B. 216.

101. Caplan, "Gender and the Concentration Camps," quote on 99.

102. Hesse, "Moringen," 160–63; Caplan, Introduction, 22–23; Füllberg-Stolberg et al., "Einleitung"; White, "Moringen-Solling (Men)" and "Moringen-Solling (Women).'"

103. Hesse, "Moringen," 164; Harris, "Role of the Concentration Camps." For a survey of abortion, see Evans, *The Third Reich in Power*, 515–20. For Hans Beimler, see chapter 1.

104. Caplan, Introduction, 33.

105. Hesse, "Moringen," 164.

106. On Lichtenburg as a men's camp, see Mette, "Schloss Lichtenburg."

107. On guard dogs see Perz, "'. . . müssen zu reißenden Bestien erzogen werden.'"

108. Endlich, "Die Lichtenburg, 1933–1939," 21–22, 52; Caplan, Introduction, 40. See also 258. More generally, see Fahrenberg and Hördler, "Das Frauen-Konzentrationslager Lichtenburg." On the recruitment of female guards, see Erpel, *Im Gefolge der SS*.

109. Fahrenberg and Hördler, "Das Franen-Konzentrationslager Lichtenburg." On "asocial" women in the camps generally, see Schikorra, *Kontinuitäten der Ausgrenzung*.

110. On Ravensbrück, see Strebel, *KZ Ravensbrück*.

111. Leo, "Ravensbrück-Stammlager," 473–75, 501. See also Bessmann, "Camp Prison."

112. Distel, "Frauen in nationalsozialistischen Konzentrationslagern," 203–4. See also Heike, "'. . . da es sich ja lediglich um die Bewachung der Häftlinge handelt . . . ': Lagerverwaltung und Bewachungspersonal," 223–36.

113. Printed in Schnabel, *Macht ohne Moral*, 114.

114. Niedersächsisches HStA Hannover, Hann. 158 Moringen, Acc. 105/96, Nr. 282. Our thanks to Kim Wünschmann and Julia Hörath for sharing this document with us.

115. WL, P.III.h.117. Sherwood-Schweitzer was born in 1900 in Halberstadt into a middle-class Jewish family. She was released from Moringen in September 1935 and eventually emigrated to England in 1939.

116. Niedersächsisches HStA Hannover, Hann. 158 Moringen, Acc. 105/96, Nr. 205. Our thanks to Kim Wünschmann and Julia Hörath for sharing this document with us.

117. Herz, *The Women's Camp in Moringen*, 82–88. It is not entirely clear when these postwar memoirs were written. Gabriele Herz (1886–1957), a Jewish woman, was married to a publisher and left Nazi Germany after her release in 1937.

118. Behnken, *Deutschland-Berichte der Sopade*, 4:713–14.

119. Haag, *Eine Handvoll Staub*, 111. Lina Haag (1907–), a Communist activist, was married to Alfred Haag, a prominent Communist politician. Held in several prisons and camps, she first published these memoirs in 1947. She is famous for securing her husband's release from Mauthausen in 1940 after a conversation with Himmler.

120. IfZ Fa 183/1, Bl. 402.

121. BAB, NS 3/415, Bl. 1. On Koegel see chapter 3.

122. Buchmann, *Die Frauen von Ravensbrück*, 15. Erika Buchmann (1902–1971), a Communist activist, was married to KPD politician Albert Buchmann. Arrested and sentenced to prison in 1935, she was transferred to Ravensbrück upon her release.

6. The Camps and the Public

1. On this problem see Kershaw, *Popular Opinion and Political Dissent*, 373–85.

2. Quoted in Noakes and Pridham, *Nazism*, 2:187.

3. Kershaw, *The "Hitler Myth,"* 48–147; Welch, *The Third Reich*, 50–89.

4. Milton, "Die Konzentrationslager der dreißiger Jahre," 136–38.

5. Welch, *The Third Reich*, 17–49; see also Hale, *Captive Press*. On Dietrich's press instructions see Herf, *The Jewish Enemy*, 22–27.

6. For some background, see also Toepser-Ziegert and Bohrmann, *NS-Presseanweisungen der Vorkriegszeit*.

7. "Göring über aktuelle Fragen," *Berliner Börsen-Zeitung*, 21 April 1934.

8. For an exploration of Nazi propaganda on declining crime rates, see Wagner, *Volksgemeinschaft ohne Verbrecher*, 214–32.

9. Cf. Gellately, *Backing Hitler*, 61–69, who claims that from the mid-1930s propaganda about the camps focused almost exclusively on the suppression of social and racial outsiders.

10. See Zeck, *Das Schwarze Korps*, esp. 305–7.

11. See also section 6.3.

12. See chapter 2 on Eicke's concerns about "atrocity propaganda."

13. For examples, see extracts from BAB, R 58/463 below.

14. See, e.g., Politisches Archiv des Auswärtigen Amts, Berlin, R 99574, Preussische Geheime Staatspolizei to Auswärtiges Amt, 12 March 1935. More generally on the German Foreign Office, see Döscher, *Das Auswärtige Amt im Dritten Reich*, 67–78.

15. For Hitler's speech on 30 January 1941, see Domarus, *Hitler*, 4:1658; Moore, "'And what concentration camps those were!,'" 672.

16. On the camps in the Boer War see I. R. Smith, *The Origins of the South-African War*; Heyningen, "Concentration Camps of the South African War."

17. Moore, "'And what concentration camps those were!,'" 651–54.

18. See also Himmler's 1937 speech to the Wehrmacht, in section 2.1.

19. Quoted in *Prager Tageblatt*, May 1934, copy in USHMM, RG 11–001M.01, Fond 500, Osobyi 1, Folder 236.

20. Toepser-Ziegert and Bohrmann, NS-*Presseanweisungen der Vorkriegszeit*, 2, 342.

21. Ernst Torgler (1893–1963), a Communist politician, and Carl von Ossietzky (1889–1938) were not released until 1935 and 1936, respectively. On Ossietzky see chapter 5.

22. Printed in Behnken, *Deutschland-Berichte der Sopade*, 2:160.

23. Politisches Archiv des Auswärtigen Amts, Berlin, R 99574.

24. This is a reference to the sinking of a German submarine by the British in 1915. The British are said to have shot the submarine's crew.

25. A reference to the British naval blockade of the North Sea during World War I.

26. A French penal colony.

27. A reference to the seizure of German colonies by the French and British in the wake of World War I.

28. "Erfolg der Vorbeugungshaft: 476 Berufsverbrecher mit fast 5000 Jahren Freiheitsstrafen," *Berliner Börsen-Zeitung*, 24 October 1935, copy in BAB, R 3001/21469, Bl. 24.

29. "Störche im K.Z.," *Das Schwarze Korps*, 12 December 1935.

30. *Trial of the Major War Criminals before the International Military Tribunal*, XXIX, ND-1956-PS.

31. IfZ, Fa 183/1, Bl. 352.

32. "K.Z. und seine Insassen," *Das Schwarze Korps*, 13 February 1936. On this article see Zeck, *Das Schwarze Korps*, 305–7.

33. Julius Streicher (1885–1946), was *Gauleiter* of Franconia and editor of the viciously anti-Semitic Nazi paper *Der Stürmer*.

34. "Saure Wochen, frohe Feste," *Das Schwarze Korps*, 3 September 1936.

35. This unit was stationed at Sachsenburg.

36. "Konzentrationslager Dachau," *Illustrierter Beobachter*, 3 December 1936, 2014–17, 2028.

37. Toepser-Ziegert and Bohrmann, NS-*Presseanweisungen der Vorkriegszeit*, IV/3, 1534–35.

38. *Der Neue Brockhaus*, 699–700.

39. "Professor Landra besucht das Konzentrationslager Sachsenhausen . . . und die Leibstandarte," *Illustrierter Beobachter*, 5 January 1939. See Aaron, "Guido Landra and the Office of Racial Studies," 366.

40. An SS unit for Hitler's personal protection.

41. IfZ, MA 312.

42. This sentence was later deleted in the script.

43. Quoted in Schley, *Nachbar Buchenwald*, 103–4.

44. Milton, "Die Konzentrationslager der dreißiger Jahre," 135; Evans, *The Third Reich in Power*, 147–48.

45. Milton, "Die Konzentrationslager der dreißiger Jahre," 138–40.

46. Milton, "Die Konzentrationslager der dreißiger Jahre," 139.

47. "Life Inside a Nazi Concentration Camp," *New York Times Magazine*, 14 February 1937. Milton, "Die Konzentrationslager der dreißiger Jahre," 139, criticizes this report for failing to comment on these Nazi propaganda pictures. In fact, the report clearly acknowledges that these were Nazi pictures, reprinted with their original captions.

48. Lipstadt, *Beyond Belief*, 79–95. On context, see also Leff, *Buried by the Times*.

49. On British reactions to Nazi repression see, for example, London, *Whitehall and the Jews*.

50. On *The Times*'s reporting on the camps, see also Kersten, "'The Times' und das KZ Dachau." Cf. Conze et al., *Das Amt und die Vergangenheit*, 26.

51. Evans, *The Third Reich in Power*, 230–31; Milton, "Die Konzentrationslager der dreißiger Jahre," 140.

52. Fröhlich, *Die Tagebücher von Joseph Goebbels*, 5:185.

53. "Dr. Niemöller Sent to Concentration Camp," *The Times*, 5 March 1938.

54. On Niemöller see Schmidt, *Martin Niemöller im Kirchenkampf*, 433–47; specifically on his imprisonment at Sachsenhausen, see Niemöller, *Martin Niemöller*, 7–18; Evans, *The Third Reich in Power*, 231–32.

55. Milton, "Die Konzentrationslager der dreißiger Jahre," 141. For another example, see "Treatment of Prisoners in Concentration Camps," *Manchester Guardian*, 3 April 1936.

56. Drobisch and Wieland, *System der NS-Konzentrationslager*, 303–5.

57. Burckhardt, *Meine Danziger Mission*, 53–63; Drobisch and Wieland, *System der NS-Konzentrationslager*, 213–15. There are other inaccuracies in Burckhardt's postwar account. For example, he claimed that the Esterwegen commandant Loritz had been arrested for mistreating prisoners following Burckhardt's official report. This was clearly not the case. See also Riedel, *Ordnungshüter*, 127–29. More generally, see also Favez, *Warum schwieg das Rote Kreuz?*, 84–89; on Burckhardt's career see pp. 82–83.

58. Milton, "Die Konzentrationslager der dreißiger Jahre," 142–43.

59. On the *Pariser Tageblatt* see Roussel and Winckler, *Rechts und links der Seine*.

60. Drobisch, 'Zeitgenössische Berichte über Nazikonzentrationslager."

61. "Die Mörder von Dachau und ihre Opfer," *Pariser Tageblatt*, 20 December 1934.

62. A reference to Hans Steinbrenner's atrocities at Dachau. See 31 and 172.

63. "The German Camps: A Paradox of Nazi Power; Renewed Plea for Justice," *The Times*, 24 January 1935.

64. A reference to the People's Court, a court set up by the Nazis in 1934 to deal with political opposition.

65. In fact, this only happened in exceptional circumstances.

66. A reference to the DNVP, the Nazis' national-conservative coalition partner in 1933.

67. SA or SS men.

68. IfZ, Fa 199/29, Bl. 145–47.

69. International Committee of the Red Cross Archives, Geneva, CR 110/4/60. Our thanks to Dr. Daniel Palmieri for sharing this document with us and to Jeff Porter for the translation from the French original.

70. Günther Tamaschke (1896–1959) was, from 1935 until 1937, in a leading position in the Inspectorate of Concentration Camps. See Tuchel, *Konzentrationslager*, 392.

71. See section 3.3.

72. He was actually arrested in the wake of the Reichstag Fire Decree of 28 February 1933.

73. In fact, Heilmann was the leader of the SPD group in the Prussian diet.

74. Heinrich Deubel (1890–1962) was commandant of Dachau in 1934–36 before being appointed commandant of the Columbia-Haus. He left the Camp SS in 1936. See Tuchel, *Konzentrationslager*, 372–73.

75. This article from the Dutch newspaper was filed and translated by the SS, copy in BAB, R 58/463, Bl. 76–77.

76. Copy in WL, PC 4, reel 73.

77. "German Political Prisoners," *The Times*, 8 January 1937.

78. *Dokumente über die Behandlung*, 23–27.

79. An annual Nazi charity campaign.

80. For example Wachsmann, "Dynamics of Destruction," 23, 25.

81. Horwitz, *In the Shadow of Death*, 31.

82. Steinbacher, *Dachau*, 33–48, 137–50. On contacts between Weimar businesses and Buchenwald, see Schley, *Nachbar Buchenwald*, 79–86. See also section 2.4 on the increasing economic autarky of the SS camps.

83. Schley, *Nachbar Buchenwald*, 40–41, 98–99, 103. See also Steinbacher, *Dachau*, 116–23.

84. Dillon, "'We'll meet again in Dachau.'"

85. For recollections of these threats, see Asgodom, *"Halts Maul—sonst kommst nach Dachau"*; Kershaw, *Popular Opinion and Political Dissent*, 73–74.

86. Schley, *Nachbar Buchenwald*, 96–97.

87. Steinbacher, *Dachau*, 150–52; Marcuse, *Legacies of Dachau*.

88. See Johe, "Das deutsche Volk und die Konzentrationslager."

89. Cf. Gellately, *Backing Hitler*, 60.

90. See the Gestapo decree on "Entlassene Schutzhäftlinge," printed in Mason, *Arbeiterklasse und Volksgemeinschaft*, 328–29.

91. Drobisch and Wieland, *System der NS-Konzentrationslager*, 234–36.

92. On Germans' reactions to the pogrom, see Longerich, *"Davon haben wir nichts gewusst,"* 123–46.

93. Dörner, *"Heimtücke,"* 255–75.

94. Drobisch and Wieland, *System der NS-Konzentrationslager*, 239.

95. StA München, Staatsanwaltschaften 4849, Bl. 2–5: Geheime Staatspolizei—Staatspolizeistelle München, 11 May 1939; StA München, Staatsanwaltschaften 4849, Bl. 7, Vernehmung des Michael S., 11 May 1939; StA München, Staatsanwaltschaften 4849, Bl. 11. Such denunciations for personal reasons were common in Nazi Germany, with people trying to settle private conflicts with the help of the authorities; see Gellately, *The Gestapo and German Society.*

96. See Evans, "Coercion and Consent in Nazi Germany."

97. Kogon, *Theory and Practice of Hell*, 40.

98. Behnken, *Deutschland-Berichte der Sopade*, 2:372.

99. BAB, R 3001/21088, Bl. 160.

100. IfZ, Fa 199/29, Bl. 148–50.

101. BAB, NS 4 BU/33.

102. Archiv Dachau, 8644.

103. BAB, NS 4 BU/33.

104. Quoted in Schley, *Nachbar Buchenwald*, 37.

105. BAB, NS 4/Fl. 342. The original document is wrongly dated 1938. Our thanks to Johannes Ibel for confirming our dating. On Salpeter, a top manager in the ss economy, see Allen, *The Business of Genocide*, 79–83.

106. Quoted in Steinbacher, *Dachau*, 179.

107. BAB, NS 4 BU/33.

108. Archiv Dachau 8643. Our thanks to Christopher Dillon for sharing this document with us.

109. FZH 353-1, copy of BayHStA Abt. II, Geheimes StA, Reichsstatthalter 823.

110. In November 1938 the Nazis demanded that German Jews pay 1 billion Reichsmark to "cover" the damages to Jewish property during the pogrom.

111. WL, B. 216.

112. Andreas-Friedrich, *Der Schattenmann*, 49–50. Ruth Andreas-Friedrich (1901–77) was a journalist and anti-Nazi activist.

113. "They" are Jewish men who had been taken to the concentration camps in the pogrom's aftermath.

114. Dokumentationsarchiv des österreichischen Widerstandes, *Widerstand und Verfolgung in Oberösterreich*, 2:587.

115. StA München, Nr. 4849, Bl. 10. Our thanks to Paul Moore for sharing this document with us.

116. BAB, NS 4 BU/31, Bl. 18.

BIBLIOGRAPHY

Archival Sources

Archiv Buchenwald
Archiv Dachau
Archiv Sachsenhausen
Bayerisches Hauptstaatsarchiv Munich
Brandenburgisches Landeshauptarchiv Potsdam
Bundesarchiv Berlin
Bundesarchiv Dahlwitz-Hoppegarten
Dokumentationsarchiv des Österreichischen Widerstands, Vienna
Forschungsstelle für Zeitgeschichte, Hamburg
Geheimes Staatsarchiv Preußischer Kulturbesitz, Berlin-Dahlem
Hauptstaatsarchiv Düsseldorf
Hessisches Staatsarchiv Darmstadt
Institut für Zeitgeschichte, Munich
International Committee of the Red Cross Archives, Geneva
International Tracing Service, Bad Arolsen
Landesarchiv Berlin
Leo Baeck Institute
National Archives, Kew
Niedersächsisches Hauptstaatsarchiv Hannover
Politisches Archiv des Auswärtigen Amts, Berlin
Staatsarchiv Chemnitz
Staatsarchiv Munich
Staatsarchiv Oldenburg
United States Holocaust Memorial Museum, Washington DC
Wiener Library, London

Published Sources

Aaron, Gillette. "Guido Landra and the Office of Racial Studies in Fascist Italy." *Holocaust and Genocide Studies* 16 (2002): 357–75.
Abraham, Max. "Juda verrecke: Ein Rabbiner im Konzentrationslager." In

Konzentrationslager Oranienburg: Augenzeugenberichte aus dem Jahre 1933. Gerhart Seger. Reichstagsabgeordneter der SPD. Max Abraham. Prediger aus Rathenow, ed. Irene A. Diekmann and Klaus Wettig, 113–67. Potsdam: Verlag für Berlin-Brandenburg, 2004.

Abzug, Robert H. *Inside the Vicious Heart.* New York: Oxford University Press, 1985.

Allen, Michael Thad. *The Business of Genocide: The SS, Slave Labor, and the Concentration Camps.* Chapel Hill: University of North Carolina Press, 2002.

Aly, Götz. *Hitlers Volksstaat: Raub, Rassenkrieg, und nationaler Sozialismus.* Frankfurt am Main: S. Fischer, 2005.

Aly, Götz, et al., eds. *Die Verfolgung und Ermordung der europäischen Juden durch das nationalsozialistische Deutschland, 1933–1945.* 16 projected vols. Munich: Oldenbourg, 2008–.

Andreas-Friedrich, Ruth. *Der Schattenmann: Tagebuchaufzeichnungen 1938–1945.* Berlin: Suhrkamp, 1947.

Arendt, Hannah. *The Origins of Totalitarianism.* 1951. San Diego: Harcourt, 1976.

Asgodom, Sabine, ed. *"Halts Maul—sonst kommst nach Dachau": Frauen und Männer der Arbeiterbewegung berichten über Widerstand und Verfolgung unter dem Nationalsozialismus.* Cologne: Bund-Verlag, 1983.

Ayaß, Wolfgang. *"Asoziale" im Nationalsozialismus.* Stuttgart: Klett-Cotta, 1995.

———, ed. *"Gemeinschaftsfremde": Quellen zur Verfolgung von "Asozialen" 1933–1945.* Koblenz: Bundesarchiv, 1998.

———. "Keiner hat die Bettler vor der Razzia gewarnt: Wie Wohlfahrtsverbände, Presse und Rundfunk Hand in Hand mit den Nazis gegen die Armen vorgingen." *Frankfurter Rundschau,* 11 September 1993, 14.

Baganz, Carina. *Erziehung zur "Volksgemeinschaft"? Die frühen Konzentrationslager in Sachsen, 1933–34/37.* Berlin: Metropol, 2005.

Baird, Jay W. *To Die for Germany: Heroes in the Nazi Pantheon.* Bloomington: Indiana University Press, 1992.

Bajohr, Frank. *Parvenüs und Profiteure: Korruption in der NS-Zeit.* Frankfurt am Main: S. Fischer, 2001.

Bankier, David, ed. *Probing the Depths of German Antisemitism: German Society and the Persecution of the Jews, 1933–1941.* New York: Berghahn, 2000.

Barkow, Ben, Raphael Gross, and Michael Lenarz, eds. *Novemberpogrom 1938: Die Augenzeugenberichte der Wiener Library, London.* Frankfurt am Main: Jüdischer Verlag, 2008.

Behnken, Klaus, ed. *Deutschland-Berichte der Sopade.* 7 vols. Frankfurt am Main: Zweitausendeins, 1980.

Beimler, Hans. *Im Mörderlager Dachau: Vier Wochen in den Händen der braunen Banditen.* Moscow: Verlagsgenossenschaft ausländischer Arbeiter, 1933.

Benz, Wolfgang. "Mitglieder der Häftlingsgesellschaft auf Zeit: 'Die Aktions-juden' 1938/39." In *Das Konzentrationslager Dachau*, ed. Wolfgang Benz and Angelika Königseder, 207–18. Berlin: Metropol, 2008.

Benz, Wolfgang, and Barbara Distel, eds. *Herrschaft und Gewalt: Frühe Konzentrationslager 1933–1939*. Berlin: Metropol, 2002.

———, eds. *Instrumentarium der Macht: Frühe Konzentrationslager 1933–1937*. Berlin: Metropol, 2003.

———, eds. *Der Ort des Terrors: Geschichte der nationalsozialistischen Konzentrationslager*. 9 vols. Munich: C. H. Beck, 2005–9.

———, eds. *Terror ohne System: Die ersten Konzentrationslager im Nationalsozialismus, 1933–1935*. Berlin: Metropol, 2001.

Benz, Wolfgang, and Angelika Königseder, eds. *Das Konzentrationslager Dachau: Geschichte und Wirkung nationalsozialistischer Repression*. Berlin: Metropol, 2008.

Bessel, Richard. "The Nazi Capture of Power." *Journal of Contemporary History* 39 (2004): 169–88.

———. "The Potempa Murder." *Central European History* 10 (1977): 241–54.

Bessmann, Alyn. "The Camp Prison at the Ravensbrück Women's Concentration Camp." In *Ravensbrück: The Cell Building*, ed. Insa Eschebach, 17–49. Berlin: Metropol, 2008.

Blasius, Dirk. *Weimars Ende: Bürgerkrieg und Politik, 1930–1933*. Göttingen: Vandenhoeck & Ruprecht, 2005.

Botz, Gerhard. *Wien vom "Anschluß" zum Krieg: Nationalsozialistische Machtübernahme und politisch-soziale Umgestaltung am Beispiel der Stadt Wien, 1938/39*. 2nd ed. Vienna: Jugend und Volk, 1980.

Braunbuch über Reichstagsbrand und Hitler-Terror. Foreword by Lord Marley. Basle: Universum-Bücherei, 1933.

Bräutigam, Helmut, and Oliver C. Gliech. "Nationalsozialistische Zwangslager in Berlin I: Die 'wilden' Konzentrationslager und Folterkeller 1933/34." In *Berlin-Forschungen*, ed. Wolfgang Ribbe, 2:141–78. Berlin: Colloquium Verlag, 1987.

Broszat, Martin, ed. *Kommandant in Auschwitz: Autobiographische Aufzeichnungen von Rudolf Höß*. 2nd ed. Stuttgart: DVA, 1961.

———. "Nationalsozialistische Konzentrationslager, 1933–1945." In *Anatomie des SS-Staates*, ed. Hans Buchheim, Martin Broszat, Hans-Adolf Jacobsen and Helmut Krausnick, 323–445. Munich: dtv, 2005.

———. *Der Staat Hitlers*. Munich: dtv, 1969.

Buchheim, Hans, Martin Broszat, Hans-Adolf Jacobsen, and Helmut Krausnick, eds. *Anatomie des SS-Staates*. Munich: dtv, 2005.

Buchmann, Erika. *Die Frauen von Ravensbrück*. East-Berlin: Kongress-Verlag, 1959.

Bullen, Roger, et al., eds. *Ideas into Politics: Aspects of European History, 1880 to 1950*. London: Croom Helm, 1984.

Burckhardt, Carl J. *Meine Danziger Mission, 1937–1939*. Munich: DW Callwey, 1960.

Burkhardt, Hugo. *Tanz mal Jude! Von Dachau bis Shanghai. Meine Erlebnisse in den Konzentrationslagern Dachau, Buchenwald, Getto Shanghai. 1933–1948*. Nuremberg: Reichenbach, 1967.

Burleigh, Michael. *Death and Deliverance: "Euthanasia" in Germany, c. 1900–1945*. Cambridge: Cambridge University Press, 1994.

Büttner, Ursula, ed. *Das Unrechtsregime: Internationale Forschung über den Nationalsozialismus, Band 1: Ideologie—Herrschaftssystem—Wirkung in Europa*. Hamburg: Christians, 1986.

Caplan, Jane. "Gender and the Concentration Camps." In *Concentration Camps in Nazi Germany: The New Histories*, ed. Jane Caplan and Nikolaus Wachsmann, 82–107. London: Routledge, 2010.

———. Introduction. In *The Women's Camp in Moringen: A Memoir of Imprisonment in Germany, 1936–1937*, by Gabriele Herz, ed. Jane Caplan, 1–55. New York: Berghahn, 2006.

———. "Political Detention and the Origins of the Concentration Camps in Nazi Germany, 1933–1935/6." In *Nazism, War and Genocide*, ed. Neil Gregor, 22–41. Exeter: Exeter University Press, 2005.

———, ed. *Short Oxford History of Germany: Nazi Germany*. Oxford: Oxford University Press 2008.

Caplan, Jane, and Nikolaus Wachsmann, eds. *Concentration Camps in Nazi Germany: The New Histories*. London: Routledge, 2010.

———. "Introduction: The Nazi Concentration Camps, 1933–1945." In *Concentration Camps in Nazi Germany: The New Histories*, ed. Jane Caplan and Nikolaus Wachsmann, 1–16. London: Routledge, 2010.

Cesarani, David. *Eichmann: His Life, Crimes and Legacy*. London: Heinemann, 2004.

Comité International de Dachau, ed. *Konzentrationslager Dachau*. Brussels: Comité International de Dachau, 1978.

Conze, Eckart, Norbert Frei, Peter Hayes, and Moshe Zimmermann. *Das Amt und die Vergangenheit: Deutsche Diplomaten im Dritten Reich und der Bundesrepublik*. Munich: Blessing, 2010.

Daxelmüller, Christoph. "Kulturelle Formen und Aktivitäten als Teil der Überlebens- und Vernichtungsstrategie in den Konzentrationslagern." In *Die nationalsozialistischen Konzentrationslager: Entwicklung und Struktur*, vol. 2, ed. Ulrich Herbert, Karin Orth, and Christoph Dieckmann, 983–1005. Göttingen: Wallstein, 1998.

Diehl-Thiele, Peter. *Partei und Staat im Dritten Reich: Untersuchungen zum Verhältnis von* NSDAP *und allgemeiner innerer Staatsverwaltung, 1933–1945.* Munich: C. H. Beck, 1971.

Diekmann, Irene A., and Klaus Wettig, eds. *Konzentrationslager Oranienburg: Augenzeugenberichte aus dem Jahre 1933. Gerhart Seger. Reichstagsabgeordneter der* SPD. *Max Abraham. Prediger aus Rathenow.* Potsdam: Verlag für Berlin-Brandenburg, 2004.

Diercks, Herbert. "Fuhlsbüttel—das Konzentrationslager in der Verantwortung der Hamburger Justiz." In *Terror ohne System: Die ersten Konzentrationslager im Nationalsozialismus, 1933–1935,* ed. Wolfgang Benz and Barbara Distel, 261–308. Berlin: Metropol, 2001.

Diestelkamp, Bernhard, and Michael Stolleis, eds. *Justizalltag im Dritten Reich.* Frankfurt am Main: Fischer, 1988.

Dillon, Christopher. "'We'll meet again in Dachau!': The Early Dachau SS and the Narrative of Civil War." *Journal of Contemporary History* 45 (July 2010): 535–54.

Distel, Barbara. "Frauen in nationalsozialistischen Konzentrationslagern—Opfer und Täterinnen." In *Der Ort des Terrors: Geschichte der nationalsozialistischen Konzentrationslager,* ed. Wolfgang Benz and Barbara Distel, 1:195–209. Munich: C. H. Beck, 2005.

Długoborski, Wacław, and Franciszek Piper, eds. *Auschwitz, 1940–1945.* 5 vols. Oświęcim: State Museum, 2000.

Dokumentationsarchiv des österreichischen Widerstandes, ed. *Widerstand und Verfolgung in Oberösterreich: Eine Dokumentation.* Vol. 2. Vienna: Österreichischer Bundesverlag, 1982.

Dokumente über die Behandlung deutscher Staatsangehöriger in Deutschland, 1938–39. London: H.M. Stationery Office, 1940.

Domarus, Max, ed. *Hitler: Reden und Proklamationen, 1932–1945.* 4 vols. Wiesbaden: Löwit, 1973.

Dörner, Bernward. *"Heimtücke": Das Gesetz als Waffe: Kontrolle, Abschreckung und Verfolgung in Deutschland, 1933–1945.* Paderborn: Schöningh, 1998.

———. "Das Konzentrationslager Oranienburg und die Justiz." In *Konzentrationslager Oranienburg,* ed. Günter Morsch, 67–77. Berlin: Edition Hentrich, 1994.

———. "Ein KZ in der Mitte der Stadt: Oranienburg." In *Terror ohne System: Die ersten Konzentrationslager im Nationalsozialismus, 1933–1935,* ed. Wolfgang Benz and Barbara Distel, 1:123–38. Berlin: Metropol, 2001.

Döscher, Hans-Jürgen. *Das Auswärtige Amt im Dritten Reich: Diplomatie im Schatten der "Endlösung".* Berlin: Siedler, 1987.

Drobisch, Klaus. "Zeitgenössische Berichte über Nazikonzentrationslager, 1933–1939." *Jahrbuch für Geschichte* 26 (1982): 103–33.

Drobisch, Klaus, and Günther Wieland. *System der NS-Konzentrationslager, 1933–1939*. Berlin: Akademie Verlag, 1993.

Dwork, Debórah, and Robert Jan van Pelt. *Auschwitz, 1270 to the Present*. New York: Norton, 1997.

Eberle, Annette. "'Asoziale' und 'Berufsverbrecher': Dachau als Ort der 'Vorbeugehaft.'" In *Das Konzentrationslager Dachau: Geschichte und Wirkung nationalsozialistischer Repression*, ed. Wolfgang Benz and Angelika Königseder, 253–68. Berlin: Metropol, 2008.

———. "Häftlingskategorien und Kennzeichnungen." In *Der Ort des Terrors: Geschichte der nationalsozialistischen Konzentrationslager*, ed. Wolfgang Benz and Barbara Distel, 1:91–109. Munich: C. H. Beck, 2005.

Ecker, Fritz. "Die Hölle Dachau." In *Konzentrationslager: Ein Appell an das Gewissen der Welt. Die Opfer klagen an*, 13–53. Karlsbad: Verlagsanstalt Graphia, 1934.

Eley, Geoff. "Hitler's Silent Majority? Conformity and Resistance under the Third Reich (Part 2)." *Michigan Quarterly Review* 42 (2003): 550–83.

Endlich, Stefanie. "Die Lichtenburg, 1933–1939: Haftort politischer Prominenz und Frauen-KZ." In *Herrschaft und Gewalt. Frühe Konzentrationslager 1933–1939*, ed. Wolfgang Benz and Barbara Distel, 11–64. Berlin: Metropol, 2002.

Erpel, Simone, ed. *Im Gefolge der SS: Aufseherinnen des Frauen-KZ Ravensbrück*. Berlin: Metropol, 2007.

Eschebach, Insa, ed. *Ravensbrück. The Cell Building*. Berlin: Metropol, 2008.

———. "Karl Otto Koch, Concentration Camp Commandant (1897–1945)." In *From Sachsenburg to Sachsenhausen*, ed. Günter Morsch, 49–54.

Evans, Richard J. "Coercion and Consent in Nazi Germany." *Proceedings of the British Academy* 151 (2006): 53–81.

———. *The Coming of the Third Reich*. London: Allen Lane, 2003.

———, ed. *The German Underworld: Deviants and Outcasts in German History*. London: Routledge, 1988.

———. "Social Outsiders in German History: From the Sixteenth Century to 1933." In *Social Outsiders in Nazi Germany*, ed. Robert Gellately and Nathan Stoltzfus, 20–44. Princeton NJ: Princeton University Press, 2001.

———. *The Third Reich in Power*. London: Allen Lane, 2005.

Fackler, Guido. "Cultural Behaviour and the Invention of Traditions: Music and Musical Practices in the Early Concentration Camps." *Journal of Contemporary History* 45 (July 2010): 601–27.

———. "*Des Lagers Stimme*": *Musik im KZ. Alltag und Häftlingskultur in den Konzentrationslagern 1933 bis 1936*. Bremen: Edition Temmen, 2000.

Fahrenberg, Henning, and Nicole Hördler. "Das Frauen-Konzentrationslager

Lichtenburg." In *Lichtenburg. Ein deutsches Konzentrationslager*, ed. Stefan Hördler and Sigrid Jacobeit, 166–89. Berlin: Metropol, 2009.

Faust, Anselm, ed. *Die "Kristallnacht" im Rheinland: Dokumente zum Judenpogrom im November 1938*. Düsseldorf: Schwan, 1987.

Favez, Jean-Claude. *Warum schwieg das Rote Kreuz? Eine internationale Organisation im Dritten Reich*. Munich: dtv, 1994.

Favre, Muriel. "'Wir können vielleicht die Schlafräume besichtigen': Originalton einer Reportage aus dem KZ Oranienburg (1933)." *Rundfunk und Geschichte* 24 (1998): 164–70.

Fleck, Christian, Albert Müller and Nico Stehr. "Nachwort." In *Die Gesellschaft des Terrors: Innenansichten der Konzentrationslager Dachau und Buchenwald*, ed. Paul Martin Neurath, 409–54. Frankfurt am Main: Suhrkamp, 2004.

Freund, Florian, and Bertrand Perz. "Mauthausen—Stammlager." In *Der Ort des Terrors: Geschichte der nationalsozialistischen Konzentrationslager*, ed. Wolfgang Benz and Barbara Distel, 4:293–346. Munich: C. H. Beck, 2006.

Freund, Julius. *O Buchenwald!* Klagenfurt: self-published, 1945.

Friedlander, Henry, and Sybil Milton, eds. *Archives of the Holocaust: Berlin Document Center*. New York: Garland, 1992.

Friedländer, Saul. *Nazi Germany and the Jews*. Vol. 1, *The Years of Persecution*. London: Weidenfeld and Nicholson, 1997.

Friedman, Tuviah. *Der Personal-Akt des SS-Obergruppenfuehrers Theo Eicke: Chef der Konzentrations-Lager im Dritten Reich. Seine Briefe an SS-Reichsfuehrer Himmler in den Jahren 1933–1943*. Haifa: Institute of Documentation in Israel for the Investigation of Nazi War Crimes, 1994.

Fritzsche, Peter. "The NSDAP, 1919–1934: From Fringe Politics to the Seizure of Power." In *Short Oxford History of Germany: Nazi Germany*, ed. Jane Caplan, 48–72. Oxford: Oxford University Press, 2008.

Fröhlich, Elke, ed. *Die Tagebücher von Joseph Goebbels, Teil 1: Aufzeichnungen, 1923–1941*. Munich: K. G. Saur, 1998.

Füllberg-Stolberg, Claus, Martina Jung, Renate Riebe, and Martina Scheitenberger. "Einleitung." In *Frauen in Konzentrationslagern: Bergen-Belsen, Ravensbrück*, ed. Claus Füllberg-Stolberg, Martina Jung, Renate Riebe, and Martina Scheitenberger, 7–12. Bremen: Edition Temmen, 1994.

Füllberg-Stolberg, Claus, Martina Jung, Renate Riebe and Martina Scheitenberger, eds. *Frauen in Konzentrationslagern: Bergen-Belsen, Ravensbrück*. Bremen: Edition Temmen, 1994.

Garbe, Detlef. "Erst verhasst, dann geschätzt—Zeugen Jehovahs als Häftlinge im KZ Dachau." In *Das Konzentrationslager Dachau: Geschichte und Wirkung nationalsozialistischer Repression*, ed. Wolfgang Benz and Angelika Königseder, 219–36. Berlin: Metropol Verlag, 2008.

———. "Neuengamme—Stammlager." In *Der Ort des Terrors: Geschichte der nationalsozialistischen Konzentrationslager*, ed. Wolfgang Benz and Barbara Distel, 5:315–46. Munich: C. H. Beck, 2007.

———. "Selbstbehauptung und Widerstand." In *Der Ort des Terrors: Geschichte der nationalsozialistischen Konzentrationslager*, ed. Wolfgang Benz and Barbara Distel, 1:242–57. Munich: C. H. Beck, 2005.

———. *Zwischen Widerstand und Martyrium: Die Zeugen Jehovahs im "Dritten Reich"*. Munich: Oldenbourg, 1994.

Gellately, Robert. *Backing Hitler: Consent and Coercion in Nazi Germany*. Oxford: Oxford University Press, 2001.

———. *The Gestapo and German Society: Enforcing Racial Policy, 1933–1945*. Oxford: Clarendon Press, 1991.

———. "Social Outsiders and the Consolidation of Hitler's Dictatorship, 1933–1939." In *Nazism, War, and Genocide: Essays in Honour of Jeremy Noakes*, ed. Neil Gregor, 56–74. Exeter: Exeter University Press, 2005.

Gellately, Robert, and Nathan Stoltzfus, eds. *Social Outsiders in Nazi Germany*. Princeton NJ: Princeton University Press, 2001.

Gerwarth, Robert. *Hitler's Hangman: The Life of Reinhard Heydrich*. New Haven: Yale University Press, 2011.

Giles, Geoffrey J. "The Institutionalization of Homosexual Panic in the Third Reich." In *Social Outsiders in Nazi Germany*, ed. Robert Gellately and Nathan Stoltzfus, 233–55. Princeton NJ: Princeton University Press, 2001.

Goeschel, Christian. "Suicide in Nazi Concentration Camps, 1933–9." *Journal of Contemporary History* 45 (July 2010): 628–48.

———. *Suicide in Nazi Germany*. Oxford: Oxford University Press, 2009.

Goeschel, Christian, and Nikolaus Wachsmann. "Before Auschwitz: The Formation of the Nazi Concentration Camps, 1933–9." *Journal of Contemporary History* 45 (July 2010): 515–34.

Göhring, Ludwig. *Dachau, Flossenbürg, Neuengamme: Eine antifaschistische Biographie*. Schkeuditz: GNN-Verlag, 1999.

Gostner, Erwin. *1000 Tage im KZ: Ein Erlebnisbericht aus den Konzentrationslagern Dachau, Mauthausen und Gusen*. Innsbruck: self-published, 1945.

Gräf, Hugo. "Prügelstrafe." *Die Neue Weltbühne* 23 (1936): 353–58.

Gregor, Neil, ed. *Nazism, War, and Genocide: Essays in Honour of Jeremy Noakes*. Exeter: Exeter University Press, 2005.

Greschat, Martin. "Kirche und Widerstand gegen den Nationalsozialismus." *Zeitschrift für Geschichtswissenschaft* 46 (1998): 875–88.

Gritschneder, Otto. *"Der Führer hat Sie zum Tode verurteilt . . .": Hitlers "Röhm-Putsch"-Morde vor Gericht*. Munich: C. H. Beck, 1993.

Gruchmann, Lothar. *Justiz im Dritten Reich: Anpassung und Unterwerfung in der Ära Gürtner, 1933–1940*. 2nd ed. Munich: Oldenbourg, 1990.

Grunewald, Michel. "Kritik und politischer Kampf: Der Fall 'Der Gegen-Angriff.'" In *Deutsche Exilpresse und Frankreich 1933–1940*, ed. Hélène Roussel, 237–47. Berne: Peter Lang, 1992.

Haag, Lina. *Eine Handvoll Staub: Widerstand einer Frau 1933–1945*. Frankfurt am Main: Fischer, 1995.

Hackett, David A., ed. *The Buchenwald Report*. Boulder CO: Westview Press, 1995.

Hahn, Judith. *Grawitz, Genzken, Gebhardt: Drei Karrieren im Sanitätsdienst der SS*. Münster: Klemm & Oelschläger, 2008.

———, ed. *Medizin im Nationalsozialismus und das System der Konzentrationslager: Beiträge eines interdisziplinären Symposiums*. Frankfurt am Main: Mabuse-Verlag, 2005.

Hale, O. J. *The Captive Press in the Third Reich*. Princeton NJ: Princeton University Press, 1964.

Harris, Victoria. "The Role of the Concentration Camps in the Nazi Repression of Prostitutes, 1933–9." *Journal of Contemporary History* 45 (July 2010): 675–98.

Hartewig, Karin. "Wolf unter Wölfen? Die prekäre Macht der kommunistischen Kapos im Konzentrationslager Buchenwald." In *Die nationalsozialistischen Konzentrationslager: Entwicklung und Struktur*, vol. 2, ed. Ulrich Herbert, Karin Orth and Christoph Dieckmann, 939–58. Göttingen: Wallstein, 1998.

Hax, Iris. "Sterilisierung und Kastration von Häftlingen des KZ Sachsenhausen." In *Medizin im Nationalsozialismus und das System der Konzentrationslager: Beiträge eines interdisziplinären Symposiums*, ed. Judith Hahn, 66–90. Frankfurt am Main: Mabuse-Verlag, 2005.

Heiber, Helmut, ed. *Reichsführer! . . . Briefe an und von Himmler*. Stuttgart: DVA, 1968.

Heike, Irmtraud. "'. . . da es sich ja lediglich um die Bewachung der Häftlinge handelt . . . ': Lagerverwaltung und Bewachungspersonal." In *Frauen in Konzentrationslagern: Bergen-Belsen, Ravensbrück*, ed. Claus Füllberg-Stolberg, Martina Jung, Renate Riebe, and Martina Scheitenberger, 221–40. Bremen: Edition Temmen, 1994.

Hennig, Eike, ed. *Hessen unterm Hakenkreuz: Studien zur Durchsetzung der NSDAP in Hessen*. Frankfurt am Main: Insel Verlag, 1983.

Hensle, Michael P. "Die Verrechtlichung des Unrechts: Der legalistische Rahmen der nationalsozialistischen Verfolgung." In *Der Ort des Terrors: Geschichte der nationalsozialistischen Konzentrationslager*, ed. Wolfgang Benz and Barbara Distel, 1:76–90. Munich: C. H. Beck, 2005.

Herbert, Ulrich. *Best: Biographische Studien über Radikalismus, Weltanschauung und Vernunft, 1903–1989*. Bonn: Dietz, 1996.

————. "Von der Gegnerbekämpfung zur 'rassischen Generalprävention':
'Schutzhaft' und Konzentrationslager in der Konzeption der Gestapo-Füh-
rung 1933–1939." In *Die nationalsozialistischen Konzentrationslager: Entwicklung und Struktur*, vol. 1, ed. Ulrich Herbert, Karin Orth, and Christoph Dieckmann, 60–86. Göttingen: Wallstein, 1998.

Herbert, Ulrich, Karin Orth, and Christoph Dieckmann, eds. *Die nationalsozialistischen Konzentrationslager: Entwicklung und Struktur*. Göttingen:
Wallstein, 1998.

Herf, Jeffrey. *The Jewish Enemy: Nazi Propaganda during World War II and
the Holocaust*. Cambridge MA: Harvard University Press, 2006.

Herz, Gabriele. *The Women's Camp in Moringen: A Memoir of Imprisonment
in Germany, 1936–1937*. Ed. Jane Caplan. New York: Berghahn, 2006.

Hesse, Hans. "Moringen." In *Der Ort des Terrors: Geschichte der nationalsozialistischen Konzentrationslager*, ed. Wolfgang Benz and Barbara Distel,
2:160–68. Munich: C. H. Beck, 2005.

————, ed. *Persecution and Resistance of Jehovah's Witnesses during the Nazi
Regime, 1933–1945*. Bremen: Edition Temmen, 2001.

Hett, Benjamin Carter. *Crossing Hitler: The Man Who Put the Nazis on the
Witness Stand*. Oxford: Oxford University Press, 2008.

Heyningen, Elizabeth van. "The Concentration Camps of the South African
(Anglo-Boer) War, 1900–1902." *History Compass* 7 (2009): 22–43.

Hirte, Chris. *Erich Mühsam: "Ihr seht mich nicht feige."* Berlin: Verlag Neues
Leben, 1985.

Hofmann, Thomas, Hanno Loewy, and Harry Stein, eds. *Pogromnacht und
Holocaust: Frankfurt, Weimar, Buchenwald. Die schwierige Erinnerung
an die Stationen der Vernichtung*. Cologne: Böhlau, 1994.

Hohmann, Joachim S., and Günther Wieland, eds. *Konzentrationslager Sachsenhausen bei Oranienburg, 1939–1944: Die Aufzeichnungen des KZ-Häftlings
Rudolf Wunderlich*. Frankfurt am Main: Peter Lang, 1997.

Hördler, Stefan, and Sigrid Jacobeit, eds. *Lichtenburg: Ein deutsches Konzentrationslager*. Berlin: Metropol, 2009.

Horwitz, Gordon. *In the Shadow of Death: Living outside the Gates of Mauthausen*. London: I. B. Tauris, 1991.

Höß, Rudolf. *Kommandant in Auschwitz: Autobiographische Aufzeichnungen von Rudolf Höß*. Ed. Martin Broszat. 2nd ed. Stuttgart: DVA, 1961.

Housden, Martyn. *Hans Frank: Lebensraum and the Holocaust*. Basingstoke:
Palgrave Macmillan, 2003.

Jäckel, Eberhard, and Axel Kuhn, eds. *Hitler: Sämtliche Aufzeichnungen, 1905–
1924*. Stuttgart: DVA, 1980.

Jahnke, K. H. "Heinz Eschen—Kapo des Judenblocks im Konzentrationslager
Dachau bis 1938." *Dachauer Hefte* 7 (1991): 24–33.

Jansen, Christian, et al., eds. *Von der Aufgabe der Freiheit. Politische Verant-wortung und bürgerliche Gesellschaft im 19. und 20. Jahrhundert: Fest-schrift für Hans Mommsen zum 5. November 1995*. Berlin: Akademie-Verlag, 1995.

Jaskot, Paul B. *The Architecture of Oppression: The SS, Forced Labor and the Nazi Monumental Building Economy*. London: Routledge, 2000.

Jellonnek, Burkhard. *Homosexuelle unter dem Hakenkreuz: Die Verfolgung von Homosexuellen im Dritten Reich*. Paderborn: Schöningh, 1990.

Johe, Werner. "Das deutsche Volk und die Konzentrationslager." In *Das Un-rechtsregime: Internationale Forschung über den Nationalsozialismus, Band 1: Ideologie—Herrschaftssystem—Wirkung in Europa*, ed. Ursula Büttner, 331–46. Hamburg: Christians, 1986.

———. *Neuengamme: Zur Geschichte der Konzentrationslager in Hamburg*. Hamburg: Landeszentrale für politische Bildung, 1982.

Jürgens, Christian. *Fritz Solmitz: Kommunalpolitiker, Journalist und NS-Ver-folgter aus Lübeck*. Lübeck: Schmidt-Römhild, undated [1996].

Kaienburg, Hermann. "Sachsenhausen—Stammlager." In *Der Ort des Terrors: Geschichte der nationalsozialistischen Konzentrationslager*, ed. Wolfgang Benz and Barbara Distel, 3:17–72. Munich: C. H. Beck, 2006.

———. *Die Wirtschaft der SS*. Berlin: Metropol, 2003.

Kaplan, Marion. *Between Dignity and Despair: Jewish Life in Nazi Germany*. New York: Oxford University Press, 1998.

Kautsky, Benedikt. *Teufel und Verdammte: Erfahrungen und Erkenntnisse aus sieben Jahren in deutschen Konzentrationslagern*. Zurich: Büchergil-de Gutenberg, 1946.

Kent, Madeleine. *I Married a German*. London: Allen and Unwin, 1938.

Kershaw, Ian. "'Cumulative Radicalisation' and the Uniqueness of National So-cialism." In *Von der Aufgabe der Freiheit: Politische Verantwortung und bürgerliche Gesellschaft im 19. und 20. Jahrhundert: Festschrift für Hans Mommsen zum 5. November 1995*, ed. Christian Jansen et al., 323–36. Berlin: Akademie-Verlag, 1995.

———. *Hitler, 1936–45: Nemesis*. London: Allen Lane, 2000.

———. *The "Hitler Myth": Image and Reality in the Third Reich*. Oxford: Ox-ford University Press, 1987.

———. *The Nazi Dictatorship: Problems and Perspectives of Interpretation*. 4th ed. London: Edward Arnold, 2000.

———. *Popular Opinion and Political Dissent in the Third Reich: Bavaria, 1933–1945*. Oxford: Oxford University Press, 1983.

Kersten, Lee. "'The Times' und das KZ Dachau: Ein unveröffentlichter Artikel aus dem Jahr 1933." *Dachauer Hefte* 12 (1996): 104–22.

Kienle, Markus. "Das Konzentrationslager Heuberg in Stetten am kalten Markt." In *Terror ohne System. Die ersten Konzentrationslager im Nationalsozialismus, 1933–1935,* ed. Wolfgang Benz and Barbara Distel, 41–64. Berlin: Metropol, 2001.

Klee, Ernst. *Das Personenlexikon zum Dritten Reich.* Frankfurt am Main: Fischer, 2003.

Klemperer, Victor. *The Language of the Third Reich: A Philologist's Notebook.* London: Continuum, 2002.

Knoch, Habbo. "Die Emslandlager, 1933–1945." In *Der Ort des Terrors: Geschichte der nationalsozialistischen Konzentrationslager,* ed. Wolfgang Benz and Barbara Distel, 2:531–70. Munich: C. H. Beck, 2005.

Knoll, Albert. "Homosexuelle Häftlinge im KZ Dachau." In *Das Konzentrationslager Dachau: Geschichte und Wirkung nationalsozialistischer Repression,* ed. Wolfgang Benz and Angelika Königseder, 237–52. Berlin: Metropol, 2008.

Koehl, Robert Lewis. *The Black Corps: The Structure and Power Struggles of the Nazi SS.* Madison: University of Wisconsin Press, 1983.

Kogon, Eugen. *The Theory and Practice of Hell: The German Concentration Camps and the System behind Them.* Trans. Heinz Norden. 1946. New York: Farrar, Straus and Giroux, 2006.

Königseder, Angelika. "Die Entwicklung des KZ-Systems." In *Der Ort des Terrors: Geschichte der nationalsozialistischen Konzentrationslager,* ed. Wolfgang Benz and Barbara Distel, 1:3–42. Munich: C. H. Beck, 2005.

Konzentrationslager: Ein Appell an das Gewissen der Welt. Die Opfer klagen an. Karlsbad: Verlagsanstalt Graphia, 1934.

Kosthorst, Erich, and Bernd Walter, eds. *Konzentrations- und Strafgefangenenlager im Emsland, 1933–1945: Zum Verhältnis von NS-Regime und Justiz; Darstellung und Dokumentation.* Düsseldorf: Droste, 1985.

Kraiker, Gerhard, and Elke Suhr. *Carl von Ossietzky.* Reinbek: rororo, 1994.

Kramer, Alan, and John Horne. *German Atrocities, 1914: A History of Denial.* New Haven CT: Yale University Press, 2001.

Krause-Vilmar, Dietfrid. "Das Konzentrationslager Breitenau, 1933/34." In *Hessen unterm Hakenkreuz: Studien zur Durchsetzung der NSDAP in Hessen,* ed. Eike Hennig, 469–89. Frankfurt am Main: Insel Verlag, 1983.

Kropat, Wolf-Arno. *"Reichskristallnacht": Der Judenpogrom vom 7. bis 10. November 1938—Urheber, Täter, Hintergründe.* Wiesbaden: Kommission für die Geschichte der Juden in Hessen, 1997.

KZ-Gedenkstätte Flossenbürg, ed. *Concentration Camp Flossenbürg, 1938–1945.* Flossenbürg: KZ-Gedenkstätte Flossenbürg, undated.

Langhammer, Sven. "Die reichsweite Verhaftungsaktion vom 9. März 1937—eine Maßnahme zur 'Säuberung des Volkskörpers.'" *Hallische Beiträge zur Zeitgeschichte* 17 (2007): 55–77.

Langhoff, Wolfgang. *Die Moorsoldaten: 13 Monate Konzentrationslager*. Zurich: Schweizer Spiegel-Verlag, 1935.

Laqueur, Renata. *Schreiben im KZ*. Hanover: Donat, 1991.

Lautmann, Rüdiger, Winfried Grikschat, and Egbert Schmidt. "Der rosa Winkel in den nationalsozialistischen Konzentrationslagern." In *Seminar: Gesellschaft und Homosexualität*, ed. Rüdiger Lautmann, Winfried Grikschat and Egbert Schmidt, 325–65. Frankfurt am Main: Suhrkamp, 1977.

———, eds. *Seminar: Gesellschaft und Homosexualität*. Frankfurt am Main: Suhrkamp, 1977.

Lechner, Silvester. "Das Konzentrationslager Oberer Kuhberg in Ulm." In *Terror ohne System: Die ersten Konzentrationslager im Nationalsozialismus, 1933– 1935*, ed. Wolfgang Benz and Barbara Distel, 79–103. Berlin: Metropol, 2001.

Leff, Laurel. *Buried by the Times: The Holocaust and America's Most Important Newspaper*. Cambridge: Cambridge University Press, 2005.

Leleu, Jean-Luc. *La Waffen-SS: Soldats politiques en guerre*. Paris: Perrin, 2007.

Lenarczyk, Wojciech, ed. *KZ-Verbrechen: Beiträge zur Geschichte der nationalsozialistischen Konzentrationslager und ihrer Erinnerung*. Berlin: Metropol, 2007.

Leo, Annette. "Ravensbrück-Stammlager." In *Der Ort des Terrors: Geschichte der nationalsozialistischen Konzentrationslager*, ed. Wolfgang Benz and Barbara Distel, 4:473–519. Munich: C. H. Beck, 2006.

Lipstadt, Deborah E. *Beyond Belief: The American Press and the Coming of the Holocaust, 1933–1945*. New York: Free Press, 1985.

Litten, Irmgard. *Die Hölle sieht Dich an: Der Fall Litten mit einem Vorwort von Rudolf Olden*. Paris, 1940.

London, Louise. *Whitehall and the Jews, 1933–1948: British Immigration Policy, Jewish Refugees, and the Holocaust*. Cambridge: Cambridge University Press, 2000.

Longerich, Peter. *"Davon haben wir nichts gewusst!": Die Deutschen und die Judenverfolgung, 1933–1945*. Munich: Siedler, 2006.

———. *Heinrich Himmler: Biographie*. Munich: Siedler, 2008.

———. *Politik der Vernichtung: Eine Gesamtdarstellung der nationalsozialistischen Judenverfolgung*. Munich: Piper, 1998.

Lüerssen, Dirk. "'Moorsoldaten' in Esterwegen, Börgermoor, Neusustrum." In *Herrschaft und Gewalt. Frühe Konzentrationslager 1933–1939*, ed. Wolfgang Benz and Barbara Distel, 157–210. Berlin: Metropol, 2002.

———. "'Wir sind die Moorsoldaten': Die Insassen der frühen Konzentrationslager im Emsland 1933 bis 1936." Diss. rer. pol., Universität Osnabrück, 2001.

Mallmann, Klaus-Michael, and Gerhard Paul, eds. *Karrieren der Gewalt: Nationalsozialistische Täterbiographien*. Darmstadt: Wissenschaftliche Buchgesellschaft, 2004.

Marcuse, Harold. *Legacies of Dachau: The Uses and Abuses of a Concentration Camp, 1933–2001.* Cambridge: Cambridge University Press, 2001.

Maršálek, Hans. *Die Geschichte des Konzentrationslagers Mauthausen.* 3rd ed. Vienna: Österreichische Lagergemeinschaft Mauthausen, 1995.

Marxen, Klaus. "Strafjustiz im Nationalsozialismus: Vorschläge für eine Erweiterung der historischen Perspektive." In *Justizalltag im Dritten Reich,* ed. Bernhard Diestelkamp and Michael Stolleis, 101–11. Frankfurt am Main: Fischer, 1988.

Mason, Timothy W. *Arbeiterklasse und Volksgemeinschaft: Dokumente und Materialien zur deutschen Arbeiterpolitik 1936–1939.* Opladen: Westdeutscher Verlag, 1975.

Matthäus, Jürgen. "Verfolgung, Ausbeutung, Vernichtung: Jüdische Häftlinge im System der Konzentrationslager." In *Jüdische Häftlinge im Konzentrationslager Sachsenhausen 1936 bis 1945,* ed. Günter Morsch and Susanne zur Nieden, 64–90. Berlin: Hentrich, 2004.

Mayer, Irene. "Berlin-Kreuzberg (Hedemannstr.)." In *The United States Holocaust Memorial Museum Encyclopedia of Camps and Ghettos,* I/A, ed. Geoffrey P. Megargee, 35–36. Bloomington: Indiana University Press, 2009.

Mayer–von Götz, Irene. *Terror im Zentrum der Macht: Die frühen Konzentrationslager in Berlin 1933/34–1936.* Berlin: Metropol, 2008.

McElligott, Anthony. "'Sentencing towards the Führer?': The Judiciary in the Third Reich." In *Working towards the Führer: Essays in Honour of Sir Ian Kershaw,* ed. Anthony McElligott and Tim Kirk, 153–85. Manchester: Manchester University Press, 2003.

McElligott, Anthony, and Tim Kirk, eds. *Working towards the Führer: Essays in Honour of Sir Ian Kershaw.* Manchester: Manchester University Press, 2003.

Meckl, Markus. "Wuppertal-Kemna." In *Der Ort des Terrors: Geschichte der nationalsozialistischen Konzentrationslager,* ed. Wolfgang Benz and Barbara Distel, 2:220–24. Munich: C. H. Beck, 2006.

Megargee, Geoffrey P., ed. *The United States Holocaust Memorial Museum Encyclopedia of Camps and Ghettos.* Bloomington: Indiana University Press, 2009.

Merson, Allan. *Communist Resistance in Nazi Germany.* London: Lawrence and Wishart, 1985.

Mette, Sandra. "Schloss Lichtenburg: Konzentrationslager für Männer von 1933 bis 1937." In *Lichtenburg. Ein deutsches Konzentrationslager,* ed. Stefan Hördler and Sigrid Jacobeit, 130–65. Berlin: Metropol, 2009.

Meyer, Hans-Georg, and Kerstin Roth. "Zentrale staatliche Einrichtung des Landes Hessen: Das Konzentrationslager Osthofen." In *Der Ort des Terrors: Geschichte der nationalsozialistischen Konzentrationslager,* ed. Wolfgang Benz and Barbara Distel, 2:181–84. Munich: C. H. Beck, 2005.

Meyer, Winfried. "Stalinistischer Schauprozess gegen KZ-Verbrecher? Der Berliner Sachsenhausen-Prozeß vom Oktober 1947." *Dachauer Hefte* 13 (1997): 153–80.

Michaelis, Herbert, and Ernst Schraepler, eds. *Ursachen und Folgen: Vom deutschen Zusammenbruch 1918 und 1945 bis zur staatlichen Neuordnung Deutschlands in der Gegenwart.* Vol. 9. Berlin: H. Wendler, n.d.

Milton, Sybil. "Gypsies as Social Outsiders in Nazi Germany." In *Social Outsiders in Nazi Germany,* ed. Robert Gellately and Nathan Stoltzfus, 212–32. Princeton NJ: Princeton University Press, 2001.

———. "Jehovah's Witnesses: A Documentation." In *Persecution and Resistance of Jehovah's Witnesses during the Nazi Regime,* ed. Hans Hesse, 149–65. Bremen: Edition Temmen, 2001.

———. "Jehovah's Witnesses as Forgotten Victims." In *Persecution and Resistance of Jehovah's Witnesses during the Nazi Regime, 1933–1945,* ed. Hans Hesse, 141–47. Bremen: Edition Temmen, 2001.

———. "Die Konzentrationslager der dreißiger Jahre im Bild der in- und ausländischen Presse." In *Die nationalsozialistischen Konzentrationslager: Entwicklung und Struktur,* vol. 1, ed. Ulrich Herbert, Karin Orth, and Christoph Dieckmann, 135–47. Göttingen: Wallstein, 1998.

Mommsen, Hans. "Der Reichstagsbrand und seine politischen Folgen." *Vierteljahrshefte für Zeitgeschichte* 12 (1964): 351–413.

Moore, Paul. "'And what concentration camps those were!': Foreign Concentration Camps in Nazi Propaganda, 1933–1939." *Journal of Contemporary History* 45 (July 2010): 649–74.

Morsch, Günter. "Formation and Construction of the Sachsenhausen Concentration Camp." In *From Sachsenburg to Sachsenhausen: Pictures from the Photograph Album of a Concentration Camp Commandant,* ed. Günter Morsch, 87–194. Berlin: Metropol, 2007.

———, ed. *From Sachsenburg to Sachsenhausen: Pictures from the Photograph Album of a Concentration Camp Commandant.* Berlin: Metropol, 2007.

———, ed. *Jüdische Häftlinge im Konzentrationslager Sachsenhausen 1936 bis 1945.* Berlin: Edition Hentrich, 2004.

———, ed. *Konzentrationslager Oranienburg.* Berlin: Edition Hentrich, 1994.

———. "Organisations- und Verwaltungsstruktur der Konzentrationslager." In *Der Ort des Terrors: Geschichte der nationalsozialistischen Konzentrationslager,* ed. Wolfgang Benz and Barbara Distel, 1:58–75. Munich: C. H. Beck, 2005.

Morsch, Günter, and Astrid Ley, eds. *Das Konzentrationslager Sachsenhausen, 1936–1945: Ereignisse und Entwicklungen.* Berlin: Metropol, 2008.

Morsch, Günter, and Susanne zur Nieden, eds. *Jüdische Häftlinge im Konzentrationslager Sachsenhausen 1936 bis 1945.* Berlin: Edition Hentrich, 2004.

Mühsam, Kreszentia. *Der Leidensweg Erich Mühsams.* Zurich: Mopr, 1935.

Müller, Joachim, and Andreas Sternweiler, eds. *Homosexuelle Männer im* KZ *Sachsenhausen.* Berlin: Verlag Rosa Winkel, 2000.

Nationale Mahn-und Gedenkstätte Buchenwald, ed. *Buchenwald: Mahnung und Verpflichtung; Dokumente und Berichte.* 4th ed. East-Berlin: VEB Deutscher Verlag der Wissenschaften, 1983.

————, ed. *Konzentrationslager Buchenwald: Post Weimar/Thür. Katalog zu der Ausstellung aus der Deutschen Demokratischen Republik im Martin Gropius Bau Berlin (West) April–Juni 1990.* Berlin: Nationale Mahn- und Gedenkstätte Buchenwald, 1990.

Naujoks, Harry. *Mein Leben im* KZ *Sachsenhausen, 1936–1942: Erinnerungen des ehemaligen Lagerältesten.* Cologne: Pahl-Rugenstein, 1987.

Der Neue Brockhaus: Allbuch in vier Bänden und einem Atlas. Vol. 2. Leipzig: F. A. Brockhaus, 1937.

Neugebauer, Wolfgang. "Der erste Österreichertransport in das KZ Dachau." In *Das Konzentrationslager Dachau: Geschichte und Wirkung nationalsozialistischer Repression,* ed. Wolfgang Benz and Angelika Königseder, 193–206. Berlin: Metropol, 2008.

Neurath, Paul Martin. *Die Gesellschaft des Terrors: Innenansichten der Konzentrationslager Dachau und Buchenwald.* Frankfurt am Main: Suhrkamp, 2004.

Niemöller, Wilhelm, ed. *Martin Niemöller: Briefe aus der Gefangenschaft. Konzentrationslager Sachsenhausen (Oranienburg).* Bielefeld: Ludwig Bechauf Verlag, 1979.

Niethammer, Lutz, ed. *Der "gesäuberte" Antifaschismus: die* SED *und die roten Kapos von Buchenwald.* Berlin: Akademie-Verlag, 1994.

Noakes, Jeremy. "Nazism and Eugenics: The Background to the Nazi Sterilization Law of 14 July 1933." In *Ideas into Politics: Aspects of European History, 1880 to 1950,* ed. Roger Bullen et al., 74–94. London: Croom Helm, 1984.

Noakes, Jeremy, and Geoffrey Pridham, eds. *Nazism, 1919–1945: A Documentary Reader.* 4 vols. Exeter: Exeter University Press, 1998–2001.

Nürnberg, Kaspar. "Außenstelle des Berliner Polizeipräsidiums: Das 'staatliche Konzentrationslager' Sonnenburg bei Küstrin." In *Herrschaft und Gewalt. Frühe Konzentrationslager 1933–1939,* ed. Wolfgang Benz and Barbara Distel, 83–100. Berlin: Metropol, 2002.

Obenaus, Herbert. "Der Kampf um das tägliche Brot." In *Die nationalsozialistischen Konzentrationslager: Entwicklung und Struktur,* ed. Ulrich Herbert, Karin Orth and Christoph Dieckmann, 841–73. Göttingen: Wallstein, 1998.

Orth, Karin. "Bewachung." In *Der Ort des Terrors: Geschichte der nationalsozialistischen Konzentrationslager,* ed. Wolfgang Benz and Barbara Distel, 1:126–40. Munich: C. H. Beck, 2005.

———. "The Concentration Camp Personnel." In *Concentration Camps in Nazi Germany: The New Histories*, ed. Jane Caplan and Nikolaus Wachsmann, 44–57. London: Routledge, 2010.

———. "Egon Zill—ein typischer Vertreter der Konzentrationslager-SS." In *Karrieren der Gewalt: Nationalsozialistische Täterbiographien*, ed. Klaus-Michael Mallmann and Gerhard Paul, 264–73. Darmstadt: Wissenschaftliche Buchgesellschaft, 2004.

———. *Die Konzentrationslager-SS: Sozialstrukturelle Analysen und biographische Studien*. Munich: DTV, 2000.

———. *Das System der nationalsozialistischen Konzentrationslager: Eine politische Organisationsgeschichte*. Hamburg: Hamburger Edition, 1999.

Papen, Felix von. *Ein von Papen spricht . . . über seine Erlebnisse im Hitler Deutschland*. Nijmegen: G. J. Thieme, undated [c. 1939].

Patel, Kiran Klaus. *Soldiers of Labor: Labor Services in Nazi Germany and New Deal America*. Cambridge: Cambridge University Press, 2005.

Pätzold, Kurt. "Häftlingsgesellschaft." In *Der Ort des Terrors: Geschichte der nationalsozialistischen Konzentrationslager*, ed. Wolfgang Benz and Barbara Distel, 1:110–25. Munich: C. H. Beck, 2005.

Perz, Bertrand. "'. . . müssen zu reißenden Bestien erzogen werden': Der Einsatz von Hunden zur Bewachung in den Konzentrationslagern." *Dachauer Hefte* 12 (1996): 139–58.

Pingel, Falk. *Häftlinge unter SS-Herrschaft: Widerstand, Selbstbehauptung und Vernichtung im Konzentrationslager*. Hamburg: Hoffmann und Campe, 1978.

———. "Social Life in an Unsocial Environment: The Inmates' Struggle for Survival." In *Concentration Camps in Nazi Germany: The New Histories*, ed. Jane Caplan and Nikolaus Wachsmann, 58–81. London: Routledge, 2010.

Poller, Walter. *Arztschreiber in Buchenwald: Bericht des Häftlings 996 aus Block 39*. Hamburg: Phönix-Verlag/Christen & Co., 1946.

Pollmeier, Heiko. "Die Verhaftungen nach dem November-Pogrom 1938 und die Masseninternierung in den 'jüdischen Baracken' des KZ Sachsenhausen." In *Jüdische Häftlinge im Konzentrationslager Sachsenhausen 1936 bis 1945*, ed. Günter Morsch and Susanne zur Nieden, 164–79. Berlin: Edition Hentrich, 2004.

Pretzel, Andreas, and Gabriele Roßbach, eds. *Wegen der zu erwartenden hohen Strafe . . . : Homosexuellenverfolgung in Berlin 1933–1945*. Berlin: Verlag Rosa Winkel, 2000.

Der Prozess gegen die Hauptkriegsverbrecher vor dem Internationalen Militärgerichtshof Nürnberg 14. November 1945. Nuremberg, 1947.

Przyrembel, Alexandra. "Transfixed by an Image: Ilse Koch, the 'Kommandeuse of Buchenwald.'" *German History* 19 (2001): 369–99.

Rabinbach, Anson. "Staging Antifascism: The Brown Book of the Reichstag Fire and Hitler Terror." *New German Critique* 35 (2008): 97–126.

Raithel, Thomas, and Irene Strenge. "Die Reichstagsbrandverordnung: Grundlegung der Diktatur mit den Instrumenten des Weimarer Ausnahmezustands." *Vierteljahrshefte für Zeitgeschichte* 48 (2000): 413–60.

Reichssicherheitshauptamt—Amt V, ed. *Sammlung der auf dem Gebiete der vorbeugenden Verbrechensbekämpfung ergangenen Erlasse und sonstigen Bestimmungen.* Berlin: Reichssicherheitshauptamt, 1941.

Ribbe, Wolfgang, ed. *Berlin-Forschungen.* Berlin: Colloquium Verlag, 1987.

Richardi, Hans-Günter. *Schule der Gewalt: Das Konzentrationslager Dachau.* Munich: Piper, 1995.

Richter, Alfred. "Wandlungen in der ss." *Die Neue Weltbühne,* 21 May 1936, 642–45.

Riedel, Dirk. *Ordnungshüter und Massenmörder im Dienst der "Volksgemeinschaft": Der kz-Kommandant Hans Loritz.* Berlin: Metropol, 2010.

———. "A 'Political Soldier' and 'Practitioner of Violence': The Concentration Camp Commandant Hans Loritz." *Journal of Contemporary History* 45 (July 2010): 555–75.

Riedle, Andrea. *Die Angehörigen des Kommandanturstabs im kz Sachsenhausen.* Berlin: Metropol, 2011.

Röll, Wolfgang. *Sozialdemokraten im Konzentrationslager Buchenwald, 1937–1945.* Göttingen: Wallstein, 2000.

Rost, Nico. *Goethe in Dachau.* Berlin: Volk und Welt, 1946.

Roussel, Hélène, ed. *Deutsche Exilpresse und Frankreich, 1933–1940.* Berne: Peter Lang, 1992.

Roussel, Hélène, and Lutz Winckler, eds. *Rechts und links der Seine. Pariser Tageblatt und Pariser Tageszeitung 1933–40.* Tübingen: Niemeyer Verlag, 2002.

Rubner, Wenzel. "Dachau im Sommer 1933." In *Konzentrationslager: ein Appell an das Gewissen der Welt. Die Opfer klagen an,* 54–82. Karlsbad: Verlagsanstalt Graphia, 1934.

Rudorff, Andrea. "Breslau-Dürrgoy." In *Der Ort des Terrors: Geschichte der nationalsozialistischen Konzentrationslager,* ed. Wolfgang Benz and Barbara Distel, 2:83–86. Munich: C. H. Beck, 2005.

———. "Gollnow." In *Der Ort des Terrors: Geschichte der nationalsozialistischen Konzentrationslager,* ed. Wolfgang Benz and Barbara Distel, 2:102–4. Munich: C. H. Beck, 2005.

———. "Gotteszell." In *Der Ort des Terrors: Geschichte der nationalsozialistischen Konzentrationslager,* ed. Wolfgang Benz and Barbara Distel, 2:104–6. Munich: C. H. Beck, 2005.

———. "Misshandlung und Erpressung mit System: Das Konzentrationslager 'Vulkanwerft' in Stettin-Bredow." In *Instrumentarium der Macht: Frühe*

Konzentrationslager, 1933–1937, ed. Wolfgang Benz and Barbara Distel, 35–70. Berlin: Metropol-Verlag, 2003.

———. "Stettin-Bredow." In *Der Ort des Terrors: Geschichte der nationalsozialistischen Konzentrationslager*, ed. Wolfgang Benz and Barbara Distel, 2:204–7. Munich: C. H. Beck, 2005.

Rüter, C. F., D. W. de Mildt, et al., eds. *Justiz und NS-Verbrechen: Sammlung deutscher Strafurteile wegen nationalsozialistischer Tötungsverbrechen.* Vol. 36. Amsterdam: Amsterdam University Press, 2006.

Sbosny, Inge, and Karl Schabrod. *Widerstand in Solingen: Aus dem Leben antifaschistischer Kämpfer.* Frankfurt am Main: Röderberg-Verlag, 1975.

Schäfer, Werner. *Konzentrationslager Oranienburg: Das Anti-Braunbuch über das erste deutsche Konzentrationslager.* Berlin: Buch- und Tiefdruckgesellschaft, n.d. [1934].

Schikorra, Christa. *Kontinuitäten der Ausgrenzung: "Asoziale" Häftlinge im Frauen-Konzentrationslager Ravensbrück.* Berlin: Metropol-Verlag, 2001.

Schilde, Kurt. "Columbia-Haus." In *The United States Holocaust Memorial Museum Encyclopedia of Camps and Ghettos*, ed. Geoffrey P. Megargee, 1/A, 59–61. Bloomington: Indiana University Press, 2009.

Schilde, Kurt, and Johannes Tuchel, eds. *Columbia-Haus: Berliner Konzentrationslager, 1933–36.* Berlin: Edition Hentrich, 1990.

Schleunes, Karl. *Twisted Road to Auschwitz: Nazi Policy toward German Jews, 1933–1939.* 2nd ed. Urbana: University of Illinois Press, 1990.

Schley, Jens. *Nachbar Buchenwald: Die Stadt Weimar und ihr Konzentrationslager 1937–1945.* Cologne: Böhlau, 1999.

Schmidt, Jürgen. *Martin Niemöller im Kirchenkampf.* Hamburg: Leibniz-Verlag, 1971.

Schmitt, Hans A. *Quakers and Nazis.* Columbia: University of Missouri Press, 1997.

Schnabel, Reimund, ed. *Macht ohne Moral: Eine Dokumentation über die SS.* Frankfurt am Main: Röderberg-Verlag, 1957.

Schneider, Hans. "Das Ermächtigungsgesetz vom 24. März 1933: Bericht über das Zustandekommen und die Anwendung des Gesetzes." *Vierteljahrshefte für Zeitgeschichte* 1 (1953): 197–221.

Schüler-Springorum, Stefanie. "Masseneinweisungen in Konzentrationslager: Aktion 'Arbeitsscheu Reich', Novemberpogrom, Aktion 'Gewitter.'" In *Der Ort des Terrors: Geschichte der nationalsozialistischen Konzentrationslager*, ed. Wolfgang Benz and Barbara Distel, 1:156–64. Munich: C. H. Beck, 2005.

Schulte, Jan Erik. *Zwangsarbeit und Vernichtung: Das Wirtschaftsimperium der SS.* Paderborn: Schöningh, 2001.

Seela, Torsten. "Die Lagerbücherei im Konzentrationslager Dachau." *Dachauer Hefte 7* (1991): 34–46.

Seger, Gerhart. *Oranienburg: Erster authentischer Bericht eines aus dem Konzentrationslager Geflüchteten.* Karlsbad: Verlagsanstalt Graphia, 1934.

Segev, Tom. *Soldiers of Evil: The Commandants of the Nazi Concentration Camps.* London: Grafton, 1990.

Siegel, Fritz. *Todeslager Sachsenhausen: ein Dokumentarbericht vom Sachsenhausen-Prozess.* Berlin: SWA Verlag, 1948.

Singer, Kurt, and Felix Burger. *Carl von Ossietzky.* Zurich: Europa-Verlag, 1937.

Skriebeleit, J. "Flossenbürg—Stammlager." In *Der Ort des Terrors. Geschichte der nationalsozialistischen Konzentrationslager,* ed. Wolfgang Benz and Barbara Distel, 4:17–66. Munich: C. H. Beck, 2006.

Smith, Bradley F., and Agnes F. Peterson, eds. *Heinrich Himmler: Geheimreden 1933 bis 1945 und andere Ansprachen.* Frankfurt am Main: Propyläen-Verlag, 1974.

Smith, Iain R. *The Origins of the South-African War, 1899–1902.* London: Longman, 1996.

Sofsky, Wolfgang. *Die Ordnung des Terrors: Das Konzentrationslager.* Frankfurt am Main: Fischer, 2004.

Springmann, Veronika. "'Sport machen': Eine Praxis der Gewalt im Konzentrationslager." In *KZ-Verbrechen: Beiträge zur Geschichte der nationalsozialistischen Konzentrationslager und ihrer Erinnerung,* ed. Wojciech Lenarczyk, 89–101. Berlin: Metropol, 2007.

Stadtarchiv, ed. *KZ-Kemna 1933–1934: Eine Quellendokumentation.* Wuppertal: Stadtarchiv, 1988.

Statistisches Jahrbuch der Schutzstaffel der NSDAP. 1937, 1938.

Steigmann-Gall, Richard. "Religion and the Churches." In *Short Oxford History of Germany: Nazi Germany,* ed. Jane Caplan, 146–67. Oxford: Oxford University Press 2008.

Stein, Harry. "Buchenwald—Stammlager." In *Der Ort des Terrors: Geschichte der nationalsozialistischen Konzentrationslager,* ed. Wolfgang Benz and Barbara Distel, 3:301–56. Munich: C. H. Beck, 2006.

———. "Juden im Konzentrationslager Buchenwald, 1938–1942." In *Pogromnacht und Holocaust: Frankfurt, Weimar, Buchenwald. Die schwierige Erinnerung an die Stationen der Vernichtung,* ed. Thomas Hofmann, Hanno Loewy and Harry Stein, 81–171. Cologne: Böhlau, 1994.

———, ed. *Konzentrationslager Buchenwald, 1937–1945: Begleitband zur ständigen historischen Ausstellung.* Göttingen: Wallstein, 1999.

Steinbacher, Sybille. *Dachau: Die Stadt und das Konzentrationslager in der NS-Zeit: Die Untersuchung einer Nachbarschaft.* Frankfurt am Main: Peter Lang, 1993.

Steinweis, Alan E. *Kristallnacht 1938*. Cambridge MA: The Belknap Press, 2009.

Stokes, Lawrence D. "Das oldenburgische Konzentrationslager in Eutin, Neu-kirchen und Nüchel." In *Terror ohne System: Die ersten Konzentrations-lager im Nationalsozialismus, 1933–1935*, ed. Wolfgang Benz and Barba-ra Distel, 189–210. Berlin: Metropol, 2001.

Sternburg, Wilhelm von. *"Es ist eine unheimliche Stimmung in Deutschland": Carl von Ossietzky und seine Zeit*. Berlin: Aufbau-Verlag, 1996.

Strebel, Bernhard. *Das KZ Ravensbrück: Geschichte eines Lagerkomplexes*. Paderborn: Schöningh, 2003.

Sydnor, Charles W., Jr. *Soldiers of Destruction: The SS Death's Head Division, 1933–1945*. Princeton NJ: Princeton University Press, 1977.

Tausk, Walter. *Breslauer Tagebuch, 1933–1940*. East-Berlin: Ruetten und Löning, 1984.

Terhorst, Karl-Leo. *Polizeiliche planmäßige Überwachung und polizeiliche Vor-beugungshaft im Dritten Reich*. Heidelberg: Müller, 1985.

Timpke, Henning, ed. *Dokumente zur Gleichschaltung des Landes Hamburg, 1933*. Hamburg: Christians, 1983.

Toepser-Ziegert, Gabriele, and Hans Bohrmann, eds. NS-*Presseanweisungen der Vorkriegszeit: Edition und Dokumentation*. Munich: K. G. Saur, 1984–2001.

Tooze, J. Adam. *The Wages of Destruction: The Making and Breaking of the Nazi Economy*. London: Penguin, 2007.

The Trial of the Major War Criminals before the International Military Tribu-nal. 42 vols. Nuremberg, 1947–49.

Tuchel, Johannes, ed. *Die Inspektion der Konzentrationslager, 1938–1945*. Ber-lin: Edition Hentrich, 1994.

———. "Die Kommandanten des Konzentrationslagers Flossenbürg—Eine Stud-ie zur Personalpolitik in der SS." In *Die Normalität des Verbrechens: Bi-lanz und Perspektiven der Forschung zu den nationalsozialistischen Ge-waltverbrechen*, ed. Johannes Tuchel, Helge Grabitz, and Klaus Bästlein, 201–19. Berlin: Edition Hentrich, 1994.

———. "Die Kommandanten des KZ Dachau." In *Das Konzentrationslager Dachau: Geschichte und Wirkung nationalsozialistischer Repression*, ed. Wolfgang Benz and Angelika Königseder, 329–49. Berlin: Metropol, 2008.

———. *Konzentrationslager: Organisationsgeschichte und Funktion der "Ins-pektion der Konzentrationslager" 1934–1938*. Boppard am Rhein: Harald Boldt, 1991.

———. "Theodor Eicke im Konzentrationslager Lichtenburg." In *Lichtenburg. Ein deutsches Konzentrationslager*, ed. Stefan Hördler and Sigrid Jacobe-it, 59–74. Berlin: Metropol, 2009.

Tuchel, Johannes, Helge Grabitz, and Klaus Bästlein, eds. *Die Normalität des Verbrechens: Bilanz und Perspektiven der Forschung zu den nationalsozialistischen Gewaltverbrechen*. Berlin: Edition Hentrich, 1994.

Tuchel, Johannes, and Reinhold Schattenfroh. *Zentrale des Terrors*. Frankfurt am Main: Büchergilde Gutenberg, 1987.

Turner, Henry A. *Hitler's Thirty Days to Power: January 1933*. London: Bloomsbury, 1997.

Union für Recht und Freiheit, ed. *Der Strafvollzug im III. Reich: Denkschrift und Materialsammlung*. Prague: Union für Recht und Freiheit, 1936.

Valentin, Dr. "Die Krankenversorgung im Konzentrationslager." *Internationales Ärztliches Bulletin: Zentralorgan der Internationalen Vereinigung Sozialistischer Ärzte* 4 (1936): 57–59.

Wachsmann, Nikolaus. "The Dynamics of Destruction: The Development of the Nazi Concentration Camps, 1933–45." In *Concentration Camps in Nazi Germany: The New Histories*, ed. Jane Caplan and Nikolaus Wachsmann, 17–43. London: Routledge, 2010.

———. "From Indefinite Confinement to Extermination: 'Habitual Criminals' in the Third Reich." In *Social Outsiders in Nazi Germany*, ed. Robert Gellately and Nathan Stolzfus, 165–91. Princeton NJ: Princeton University Press, 2001.

———. *Hitler's Prisons: Legal Terror in Nazi Germany*. New Haven CT: Yale University Press, 2004.

———. "Introduction: Eugen Kogon and the ss State." In *The Theory and Practice of Hell: The German Concentration Camps and the System behind Them*, by Eugen Kogon, trans. Heinz Norden, xi–xxi. New York: Farrar, Straus and Giroux, 2006.

———. "Looking into the Abyss: Historians and the Nazi Concentration Camps." *European History Quarterly* 36 (2006): 247–78.

———. "The Policy of Exclusion: Repression in the Nazi State, 1933–1939." In *Short Oxford History of Germany: Nazi Germany*, ed. Jane Caplan, 122–45. Oxford: Oxford University Press 2008.

Wagner, Patrick. "'Vernichtung der Berufsverbrecher': Die vorbeugende Verbrechensbekämpfung der Kriminalpolizei bis 1937." In *Die nationalsozialistischen Konzentrationslager: Entwicklung und Struktur*, vol. 1, ed. Ulrich Herbert, Karin Orth, and Christoph Dieckmann, 87–110. Göttingen: Wallstein, 1998.

———. *Volksgemeinschaft ohne Verbrecher: Konzeptionen und Praxis der Kriminalpolizei in der Zeit der Weimarer Republik und des Nationalsozialismus*. Hamburg: Christians, 1996.

Walk, Joseph, ed. *Das Sonderrecht für die Juden im NS-Staat: Eine Sammlung der gesetzlichen Massnahmen und Richtlinien—Inhalt und Bedeutung*. Heidelberg: Müller, 1981.

Wegner, Bernd. *Hitlers politische Soldaten: Die Waffen-SS, 1933–1945*. Paderborn: Schöningh, 1982.

Welch, David. *The Third Reich: Politics and Propaganda*. London: Routledge, 1993.

White, Joseph Robert. "Introduction to the Early Camps." In *The United States Holocaust Memorial Museum Encyclopedia of Camps and Ghettos, 1933–1945*, I/A, ed. Geoffrey P. Megargee, 3–16. Bloomington: Indiana University Press, 2009.

———. "Moringen-Solling (Men)." In *The United States Holocaust Memorial Museum Encyclopedia of Camps and Ghettos, 1933–1945*, I/A, ed. Geoffrey P. Megargee, 125–28. Bloomington: Indiana University Press, 2009.

———. "Moringen-Solling (Women)." In *The United States Holocaust Memorial Museum Encyclopedia of Camps and Ghettos, 1933–1945*, I/A, ed. Geoffrey P. Megargee, 128–31. Bloomington: Indiana University Press, 2009.

Wickert, Christl. "The Formation of the SS in Early Concentration Camps, 1933–1937: The Example of Karl Otto Koch." In *From Sachsenburg to Sachsenhausen: Pictures from the Photograph Album of a Concentration Camp Commandant*, ed. Günter Morsch, 195–201. Berlin: Metropol, 2007.

Wildt, Michael. "Violence against Jews in Germany, 1933–1939." In *Probing the Depths of German Antisemitism: German Society and the Persecution of the Jews, 1933–1941*, ed. David Bankier, 181–212. New York: Berghahn, 2000.

Wilhelm, F. *Die Polizei im NS-Staat*. Paderborn: Schöningh, 1997.

Wißkirchen, Josef. "Brauweiler." In *Der Ort des Terrors: Geschichte der nationalsozialistischen Konzentrationslager*, ed. Wolfgang Benz and Barbara Distel, 2:70–73. Munich: C. H. Beck, 2005.

Wohlfeld, Udo. "Im Hotel 'Zum Großherzog': Das Konzentrationslager Bad Sulza, 1933–1937." In *Instrumentarium der Macht. Frühe Konzentrationslager 1933–1937*, ed. Wolfgang Benz and Barbara Distel, 263–75. Berlin: Metropol, 2003.

———. "Das Konzentrationslager Nohra in Thüringen." In *Terror ohne System: Die ersten Konzentrationslager im Nationalsozialismus, 1933–1935*, ed. Wolfgang Benz and Barbara Distel, 105–22. Berlin: Metropol, 2001.

Wright, Jonathan. *Gustav Stresemann: Weimar's Greatest Statesman*. Oxford: Oxford University Press, 2002.

Wünschmann, Kim. "Cementing the Enemy Category: Arrest and Imprisonment of German Jews in Nazi Concentration Camps, 1933–8/9." *Journal of Contemporary History* 45 (July 2010): 576–600.

Zámečník, Stanislav. "Dachau-Stammlager." In *Der Ort des Terrors: Geschichte der nationalsozialistischen Konzentrationslager*, ed. Wolfgang Benz and Barbara Distel, 2:233–74. Munich: C. H. Beck, 2005.

———. "Das frühe Konzentrationslager Dachau." In *Terror ohne System: Die ersten Konzentrationslager im Nationalsozialismus, 1933–1935*, ed. Wolfgang Benz and Barbara Distel, 13–39. Berlin: Metropol-Verlag, 2001.

———. *Das war Dachau*. Luxemburg: Comité International de Dachau, 2002.

Zarusky, Jürgen. "Juristische Aufarbeitung der KZ-Verbrechen." In *Der Ort des Terrors: Geschichte der nationalsozialistischen Konzentrationslager*, ed. Wolfgang Benz and Barbara Distel, 1:345–62. Munich: C. H. Beck, 2005.

Zeck, Mario. *Das Schwarze Korps: Geschichte und Gestalt des Organs der Reichsführung SS*. Tübingen: Max Niemeyer Verlag, 2002.

Zegenhagen, Evelyn. "Buchenwald Main Camp." In *The United States Holocaust Memorial Museum Encyclopedia of Camps and Ghettos*, I/A, ed. Geoffrey P. Megargee, 290–95. Bloomington: Indiana University Press, 2009.

INDEX

concentration camps—definition and terminology, xiv, xv, 301–2

concentration camps—portrayals and perceptions: contemporary view, ix, x, xi; as educational institutions, 57, 347n141; German newspaper coverage of, 49, 57–58, 289, 294–96; German public opinion and, 49–52, 317–28; as humane and civilized, 49, 52, 57, 302–3; in international media, 304–5, 306, 308–10, 314–16. *See also* Nazi propaganda

concentration camps—purpose and function: Himmler on, 78; Hitler on, 9; Inspectorate of Concentration Camps on, 160; political repression and deterrence, 8–9, 49, 229, 291; as sites of social discipline, 8, 290

concentration camps—ss system, xix–xxv, 71–139; administrative structure, 142–43; Dachau as model for, xvii, 6, 71–72, 142, 148; Eicke and, xxvii, 6, 71–72, 73, 76, 141–43, 146–49, 159, 195; extralegality of, 29–30, 72, 74, 75, 110–112, 308; Himmler and, xxvii, 7, 8, 71–72, 73–75, 85–89; transformation into mass murder sites, ix, x, xi, xxiv, 209

Confessing Church, 210, 213–14, 305

corruption: among Camp ss, 169, 185, 187; among prisoners, 251

crime statistics, 27, 296, 303

cultural activities: music, 30, 209–10; reading, 212–13; theater performances, 30, 40–41

Czechoslovakia, xxi, 211–12

Dachau camp, 66, 85, 321; arrival of prisoners at, 197–98, 201–2, 260–61, 272–73; beatings and floggings in, 43–44, 178–79, 197–98, 201–2, 216, 325–26; canteen in, 205–6; cultural activities at, 30; daily schedule in, 192; design and grounds, 33, 75; economic enterprises at, 131, 135; Eicke as commandant of, 6, 39, 144, 148; escapes from, 327–28; establishment of, x, xvi, xx, 5, 10; food for prisoners in, 29, 199; forced labor in, 14, 90, 131, 134–35; funding for, 80; geographical remit of, 75, 91; homosexuals in, 98–99, 255, 260; housing for prisoners, 34, 222, 232, 235; hygienic conditions in, 29; Jehovah's Witnesses in, 241; Jews in, 96, 97, 104, 190, 236–37, 264, 269–70, 272–73; jurisdiction within, 14–15; and local population, 51, 53, 317–18, 325; as model for other camps, xvii, 6, 71–72, 142, 148; murder of sa men in (1934), 76–77; Nazi propaganda on,

290–91, 293–94, 296–97, 300–301; prisoner classification, 232, 235–38; prisoner deaths and murders, 5, 21–22, 110, 190, 307–8; prisoner numbers in, xviii, 25, 72; prisoner self-justice in, 47–48; regulations, xix, 12–15, 145; social outsiders sent to, 43, 101, 236, 253, 254, 257–58, 259, 260–61, 293–94; ss guards in, 39, 323; staged visits to, 313, 314–15; sterilizations and castrations in, 258–59, 301; types of punishments in, 226–28

Daluege, Kurt, 66–67, 77–78, 347n159

Dammert, Hans, 30–32

d'Angelo, Karl, 12

Daniels, adjutant, 58

Day of the German Police, 292

death penalty, xix, 5, 14, 145, 195, 341n30

death rates, x, 5, 190; of Jews in camp, 264

Death's Head Division, 146

Death's Head Units. *See* Camp ss

Decree against Malicious Attacks, 50, 60–61, 320–21

Decree for the Protection of People and State, xiii, 1, 9–10, 11, 12, 23, 25

Deller, Hans, 76–77

Deubel, Heinrich, 313, 372n74

Deutscher Kurzwellensender, 62–64

Deutsches Recht, 124–25

Deutschlandsender, 62–64

Deutschnationale Volkspartei (German National People's Party, DNVP), xii, 2, 289, 310

Devil's Island, 294

Diels, Rudolf, 24, 115, 239, 242

Dietrich, Otto, 289, 291, 301

Dietrich, ss guard, 224

discipline: within Camp ss, 145, 159, 161, 162, 163, 171, 172–73; Nazi propaganda on, 300; for prisoners, 5, 13, 88, 145, 151, 189, 301. *See also* punishment, disciplinary

disease, 190, 193, 195–96, 197, 237

drunkenness, guard, 39, 200, 217, 319, 323

Dünkmann, ss guard, 114

Dürrgoy camp, 54–55

Ebert, Friedrich, 39

Ebert, Fritz, 56–57, 347nn137–39

Ebert, Louise, 51, 56–57, 347n136

Ecker, Fritz, 39, 47–48, 344n92

education: Camp ss platoon for, 145, 146, 165–66; Himmler on, 87, 88, 165–66

Eichmann, Adolf, 96, 104, 352n90

Eicke, Theodor, 129, 279; on agitators, 153, 155; on arbitrary punishments, 145, 147,

Frank, Hans, 15–16, 21–22, 342n43
Franz, Wilhelm (Willy), 21–22, 39, 345n93
Fräser, G. H., 66
Freund, Julius, 207–8
Frick, Wilhelm, xviii, 7, 9–10, 83–84; on abuse of protective custody, 23, 116; concerned with Himmler's influence, 72, 110; decree on preventive custody by, 102–3
Frieda K., 277, 280
Friedrichs, Special Commissioner, 53
Fritsch, Dr., 299
Fritz S., 126, 127, 355n147
Frommhold, Ernst, 214–15
Fuhlsbüttel camp, 4, 17–19, 30, 35–37, 342n46
funding, 20, 73, 113–14; of Dachau, 80; of Death's Head Units, 141, 158; of Oranienburg, 54; Pohl and, 79–80, 113, 129, 135, 138, 141; of Sachsenhausen, 89

Gebhard, Dr., 196, 218
Der Gegen-Angriff, 44–45, 239, 243, 345n105
German public, 317–28; ambivalence about concentration camps, 51, 319, 324; knowledge and rumors about camps, 50–52, 317, 320; Nazi concern over, 110; opposition to Nazis among, 321; support for concentration camps among, 319; sympathy for released prisoners among, 326
Gersch, Rottenführer, 222, 224
Gerstenberger, SA guard, 60
Gestapa. See Gestapo
Gestapo, xxi–xxii, 75, 89, 96, 248, 305; and concentration camps, xvi, 73, 85, 125, 143, 291; database of, 74, 80–81, 99; Himmler control over, 7, 74, 83–84; and judicial system, xviii, 112, 113; on prisoner classification, 232–33; propaganda efforts of, 294, 297; relations with SS, 73, 113; roundup of Jews by, xxiii, 97, 264
Gleiwitz, 106
Glücks, Richard, 146
Goebbels, Joseph, 107, 287, 293, 294, 305, 325–26
Goerke, Amtsrat, 198
Goethe, Johann Wolfgang von, 91
Göring, Hermann, xvii, 67, 116, 295; on eliminating Communist threat, 290; and establishment of Prussian state camps, xvi, 6; on forced labor, 133–34; and prisoner amnesty, 22–23, 68, 72; on unauthorized concentration camps, 24; on work-shy elements, 126
Gostner, Erwin, 92–93

Gotteszell penal institution, 42
Gräf, Hugo, 194–95, 360n17
Grauert, Ludwig, 1, 11–12, 79–80, 133, 342n37
Grawitz, Ernst-Robert, 137, 356n173
Grynszpan, Herschel, 96–97, 272, 368n98
Grzesinski, Albert, 34, 344n82
Gürtner, Franz, 9–10, 119–20, 123, 128–30; concerned about SS extralegal power, 72, 109, 111, 116–18; on construction of Buchenwald, 127
Gussak, Adolf, 204–5
Gütt, Arthur, 86, 350n47
Gypsies, 105–6, 112–13, 234, 253, 286

Haag, Lina, 285, 369n119
habitual and professional criminals, so-called: arrest of, 98, 105; arrival in camps of, 43, 46–47, 260–61; in concentration camps, xxiii, 103, 231, 233, 255–56, 273, 312; decrees on preventive custody for, 20–21, 102–3; Himmler on, 87–88; Nazi propaganda about, 66–67, 295–96, 300; political prisoners' relations with, 229, 245–47, 309; prisoner self-justice against, 47–48; wearing of green triangle by, 232, 234
Hamburg, 4, 136–37, 138
Handschuh, Hugo, 21–22
heating, 35, 275, 312
Heilmann, Ernst, 33, 42, 304, 311, 313, 344n78
Heines, Edmund, 54–55, 347n133
Heinle, Ottmar, 163
Hermann, SS guard, 115
Herz, Gabriele, 278, 283–84, 369n117
Herzogsägmühle Central Rambler's Hostel, 253, 259
Hess, Rudolf, 115–16, 354n127
Het Volk, 314
Heydrich, Reinhard, 7, 113, 291–92; on arrest of asocial elements, 105–6; on database for state enemies, 80–81; and detention of Communists, 74, 79; and mass arrest of Jews, 97, 108; and prisoner releases, 89, 108; on transferring state prisoners to concentration camps, 128–29
Hierl, Konstantin, 85–86, 133–34, 355n164
Himmler, Heinrich, 247, 314; barring of prisoners' attorney representation by, 111, 123; on camp guard conduct, 168–69; on character and tasks of SS, 85–89; and Communists, xxii, 79, 86; and creation of SS camp system,

pack drills, 29, 191, 217, 265; in Dachau, 227, 237; in Esterwegen, 267; in Hohnstein, 196; in Lichtenburg, 219–20; in Oranienburg, 33

Papen, Felix von, 76, 349n24

Papenburg camps, 19, 20. *See also* Emsland

parades, 54–55, 166, 200, 201

Pariser Tageblatt, 307–8

Pariser Tageszeitung, 215

penal labor, 205, 227, 234

People's Court, 121, 354n136

Perg, 327

Pfundtner, Hans, 104, 352n89

pillorying, 195, 216, 226, 227–28

pimps, 105–6, 233

Pohl, Oswald: biographical information, 349n32; on Buchenwald brickworks, 136–37; and concentration camp funding, 79–80, 113, 129, 135, 138; Eicke and, 113, 148

political prisoners, xxiv, 19, 239–52; as category, 233, 236, 237; conduct of, 47; conflicts between Communists and Social Democrats, 34, 42, 44–45, 240, 345n99; Jehovah's Witnesses as contingent of, 241–42; numbers of, xviii, 8, 312; organization and leadership of, 244–47; political activities and resistance by, 209, 239, 250–52; as prisoner functionaries, 230, 251–52; relations with social outsiders, 43, 229, 245–47, 250–52, 276, 309; self-administration by, 251; solidarity among, 42, 240, 247, 273; strips and patches worn by, 232, 238, 249; women as, 283; working-class composition of, xxii, 231

political violence, xii, xiii, 141

Poller, Walter, 240, 249–50

Presidential Emergency Decree, 9, 341n30

preventive police custody, xxiii, 106–7, 261, 262, 300; decrees on, 20–21, 102–3, 105

prisoner arrival, 29, 30–31, 191–92, 255, 264–65; at Buchenwald, 249–50, 270, 273–74; at Dachau, 197–98, 201–2, 260–61, 272–73; at Esterwegen, 34–35, 197, 266–67; at Lichtenburg, 46–47, 285

prisoner categories and classification, 14, 18–19, 36, 231–38; denotation of, through strips and patches, 200, 231, 232, 234, 237–38, 246, 249, 255; and prisoner hierarchy, 189, 232

prisoner deaths, 73–74, 149, 271; in Buchenwald, 193, 327; in Dachau, 5, 190, 317, 320; investigations into, 6, 15–16, 21–22; in Kemna, 28; in Mauthausen, 190; during World War II, x, xi, xxiv

prisoner functionaries, 200, 232, 279; in Buchenwald, 193, 202–4, 229–30; Communists as, 208, 229, 230; Kapos, 189–90, 208, 230, 231, 251, 252, 275; political prisoners as, 230, 251–52; professional criminals as, 229–30; responsibilities of, 189, 193, 202–4; senior block prisoners, 201, 202–4, 235, 251

prisoner numbers, xi, xxii, xxiv, 8, 16–17, 316, 333; in 1933–34, xv, xviii, 2, 8, 72; in 1936, 85, 86; in 1937–39, xi, xx–xxi, xxiv; in 1942–45, x; at Buchenwald, xx–xxi; at Dachau, xviii, 25; Himmler on, 88; at Lichtenburg, 312; of political prisoners, xvii, 8, 312; of women, 309

prisoner releases, xxiii, 20, 26, 29, 308, 310, 321, 326, 339n46; in 1933, xv–xvi, 22–23, 68, 72; in 1939, 166; Heydrich on, 89; Himmler on, 74, 81–83, 86, 88, 93–94, 264

prisoners: behavior instructions for, 152–53, 199–200; clothing and uniforms, 29, 190, 195; criminalization of, 105, 246, 255; daily schedule of, 29, 90, 189, 191, 192, 193–94, 198, 271; free time, 200, 212–13; resistance by, 209, 210; roll call for, 29, 143, 192, 202–3, 265; second-time, 83, 232, 234, 235–36, 238; self-assertion of, 209–15; self-justice of, 42, 47–48; sick and elderly, 189, 237, 270; society of, 191, 231; socioeconomic differences among, 193; theft from, 39, 168, 173–74; washing, 192, 194–95, 202

professional criminals. *See* habitual and professional criminals, so-called

prostitutes, xxiii, xxiv, 105–6, 285

protective custody (*Schutzhaft*), xiii, 11–12; address to detainees about, 17–18; ambiguity and arbitrariness of, 2, 26; in Bavaria, xvi, 4, 5, 8, 24–27, 297–98; complaints from officials about, 23, 24–26; conference on, 129–30; early sites for detention, x, xiv, xviii, 3, 4–8, 19–20, 24, 52–53; Gürtner on regulation of, 119–20; legal basis and decrees, xiii, 1, 43, 102–3, 124–25; in Prussia, xx, 11–12, 24, 26, 295–96; SA men in, 77–78; for social outsiders, xviii–xix, 8, 25, 27, 97–98, 103–4, 109–10, 253–62; women in, 42, 280

Protestant clergymen, 118–19, 210, 213–14

Prussia: Ministry of the Interior in, xvi, 6–7, 11–12, 19–21; protective custody prisoners in, xx, 24, 26, 295–96; state camps in, xvi, 6–7, 43

punishment, disciplinary, 32, 216–17; cleaning straw by hand, 281; collective, 215, 217, 225;

homosexuals within, 99, 102; judicial system collaboration with, xviii, 112–13; judicial system conflicts with, xix, 6–7, 110–12; and SA, xvii, 71, 183; standardization of prisoner classification by, 231; virulent anti-Semitism of, 43, 263; during Weimar Republic, xii. *See also* Camp SS

Schwarz, Hans, 250–52, 366n47

Das Schwarze Korps, 211, 214, 272, 291, 296–97, 298–300

Schwister, county court chief president, 130

second-time inmates, 83, 232, 234, 235–36, 238

security confinement, 126, 139, 355n149, 356n178

Seger, Gerhart, 32–33, 42, 44–45, 343n74

Serelmann, Dr., 196

Severing, Carl, 32, 344n76

sexual harassment, 318–19, 324–25

Sherwood-Schweitzer, Frieda, 278, 280–81, 369n115

shootings while "trying to escape," 35, 120, 127–28, 129, 211, 271

Siebert, Ludwig, 16, 24, 26

Simon, Max, 220

Smallbones, R. T., 316

smoking and tobacco, 18, 29, 83, 218–19

Social Democrats, 10, 32, 33, 36, 49; arrests and preventive detention of, xii, 1, 2, 42, 239; Communists' conflict with, 34, 42, 44–45, 240, 345n99; Gestapo database on, 80, 81; at Oranienburg, 44–45, 62. *See also* Sopade

Socialist Workers Party (SAP), 81, 245, 350n36

Society of Friends (Quakers), 78, 349n28

solitary confinement, 13, 18, 23–24, 36, 210, 216

Solmitz, Fritz, 30, 35–37, 344n88

songs and singing, 243–44; as clandestine resistance, 239; Nazis and, 88, 207–8, 365n18

Sonnenburg camp, 19, 20, 60

Sopade: on Columbia-Haus, 199–200; on Dachau, 134–35, 222, 235–38, 321; on Esterwegen, 197; on Lichtenburg, 200, 219–20; on Moringen, 284–85. *See also* Social Democrats

Sorge, Gustav, 242, 365n28

Spatzenegger, SS guard, 221

special courts (*Sondergerichte*), 26, 343n60

Speer, Albert, 136

SS. *See* Schutzstaffel (SS)

Stabswache, 76, 349n25

staged visits, 64, 281, 287–88, 304; by American Consul, 68–69; to Dachau, 313, 314–15; to Hohnstein, 64, 67–68; by International Red Cross, 306–7, 312–13; to Sachsenhausen, 291, 302

Stahlkopf, Hans, 33, 76, 344n77

state prisons, 5, 106, 109; number of inmates in, xviii; protective custody prisoners in, xx, 4; security confinement in, 126, 139, 355n149, 356n178; transfer of detainees to concentration camps, 112, 121–22, 125, 126, 128–29, 256

Steinbrenner, Hans, 39, 43–44, 176, 177–78, 307, 345n94

sterilizations, 109, 254, 258–59, 301

Stettin-Bredow camp, 7, 110, 113–16, 117

storks, 296–97

Streicher, Julius, 272, 298, 371n33

Stresemann, Gustav, 34, 344n86

Sturmabteilung (Stormtroopers, SA), xii, 55, 76; decline of, after Röhm purge, xvii, 71, 73, 77–78; execution of men from, 73, 76–77; as guards, 36–38, 54, 58; running of camps by, xiv–xv, 32–33; SS comparison to, 183

Der Stürmer, 272

Sudetenland, 137, 212

Tamaschke, Günther, 312, 372n70

Tarré, SS guard, 249

Taus, Karl, 167, 175

Tausk, Walter, 54–55, 346n131

theater performances, 30, 40–41

Thiele, Herbert, 90–91

Thunig, Ewald, 134

Thüringer Gauzeitung, 303

Thuringia, xx, 1, 10, 75

The Times (London): German ambassador on, 310–11; and Ludwig Levy, 50, 61–62; reportage on concentration camps, 305, 306, 308–10, 315–16, 348n151

Torgler, Ernst, 289, 293, 370n21

transport to camps, 101, 191, 197, 264, 273, 327

Treptow, SS guard, 115

Trinkl, Maria, 324

Tuchel, Johannes, xv

Valentin, Dr., 195–97

van der Lubbe, Marinus, 60–61, 347n148

Versailles treaty, 294

Vienna, 92

Index